Between
Dictatorship
and
Democracy

Russian and Eurasian Books
from the Carnegie Endowment for International Peace

Russia's Restless Frontier: The Chechnya Factor in Post-Soviet Russia
Dmitri Trenin, Aleksei V. Malashenko, with Anatol Lieven

Putin's Russia
Lilia Shevtsova

Ambivalent Neighbors: The EU, NATO and the Price of Membership
Anatol Lieven and Dmitri Trenin, Editors

The End of Eurasia: Russia on the Border between
Geopolitics and Globalization
Dmitri Trenin

Kazakhstan: Unfulfilled Promise
Martha Brill Olcott

Russia after the Fall
Andrew C. Kuchins, Editor

Gorbachev, Yeltsin, and Putin: Political Leadership in Russia's Transition
Archie Brown and Lilia Shevtsova, Editors

Belarus at the Crossroads
Sherman W. Garnett and Robert Legvold, Editors

Yeltsin's Russia: Myths and Reality
Lilia Shevtsova

To read excerpts and find more information on these and
other publications visit **www.ceip.org/pubs**.

Between Dictatorship and Democracy

Russian Post-Communist Political Reform

Michael McFaul, Nikolai Petrov, and Andrei Ryabov

*with Mikhail Krasnov, Vladimir Petukhov, Viktor Sheinis,
and Elina Treyger*

CARNEGIE ENDOWMENT FOR INTERNATIONAL PEACE
Washington, D.C.

Carnegie Endowment for International Peace
1779 Massachusetts Avenue, N.W., Washington, D.C. 20036
202-483-7600, fax 202-483-1840
www.ceip.org

The Carnegie Endowment normally does not take institutional positions on public policy issues; the views and recommendations presented in this publication do not necessarily represent the views of the Carnegie Endowment, its officers, staff, or trustees.

To order, contact Carnegie's distributor:
The Brookings Institution Press
Department 029, Washington, D.C. 20042-0029, USA
1-800-275-1447 or 1-202-797-6258
Fax 202-797-2960, E-mail bibooks@brook.edu

Composition by Oakland Street Publishing. Text set in ITC Berkeley.
Printed by Maple-Vail Book Manufacturing Group.

Library of Congress Cataloging-in-Publication Data

McFaul, Michael, 1963-
    Between dictatorship and democracy : Russian post-communist political
reform / Michael McFaul, Nikolai Petrov, and Andrei Ryabov ; with
Mikhail Krasnov, Vladimir Petukhov, Viktor Sheinis, and Elina Treyger.
    p. cm.
Includes bibliographical references and index.
    ISBN 0-87003-206-2 (pbk.) — ISBN 0-87003-207-0 (cloth)
1. Russia (Federation)—Politics and government—1991- 2.
Democracy—Russia (Federation) 3. Post-communism—Russia (Federation)
I. Petrov, Nikolaæi (Nikolaæi Vladimirovich) II. Rëiiabov, Andreæi. III. Title.
JN6695.M39 2004
320.947—dc22   2003026788

09 08 07 06 05 04   5 4 3 2 1   1st Printing 2004

Contents

Foreword vii

Preface. ix

Acknowledgments. xi

Abbreviations and Acronyms xii

---

1   Introduction 1
     Michael McFaul, Nikolai Petrov, and Andrei Ryabov

2   Elections. 23
     Michael McFaul and Nikolai Petrov

3   The Constitution. 56
     Viktor Sheinis

4   Legislative–Executive Relations. 83
     Andrei Ryabov

5   Political Parties 105
     Michael McFaul

6   Civil Society 135
     Michael McFaul and Elina Treyger

7   The Mass Media 174
     Andrei Ryabov

8. The Rule of Law 195
    Mikhail Krasnov

9. Federalism 213
    Nikolai Petrov

10. Regional Models of Democratic Development 239
    Nikolai Petrov

11. Public Attitudes About Democracy 268
    Vladimir Petukhov and Andrei Ryabov

12. Postscript: The 2003 Parliamentary Elections and the Future of
    Russian Democracy. 292
    Michael McFaul, Nikolai Petrov, and Andrei Ryabov

Notes 299

Index 343

About the Authors 363

The Carnegie Endowment for International Peace 365

Foreword

The initiation of political liberalization in the Soviet Union under Mikhail Gorbachev had profound and unexpected consequences for both the USSR and the world. Gorbachev aspired to make the Soviet regime more accountable to its citizens, more pluralistic, and more effective. He did not achieve his aims. Instead the Soviet Union collapsed altogether and Gorbachev was deposed as its last leader.

After the Soviet Union dissolved in December 1991, a newly independent Russia seemed to be making its way from autocracy to democracy. Russian President Boris Yeltsin called himself a democrat and pledged to build democratic institutions. Leaders in Western democracies cheered him on, believing that democratic change would make it possible to integrate Russia into the international community of democratic states and end the Cold War once and for all.

More than a decade later, however, democracy has not consolidated in Russia. Some democratic practices have taken root, including, in particular, the idea that national leaders must be elected. For a country ruled by autocrats for hundreds of years, this change is no small achievement. Yet the path from communist rule to democracy has proven to be longer, rockier, and less straightforward than most imagined back in 1991. Indeed, the Russian regime may no longer be "in transition." If it is in motion at all, its trajectory recently appears to be in an antidemocratic direction.

Exactly what kind of political system is in place in Russia today? What factors have contributed to democratization and autocratization over the last two decades? And is this regime stable or still changing and in what direction? These are the questions that Michael McFaul, Nikolai Petrov,

Andrei Ryabov, and their collaborators seek to answer in *Between Dictatorship and Democracy*. As the title implies, the authors believe that the regime can neither be called a democracy nor a dictatorship, but floats somewhere in between. By analyzing nearly every component of the Russian political system, the authors attempt to provide a nuanced and comprehensive evaluation. In the United States, the debate about Russia is all too often artificially simplified into "optimists" and "pessimists" or those who are "pro-Russia" and those who are "anti-Russia." Readers seeking definitive judgments to affirm their side of this black and white debate will be disappointed. While the authors agree on what Russia's political system is not, they do not see eye to eye on what it is or on how to explain political change in Russia over the last two decades. The mix of American and Russian authors in this volume enriches the diversity of views on a still highly important and uncertain pathway of change.

The authors do agree on two general conclusions. First, Russia has experienced some degree of democratization. Beginning in the late 1990s, political liberalization did occur. To argue that the Russian regime is the same as it ever was ignores some momentous historical developments that this book describes and explains in detail. Second, the political regime has become less democratic over the last several years under President Vladimir Putin. While some important political and legal reforms have begun under Putin, which in the long run may help to improve the rule of law and the effectiveness of the state, these gains have been overshadowed by a series of policies and actions that have resulted in less pluralism today than a decade ago.

With Russia's political system still very much in flux, this book represents only the latest in a continuing series of assessments by scholars of Russia's domestic politics at the Carnegie Endowment's Moscow Center. Future projects will examine issues of civil society development, electoral behavior, regional democratization, federalism, and the evolution of political parties in even greater depth.

Jessica T. Mathews
President
Carnegie Endowment for International Peace

Preface

This book has a Moscow-centric bias. Although Michael McFaul now lives elsewhere, the original idea behind writing this book was to present a Moscow-anchored perspective on Russia's political trajectory over the last decade. The perspectives of most books on the subject, almost all written in English, are shaped by debates and traditions formed in Cambridge, Washington, D.C., Palo Alto, or Oxford. Often these perspectives are presented through American, and sometimes British, social scientific jargon or mathematical models. American foreign policy considerations frequently shape analyses coming out of Washington. Even though it is an American-Russian collaboration, ours is a distinctly Moscow-anchored view. With this view comes a different approach to causation, citation, and discourse. Rather than trying to forge every chapter into an American style, we have allowed pluralism in method and approach.

Originally Michael McFaul, Nikolai Petrov, and Andrei Ryabov set out to write this entire book collaboratively. We soon realized, however, that we did not have the collective expertise to cover all the necessary topics. Consequently, the authorship of the chapters is extremely complex. Petrov was the lead author on chapters 9 (federalism) and 10 (regional models of political development). Ryabov took the lead on chapters 4 (legislative-executive relations), 7 (the media), and 11 (public attitudes about democracy). McFaul assumed primary responsibility for the introduction and chapters 2 (elections), 5 (political parties), and 6 (civil society). We then recruited Viktor Sheinis, one of the authors of the Russian Constitution, to write chapter 3 on constitutionalism. In a similar vein, we were lucky to recruit Mikhail Krasnov to write about the rule of law, since he was Yeltsin's adviser on legal affairs for much of the 1990s. In addition, Vladimir Petukhov collaborated in the writing and provided much of the data for chapter 11. Elina Treyger also collaborated with McFaul in writing the chapter on civil society. In the final drafting, however, we relaxed authorship claims. McFaul, Petrov, and Ryabov did not simply edit, but significantly revised all the chapters.

Acknowledgments

The authors wish to thank Eric Bahn, Kate Dornbush, Gordon Hahn, Tatyana Krasnopevtseva, Tatyana Shmygol, Aleksei Titkov, Anya Vodopyanov and especially Katherine Kelman for their research and editorial assistance in preparing this book. As well, Toula Papanicolas provided excellent administrative support in Washington. The authors are also grateful to the two reviewers of this manuscript and the participants at several seminars at the Carnegie Moscow Center for their valuable suggestions for revisions, expansion, and contraction. The authors wish to thank the Carnegie Endowment for International Peace; the Hoover Institution; the Bradley, Mott, and Starr foundations; and the Carnegie Corporation of New York for supporting this unique project. Finally, the authors are grateful to Sage Publications for allowing them to reprint a revised version of chapter 5.[1]

Abbreviations and Acronyms

CPD	Congress of People's Deputies
CPRF	Communist Party of the Russian Federation
CPSU	Communist Party of the Soviet Union
FNPR	Federation of Independent Trade Unions of Russia
FSB	Federal Security Service
KGB	State Security Committee
KKN	Constitutional Oversight Committee
LDPR	Liberal Democratic Party of Russia
NGO	nongovernmental organization
NTV	Independent Television
ORT	Public Russian Television
OVR	Fatherland-All Russia
RIISNP	Russian Independent Institute of Social and Nationalities Problems
RSFSR	Russian Soviet Federative Socialist Republic
RTR	Russian Television and Radio
SMD	single-mandate district
SPS	Union of Right Forces
TV-6	Television-6
VTsIOM	All-Russian Center for Public Opinion Research

1

Introduction

Michael McFaul, Nikolai Petrov, and Andrei Ryabov

Is Russia a democracy? Will Russia be a democracy in ten years? Was Russia ever a democracy? This book seeks to give comprehensive and nuanced answers to these difficult, controversial questions. They are difficult to answer because Russia's political system is neither a full-blown dictatorship nor a consolidated democracy, but something in between. They are controversial because the answers have implications for both theorists and policymakers in Russia as well as in the United States.

Our method is not to present tedious, long semantic debates about the adjectives that should modify either democracy or dictatorship when describing the Russian regime.[1] Instead, in place of a simplistic label we offer an entire book devoted to describing the contours of the political regime in Russia. Moreover, we focus on the trajectory of the political system since 1991 and not only on a snapshot of the regime as it appears today. Our aim is to describe the formal institutions of the democratic regime that appeared in Russia just before the collapse of the Soviet Union and then to explain their evolution (or lack thereof). Our story is about negative trends, beginning in the mid-1990s, but accelerating during the Putin era. The chapters attempt to explain the factors that have pushed Russia's democracy in the wrong direction.

Identifying an erosion of democratic practices implies that some form of democracy existed in Russia in the first place. To varying degrees all the chapters make this assumption. In other words, in answer to the question of whether Russia ever had a democracy, we respond in the affirmative. We fully agree with those who have added qualifiers to the word democracy when describing Russia's regime at any time during its post-communist existence and argue that Russia is not and never has been a liberal democracy. Yet in contrast to many critics of the current regime, a basic hypothesis of this book is that Russia underwent a transition from communist rule to some form of democratic rule in the 1990s.[2] Democratization did occur. Electoral democracy did emerge. Even though the trajectory has continued in an antidemocratic direction for several years, especially lately, we also posit that the political system still retains some democratic features. Whether these democratic traits are significant enough to label Russia a democracy is debatable. The three principal authors of this book have competing answers, but all agree with two observations: first, Russia is not a dictatorship; and second, Russia is moving in an autocratic direction.

Defining Democracy and Dictatorship

Following Joseph Schumpeter, we define democracy as "the institutional arrangement for arriving at political decisions in which individuals acquire the power to decide by means of a competitive struggle."[3] We also concur with Adam Przeworski's refinement of Schumpeter by adding that this process of electing leaders must occur under certain or fixed rules, but with uncertain outcomes that cannot be reversed.

> The crucial moment in any passage from authoritarianism to democratic rule is the crossing of the threshold beyond which no one can intervene to reverse the outcomes of the formal political process. Democratization is an act of subjecting all the interests to competition, of institutionalizing uncertainty. The decisive step toward democracy is the devolution of power from a group of people to a set of rules.[4]

Following Larry Diamond, we consider political regimes that meet this minimal definition to be electoral democracies.[5]

Elections are a necessary but insufficient condition for democracy. Terry Karl and others have warned rightly about the "fallacy of electoralism": an overemphasis on elections with an accompanying neglect of other institu-

tions that make democracies work.[6] While deploying this minimal definition of democracy we nonetheless have higher standards in mind when
evaluating the democratic quotient of Russia's polity. Implicit in our comparative analysis of the rule of law, civil society, and the party system in
Russia is a higher model or ideal type of liberal democracy rather than a
minimal standard of *electoral democracy*.[7] Liberal democracy is harder to
define than electoral democracy because scholars disagree about the components. Larry Diamond has gone the furthest in articulating the attributes
of liberal democracy. Because his criteria constitute the implicit standard by
which we judge Russia throughout the book, the complete list of liberal
democratic features as stated by Diamond is worth restating:

1. Control of the state and its key decisions and allocations lies, in
   fact as well as in constitutional theory, with elected officials (and
   not democratically unaccountable actors or foreign powers); in
   particular, the military is subordinate to the authority of elected
   civilian officials.

2. Executive power is constrained, constitutionally and in fact, by
   the autonomous power of other government institutions (such as
   an independent judiciary, parliament, and other mechanisms of
   horizontal accountability).

3. Not only are electoral outcomes uncertain, with a significant opposition vote and the presumption of party alteration in government,
   but no group that adheres to constitutional principles is denied the
   right to form a party and contest elections (even if electoral thresh-
   olds and other rules exclude small parties from winning representations in parliament).

4. Cultural, ethnic, religious, and other minority groups (as well as
   historically disadvantaged majorities) are not prohibited (legally or
   in practice) from expressing their interests in the political process
   or from speaking their language or practicing their culture.

5. Beyond parties and elections, citizens have multiple, ongoing
   channels for expression and representation of their interests and
   values, including diverse, independent associations and movements, which they have the freedom to form and join.

6. There are alternative sources of information (including independent media) to which citizens have politically unfettered access.

7. Individuals also have substantial freedom of belief, opinion, discussion, speech, publication, assembly, demonstration, and petition.

8. Citizens are politically equal under the law (even though they are invariably unequal in their political resources).

9. Individual and group liberties are effectively protected by an independent, nondiscriminatory judiciary, whose decisions are enforced and respected by other centers of power.

10. The rule of law protects citizens from unjustified detention, exile, terror, torture, and undue interference in their personal lives not only by the state but also by organized non-state or anti-state forces.[8]

Some of these components of liberal democracy do exist in the Russian polity. Even though nonelected officials from the Federal Security Service (FSB, formerly the KGB) have assumed an increasingly large role in the federal government in recent years, elected officials do still control the highest levels of the Russian state (Diamond's first condition).[9] Russia also meets Diamond's third condition of a liberal democracy in that individuals and political parties that adhere to the constitution are allowed to participate in elections, but as discussed in chapter 2, some parties were not allowed to participate in the 1993 parliamentary elections, one group was denied access to the ballot in the 1999 parliamentary vote, and others have been scratched from the ballot in regional contests. Those Chechen groups labeled as terrorists, which included the group to which the last elected president of Chechnya belonged, also do not have this right. The Russian regime does a better job of meeting Diamond's fourth condition in that most religious, ethnic, and cultural groups can express their views openly and organize to promote their interests, but again the one exception is Chechnya. Likewise, most citizens are equal under the law (Diamond's eighth criterion), and most individuals can express their beliefs, assemble, demonstrate, and petition (Diamond's seventh criterion). Note that every attribute of liberal democracy in Russia listed here contains some qualifying language. Thus while most Russians enjoy the rights and freedoms associated with liberal democracy, not all do. If all do not enjoy these rights, then the regime is not liberal.

Other components of liberal democracy simply do not exist in Russia. The regime does not exhibit Diamond's second criterion in that executive power is only weakly constrained. Some electoral outcomes, such as contests for executive power at the national and regional levels, are becoming less and less uncertain, a violation of Diamond's third criterion. The Russian polity also fails to meet Diamond's fifth, sixth, ninth, and tenth conditions in that citizens do not have multiple channels for representation of their interests, primarily because pluralist institutions of interest intermediation are weak and mass-based interest groups are marginal; alternative sources of information are dwindling; individual and group liberties are only weakly protected; and citizens, especially in Chechnya, are unjustly detained, exiled, and tortured.[10] As chapters 4 through 10 show, the institutions and practices that make liberal democracies work are either weak or absent. In addition, as discussed in chapter 11, a deeper attribute of democratic stability—a normative commitment to the democratic process by both the elite and society—is present but not strong in Russia. Even though all major political actors recognize elections as "the only game in town" and behave accordingly, antidemocratic attitudes still linger in elite circles and in society as a whole. In sum, Russia's post-communist regime has never been a liberal democracy, and in recent years the regime has become less liberal.

By embracing this model of an ideal type of liberal democracy, analysis usually focuses on how Russia's regime falls short.[11] Some might call the use of this standard ethnocentric or American-centric. We disagree. We see the deployment of lesser criteria as analytically circumspect and politically self-defeating for those in Russia and the West seriously committed to further democratization in Russia.

If Russia's regime has not consolidated into a liberal democracy, is it nonetheless an electoral democracy? Was it ever an electoral democracy? Chapter 2 answers this question. This chapter and others take as the starting point of analysis that Soviet and then post-communist leaders rejected authoritarianism in the late 1980s and early 1990s and took steps toward building an electoral democracy. In the 1990s, the Russian regime had the basic features of an electoral democracy in that elections took place under a universally recognized set of rules, their results were not entirely certain beforehand, and no authority intervened after election day to reverse the outcome of the vote. As chapter 2 discusses in detail, however, the playing field for competitors was never equal and has become increasingly less so over time. Nonetheless, competitive elections determined Russia's rulers. The regime that emerged in the 1990s was qualitatively different from the communist and tsarist dictatorships.

After making this first claim about the collapse of dictatorship and the emergence of electoral democracy in Russia in the 1990s, the second step in our analysis is to describe and explain the weakening of democratic practices in the latter part of the 1990s, and especially during the Putin era. This erosion has mostly occurred within those institutions typically associated with liberal democracy, which were weak to begin with, but have recently become even weaker. Yet, as chapter 2 explores in detail, democratic erosion is also apparent at the core of electoral democracy. Particularly disturbing was the 1999–2000 national electoral cycle, in which the state played a prominent role in determining the results. If this trend continues, then the playing field will become so lopsided as to make the results of votes obvious beforehand. Without competition, elections become meaningless. As Przeworski has eloquently stated, "Democracy is a system in which parties lose elections."[12] If those in power never lose, then Russia will no longer be an electoral democracy.

In tracing the antidemocratic trajectory of Russia's political system our analysis stops short of labeling the current regime a dictatorship. If Russia were a dictatorship, then oligarchs, governors, and government officials would have not invested the time and energy that they did in the last electoral cycle. As several chapters in this book will echo, Vladimir Putin's victory in 2000 and the process that produced that victory were not positive steps for democratic consolidation in Russia. Yet generalizing about the long-term future of Russian democracy from this one election and the policies that have followed from it would be premature. Even in established liberal democracies, the same party can stay in power for decades. Only time will tell if Putin's first election victory was the beginning of the creation of a one-party state or just an accidental consequence of a popular war against Chechnya, hopes for the future, and a weak opposition.[13] Moreover, as discussed in chapter 11, the Russian people at this period in history actually want a tough leader who promises to build a stronger state. Such desires are common after years of revolutionary turmoil.[14] Those who claim that Putin's election was undemocratic must demonstrate that the people were prevented from voting someone more desirable for the majority into office. The demand for some other kind of candidate does not appear to have been robust, and most certainly was not expressed by a majority of Russian voters in 2000 and 2004.

Yet, some uncertainty remains about who will replace him in 2008. The absence of greater competition in the 2000 and 2004 campaigns was worrisome, but speculation that Putin might stay on past 2008 is even more worrisome. All these concerns, however, pertain to possible future transgressions of the basic rules of the game in an electoral democracy. In sharing these worries, we still are not ready to call Russia an autocratic regime.[15] The trend, however, is clearly in the autocratic direction.[16]

Quality of Democracy Versus Stability of the Regime

Analysts of democratization frequently conflate two different properties: the quality of democracy and the stability of democracy. The phrase "democratic consolidation" implies that quality and stability are two sides of the same coin. They are not, at least not in new democracies. It is true that the most democratic regimes in the world are also the most stable. Once a country obtains a 1, 1 rating from Freedom House—the highest score on political institutions and civil liberties on a scale from 1 to 7—the regime rarely backslides to 2, 2, let alone all the way back to full-blown dictatorship (7,7).[17] A "democracy is significantly more likely to become consolidated if it is liberal."[18] Consequently, factors or developments that enhance the quality of democracy also promote its stability. However, the road to democratic nirvana is not clearly delineated, nor is it certain that every country will eventually reach the promised land.

Much of the recent literature on democratization implicitly suggests a linear progression of different phases: liberalization, followed by democratic transition, followed by democratic consolidation. In the 1990s, however, many new democracies did not follow this sequence and a number of transitions from authoritarian rule did not produce democratic regimes. In the wake of authoritarian collapse, some states managed to meet the minimum criteria of electoral democracy but failed to consolidate the institutions of liberal democracy. The momentum for regime change can stop long before the outlines of liberal democracy emerge.[19] Diamond referred to this condition of many new electoral democracies as the "twilight zone between persistence without legitimization and institutionalization."[20] Even though liberal democracy is the most stable type of regime, many less perfect regime forms have shown remarkable persistence. They might be moving toward consolidation, even if the regime type is not liberal democracy. Liberal democracies rarely collapse, but illiberal democracies or partial democracies are not necessarily prone to collapse either. A political system can be stable without being liberal.[21] Likewise, an electoral democracy can be stable without being a liberal democracy.[22]

Russia is one of those regimes in the twilight zone. The absence of democracy-supporting institutions means that the regime is more fragile than a liberal democracy. At the same time, the regime has shown remarkable stability since 1993, even if it has not made progress in strengthening liberal democratic institutions. Stephen Hanson has defined consolidation as a condition in which "the enforcers of democratic institutions themselves can be counted on with very high probability to behave in ways compatible with, and oriented toward the perpetuation of *formal* institutional rules."[23] If the word formal is emphasized, then Russia meets this definition of consolidation, even if the regime type is not a liberal democracy. The crises challenging this political system—including two wars in Chechnya, the August 1998 financial crisis, and the retirement of Russia's first post-communist leader—have been enormous.[24] Yet the constitution has survived and elections have remained the only means for coming to power. Above all, no major actor, including Putin and his FSB entourage, has an interest in overturning the formal rules of the game of the Russian polity.[25] While different actors want to change the specific form of the constitution and the specific rules governing elections, all major actors have demonstrated an interest in preserving the constitution and elections.[26] Since 1993, Russian leaders have certainly violated these rules on occasion, but violations alone are not evidence of institutional failure. A system is under siege only when a major actor or set of actors champions an alternative institutional design.[27] To date, such a threat has not emerged to the political system that has consolidated in Russia since 1993.

While the formal institutions of electoral democracy seem to be stable, the democratic content of these institutions has eroded. Russia's constitution allows for the preservation of the formal, meta-rules of the political system at the same time that the informal, smaller rules of the polity are changing. As Duma Deputy Vladimir Ryzhkov explained in discussing the democratic reversals under Putin:

> The lesson of the last three years is that Russia's federal foundation can be undermined without trampling too rudely on the Constitution. Budget revenues were centralized and federal districts created without violating the constitution. The Federal Council was reformed and defanged, and a new law on regional government passed that allows

Moscow to dismiss elected regional leaders and dissolve regional legislatures—all without violating the Constitution. Planned reform of
relations between the federal center and local governments could well
become the next step in the ongoing building of the executive change
of command. Thus a Constitution containing the most liberal of principles and freedoms was used to establish a regime controlled by an
elected president wielding practically unchecked power... The Constitution is like a play that allows plenty of room for the director's
interpretation. On the basis of a single document, Russia's political
elite can create a hymn to freedom and a stirring tale of "order" lost
and found.[28]

Putin's advisers have a term for this transformation of democratic practices without altering formal democratic rules: "managed democracy." As
described in detail in this book, the campaign to impose managed democracy has had serious negative consequences for the quality of democracy.
The destabilizing consequences of this campaign, however, are less apparent. Above all, society is not demanding a more liberal democratic order.[29]
Whereas some pockets of civil society have tried to resist authoritarian
creep, the vast majority of Russian society has demonstrated little interest
or capacity to withstand Putin's antiliberal reforms.

Compared with What?

When assessing Russian democracy and its prospects, the real question is:
"compared with what?" Compared with American democracy today, Russian
democracy has a long way to go. Compared with Poland's democracy today,
Russian democracy is way behind. Compared with the U.S. polity a decade
after the signing of the Declaration of Independence, Russia's current political system does not seem so far behind. Compared with its own past, be it
Soviet communism or tsarist absolutism, the current system is vastly more
democratic. In prerevolutionary Russia, peasants did not vote, did not read
independent newspapers, and did not travel freely. Nor did Soviet citizens.
Princes were not removed from power by the ballot box like the hundreds
of Duma deputies in the December 1999 election. Only one-third (157 out
of 450) of those who served in the Duma in 1995–1999 returned to serve
again in 2000, a giant turnover rate compared with the U.S., where over 90

percent of incumbents are re-elected every two years.[30] The next time you
hear in the House of Representatives someone argue that elections in Russia
do not matter—that they are just like the charades of Soviet times—ask one
of these electoral losers if they agree. Moreover, remember that two-thirds
of an extremely educated population opted to participate in these parliamentary and presidential elections. If the elections were meaningless, then
why did these people bother to show up?

Compared with other states that emerged from the Soviet Union, Russia
appears to have made progress in building a democratic political order. The
degree of freedom of speech in Russia towers above that in Uzbekistan; the
consequences of elections in Russia are much greater than in Kazakhstan.[31]
At the same time, Russia's regime today lags far behind the progress made
toward consolidating liberal democracies in east Central Europe and the
Baltic states. By the standards of the post-Soviet world, Russian democracy
is performing rather well. By the standards of post-communist Europe, however, Russia is in the middle of the pack but is gradually slowing its pace. The
observation that Russia is somewhere near the median in its neighborhood
and among transitions from communist rule suggests that factors not specific
to Russia may be at work in determining regime type in this region.

Is Democratization Even the Right Lens?

The phenomenon of change in the former Soviet Union and Russia is big
enough and complex enough to attract a whole range of theories and comparisons. In the late 1980s and early 1990s, those interested in models of
democratization were the first to join the mission of explaining post-
communist change. Philippe Schmitter and Terry Karl pronounced, "Political scientists with expertise in other parts of the world tend to look upon
these events in Eastern Europe with 'imperial intent,' i.e., as an opportunity
to incorporate (at long last) the study of these countries into the general corpus of comparative analysis."[32] Because Schmitter and Karl and many others believed that change in Eastern Europe and the former Soviet Union was
analogous to the kind of regime change occurring elsewhere, these theorists
tried to explain these new transitions using narratives and analytical frameworks developed from studies of Latin America and southern Europe.[33]

Like the process of regime change, intellectual trajectories are also path
dependent.[34] In American political science in the 1980s, "transitology" had

eclipsed other traditions, theories, and models of regime change. The four-volume study of transitions from authoritarian rule in southern Europe and Latin America edited by O'Donnell, Schmitter, and Whitehead was published in 1986.[35] It received high acclaim and has became one of the most cited works in comparative politics. When communist regimes in Eastern Europe began to tumble just a few years later, it was only natural that these scholars of democratization and their analytical frameworks would move into the theoretical vacuum of Sovietology.[36] The rhetoric of Russia's revolutionaries encouraged the comparison. Because Boris Yeltsin and his anticommunist supporters had declared their commitment to democracy upon assuming power, many assumed that Russia was part of the so-called third wave of democratization that began (allegedly) on April 25, 1974, with the fall of Portugal's dictatorship.[37] Russian political reform would therefore follow a path to democracy similar to transitions in Latin America and southern Europe.

"Transitology" has offered many heuristic devices, approximate analogues, and analytical road maps useful for describing and explaining transitions in formerly communist countries. Russell Bova, for instance, argued, "However unique these developments [in Eastern Europe] have been on one level, the transition from communism may, nevertheless, be usefully viewed as a sub-category of a more generic phenomenon of transition from authoritarian rule."[38] If Russia's revolutionaries aspired to consolidate a democratic polity, the new Russian regime may deliberately and consciously repeat processes of democratization observed in other countries, adding yet another reason for comparing Russia with other democratic transitions.

Nevertheless, the democratization metaphor has several shortcomings when used as a tool to describe and explain Soviet and post-Soviet change in the last two decades. Political change has been only one component of the grand transformation in Russia at the end of the twentieth and beginning of the twenty-first centuries. In parallel, economic transformation and decolonization have also been under way.[39] Analogies of democratization from Latin American or southern Europe do not capture the scale of change taking place in post-communist Russia. On the contrary, one of the conditions for successful democratization in Latin America and southern Europe was that economic transformation (usually framed in these countries as the transition from capitalism to socialism) was not allowed to occur simultaneously.[40] State institutions in noncommunist authoritarian regimes also supported a market economy based on private property rights. As such, noncommunist societies were organized according to the logic of a capitalist, market system. In some transitions to democracy economic reform has accompanied, as well as precipitated, transitions to democracy in capitalist economies. In none of the recent transitions to democracy in Latin America, Africa, southern Europe, or Asia has full-scale transformation of a command economy been an agenda item.

The democratization lens has another problem, already alluded to. The end point of transition is assumed to be democratization. In reality, the experience of the post-communist world is that the transition from autocracy can lead to democracy as well as to new forms of autocracy.[41] It is regime change, but not necessarily democratic regime change.

Revolution is a more apt description of the phenomenon that first began in Russia nearly two decades ago and is still under way. During this period, the Russian state and the surrounding states of the former Soviet Union and Eastern Europe have undergone monumental political, economic, and social change rivaled only by the French Revolution or the Bolshevik Revolution in scope or consequence. The old Soviet polity, consisting of a state subordinated to the Communist Party of the Soviet Union, was destroyed. In the vacuum, new political institutions are emerging, including elected parliaments and executives, separation of powers between the legislative and executive branches, and several political parties. While the final end point of this political transformation is still uncertain, thus far a qualitatively new kind of regime has replaced the Soviet dictatorship. Likewise, the old Soviet command economy, in which the party-state controlled virtually all production and distribution, has also collapsed. It is being replaced by a system based on private property, free prices, and market forces. In short, a developing Russian capitalism is replacing Soviet communism. Moreover, these transformations have advanced by confrontational means, at times even violent confrontational means.[42] They have not resulted from cooperative arrangements. Rapid, simultaneous, and conflictual transformation of both the polity and economy is the definition of a revolution, but remember that most social revolutions ended in dictatorship, not democracy.[43] The application of theories of revolution to the Russian case, a seemingly rich research agenda, has only recently begun.[44] American political scientists have tended to shy away from this grandiose (and difficult to explain) label for examining the collapse of communism in Europe and Asia.[45] Russian scholars, and even some politicians, have been much more willing to deploy the discourse of revolution to events and processes under way in their country over the last two decades.[46]

Decolonization is another useful framework.[47] In the post-communist world, three multi-ethnic states—the Soviet Union, Yugoslavia, and Czechoslovakia—had to collapse before democratic or autocratic regimes could consolidate. Twenty-two of the twenty-seven states in the post-communist world did not exist before communism's collapse. Rather than an extension of the third wave of democratization, this explosion of new states is more analogous to the wave of decolonization and regime emergence that followed World War II throughout the British, French, and Portuguese empires, and like this earlier wave of state emergence, the delineation of borders may have been a necessary condition, but certainly was not a sufficient condition, for democratization. Most of the new postcolonial states that formed after World War II claimed to be making a transition to democracy, but only a few succeeded in consolidating democratic systems. Similarly, in the post-communist world the consolidation of liberal democracy has been the exception, not the rule.

Though sympathetic to these other frameworks, we have written a book about Russian regime change and not a book about Russia's second revolution or decolonization. The focus is on political change, because this is the dimension of Russia's triple transformation that remains most unsettled and least complete. The Soviet empire has collapsed and will never be reconstituted. Belarus may join Russia again, and Russia's internal borders in the Caucuses are still hotly contested, but the coercive subjugation of states and people adjacent to Russia's borders appears unlikely. Even though thousands of lives have been lost as a result of this empire's dissolution, Russian decolonization has been relatively peaceful when compared with the collapse of other empires.[48] The Soviet command economy is also extinct. Today Russia has a market economy.[49] This market system is severely flawed, but the key practices and institutions of the Russian economy today look more like those of other capitalist economies and less like the practices and institutions of the Soviet era.[50] Even the Communist Party of the Russian Federation now endorses the basic tenets of capitalism.

The final settling point of political transformation, however, is still uncertain. The autocratic institutions of the Soviet regime have collapsed, but what set of institutions will replace this old system has not been fully determined. Our book aims to shed light on possible trajectories. One possible outcome is the creation of a new kind of autocratic regime, different from Soviet dictatorship, but dictatorship nonetheless. Such a return to the past does not seem likely when discussing either the Russian economy or Russia's relations with its former colonies. Therefore paying greater attention to the future of Russia's political system, while giving less attention to the future of Russia's borders or Russian capitalism, seems appropriate.

Explaining Regime Type and Its Trajectory

In this book we deliberately did not superimpose an equation of independent and dependent variables from American political science onto our analysis of Russia's polity. The Russian authors involved in this project resisted this form of American hegemony. Nonetheless, several common factors that influence the formation of Russia's political system do emerge.

A Nondemocratic Inheritance

The actors and institutions that make democracy work were far less developed in Russia at the time of transition from communist rule than in other transitions to democracy in Latin American, southern Europe, and even post-communist East Central Europe. Many cases in these other regions were actually instances of redemocratization as countries resurrected democratic constitutions, political parties, and civil society.[51] Russia, however, had no such democratic institutions, parties, or civil society to rekindle.[52] The lack of democratic social capital was particularly glaring. No political system has ever been more hostile to civil society than the communist totalitarian regime Stalin erected. Although pre-Soviet Russia also accorded the state pride of place and limited the arenas of autonomous society, even the tsars permitted important nongovernmental organizations to exist, especially after 1861. The Soviet Union did not. Because Marxist theory predicted an end to all political and social conflict after the proletarian revolution, organization for the sake of any particularistic interest had no place in a communist society. Divergent group interests were to be transcended; the interests of all became the interests of one, embodied in the state. In keeping with ideological dictates, the Soviet state's most salient characteristic became destruction of the space between the individual and the state, the space that in noncommunist states is occupied by civil society organizations, such as trade unions, social networks, private business associations, public associations, clubs, and religious groups. These institutions were either rooted out altogether or absorbed into the sprawling state and the Communist Party, so that all social exchange was carried out under the guise of the party-state. This system atrophied slowly and consistently after Stalin's death. Nonetheless, we should not be surprised that the shadow of seventy years of communist rule still remains a decade later.

Similarly, Russian democrats could not dust off democratic constitutions of previous eras or breathe new life into old political parties of a democratic orientation.[53] Instead, Russia inherited social capital and institutional legacies from the Soviet era (and before) that impeded democratic consolidation.[54] Russia was not even starting with a blank slate, but with a cluttered political landscape that had to be cleared before the construction of democracy could begin. The process still has not ended. Lingering antidemocratic legacies feature prominently in many of the chapters.

The Process of Transition

In addition to an antidemocratic inheritance, Russia made the transition from communist rule by a process that did not facilitate the emergence of democratic institutions. The mode of transition affects the kind of regime that emerges.[55] The nature of Russia's transition from communist rule—protracted, conflictual, and imposed by the winners of the contests rather than negotiated—has impeded the consolidation of liberal democratic institutions and liberal democratic values. In other words, a causal relationship exists between the kind of transition and the kind of democracy that emerges.

The democratization literature has identified pacted transitions as those most likely to produce liberal democracy. Pacted transitions occur when the balance of power between the ancien regime and democratic challengers is relatively equal. In summing up the results of their multivolume study, O'Donnell and Schmitter asserted that "political democracy is produced by stalemate and dissensus rather than by prior unity and consensus."[56] Philip Roeder has made the same claim in his analysis of post-communist transitions: "The more heterogeneous in objectives and the more evenly balanced in relative leverage are the participants in the bargaining process of constitutional design, the more likely is the outcome to be a democratic constitution."[57] When both sides realize that they cannot prevail through the use of their own unilateral power, they agree to seek mutually beneficial solutions. Democratization requires a stalemate, "a prolonged and inconclusive struggle."[58] As Daniel Levine formulated, "[D]emocracies emerge out of mutual fear among opponents rather than as the deliberate outcome of con-certed commitments to make democratic political arrangements work."[59] Moderate, evolutionary processes are considered by transitologists as good for democratic emergence; radical revolutionary processes are considered bad. Cooperative bargains produce democratic institutions; noncoopera-tive processes do not.[60] As Przeworski concludes, "Democracy cannot be dictated; it emerges from bargaining."[61]

Such processes work best when they are protracted, slow, and deliberate. Drawing on earlier experiences of democratization, Harry Eckstein asserted that post-communist "democratization should proceed gradually, incre-mentally, and by the use of syncretic devices ... Social transformation is only likely to be accomplished, and to be accomplished without destructive dis-orders, if it spaced out over a good deal of time, if it is approached incre-mentally (i.e., sequentially), and if it builds syncretically upon the existing order rather than trying to eradicate it."[62] Advocates of this theoretical approach assert that "conservative transitions are more durable" than radi-cal transformations.[63]

Russia's regime, however, did not emerge from bargaining over a long period. It emerged abruptly from conflict in a short period.[64] The transition from communist rule first began when Mikhail Gorbachev initiated a series of liberalization measures, including greater freedom of speech, elections, and a new relationship between the Communist Party of the Soviet Union and the Soviet state. As the head of a totalitarian regime, Gorbachev imposed these reforms from above, but eventually these measures gave rise to new and inde-pendent political actors with more radical agendas for change.[65] Although Gorbachev and other reformers within the old Soviet regime periodically attempted to negotiate with moderates in Russia's democratic movement, they did not succeed in reaching a transition agreement. Instead, regime hard-liners tried to roll back reform by decreeing emergency rule in August 1991, an action that Russia's democratic forces succeeded in defeating.

The failed August 1991 coup created another propitious moment for an attempt at democratic transition. Led by Yeltsin, Russia's democratic forces had a unique window of opportunity to design democratic institutions by negotiating a new set of political rules with their communist opponents. The holding of new elections and the adoption of a revised constitution might have helped to legitimate a democratic order, but Yeltsin decided not to take this course. Indeed, Yeltsin devoted little time to designing new political institutions, focusing instead on dismantling the Soviet Union and initiating economic reform. Opposition to Yeltsin's policies, particularly his economic policies, grew over time. In the murky institutional context of the first Russian republic, the conflict between Yeltsin and his opponents eventually became a constitutional crisis between the Russian president and the Russian Congress, which ended tragically in the fall of 1993 after another military confrontation between groups with conflicting visions of Russia's political system. Yeltsin once again prevailed in this standoff, but at a much higher price than in 1991: dozens of Russian civilians were killed.[66]

Unlike in 1991, Yeltsin used his temporary political advantage in the fall of 1993 to institute a new political order. In November of that year he issued a new constitution and announced that a referendum on it would take place in December 1993. Viktor Sheinis, one of the authors of this constitution, discusses the basic features of this document in chapter 3. At the same time, voters were asked to elect representatives to a new bicameral parliament. Yeltsin and his side dictated the new rules. The opposition had only two options: accept the new rules dictated by Yeltsin or return to the barricades. Their acquiescence was a positive step for democracy. That these rules were not negotiated, however, had negative consequences for Russian democracy. Most important, as detailed in chapter 4, the 1993 constitution gave the president extraordinary powers. The executive branch not only faced few checks on its power, but the president also acquired the resources to maintain his or his successor's position of power.[67]

Concentrated power in the hands of the president did not result from a Russian cultural or historical proclivity for strong leaders.[68] The office of the presidency and then the considerable powers assigned to this presidential office emerged directly from the transition process.[69] A different kind of transition might have produced a different balance of power between the man in the Kremlin and everyone else.

The Political Economy of Post-Communism

Another barrier to democratic development in Russia is the structure of organized interests in the economy that has emerged in response to Russia's particular transition from communism to capitalism. The kinds of economic reforms pursued have influenced the type of political system that has emerged. When the Soviet Union collapsed in 1991, the people and organizations that had benefited from the Soviet economy did not cease to exist. On the contrary, these groups organized to defend their interests. The directors of state enterprises, in cooperation with trade unions organized during the Soviet era, moved aggressively to defend their property rights at the enterprise level. This coalition proved to be an effective interest group during the first years of the post-Soviet era.[70] Later in the decade a new group of economic actors—the oligarchs—emerged as a result of insider privatizations allowed by the government.[71]

These "red directors'" control over mammoth Soviet era enterprises and the avarice of the oligarchs squeezed the middle class as an economic force, a highly deleterious development for Russian democracy. If Barrington Moore's dictum "no bourgeoisie, no democracy" still holds, then Russia cannot be a democracy.[72] Nor has the Russian labor movement organized to press for democratization.[73] As discussed in chapter 6, this structure of ownership and socioeconomic organization has impeded the emergence of civil society, because the middle class often provides the bulk of funding and participation for nongovernmental organizations in developed democracies. Because the oligarchs are highly dependent on the state, they have remained loyal to those in the state, using their resources to help incumbents when necessary. When some of the oligarchs have attempted to play a role in politics autonomous from the state, the state has moved quickly to check their political activities and erode their economic fortunes. Russia's per capita gross national product has not reached the levels generally thought to be conducive to democratic stability.[74] On the contrary, the Russian economy endured a severe depression for most of the 1990s, making resources for nonessential activities scarce for most of the population. People have had neither the time nor the money to support participatory democracy.

The Reemergence of the State

Another factor that features prominently in many of the chapters is the reemergence of the state as a major player in Russian politics. The latent power of the Russian state in political affairs was always apparent, but it has only recently been deployed in ways that have negative consequences for democratic development.

Many considered the Soviet Union to be one of the strongest states in the world. Unconstrained by societal demands, Soviet leaders had the power to distribute resources as they saw fit. They also faced few external constraints in relation to decision making, as the USSR was a military superpower anchoring a bloc of states relatively insulated from the international capitalist system. Accompanying this autonomy was genuine state capacity. While inefficient and corrupt, the state still dominated every aspect of life within the Soviet Union and had the ability to project power internationally. If someone wanted something done within the Soviet Union, the state was the only means available.

In the early years after the Soviet Union's collapse, the new Russian state appeared weak and broken. Decisions made in Moscow seemed to have little consequence outside the "garden ring," the inner boulevard of the Russian capital. Basic services traditionally provided by the state, such as a single currency, a common market, security, welfare, and education, were no longer public goods. State employees had to negotiate and strike just to be paid for work already completed. Contractual arrangements had be self-enforcing to succeed. Mafias, security firms, and private armies assumed major responsibilities for providing security, in essence challenging the state's monopoly on the use of force. For a time, many transactions were conducted using barter or U.S. dollars, thereby marginalizing the role of the national currency. Finally, after the August 1998 financial meltdown, individual regions imposed trade barriers and export quotas, defying the notion of a national economy. Many cited this state weakness as an impediment to democratization and liberal practices.[75]

The institutional coherence of the Russian state was also weak and ill-defined. Fractures emerged both between different levels of government and between different branches of the central government, dramatically undermining the state's autonomy as an independent actor.[76] With no constitutional delineation of rights and responsibilities between central and local authorities, regional governments seized the moment of Soviet collapse to assume greater political and economic autonomy. In March 1992, two autonomous republics, Tatarstan and Chechnya, declared their independence from the Russian Federation. Others soon followed. The Russian central state, only just constituted months before, had little capacity to counter these assertions of subnational authority. The stalemate between different branches of the central government precipitated an even greater state crisis. Soon after economic reform began in January 1992, the Russian Supreme Soviet and the Russian Congress of People's Deputies began a campaign to reassert their authority as the "highest state organ."[77] With no formal, or even informal, institutions to structure relations between the president and the Congress, the state virtually ceased to function. The polarization between branches of government occurred because of the deep ideological

divide between opposing camps. Polarization, in turn, produced state inca-
pacity.

In many spheres the state remains weak, divided, and ineffective. The
general trajectory since 1993, however, has been toward consolidating the
state internally and lessening political divisions among those running it.
The 1993 constitution outlined the basic institutional division of power
within the national government and between central and regional powers.
This clarity, in turn, has facilitated greater coherence in the policy-making
process, especially because the executive branch of government has such
clearly articulated advantages in relation to other branches. Equally important, the ideological divides that polarized the national government in the
early 1990s no longer exist. Beginning in 1999, economic growth has also
given the state a new flow of income that officials in power earlier in the
decade did not enjoy.

In parallel, however, old state structures that never reformed or disappeared have regained some of their power from the Soviet era. Most dramatic has been the rise of the FSB. One of its own now runs the Kremlin and
nearly a hundred more have crossed into civilian service to assume senior
positions in the government.[78] The Ministry of Defense is one of the least
reformed bureaucracies left over from the Soviet days. While Russia's armed
forces have demonstrated a limited capacity to project force in Chechnya,
the military's influence on political decisions has grown significantly in
recent years. The Ministry of Internal Affairs is another unreformed branch
of government whose capacity to influence political outcomes has grown
with time.

This rising state has not been accompanied by a commensurate strengthening of society, and most certainly not of political society. The balance of
power between the state and civil society is heavily skewed in favor of the
former. Especially in recent years, the state has begun to creep back into arenas considered privatized earlier in the decade. As discussed throughout the
book, the state under Putin has played a direct role in influencing electoral
outcomes, creating parties, organizing civil society, and obtaining control of
national media outlets.

Putin's move to strengthen the state is not surprising. Like all revolutions
in their later stages, the consolidation of regime change requires greater
state power, more order, and even a return of some old practices, that is, a
Thermidorean reaction.[79] The rise of state capacity need not be directly and

negatively correlated with democracy. Democracies need capacious states to defend individual liberties. The state's re-penetration into realms society has only recently reclaimed, however, is not the kind of state capacity needed for democratic development. On the contrary, the reconstitution of a coherent and powerful state, albeit only in certain spheres, has eroded democratic development, not enhanced it.[80]

Individual Actions, Policies, and Choices About Institutions

After recognizing the negative consequences for democratic development of the Soviet inheritance, the nature of Russia's transition, and the rise of the state, many chapters add another important factor: individuals and the policies they pursued. In addition to structural factors, individuals can play an instrumental role in crafting the political institutions of a regime in transition. In stable institutional settings in which individuals select from the same menu of choices over multiple iterations, the role of particular individuals is minimal. In stable settings the preferences and power of social groups are also relatively fixed, thereby constraining the leaders who represent these groups. In uncertain institutional settings, however, the causal role assigned to unique individuals is greater.[81]

Yeltsin's leadership style, his norms, and his policy preferences had huge consequences for the trajectory of Russian democracy in the 1990s.[82] Not all democratic failures and shortcomings in post-communist Russia can be blamed on the long shadows of Ivan Grozny or Joseph Stalin. Yeltsin made his contributions too, as did his close allies and his ardent enemies. Yeltsin also made positive contributions to democratic development that might not have occurred with another leader. Democracies do not just emerge organically as a result of modernization. People make them.

People can also undo them. The impact of a single leader on regime trajectory has become even more apparent during the Putin era, because Putin has good health, youth, energy, and popularity. While these attributes have given him the capacity to have a fundamental impact on the evolution of Russia's political system, they did not determine his course of action.[83] On the contrary, another individual in the Kremlin with these same attributes might have pushed Russia in a more democratic direction. As several chapters highlight, Putin's role and policies cannot be under-emphasized.

That Putin's rise to power has had such a major impact on the regime suggests that the current political system is not consolidated. This condition
gives some cause for hope. As will become clear, the trajectory of democracy
in Russia today is in a negative direction, yet this regime has not consolidated into a full-blown dictatorship.[84] Whether Putin wants to move toward
creating such a regime still remains in question. Whether he could is also
not certain.

2

Elections

Michael McFaul and Nikolai Petrov

Competitive elections are the cornerstone of any democracy. Elections alone do not make a country a democracy, but they are an essential component of the democratic process. In seeking to describe regime types, analysts have invented many adjectives to qualify the word democracy, but all descriptions on the democratic side of the ledger, including electoral democracies and illiberal democracies, still recognize competitive elections as the critical variable that distinguishes autocracies from democracies.[1]

The advent of competitive elections in the Soviet Union and then Russia certainly contributed to the reclassification of the country as a democracy.[2] In the early 1990s, Russia met Joseph Schumpeter's minimalist definition of democracy as a political regime in which the major positions of power are filled "through a competitive struggle for the people's vote."[3] Since the first semicompetitive election in the Soviet Union in the spring of 1989, Russians have voted a lot. They have cast votes in five national parliamentary elections (1989, 1990, 1993, 1995, and 1999); three presidential elections (1991, 1996, and 2000); four referenda (two in 1991 and two in 1993); four rounds of elections for regional legislatures (1990, 1993–1994, 1996–1997, and 2000–2001); and two rounds of gubernatorial elections (1996–1997 and 2000–2001). These elections can be grouped into four large electoral cycles: the Gorbachev era (1989–1991), the 1993–1994 founding elections, the 1995–1997 electoral cycle, and the 1999–2001 electoral cycle.

Every election since the Soviet collapse has included more than one candidate. In the parliamentary elections, voters selected from dozens of choices both from the party list and from individual single-mandate candidates as provided by Russia's mixed electoral system. Furthermore, Russia now has an estimated 3,000 elections every four years to a total of about 20,000 elective offices.[4] Roughly 2 million people, or about 2 percent of adult population, are directly involved in the electoral process. In addition, with the exception of the 2000 presidential vote, the outcomes of these elections at the national level have been uncertain. The sheer number of candidates, the high voter turnouts, and the amount spent in these electoral competitions suggest that their outcomes have consequences well understood by all. Since 1993, elections have also taken place on time and under the rule of law.[5] An important factor is that the laws governing elections have not changed radically before each election.

Yet paradoxes and anomalies are apparent in the election process that over time call into question the democratic function of these events in the political system. In particular, since the collapse of the Soviet Union, presidential elections in post-communist Russia have never produced a change in "party." Boris Yeltsin won the first two presidential elections and his handpicked successor, Vladimir Putin, won the third election. He will win again in 2004. Because the presidency is the most powerful office in the Russian political system, this continuity over time—despite extreme discontinuity in economic and social affairs—is curious, if not alarming. It cuts against the grain of electoral patterns in the most democratic parts of the post-communist world, where the winners of the first round of competitive elections were often replaced by former communists in the second round of competitive elections. In east Central Europe, economic depression caused by the costs of transition triggered this swing of the pendulum. The Russian people endured an even greater economic depression, but did not "throw the bastards out." Why not?

In this chapter we argue that three factors have contributed to this rather strange outcome. First, the Soviet leadership, and Mikhail Gorbachev in particular, did not introduce semicompetitive elections into the political practices of the USSR and then Russia as a means of democratizing the polity. Rather, the goal of these elections was to purge the conservative ranks of the Communist Party of the Soviet Union (CPSU) from their positions of power within state structures as a way to liberate these state institutions and thereby make them available as instruments for executing Gorbachev's economic reforms. As is often the case in new democracies, the electoral process then produced unexpected outcomes and unlikely winners such as Yeltsin. Over time, however, these same Soviet era elites who were initially threatened by elections learned how to regain control of them. Consequently, Russian elections have become less competitive and less free over time, at least in those elections that have the most meaning: presidential elections and elections for executives at the regional level. Parliamentary elections at all levels have been more competitive and less corrupt, in part because parliaments have less power than in the Russian political system.

Second, old elites have been able to reduce the uncertainties associated with competitive elections over time because they have regained control of the state and its resources and learned to use the state's resources to achieve the electoral outcomes they want. Business people, and even some mass associations, such as trade unions, environmental groups, and consumer protection organizations, have spent private resources to influence electoral outcomes, but their resources have never matched those of the state. With time, the imbalance between state and society has become more pronounced, not less. The state's power was demonstrated most dramatically in the 1999 parliamentary elections, when by maintaining control of the two largest television networks, the Kremlin managed to invent a party— Unity—from scratch, which won nearly a quarter of the vote. These same resources helped to propel Putin to elected power in the Kremlin after he had already acquired control of the state through a nonelectoral process.

Third, the lopsided outcomes in favor of incumbents have not resulted just from the deployment of state resources (known as "administrative resources" in Russia) during the campaign. Those already in power have increasingly benefited from the fact that those loyal to them in the state count the votes. In successful transitions to democracy, the completion of several electoral rounds tends to make the electoral process more democratic. Because they are new events, founding elections in democratic transitions are often marred by irregularities. Outgoing dictators wield their control of the state apparatus to falsify results and terrorize voters. Often, first elections are deliberately not fully democratic, but instead serve as an interim step between dictatorship and democracy. Over time, however, these constraints on and irregularities in the democratic process fade. Practice makes perfect. In Russia, however, the trend has been in the opposite direction.

The combination of these three factors means that elections have become less free and fair today than they were a decade ago. Some even call into question whether Russia can be considered an electoral democracy.[6] We are close to tossing Russia back into the authoritarian category ourselves.

To demonstrate the changing function of elections in the Soviet Union and Russia over the last decade, this chapter proceeds as follows. The next section discusses the function of elections in the Gorbachev era, showing that the Soviet Union's last leader used elections as a means for ends besides democracy, though with unintended consequences. The second section discusses the intended purpose of elections in 1993, which in many ways were Russia's founding elections. The third section explores the democratic nature of elections in the 1995–1997 electoral cycle, which may have been the most competitive and consequential in Russia's brief democratic history. The fourth section contrasts the 1999–2001 election cycle with the previous two cycles, showing how Russia's elections have become less free and fair over time. The final section concludes.

The Gorbachev Era: Elections as a Political Weapon

In most successful transitions from authoritarian rule to democracy, the first or founding election marks the completion of the transition phase and the beginning of regime consolidation. To get to a founding election, reform-oriented elites (called soft-liners in the literature on democratization) from the old regime and moderates from civil society often negotiate pacts that limit the issues allowed to be contested after the first vote. [7] A pact "lessens the fears of moderates that they will be overwhelmed by a triumphant, radical, majority which will implement drastic changes."[8] Limitations on economic transformation, for instance, are often a critical component of successful pacts that in turn produce the first election after authoritarian rule or a founding election. As O'Donnell and Schmitter famously remarked, "[A]ll previously known transitions to political democracy have observed one fundamental restriction: it is forbidden to take, or even to checkmate, the king of one of the players. In other words, during the transition, the property rights of the bourgeoisie are inviolable."[9]

Generally the boundaries of a state must also be agreed upon before elites can make a successful bargain for creating a democratic polity.[10] If who is a citizen of the state and who is not is unclear, then how can elections be organized?

Finally, in many of the so-called third wave transitions to democracy, political liberalization and the rebirth of civil society preceded the first elections. Moreover, "mobilization following initial liberalization is likely to bring political parties to the forefront of the transition and make the convocation of elections an increasingly attractive means for conflict resolution."[11] A founding election marks the end of the transition period and the beginning of the new democratic regime. Before this founding election, the basic rules of the game for governing the country have been agreed upon by those involved in negotiating the regime change.

The function of competitive elections and the timing of their introduction in the Soviet Union and then Russia did not follow this transitions script. Most important, the convocation of elections did not demarcate the end of the transition period. These first Soviet era competitive elections took place midstream in the process of regime change, at which time the basic institutional framework of the new polity had not been established. Indeed, elites competing in these elections did not even share a common definition of the state's borders. These elections also took place while Soviet and Russian elites were debating the fundamental organization of the economy, before the blossoming of civil society, and before the formation of political parties. In this context, elections served to polarize politics rather than to bring closure to the struggle between opposing actors involved in redefining the new rules of the game for the Soviet and Russian regimes. Every vote was a referendum on the Soviet ancien regime.[12] Every vote was also a tactical tool that both sides in these polarized debates deployed to advance their immediate political aims. Neither side made the electoral process an actual goal of the political struggle.

The first semicompetitive elections in Soviet history occurred in the spring of 1989. Soviet voters were given the opportunity to select a portion of the representatives to the USSR Congress of People's Deputies (CPD), at that time the Soviet state's parliament. The decision to convoke these elections did not occur as the result of a bargain between soft-liners in the Soviet state and moderates representing societal opposition. At the time, the level of mobilization within society not directly controlled by the state was modest. General Secretary of the CPSU Gorbachev initiated these semicompetitive elections.

Gorbachev did want to liberalize the Soviet political system as an end in and of itself. Nonetheless, his decision in the summer of 1988 to introduce semicompetitive elections to the USSR CPD was instrumental. Beginning in 1987, and then more earnestly in 1988, Gorbachev had begun to pursue serious economic reform under the banner of perestroika. Initially, he believed that the Communist Party might be the vanguard organization that would implement these reforms. By the summer of 1988, however, Gorbachev and his liberal advisers had come to see many of the top leaders of the CPSU as the enemies of reform. Rather than spearheading his initiatives, in Gorbachev's estimation party leaders were impeding perestroika. He therefore switched course. By using elections he aimed to free the Soviet Union's formal state institutions of conservative Communist Party bosses. For decades, these legislative organs simply rubber-stamped and helped to implement decisions taken by the CPSU. Gorbachev wanted to reinvigorate the soviets (councils) through the electoral process, a process that might also give greater legitimacy to these bodies.

Unable to garner support for his reform ideas within the upper echelons of the CPSU, Gorbachev hoped to take away governing power from the Communist Party and instead give it to the soviets.[13] He predicted that a newly elected USSR CPD would be more sympathetic to his reform agenda than the CPSU. He also planned to transfer his political base from the Communist Party to this legislative body. General Secretary Gorbachev would also become Speaker Gorbachev and then President Gorbachev, and eventually, if all went according to plan, these state positions would become more important than his party post.

To maintain control of the process, Gorbachev did not permit these first elections to be free and fair. One-third of the 2,225 seats in the Congress were allocated to "social organizations," which included everything from the CPSU to the Soviet Academy of Sciences.[14] The remaining seats, divided equally between districts determined by territorial divisions and districts carved according to population, in principle were all contested. In practice, however, the cumbersome electoral procedures made the nomination of "democratic" challengers virtually impossible. To be nominated, candidates had to be endorsed by either a workers' collective or a public meeting of at least 500 people. Following their nomination, district electoral committees had the power to disqualify any candidates—a power exercised against almost half of all candidates.[15]

Nonetheless, these elections constituted a direct threat to the CPSU elite, because only the Party's top 100 officials were elected through the social organization list. The elections brought new people into the political process: an estimated 88 percent of successful candidates were elected for the first time.[16] Only nine out of thirty-two CPSU first secretaries won in contested races. Out of seventy-five secretaries running unopposed, six nevertheless lost because they failed to receive the required 50 percent threshold of support.[17] The failure of the CPSU's *nomenklatura* was most impressive in Leningrad, where both the first and second secretaries and most other lower-level party officials failed to win seats. At this stage, elections were doing what Gorbachev had hoped, that is, weakening or eliminating from power the CPSU's most conservative bosses.

While local CPSU leaders were humiliated, their losses did not translate directly into gains for new political actors—or democrats as they were then labeled. Eighty-five percent of the new Soviet legislature were members of the CPSU, while none belonged to an alternative political party at the time of the elections.

For Gorbachev and his allies within the Politburo, the 1989 elections to the Soviet Congress were the most important elections. The electoral process had sparked mass interest in politics. Tens of thousands of people participated in the nominating process and voter turnout was an outstanding 89.8 percent of eligible voters in the USSR—and most newcomers to the political process were Gorbachev supporters. Once the new Congress convened, deputies quickly elected Gorbachev first as chairman of the Congress and later as president of the Soviet Union, a newly created post designed to give him executive authority within the state that would be autonomous from both the CPSU and the Congress. As a tool for strengthening Gorbachev, elections were certainly paying dividends at this stage in the reform process.

Consequently, for Gorbachev and his team, the elections to soviets at the republic, regional, city, and district levels to be held in the spring of 1990 seemed like an afterthought. The idea to hold these elections was consistent with Gorbachev's overall strategy of seeking to empower state institutions at the party's expense. He could not liberate the state from the party at the national level of government and not do the same at lower levels of government. Nonetheless, Gorbachev and his colleagues did not approach these elections with the same level of attention that they devoted to the 1989 elections.[18]

The electoral law created a large Russian Congress of 1,068 delegates from which a smaller Supreme Soviet would be selected. The Russian electoral law, however, differed from the rules governing the election to the Soviet Congress in that no seats were set aside for social organizations.[19]

Even though Gorbachev was worried about alienating conservative forces with direct elections in 1989, this concern had either subsided or been taken over by other worries in 1990. Instead, all seats were filled in first-past-the-post elections in two kinds of electoral districts, one defined by territory (168 seats) and the other by population (900 seats). If no candidate won 50 percent of the vote in the first round, a runoff between the top two finishers occurred two weeks later. These elections to the Congress occurred simultaneously with elections for soviet deputies at lower levels. The 1990 elections were the first truly democratic elections in Soviet history.

The nominating procedures still disadvantaged outsiders, however. As in the 1989 elections, workers' collectives at enterprises were granted primary power to nominate candidates. Because workers' collectives still reported to CPSU secretaries within enterprises and institutes, the Communist Party could filter out unwanted candidates, but by 1990 the party no longer wielded hegemonic control over every institute and factory. In addition, voters could nominate candidates at a public meeting of 300 people instead of the 500 required for the 1989 election.

Formally, parties did not compete in this election, because noncommunist parties were just forming. (Article 6 of the Soviet Constitution, which had guaranteed the CPSU the leading role in Soviet society, was repealed in February 1990—just weeks before the election—not giving new political parties enough time to organize.) Nonetheless, these elections stimulated an explosion of grassroots political activity throughout Russia.[20] The sheer number of seats contested meant that a large segment of the population was involved in the nomination and campaign process and that each district contest had its unique characteristics. At the same time, two main camps formed: the democrats and the communists.

The democrats—a label used at the time by both their friends and their enemies—had begun to organize as a united political force well before the spring of 1990. In January 1990 they founded a new organization, Democratic Russia, which assumed primary responsibility for coordinating candidate recruitment and campaign activity for the nascent democratic movement. Democratic Russia ran against the status quo. Its slogans stressed that it opposed the Communist Party, opposed corruption, and even opposed Gorbachev. The articulation of concrete alternative programs was not necessary at this stage in Russia's transition. Opposing the status quo was sufficient.

The second main player in the 1990 elections was the CPSU. Split between reformists and conservatives, it did not orchestrate a national campaign or participate as an electoral party. Gorbachev and his immediate circle incorrectly assumed that the republic-level soviets were not as important as the USSR Congress of Peoples Deputies, and many CPSU officials campaigned as challengers to and opponents of those in power.

Compared with the 1989 elections, Russia's democrats, who won roughly one-third of the 1,068 seats in the Russian Congress, viewed the 1990 elections as tremendous victories.[21] Communists won about 40 percent of Congress seats, while centrists occupied what Russians refer to as the *boloto* (swamp) in the middle. These democrats were no longer Gorbachev loyalists. Many of them were people brand new to the Russian political process. A former Politburo candidate member, Yeltsin, became the de facto leader of the democratic forces and was subsequently elected chairman of the Russian Congress. But by this time Gorbachev loathed Yeltsin and did not want to see him back in politics in such a powerful position.

Elections were now producing unintended consequences for those who had initiated them. The results for Gorbachev were even worse in republics such as Estonia, Latvia, Lithuania, Armenia, and Georgia, where anticommunist fronts won solid majorities. If the 1989 elections had made Gorbachev much stronger, the 1990 elections made him much weaker.

The 1990 elections served to further open up the political process to new individuals and new political forces. At this stage in Russia's political transformation, elections still served a liberalizing function. The 1990 elections also stimulated the emergence of proto-party politics. In these elections, Democratic Russia occupied center stage as a national campaign and as a united front of those opposed to the old Soviet order. Organizationally and ideologically, Russian politics had become polarized into those supporting the old order and those behind Democratic Russia. Significant third positions or third parties had not emerged.

Soon after the 1990 vote, the central cleavage in Soviet politics became territorial jurisdiction. The Russian CPD, as well as supreme soviets in several other republics, declared their independence from the Soviet Union. This polarization remained until the collapse of the Soviet Union. The next two elections, the referendum on the fate of the Soviet Union in March 1991 and the June 1991 presidential elections in Russia, were episodes in this polarized struggle. Gorbachev organized the March 1991 referendum as a way to strengthen his hand in negotiating a new federal treaty with the republics. In asking voters if they approved of a new, reformed Union, Gorbachev did help his cause. In those republics that conducted this referendum, 76.4 percent of all voters supported the preservation of the Union. In Russia, 71.3 percent voted yes, while only 26.4 percent voted no. Yeltsin dismissed the referendum as a simple ploy for "preserving the imperial and unitary essence of the system."[22] At the same time, Yeltsin did not campaign against the vote, but instead pushed for an additional question to be added to the Russian ballot that asked voters if they supported the idea of creating a Russian presidency. A large majority answered yes, and three months later Yeltsin won Russia's first presidential election in a landslide, first-round victory over five other candidates.[23]

In the Russian Federation, the basic procedures for both the elections were generally free and fair.[24] Neither of these votes, however, could be considered normal events punctuating the end of a democratic transition. Both were extraordinary events that occurred suddenly as the direct consequence of immediate political struggles, and neither vote helped to end the transition. Gorbachev's referendum was obviously a special event. Few countries ask their voters if they want to dissolve the state or not. The Russian presidential vote was also a political tactic designed to strengthen Yeltsin's hand.[25] The CPD had elected Yeltsin as chairman by a slim margin in the spring of 1990, but by the spring of 1991 his support within the Congress had fallen dramatically. By the opening session of the Third Congress in March 1991, a petition had circulated to remove him as chairman, which could be done by a simple majority vote. Because Yeltsin remained extremely popular among Russian voters, his aides concocted the idea of creating a Russian presidency. Unlike the Soviet president, Russia's president was to be directly elected by the people, a mechanism that ensured Yeltsin victory. This new office—complete with autonomy from the Congress and legitimacy from the people—was designed to give Yeltsin more power in his battles with his communist and Soviet government enemies. Yeltsin was elected to this new office well before the Russian Constitution had been amended to spell out the president's powers. In other words, elections were occurring before the political rules of the game had been codified or agreed upon. The push to create a Russian presidency was a response to a concrete political situation, not the result of a carefully plotted strategy, a philosophy about the need for direct elections of executives, or a normative commitment to a separation of powers or to checks and balances.[26]

In August 1991, a mere two months after the Russian presidential elections, conservative forces in the Soviet government upset with Gorbachev's plans for transforming the USSR's federal organization tried to seize power in a military coup. Their efforts failed miserably, and instead helped to precipitate the end of the Soviet Union in December 1991. The August 1991 coup attempt in effect took one major issue of contestation off the table: no more referenda about the fate of the Soviet Union would be held. Rather than asking voters about their opinions again, Yeltsin took the initiative to negotiate the end of the Soviet Union once and for all.

Throughout the tumultuous period between the first semicompetitive elections in 1989 and the collapse of the Soviet Union in December 1991, elections took place in the context of a social revolution. Unlike transitions to democracy in Latin America and southern Europe, the transition from Soviet communist rule was not only about crafting new democratic institutions. Negotiations about new rules of the game for the political system occurred at the same time that the Soviet command economy was being transformed into a market system and the Soviet state was being dissolved. During this kind of regime change, elections were not part of the goals or objectives of the political conflict (as in many cases of democratization elsewhere), but rather the means for obtaining other ends. During these last years of the Soviet Union, the goal of consolidating democratic institutions was less important to most actors than the debates about economic transformation or Russian independence. Securing or impeding these latter two objectives defined most of the drama of Russia's transition from Soviet communist rule. Yeltsin and his allies used elections to gain access to political power as a way to pursue economic transformation and Soviet dissolution. Consequently, elections in the Soviet Union and Russia did not provide the same positive force for the development of democratic institutions and practices in Russia as elections have performed in other democratic transitions.

Russia's Belated Founding Election, December 1993

After the failed August 1991 coup attempt, there was much discussion among Russia's democrats about whether Yeltsin should convene new elections, particularly for the Russian parliament. Some within Democratic Russia argued that Yeltsin needed to seize advantage of his immense popularity in the wake of his successful stance against the coup attempt. They reasoned that the popularity of Yeltsin and Democratic Russia would decline quickly once they initiated the painful steps involved in economic reform. Others pushed for a referendum on the newly penned Russian Constitution. Yeltsin did neither.[27]

During this tumultuous period Yeltsin did initiate several major political changes. He banned the CPSU, subordinated Soviet ministries to the

Russian state, and, most dramatically, in December 1991 dissolved the USSR. But he did not push for ratification of a new constitution even though he had a draft in hand, and he refrained from convoking a post-communist founding election. Instead, Yeltsin and his new government used their political mandate to initiate economic transformation. Eager to avoid what they perceived as Gorbachev's mistake of putting politics before economics, Yeltsin's team concentrated their energies on dismantling the Soviet command economy and creating a new market system. Indeed, many in Yeltsin's new government believed that economic transformation was a precondition for democracy. Without private property, Russian voters had no private political rights to defend. The most vocal proponents of this logic advocated a Pinochet type of dictatorship as an interim regime between command communism and capitalist democracy.

The failure to secure a new electoral mandate to rule or a popular ratification of the rules of the game for governing Russia had destabilizing consequences for the new state. As discussed in later chapters in more detail, poorly defined political institutions fueled ambiguity, stalemate, and conflict both between the federal and subnational units of the state, and then, more consequentially, between the president and the Congress of Peoples Deputies. Institutional ambiguity between the president and the Congress did not have an immediate impact on politics, because at that time most deputies in the Congress supported Yeltsin. Yeltsin considered Ruslan Khasbulatov, his successor as chairman of the Congress, a close ally. After price liberalization and the beginning of radical economic reform in January 1992, however, the Congress began a campaign to reassert its authority over the president. The disagreement about economic reform in turn spawned a constitutional crisis between the parliament and the president. With no formal, or even informal, institutions to structure relations between the president and the Congress, political polarization occurred once again.[28]

In this renewed polarized context, both sides attempted to use elections to bolster their respective sides. For most of the winter of 1993, the Congress and Yeltsin argued about questions to be asked in a new referendum. Both sides feared a new direct election, but both were also eager to secure a new popular mandate. In response to a series of constitutional amendments proposed by the Congress that Yeltsin deemed illegitimate, he threatened to use the election weapon yet again. He called for a referendum, scheduled for January 1993, to answer the question, "Whom do you trust to take the country out of economic and political crisis [and] restore the

Russian Federation: the present composition of the Congress and the Supreme Soviet or the President?" According to Yeltsin, the winner of this electoral duel would remain in power with a mandate to control the course of reforms and the loser would be forced to face new elections in April 1993. The Constitutional Court declared Yeltsin's referendum question unconstitutional, which then set the stage for dueling referendum proposals from the Congress and Yeltsin on everything from impeachment to land reform. Eventually they reached a compromise to ask the following four questions in an April 1993 referendum.

- Do you trust Russian President Yeltsin?
- Do you approve of the socioeconomic policy conducted by the Russian president and by the Russian government since 1992?
- Should a new presidential election be conducted in advance of the scheduled date?
- Should a new parliamentary election be conducted in advance of the scheduled date?

As specified in the agreement between Yeltsin and the Congress, the outcome of the first two questions had no obvious consequences, while the third and fourth questions needed a majority of all eligible voters (and not just a majority of those voting) to be considered binding.

Given the sharp downward turn in real incomes, skyrocketing inflation, and extreme uncertainty about Russia's economic future, most predicted that Russian voters would act similarly to voters in other post-communist transitions and use this ballot to protest the pain of economic transformation. Amazingly, they did not. On the first question, 58.7 percent of voters affirmed their trust in Yeltsin, compared with 39.3 percent who did not. Even more amazingly, 53 percent expressed their approval of Yeltsin's socioeconomic policy, while 44.5 percent disapproved. Regarding questions three and four a plurality (49.5 percent) supported early presidential elections, while a solid majority (67.2 percent) called for new parliamentary elections. These results reflected the highly polarized nature of Russian politics at the time. In essence, voters were being asked their opinion about the revolution midstream in the revolution. Like votes during the Gorbachev era, this vote did not create momentum toward the consolidation of a new democratic polity, but served as a gauge of popular support for diametrically opposed sides.[29]

Yeltsin won this referendum, but not overwhelmingly. Although surprised with the results, the anti-Yeltsin coalition still believed that it was gaining popular support, because Yeltsin's percentage of support in this vote was lower than in his 1991 electoral victory. Consequently, the referendum did not prove to be decisive in resolving the political confrontation that was paralyzing the Russian state.

Tragically, the impasse between president Yeltsin and his opponents in parliament only ended after the use of force. On September 21, 1993, Yeltsin issued Presidential Decree Number 1400, which dissolved the Russian Congress and called for a referendum to adopt a new constitution. Once again a politician was convoking elections in an ad hoc manner for immediate political purposes. The Congress rejected Yeltsin's decree as unconstitutional and instead impeached him and appointed his vice president, Aleksandr Rutskoi, as the new president. In a replay of August 1991, the situation was only resolved when one side—Yeltsin's side—prevailed in a military conflict.

After Yeltsin's successful use of force against the Congress, which ended on October 4, 1993, the president used his unquestioned power to dictate the new rules of the game: he violated fundamental democratic principles by dissolving an elected parliament through unconstitutional means, he showed the same disregard for the electoral process by dissolving regional soviets, and he removed three out of eight regional heads of administration who had been elected several months earlier.[30] At the same time, Yeltsin seemed eager to establish new political rules in which elections would play a crucial role. He published a draft constitution and called for a referendum on the constitution in December. Not surprisingly, the new draft constitution gave the president extraordinary powers, compelling some to label the regime a super-presidential system.[31] After October 4, Yeltsin also announced that elections for a new bicameral parliament would take place in December.[32]

Earlier in the crisis, Yeltsin had announced his intention to hold a new presidential election in June of the following year, which was earlier than scheduled, but he later reneged on this promise. With no parliament in place at the time, Yeltsin used decrees to put new electoral laws in place. Yeltsin fiated into place a new electoral system, which stated that the new lower house of parliament, the State Duma, would be elected according to a mixed system: half of the 450 seats were to be determined by a first-past-the-post system in newly drawn up electoral districts (similar to elections of House representatives in the United States), while the other half were to be allocated according to a system of proportional representation.[33] Parties had to win at least 5 percent of the vote to win seats on the proportional representation ballot.[34] For the Federation Council, the upper house, the presidential administration decreed that voters in each region (republic, *oblast*, or *krai*) would cast two votes for their senatorial candidates on one list. The top two finishers in each region would win.

The December 1993 elections served as a founding election for Russia's new political system. Above all, their objective was to ratify a new set of political rules of the game. Yeltsin's draft constitution outlined difficult procedures for amending it, meaning that adoption of this constitution was likely to produce a lasting set of political institutions for post-communist Russia. Since 1993, the constitution has yet to be amended. The December 1993 vote was also the first election in Russia's brief democratic history in which political parties had the opportunity to participate fully. The incorporation of proportional representation into the electoral system for the Duma gave parties an additional incentive to organize and to participate in this vote.

To serve as a founding election the vote had to be legitimate and all major political forces had to participate, but some extreme nationalist and communist groups decided to boycott the elections, and some people could not participate because they were still in jail after the October 1993 conflict. Russia's major communist party, the Communist Party of the Russian Federation (CPRF), along with its rural partner, the Agrarian Party of Russia, decided to participate in these electoral contests, even though they had just been on the opposite side of the barricades from the man who was calling for and setting the rules for these elections. Their agreement to participate had major consequences. Most important, it helped to legitimate the constitution. Even though the CPRF formally called upon its supporters to vote against the new constitution, its participation in the parliamentary vote suggested that it was planning to participate in Yeltsin's new polity. Its participation also had positive consequences for the acceptance of elections as the only legitimate means for coming to power. From 1993 on, national elections for the Duma have occurred as scheduled and under rules previously agreed to by all participants. Despite numerous attempts to change it, the electoral law governing the composition of the Duma has remained basically unchanged since 1993, a milestone for democratic consolidation and stability.[35] The Federation Council has not enjoyed such stability. As discussed in the following sections, the rules for selecting senators have changed virtually every electoral cycle.

At the same time, the 1993 vote introduced several antidemocratic practices into the electoral process. First, the president issued a decree to establish the electoral rules; a democratic process did not generate them. The same must be said for the constitution. It did not emerge out of debate and compromise, but instead was drafted by the winners of the October 1993 military standoff. Voters then had only two choices—pass or reject—and had to make this decision with almost no time to become familiar with the draft. Second, whether a majority of eligible voters did indeed vote yes on the constitutional referendum remains a mystery. Officially, 58.4 percent of the voters supported Yeltsin's constitution while 41.2 percent opposed it. Turnout was reported to be 54.8 percent, ensuring that the referendum was valid. Many observers, including one particularly active and vocal member of the Central Election Commission, Aleksandr Sobyanin, claimed that these results had been falsified.[36] In particular, Sobyanin and others presented evidence that claimed to show that the Yeltsin administration had inflated the turnout, because Russia's law governing referenda required more than 50 percent of all eligible voters to participate for the referendum to be valid.[37] Such claims of falsification had not seriously tainted previous Soviet elections in 1989 and Russian elections in 1990. Finally, the 1993 elections were the first time since 1989 that the state had actively intervened to eliminate candidates from the ballot. Of the twenty-one electoral blocs that submitted signatures to qualify for the ballot, eight were disqualified, including three prominent nationalist electoral blocs.

The results of the constitutional referendum went according to plan. Elections to the Federation Council also produced few surprises. The range of competitive candidates had narrowed. Only eight of the sixty-six heads of administration who competed in these elections lost and only a handful of candidates who were not affiliated with either the old or the new regional elites won. The two-mandate ballot also created opportunities for falsification. Unaccustomed to voting for more than one candidate, many voters marked only one name, giving local electoral commissions an easy opportunity to mark a second name during ballot counting.

The Duma elections, however, did not go according to plan. Yeltsin had agreed to the mixed electoral system because his aides had advised him that proportional representation would be of the greatest benefit to the pro-presidential electoral bloc on the ballot, Russia's Choice. Several prominent members of Yeltsin's government were on the party list for Russia's Choice.

Some polls predicted that Yeltsin's allies might win a majority of seats in the new parliament.

These predictions were grossly flawed. As expected, the proportional representation vote did stimulate the formation of a party system at the national level. Quite unexpectedly, however, an extremist nationalist party initially dominated the final arrival of multiparty politics. Vladimir Zhirinovsky's Liberal Democratic Party of Russia won almost a quarter of the popular vote. Russia's Choice secured a paltry 15 percent, or less than half of what it had expected, while the other democratic parties each won less than 10 percent of the popular vote. The CPRF and its rural spin-off, the Agrarian Party of Russia, combined to win nearly 20 percent of the party list vote.

Elections for Duma single-mandate seats did not parallel the proportional representation ballot. Successful candidates were predominantly from the old Soviet *nomenklatura*, although they made up a smaller percentage of victors than in the Federation Council. In rural areas Agrarian candidates won; in the "red belt," Russia's poor, rust-belt region, communists dominated; and in major urban areas candidates supported by the local party of power prevailed. "Outsiders"—whether democrats, nationalists, neocommunists, or centrists—fared poorly.

Compared with the referendum vote, little evidence of fraud was apparent in the Duma elections. This may have reflected the Yeltsin administration's lack of concern about this election, because real power remained vested in the Kremlin and Yeltsin also had a loyal Federal Council.

The 1993 elections produced four conflicting results for democratization in general.[38] First and foremost, the vote helped to establish elections as the only game in town. Antisystemic or extraconstitutional challenges to the regime subsided significantly after the 1993 elections. Second, the vote also exhibited how an increasingly powerful state could manipulate elections and electoral outcomes. In eliminating several blocs from the party list, Yeltsin and his government demonstrated their weak normative commitment to free and fair elections. In allegedly falsifying the results of the constitutional referendum, Yeltsin and his allies indicated that they were willing to violate even the basic rules of democratic behavior if the stakes were high enough. Third, the 1993 electoral system for the Duma gave rise to parliamentary party formation. Fourth, Zhirinovsky's surprising victory implied that the state could not control every aspect of the electoral process. In retrospect, some observers speculated that Yeltsin and his government wanted Zhirinovsky to succeed in 1993, since the Liberal Democratic Party of Russia eventually became (for the right price) a loyal Kremlin supporter on key parliamentary votes.[39] In December 1993, however, his surprising electoral victory fueled doubt within the Yeltsin ranks about the president's ability to hold on to power through the ballot box. Above all, Zhirinovsky's surprising showing was a protest vote against the status quo. Yeltsin aides took comfort in the fact that the next presidential election would not take place until 1996.[40] But suddenly in December 1993, June 1996 seemed a lot closer, as uncertainty about the result of the 1996 presidential elections grew. Elections in Russia seemed to be gravitating toward their function in other democracies.

Uncertainty and the Rise of the State, the 1995–1997 Electoral Cycle

By several measures, the 1995 parliamentary elections and the 1995–1997 gubernatorial elections rank as the most competitive, free, and fair elections in Russian history. By contrast, the 1996 presidential election was less free and less fair than the previous presidential vote in 1991. In other words, the same electoral cycle could exhibit both positive and negative trends in the democratic function of elections.

The Competitive Duma Elections

The parliament elected in 1993 was an interim body whose term expired after two years. The institutional context for the 1995 parliamentary elections was much more stable than in 1993. Opposing political forces had not been warring with each other just months earlier, but had grown comfortable with parliamentary practices under a constitution and were eager to return to power. Several individuals and groups that had boycotted the 1993 elections, including the radical communists led by Viktor Tyulkin and Viktor Anpilov, decided to participate in the 1995 vote. The number of those still dedicated to seizing power by nonelectoral means was dwindling. The 1995 Duma elections took place under the same basic electoral rules as the 1993 vote. A new law, which preserved the same balance of seats between single-mandate districts and proportional representation, had replaced Yeltsin's electoral decree mandating a mixed electoral system.[41]

This continuity remained despite attempts by Yeltsin's supporters to increase the number of single-mandate seats and to decrease the number of seats allocated according to proportional representation.[42] The power of the federal state was growing, but was not yet strong enough to alter the basic composition of the Duma. The boundaries of the single-mandate districts did change: a quarter of all districts disappeared entirely, and another seventh were reconfigured.[43]

While the basic rules governing the electoral process did not change between 1993 and 1995, the numbers of participants and the balance of support between competitors changed dramatically. The number of electoral blocs that registered for the ballot rose from thirteen in 1993 to forty-three in 1995.

Early in the campaign period, the Yeltsin administration openly promoted the formation of two new electoral blocs dominated by former CPSU apparatchiks who had switched allegiance to Yeltsin's consolidating party of power. Viktor Chernomyrdin's Our Home Is Russia bloc was supposed to represent the right-of-center, while Ivan Rybkin was ordered by the Kremlin to form a left-of-center bloc. The Kremlin's project failed to shape the contours of the multiparty system. One component of the Kremlin's party of power did not even reach the 5 percent threshold, while the prime minister's party won a paltry 10 percent.

In 1995, the main competition was for the opposition vote. To steal votes away from Zhirinovsky, several new nationalist and patriotic groups appeared on the ballot in 1995, of which the most important were the Congress of Russian Communities, headed by Yuri Skokov and General Aleksandr Lebed; *Derzhava* [Power], led by former vice president Aleksandr Rutskoi; and Power to the People, headed by former Soviet premier Nikolai Ryzhkov and Sergei Baburin. Many new entrants also competed for the communist vote, including the coalition of radicals headed by Anpilov and Tyulkin known as Communist–Working Russia–for the Soviet Union. The most successful opposition party in 1995 was not Zhirinovsky's or any of the new electoral blocs, but yet again was the CPRF, which between 1993 and 1995 had devoted tremendous energy and resources to rebuilding networks and structures left over from decades of rule by the CPSU.

The CPRF made impressive gains, winning almost a quarter of the popular vote and reclaiming its role as the leader of the opposition.[44] Buoyed by party identification on the ballot, CPRF candidates also dominated single-mandate races, winning an astonishing 58 seats. Zhirinovsky won less than half his 1993 total, but still placed second with 11 percent of the popular vote. Chernomyrdin's Our Home Is Russia was the only reformist party to break through to double digits. Grigory Yavlinsky's Yabloko, the self-proclaimed leading party of Russia's democratic opposition, won a meager 7 percent, almost a full percentage point less than Yabloko's 1993 showing. Former acting prime minister Yegor Gaidar and his Democratic Choice of Russia suffered the greatest setback in 1995, winning only 3.9 percent of the popular vote, or less than one-third of its 1993 total.

These results appeared to signal a major victory for opposition forces, a major setback for democratic parties, and a firm rebuff of both Yeltsin and Prime Minister Chernomyrdin.[45] The 1995 parliamentary vote also produced a less noticeable change than earlier Soviet and Russian elections. In 1995, leaders and parties from the old Soviet *nomenklatura* now dominated both the reformist and opposition wings of Russia's polarized political spectrum. New political actors with weak ties to the old Soviet elite on both sides—whether Zhirinovsky, Yavlinsky, or Gaidar—had been pushed even further to the margins. Finally, electoral support for apolitical, ideologically vague, centrist parties and blocs collapsed. Whereas these kinds of parties and personalities had won almost a quarter of the popular vote on the party list ballot and roughly a third of the single-mandate seats in 1993, they were obliterated on both ballots in 1995. Once again, Russian politics looked increasingly bipolar rather than multipolar.

Pockets of falsification, including massive irregularities in Chechnya, tainted the electoral results. Our Home Is Russia also violated spending limits and dominated the national television airwaves. On the whole, however, all major political actors accepted the results as valid.

The Federation Council: Two Steps Backward

In contrast with the electoral law for the State Duma, the rules governing the formation of the Federation Council changed dramatically between 1993 and 1995 in a nondemocratic direction. The new law stipulated that the Federal Council would consist of two officials from each subnational territory: the chair of the legislature and the head of administration. Rather than direct elections to the Federal Council, regional executives (presidents in republics and governors in *oblasts* and *krais*) and heads of regional parliaments pushed for direct elections for their regional offices, followed by automatic appointment to this national body. Such a formulation gave governors increased local legitimacy and greater autonomy from Yeltsin and Moscow, because elected governors would be harder to dismiss than appointed ones. It also meant that parties would have a marginal role in the upper house, since few *oblast* and *krai* governors or republican presidents publicly identified with political parties. This new formulation also gave governors a direct voice in national legislative affairs, blurring the divisions both between executive and legislative powers and between national and subnational units of the federal system. After 1995, the Federation Council emerged as a powerful lobby for regional interests.[46]

The 1996 Presidential Election

As the 1996 presidential election approached, Gennady Zyuganov looked poised to present a major challenge to Yeltsin, the widely unpopular incumbent. At the same time, the reemergence of the Communist Party as the main opposition force allowed those in power to frame the 1996 contest yet again as a referendum between communism and anticommunism. With the contest framed in this way, Yeltsin could assert that he was the only anticommunist candidate capable of defeating Zyuganov, who everyone rightly believed was certain to advance to the second round.[47] By March 1996 Yeltsin had reasserted his claim to the reformist electorate, setting the stage for a second-round runoff between Zyuganov and Yeltsin. In a field of a dozen candidates, Yeltsin barely managed to win more votes than his communist opponent: in the first round Yeltsin won 35 percent of the vote, while Zyuganov captured 32 percent. Lebed came in third with a distant 14 percent. However, when the vote became a binary choice between the communist and the anticommunist, the vast majority of Russians still favored moving forward, not backward. In the second round, Yeltsin's entire campaign message painted him as the lesser of two evils. Yeltsin's team also unleashed a hard-hitting, negative media blitz against Zyuganov and his party that successfully defined the election as a referendum on seventy years of Soviet communism and deftly avoided letting the vote be about Yeltsin's record.[48] Yeltsin won easily in the second round, winning 54 percent of the popular vote compared with Zyuganov's 40 percent. In contrast with electoral trends in many parts of post-communist Europe, Russian voters opted to retain their first democratically elected leader for a second term.

To help voters understand the 1996 election in these binary, polarized categories, Yeltsin spent massive resources on television, radio, and print media. More than any previous competitive election in the USSR or Russia, the state's resources played a pivotal role in determining the outcome of the 1996 vote. Russia's first channel, ORT, owned in part by the state but controlled at the time by Kremlin loyalist Boris Berezovsky, and Russia's second channel, RTR, 100 percent state owned, were completely loyal to Yeltsin. As Russia's two largest television networks, these were invaluable tools for the Kremlin in casting Zyuganov as a dangerous communist who would disrupt people's lives even more if he came to power. Every nightly news program reported favorably and often on the Yeltsin campaign. These same programs either ignored or aired negative news about other candidates. Russia's third largest television network, NTV, was privately owned by Vladimir Gusinsky, but it too unabashedly backed Yeltsin, in part to keep Zyuganov out of the Kremlin, and in part because it hoped for Kremlin favors after the election should Yeltsin win. The same logic applied to all of Russia's oligarchs, who stood to lose the most from a Zyuganov victory and to gain the most from a Yeltsin victory. Even though accurate figures have never been gathered, the financial support these oligarchs offered ensured that Yeltsin's campaign grossly violated campaign funding limits. It was state power—specifically Yeltsin's remaining power to give away state properties—that secured support from the oligarchs in this election.[49]

Yeltsin also deployed more traditional tactics of distributing government pork (or promising to distribute government pork) to obtain support from regional heads of administration.[50] On the campaign trail, Yeltsin made a habit of promising every region he visited something special in return for its electoral support. During the campaign, Yeltsin also raised pensions and increased the salaries of government employees. Although not illegal, this use of state funds for personal electoral gain did not strengthen the democratic process.

Yeltsin and his campaign also threatened to use state power in the most egregious violation of democratic practices. Throughout the entire campaign period, some officials in Yeltsin's government openly advocated postponing the vote altogether. In his memoirs, Yeltsin admits that he seriously considered canceling the election. Only a last minute intervention by his daughter and his campaign manager, Anatoly Chubais, convinced him to stay the electoral course.[51] Nonetheless, even though Yeltsin ultimately abided by the electoral process and fired the advocates of postponement from his administration, the specter of postponement cast a long, undemocratic shadow over the electoral process. Some Communist Party campaign officials asserted that Zyuganov essentially gave up toward the end of the race, believing that he had no chance of taking power.

Finally, scattered reports of falsification surfaced throughout Russia, especially in the national republics, where swings of support away from Zyuganov to Yeltsin between the first and second rounds of the election were dramatic. In Dagestan, Tatarstan, and North Ossetia, Zyuganov won fewer votes in the second round than he did in the first. Official reports cite a 74.5 percent turnout for Chechnya, where the war was still going on, with 74 percent of these votes going to Yeltsin.[52]

As discussed in greater detail in chapter 5, the 1996 presidential election also underscored the ancillary role political parties played in determining electoral outcomes. Two of the top three candidates—Yeltsin and Lebed— ran without a party affiliation. Even Zyuganov, who ran as the CPRF candidate, tried to distance his campaign from his party by creating the National Patriotic Bloc.

The electoral process in 1996 looked less democratic than earlier votes, raising questions about whether the incumbent regime was still a positive force for further democratic consolidation.

Regional Elections

The atmosphere of intense polarization and heightened confrontation during the 1996 presidential campaign virtually disappeared after the election. Zyuganov and his party accepted defeat, participated in Yeltsin's inauguration, and then overwhelmingly approved of Chernomyrdin as Yeltsin's choice for prime minister. Zyuganov then announced the formation of a new political organization, the National Patriotic Union of Russia, which intended to be more moderate, centrist, and nationalist than the CPRF. Above all, Zyuganov proclaimed that his new political organization should be viewed as a supporter of the current system and had no revolutionary ambitions to undermine the regime. The National Patriotic Union of Russia announced plans to support a dozen candidates in the upcoming cycle of fifty-two gubernatorial elections, but the new organization specifically avoided backing extremist challengers, even if this moderate policy at times clashed with the plans of more radical local Communist Party officials.

The gubernatorial elections were virtually devoid of ideology, political platforms, or national issues.[53] Instead competency, name recognition, and relations with the Kremlin emerged as factors that decided electoral outcomes.

With few exceptions, these gubernatorial races were still contests between an incumbent loyal to Yeltsin and a communist challenger, but the differences separating such candidates became increasingly difficult to recognize. The elections were extremely competitive and incumbents lost in roughly half of the fifty races. Most amazingly, all the losers left office peacefully.

New political groups and parties independent of the new party of power and the old party of power (the communists) played only a marginal role in local legislative elections. In most regions, executives at the city and district levels or representatives loyal to the regional head of government constituted the majority in local assemblies.

The 1999–2001 Electoral Cycle: Narrowing the Function of Elections

In consolidating democracies, elections become more competitive and more consequential over time. In Russia, the opposite trend has occurred.

The 1999 Duma Elections

The prelude to the 1999 parliamentary election and the 2000 presidential election was filled with uncertainty about who would win. The combination of the August 1998 financial crash, the subsequent instability in the government, and Yeltsin's declining health created the appearance of weakness and disarray in the Kremlin. Those in power looked vulnerable. Just a year before the presidential election, they had not produced a candidate to replace Yeltsin. Rumors swirled that Yeltsin would violate or change the constitution and run for a third term, but few believed that the sitting president could win a free and fair election. The Kremlin's lack of a game plan for staying in power eventually triggered defection among many of those considered to be part of the ruling party of power. Moscow mayor Yuri Luzhkov made clear early on that he planned to participate in the next electoral cycle as an opposition candidate. Former prime minister Yevgeny Primakov eventually joined Luzhkov's *nomenklatura* opposition coalition, Fatherland-All Russia (OVR). As the candidate supported by the CPRF, for prime minister in September 1998, Primakov was Yeltsin's nemesis.

After a brief flirtation with the CPRF, Primakov joined OVR instead and agreed to participate in the 1999 parliamentary elections as steps toward winning the 2000 presidential election. At the beginning of the fall 1999 campaign, Primakov was ahead of all other presidential contenders by a large margin. For the first time in its post-communist history, Russia appeared poised to hand over presidential power from one political group to another through the ballot box.

Those close to Yeltsin in the Kremlin—called "the family" by many Russian media outlets—were not going to vacate their fortress without a fight. Because Primakov decided to compete in the 1999 parliamentary vote as a way to build momentum for 2000, his enemies in and close to the Kremlin decided to join the battle against the former prime minister in the parliamentary election as well. As a result, the 1999 election was the first time that the federal government became actively involved in a parliamentary contest.

The power of the Kremlin played a tremendous role in shaping the outcome of the 1999 election. Working closely with figures in the presidential administration, Russian tycoon Berezovsky invented a new pro-presidential electoral bloc, Unity.[54] State resources contributed to this new electoral bloc, often referred to in the Russian press at the time as a "virtual" party. Berezovsky hired the best electoral consultants money could buy and then deployed the full force of his ORT television station to promote Unity and destroy OVR. To a lesser degree, RTR assumed a similar mission. ORT newscasters and commentators, led most famously by Sergei Dorenko, unleashed the most vicious personal attacks of any Russian campaign against OVR leaders. Opinion polls suggest that this negative campaigning had consequences for OVR in the parliamentary vote. OVR began the fall electoral campaign hoping to capture as much as a quarter of the popular vote, but ended the campaign season with only 13 percent.

Indirectly, another arm of the state—the armed forces—contributed to the rise of Unity and the eventual presidential winner, Putin. Russian armed forces responded to an attack by Chechen rebel forces against Dagestan and alleged terrorist attacks against Russian civilians in Moscow and elsewhere by invading Chechnya in September 1999. At the time, Prime Minister Putin had a negligible approval rating; however, the war effort—especially as portrayed on ORT and RTR—was popular, and soon catapulted Putin's popularity into double digits and above all other presidential contenders. Putin in turn endorsed Unity. The blessing of the popular prime minister helped the virtual electoral bloc win nearly a quarter of the popular vote, an outcome no one had predicted at the beginning of the campaign.

The results of the 1999 parliamentary vote radically altered the balance of power within the Duma and determined the winner of the 2000 presidential race. As in 1995, the CPRF won the largest percentage of any party, 24 percent, an outcome that ensured Zyuganov a second-place finish yet again in the presidential contest the next year. Unity placed second with 23 percent, followed by OVR in distant third place with 13 percent. OVR's showing was so poor that Primakov decided not to run in the 2000 presidential election. The newly revamped liberal coalition, the Union of Right Forces, surprised many by winning more than 8 percent of the popular vote, almost double the total of its chief liberal rival, Yabloko. Zhirinovsky's Liberal Democratic Party of Russia continued to fade, winning only 6 percent of the party list vote and just barely crossing the 5 percent threshold.

When the distribution of seats from single-mandate races was added into the equation, the balance of power within the parliament had moved in a decisively pro-Putin direction. The Communist Party still controlled a solid minority of seats, but it could not construct opposition majorities to Kremlin initiatives. Putin further weakened the Communist Party's opposition by courting individual leaders in an attempt to divide the party. The speaker of the Duma elected in 2000, Communist Party member Gennady Seleznov, turned out to be more loyal to Putin than to the Communist Party that had helped put him in power.[55] The combination of a loyal Unity, a divided and weakened Communist Party, a sometimes supportive Union of Right Forces (SPS), and strong backing from independents and other smaller factions produced a parliament solidly supportive of Putin on major issues.

The 2000 Presidential Election

The results of the 1999 parliamentary election indicated that Putin was going to win the 2000 presidential election. The only question was whether he would win in the first or second rounds. Upon naming Putin prime minister in August 1999, Yeltsin had hinted that he hoped Putin would replace him as president the following year. Yeltsin gave his heir one last boost by resigning as president on December 31, 1999, an act that moved the date of the presidential election from June to March. As Putin's popularity peaked in January and slowly declined until election day in March, Yeltsin's decision to resign was critical in helping Putin win the 2000 presidential election in the first round.

During the abbreviated campaign period in 2000, Putin continued to enjoy the unequivocal support of ORT and RTR. Though Putin did not run an official campaign, which he considered demeaning for a sitting president, these television stations documented his every move in glowing terms. His opponents, by contrast, received no attention at all from these Kremlin-friendly media outlets. Most oligarchs and regional heads of administration also stumbled over each other in trying to show their support for Putin. Since everyone knew he was going to win, they all wanted to jump on the bandwagon. The presumption of inevitable victory allowed Putin to avoid outlining his policy ideas. Voters in 2000 had less information about the front-runner and eventual winner than in any previous presidential vote.

Reports of falsification in Russia's regions traditionally known for practicing fraud were widespread. That Putin just barely won more than 50 percent of the popular vote in the first round also fueled speculation of massive fraud. Turnout was high for an election lacking any intrigue, especially when compared with the competitive parliamentary elections held three months earlier. Even though presidential candidates Zyuganov and Yavlinsky won roughly the same or an even bigger share of votes in 2000 compared with their parties' achievements in 1999 (29.2 percent for Zyuganov in 2000 compared with 24.3 percent for CPRF in 1999; 5.8 percent for Yavlinsky in 2000 compared with 5.9 percent for Yabloko in 1999), both made statements about being robbed of votes in the 2000 election.[56]

Regional Elections

Incumbent governors were much more successful in this electoral cycle. Incumbents lost in roughly half of the gubernatorial elections in 1995–1997, but lost in only a third of the races in 1999–2001. In sixty-four regions where elections were held in both 1995–1997 and in 1999–2001, thirty-two governors were replaced in the first cycle and only twenty-one in the second. Two factors explain most of the change. First, unlike in the 1995–1997 electoral cycle, powerful leaders were fighting for reelection. Second, these incumbents had already survived one election and therefore had experience in organizing campaigns and winning. However, a third, less benign, factor also helps account for the change. Since Putin came to power, regional elections were increasingly decided not at the polling stations and not on the day of voting, but earlier—either in government offices or in courts. At least one-third of the changes in governorships took place under strange circumstances in which incumbent governors under pressure either refused to participate in the race (and those who stepped aside were often rewarded with a seat on the Federation Council), or were not allowed to participate in the election because of a court decision.

While regional heads of administration generally had an easier time getting elected in this electoral cycle than in the previous one, they also suffered from a loss of political power within the federal government. Putin's ability to assemble super-majorities in the Duma—that is, majorities capable of overriding vetoes of bills by the Federation Council—gave him the capacity to alter the organization of the national system of government, and reorganize he did. To everyone's surprise, Putin made reform of the Federation Council one of his top political goals in his first months in office. The Russian Constitution states that the Federation Council will consist of two representatives from each region. The constitution does not specify how these representatives should be selected. As already discussed, in 1993 Federation Council members were elected directly by the people. In the interim between the 1993 and 1995 parliamentary votes, however, regional leaders succeeded in changing the law governing the formation of the Federation Council to give them even greater control of the upper house of parliament. Soon after coming to office, Putin proposed a third reformulation for constituting the Federation Council. Instead of direct elections or personal representation of regions by governors and legislative heads, Putin's plan called for appointing two representatives from each region.[57] Federation Council members resisted this reform, knowing that they would lose their apartments and offices in Moscow, their immunity as members of the national parliament, and their influence in the corridors of power of the Russian government. After a fierce battle in which the Duma threatened to override a Federation Council veto and Kremlin officials apparently threatened governors with criminal investigations if they did not support Putin's plan, the Federation Council ratified the new formulation in July 2000.

The new constitution of the upper house weakens another institutional check on the president's power. Because Federation Council members are not elected, they do not have the same political authority or public standing as elected officials. The new formula also makes it more difficult for regional leaders to coordinate their actions in relation to the federal government. Indeed, anecdotal evidence suggests that increasing numbers of senators are de facto nominated by the Kremlin and not by regional governors and legislators. Several new senators had never even visited their region until their nomination to the Federation Council.[58] This new formulation gives considerable powers—including the ratification of several federal appointments that only the Federation Council votes on—to nonelected officials. Over time, this lack of legitimacy could undermine the council's ability to make independent decisions. Some have speculated that this new formation of the council is an interim step toward Putin's ultimate goal of abolishing the upper house altogether.

The Rising Role of the State

In the 1999–2001 electoral cycle, the timetable and basic rules for governing elections did not change dramatically for the Duma, presidential, and regional elections. By 1999–2000 elections were no longer ad hoc weapons to be deployed or suspended for immediate political gain. Elections for the Duma and president were becoming normal, anticipated events of the political system. By contrast, the rules for constituting the Federation Council changed yet again in this electoral cycle. That the rules for forming the upper house have changed three times in as many electoral cycles is not a good sign for democratic consolidation.

Democratic consolidation faces other barriers also. Regrettably, fraud still remained as a "normal" feature of elections, especially for elections of consequence like the presidential vote. Although claiming that fraud actually affected the outcome of either the parliamentary or presidential vote would be difficult, its continued practice is disturbing. A decade after instituting elections such antidemocratic practices should be declining. They are not.

The most disturbing trend in the 1999–2000 electoral cycle was the continuing rise of the state (and resources friendly or closely tied to the state) as a major player in determining winners and losers. In this cycle, the Kremlin actively engaged in the parliamentary race for the first time, and it did so in a disturbing way, using negative campaign techniques never before witnessed in a Russian election. The tremendous resources of the federal government and its regional allies dwarfed the electoral resources of any other party or candidate. The result was no transfer of power between different parties or political groups.

The state also wielded its power in determining winners and losers in regional elections in a more direct way by disqualifying candidates and removing others from the ballot. Such practices clearly violate the basic principles of electoral democracy.

Conclusion

Elections have not contributed to democratic consolidation in a linear way. In the last years of the Soviet Union and the first years of independent Russia, elections helped to remove or weaken communist incumbents and open political opportunities to noncommunist challengers. The function of elections in those early years of revolutionary change, however, was somewhat different than the function of elections in established democracies. In the context of major social, political, and economic upheaval, the convocation of elections has often served an immediate political purpose. They were not simply ways to determine leaders. The same was true in the Soviet Union and then Russia. They were used and manipulated in the heat of battle over major issues such as the fate of the Soviet Union or the course of economic reform. The ad hoc nature in which elections occurred or did not occur underscored the political motivations behind them: the dates of the first six national elections in the Soviet Union and then Russia—the election to the Soviet CPD in 1989, the election to the Russian CPD in 1990, the referendum in March 1991, the Russian presidential election in June 1991, the referendum in April 1993, and the constitutional referendum and parliamentary elections in December 1993—were all determined just months before these votes.

Since 1993, national elections have become more regular and anticipated events, conducted in the context of a constitutional system recognized by most and guided by electoral laws approved through a democratic process. These are positive developments for Russian democracy. In addition, the major stakeholders in Russia's political and economic system continue to devote major resources to these electoral processes, which suggests that the outcomes of these elections are not predetermined and have consequences. Concurrently, the number and power of those seeking to change the system by revolutionary means has decreased dramatically. For those out of power seeking to gain power, elections have become the only game in town. Voter turnout has dropped dramatically since the early years when nearly every eligible voter turned up at the polls. Nonetheless, voter turnout remained solid even in the late 1990s, averaging more than 60 percent in national elections. Evidently voters also believe that these elections matter.

Stability in the electoral calendar and electoral procedures has been paralleled by increasing stability in the outcomes of elections, at least for the elections of greatest consequence. In the late Soviet period and early post-

Soviet Russia era, elections played an instrumental role in undermining entrenched elites and empowering challengers who had never participated in politics before. Over time, however, the entrenched elites have figured out how to play the electoral game without losing. Most important, the most powerful office in the country—the presidency—has not seen a turnover of power. The rate of victories by incumbents in elections for regional heads of administration has also grown dramatically over time. Just as the Soviet economic elite was first threatened by free prices and privatization, but then learned how to benefit from these new economic practices over time, the Soviet political elite has also learned how to use, if not manipulate, elections to maintain political power. While elections initially helped to open up the political process to new political forces, elections later served to consolidate the grip of the ruling elite on political power. The top performers in both the 1999 parliamentary elections and the 2000 presidential votes were all actors and organizations with clear Soviet era identities. Strangely, representatives from the Soviet system's two most important (and some would say most notorious) organizations—the Communist Party and the KGB—captured the lion's share of all votes cast in the 2000 presidential election.

The reconsolidation of the Soviet elite in Russian political life has effectively crowded out new actors and new political organizations, particularly new political parties. Parliamentary elections have continued to produce turnover and competition, but this is precisely the state institution that has the least amount of power in the political system.[59]

Incumbents in democracies all over the world enjoy tremendous electoral advantages. For instance, in the 2002 elections for 435 seats to the U.S. House of Representatives, incumbents seeking reelection won 98.9 percent of the time. Before the election fewer than thirty House races were even considered competitive.[60] Parties of power have remained in power for decades in countries typically recognized as liberal democracies. The first rounds of elections in an independent United States did not produce a turnover in the party of power until 1800, twenty-four years after the publication of the Declaration of Independence. Analysts of the Russian electoral process should therefore be careful about making generalized statements about the function of elections in Russia based on a single electoral cycle.

This said, the way in which Russian elites have begun to deploy state resources to stay in power does represent a greater challenge to the democratic process than some of these other examples of incumbent entrenchment in liberal democracies. The tremendous resources of the state, and especially its control over the media, give those already in power a tremendous and unfair advantage. Moreover, complaints about electoral fraud call into question the state's politicized role in counting the vote. Expectations about electoral fraud or postponement were much lower in 1990 or 1991 than they were in 1995 or 1996. Indeed, the specter of postponement lingered until polling day both before parliamentary elections in 1995 and presidential elections in 1996. Claims of falsification have increasingly blemished the legitimacy of most elections at both the national and regional levels.

Finally, the state's growing role in determining who gets on the ballot and who does not is a disturbing trend. Farcical elections in Chechnya in 1995 and 2003, along with republican presidential elections with only one candidate in Kalmykiya in 1995 and Kabardino-Balkaria and Tatarstan in 1996, suggest that Russia's electoral procedures have not improved since the first semifree and quasi-fair elections in 1989. Likewise the ouster of an elected president in Mordovia in 1993; the removal of elected governors in Bryansk, Blagoveschensk, and Chelyabinsk the same year; and the displacement of elected mayors in many others places (the most scandalous cases of which include Vladivostok in 1994, Izhevsk and Ryazan in 1996, and Nizhny Novgorod in 1998) were all blatant violations of the will of the people. The removal of gubernatorial candidates in Kursk and Saratov in 2000, in Rostov-on-Don in 2001, Ingushetiya in 2002, and in Chechnya in 2003, as well as abuses of campaign finance laws and intimidation tactics by local executives, indicate that competitors in Russian elections do not yet enjoy a free and level playing field. All these disturbing trends reflect the growing role of the state and the declining role of society in determining electoral outcomes. More than a decade after the collapse of the Soviet Union, the state's dominance over society is still overwhelming.

How stable is the institution of democratic elections in Russia? Debate concerning this question has been significant since Putin's inauguration as president and the development of what many see as a mild version of a quasi-police regime. Nonetheless, the abolition of elections as a political mechanism seems unlikely, since too many parties are interested in preserving the process. The political elite needs elections in their present form to legitimize their rule, while those involved in the business of campaigning have a strong vested interest in retaining elections. International norms also place pressure on the Russian elite to continue the formal practice of elections, and society still values elections. In polls conducted during the 1999–2000 electoral cycle, an overwhelming 86 percent of respondents answered that electing the country's leaders was important, while only 10 percent responded that this was not important. When asked about citizens' responsibilities, 86 percent fully agreed or agreed that each citizen has a duty to vote in elections, while only 6 percent disagreed or completely disagreed.[61] A complete abandonment of elections would not be popular.

Consequently, elections are likely to perform a quasi-democratic function in post-communist Russia. Incumbents will continue to enjoy unfair advantages in the campaign period. In close elections they are also likely to benefit from the control of those state institutions that have demonstrated a capacity to falsify elections. Elections for less important state institutions will remain more competitive, although the current president's disdain for any autonomous sources of power may limit the freeness and fairness of parliamentary elections over time. Elections of limited consequence, however, are still better than no elections at all. As dictators in Kenya and the former Yugoslavia recently learned, the charade of elections can change unexpectedly into a much more meaningful procedure during periods of crises. Elections in Russia today have less meaning than they did several years ago, but they have not been completely stripped of meaning and consequence.

3

The Constitution

Viktor Sheinis

Russia's 1993 constitution was drafted to work around the constitution that was already in existence. It was approved by means of a referendum whose official results raised serious concerns about falsification. The referendum was conducted during a brief period of suppression of one of the opposition political forces and brought to an end a period of violent conflict between the president and the parliament. Unlike many states in transition, Russia was given a constitution written by the winners of the October 1993 showdown instead of a document approved through consensus. Therefore the continuation of debate about the 1993 constitution in political and academic circles, not only in Russia, but also in the West, is not surprising.

Time may show that the constitution will not withstand the influence of those who question its validity. However, despite its relatively recent confirmation in historical terms, it has demonstrated its survivability in comparison with constitutions other countries adopted during periods of revolutionary upheaval, such as France after 1789 or Russia after 1917. Moreover, it has turned out to be adequate for the conditions of contemporary political development in Russia. This chapter reviews the political give and take process that produced the constitution and assesses the constitution's strengths and weakness as well as the reasons behind them. It also cautions that any drastic changes in the near future could be harmful to the viability of the constitutional order.

The Road to the 1993 Russian Constitution

Understanding the achievements and flaws of today's constitutional system in Russia is impossible without examining the history of the 1993 constitution, a history that is dramatic, contradictory, and instructive.[1] The First Russian (Russian Soviet Federative Socialist Republic or RSFSR) Congress of People's Deputies (CPD) set up the Constitutional Commission in June 1990 and charged it with preparing a new constitution. The composition of the commission replicated the balance of political forces in the Congress, but with 102 members, the commission was too large to carry out the serious work of drafting a complex political and juridical document. The commission consisted of representatives from each of Russia's eighty-eight regions along with fourteen elected deputies mostly from Moscow and Leningrad. Yeltsin formally served as chairman of the commission, which also included lawyers, political scientists, philosophers, historians, and economists. The members of the commission's working group formed a nucleus that was capable of drafting a new constitution and was relatively homogeneous in terms of its sociopolitical orientation. This nucleus, several of the deputies, and additional expert lawyers brought into the working group who were well known for their consistent democratic stance—altogether some 15 to 20 people—carried out the real development of the text of the new constitution. Oleg Rumyantsev, the Commission's executive secretary, headed the working group.

A plenary meeting of the Constitutional Commission was required to approve each version of the draft constitution proposed by the working group. It was on these occasions that numerous disputes immediately arose. The working group presented the first version of the draft constitution on October 12, 1990.[2]

The acting constitution in 1990—the 1978 RSFSR Constitution, an offspring of the 1977 USSR "Brezhnev" Constitution—was the least useful source for a starting point. Even though it had been somewhat modified at the time of Mikhail Gorbachev's perestroika, its text still contained all the usual Soviet attributes: a pompous and insipid preamble; the notorious Article 6 (the Communist Party of the Soviet Union [CPSU] is the country's "leading and directing force" and the "nucleus of the political system and state and social organizations"), which by 1990 had already been excluded from the USSR Constitution; the confirmation of state ownership as the foundation of the economic system; the absence of guarantees of basic civil rights; and so on.[3]

The 1978 constitution had established a two-tier, quasi parliament as the apex of state power. It consisted of a periodically convened CPD (which had exclusive power to change the constitution), whose 1,068 members were elected through the majoritarian or Westminster system of single-seat districts. The other tier was a continuously sitting, bicameral Supreme Soviet whose members were elected from among CPD deputies. The federal structure was defined by asymmetry between its constituent administrative-territorial units. Perhaps the most notable element of this constitution was Article 104, which in principle excluded any separation of powers and stated that the Congress was "authorized to review and decide any question." This bastion of totalitarian rule held out until the very end, even after a series of amendments to the constitution established the principle of the separation of powers.

The First Congress, held in June 1990, adopted a series of important documents of a constitutional character. Most important, deputies approved the Declaration of Sovereignty, which for the first time established the supremacy of the constitution and the laws of the RSFSR over the laws of the Soviet Union and was effective over the federation's entire territory. In retrospect, this was the first legally formulated step toward the fall of the communist regime and the collapse of the Soviet Union.

The work of the Constitutional Commission continued for more than three years throughout the period of Soviet demise. During this time the commission introduced several successive versions of the draft constitution for discussion. Eventually, the draft that emerged was distinct in structure, conception, and content from all previous Soviet constitutions.

Two problems became the focus of discussion: the federal structure and the organization of the central government. According to early versions of the draft, Russia was to be a federation of fifteen to twenty-five regions formed by merging the existing eighty-nine autonomous regions, *krais*, and *oblasts*. The republics were to enjoy equal rights and have equal obligations. The constitution also raised the possibility of federal territories that could become republics after demonstrating their capacity to independently carry out the functions of a republic and participate fully in federal government bodies. By strengthening the republics' independence, the draft expressly established Russia as a constitutional, not a treaty-based, federation, based on a constitution approved by all its citizens.

From the beginning, the Constitutional Commission designated two approaches to the structure of the federal government, and the differences between these two approaches were so fundamental that the draft versions had to be presented separately. The first approach, labeled the president as head of the executive branch approach, was inspired by the head of the group of experts, Valery Zorkin, and was supported by a majority of the deputies who were members of the working group. According to this approach, the president would head the government as well as form and lead the apparatus of the federal executive branch. This version did not foresee an office of chair of the government, and gave the president the right to nominate ministers, whose appointment—but not removal—would be subject to parliamentary approval. This version did not mention the government and placed its functions in the category of presidential powers.[4]

A convinced proponent of presidentialism, Zorkin insisted that given Russia's conditions only a presidential republic could secure the necessary political stability and balance of powers. Zorkin and his supporters eschewed not only the parliamentary, but also the semipresidential model similar to the French model, claiming that "it shares the fate of all half-measures and half-versions."[5]

Leonid Volkov, Revol't Pimenov, and I proposed the second approach, referred to as the government accountable to parliament approach. It limited the president's role in the formation and activity of the government. The chief executive would present "a candidate for the head of government who was approved by groups making up the lower house" to the lower house of parliament. The lower house would have the right to confirm the chair's mandate to form a government, to confirm its members, to take a vote of confidence or no confidence in the government, and to force its resignation.[6]

Beginning in the fall of 1990, the working group's draft faced many hindrances. It did not have the opportunity to be approved at the Constitutional Commission's plenum. After the publication of 40 million copies of the draft, a flood of letters and proposals poured into the commission, the majority in favor of the draft constitution, but the draft's opponents had also mobilized. The communist daily *Sovetskaya Rossiya* branded the working group as a "burial team" and the draft constitution as a "hymn to unconsciousness," calling for "no constitution of thieves and robbers." The fact that the title of the state, as written in the constitution, did not contain the words "Soviet" and "socialist" provoked hysteria.[7] Under the growing onslaught Boris Yeltsin and his closest advisers flinched, and discussion of the draft was removed from the confirmed agenda of the Second RSFSR CPD scheduled for the end of 1990.

The surge toward democracy immediately after the events of August 1991 was the time when a democratic constitution was most likely to pass, and this moment was lost. The draft continued being "finished" for the next Congress and eventually dissipated in the meat-grinder of voting in the Supreme Soviet. As a result, by the end of 1992 Russia had an eclectic, compromise-ridden text, whose norms were often less precise and politically less progressive than those of the initial versions. The working group was subjected to furious attacks, especially in the Supreme Soviet's Council of Nationalities, and continuously reworked the draft for three years, from 1990 to 1993, in order to get the approval of the increasingly vengeful and aggressive CPD.[8]

The draft's main problem lay not in its compromises with those who supported state administration of the economy and social paternalism, or with regional elites. As experience would soon show, it lay in its inability to consolidate existing institutions. The compromising nature of the draft was a weakness, not a strength.

Criticism focused on various aspects of the draft. In the eyes of some critics the draft was bourgeois, while to others it was socialist. Some blamed the draft's authors for breaking up Russia, and others charged them with violating rights of autonomy. Claims that the president had been endowed with the power of an absolute monarch were accompanied by claims that the constitution's drafters were restoring Soviet power.

From late 1990 the constitutional process followed a roundabout path. Because the 1978 constitution was completely incapable of dealing with the revolutionary changes that were going on in society, each Congress made attempts to alter it. These attempts proceeded, at least until 1992. They somewhat smoothed the edges of the revolutionary situation, but were vastly insufficient.

The refashioning of the old constitution occurred as follows. At the Second Congress in December 1990, a statute on multiple forms of ownership and on equal protection for all forms of ownership was introduced as a replacement for the socialist basis of the economic system. It changed "citizens' property" to "personal property" (the majority of the Congress still could not cope with the concept of "private property"). It also resolved the continuing debate over land ownership through the adoption of a compromise formula: the sale of land was permitted, but only ten years after its purchase, and even then, only to the state.[9]

The Fourth Congress in May 1991 changed the constitution to establish the post of president of the RSFSR as the highest office in the land and as head of the executive branch. The president had the right to introduce legislation (which the Council of Ministers lost) and to veto laws (which the Congress could still override with a simple majority vote). With the agreement of the Supreme Soviet, the president could now nominate the chair of the Council of Ministers and, without its agreement, the remaining ministers. The president was also to lead the government and gained the power to declare a state of emergency, although this was subject to confirmation by the Supreme Soviet.

At the same time, the president's powers were somewhat circumscribed. The president could neither disband the Congress nor the Supreme Soviet, which were guaranteed to serve out their terms, nor could the president change the state's territorial-administrative structure. The constitution included a procedure for impeaching the president.[10]

As a result, certain vital segments of the infrastructure of a presidential republic that are present in the current constitution were put in place as early as 1991, before the August coup attempt. A desire to confront the reform communist leadership at the helm of the Union motivated a majority of both democrats and nationalists in the Congress to support these cardinal constitutional changes.

The main focus of all the subsequent sessions of the Congress then became a tug of war between the president and the deputies or, more precisely, the latter's gradually increasing antipresidential majority. The president insisted on additional powers and received many of them at the Fifth Congress, including the right to unilaterally reorganize the top executive bodies, to nominate the heads of regional governments, and even to issue decrees that contradicted the law. Such decrees would come into force if the Supreme Soviet did not reject them within seven days.[11]

Despite the growing tensions, constitutional reforms independent of the work of the constitutional commission continued. At the Sixth Congress in April 1992, extensive further changes were introduced to the constitution. A new title for the state was confirmed, doing away with terms such as Soviet and socialist. Several clauses regarding the bases of the constitutional system (people's power, federalism, republican form of rule, and separation of powers) and human rights and freedoms were borrowed from the Constitutional Commission's working draft. These were concepts absent from any Soviet constitution.[12] Guided by the federal treaties that state leaders signed with regional leaders in March 1992, the Congress also founded a new, awkward, three-tier federal structure. At the top were the republics or "states possessing on their territory the entire panoply of state power."[13] The republics were guaranteed increased representation in federal government bodies. Congress also proposed setting up an upper chamber of parliament with imbalanced representation in favor of the autonomous republics.

Open conflict between Yeltsin and the Congress majority erupted at the Seventh Congress in December 1992, resulting in the reversal of the compromises made earlier. In response, Yeltsin undertook a series of attempts to remove the Congress from the political arena, which in turn made the Congress increasingly aggressive. In 1993 a deep constitutional crisis ensued, and both sides could no longer be contained within the existing constitutional framework. The constitution was speckled with a multitude of amendments while at the same time it preserved many of the anachronisms that contradicted them. Thus both sides relied on the document to justify or condemn any action.

From the point of view of formal juridical norms, the Congress's stance was stronger, and the Congress acted with more refinement. However, its action were clearly not guided by high-minded legal considerations, but by a desire to seize power from the hands of hated pro-Yeltsin forces, to negate the results of the referenda of 1991 and 1993, and to reverse the reforms and the constitutional process itself. Thus the Congress did not hurry to approve any versions of the constitution. The politically irresponsible majority that had coalesced by 1993 was more comfortable with the patchwork quilt that the 1978 Soviet era constitution had become. "The majority of deputies preferred to cling to the old text since the adoption of a new Constitution would entail the dissolution of Congress and the end of their deputy mandates," noted British scholar G. D. G. Murrel.[14] The Congress and its majority were completely satisfied with a situation in which an amendment appeared in the morning and became part of the constitution by noon.

The Supreme Soviet formed the new Committee for Constitutional Legislation under the chairmanship of Vladimir Isakov, who had been removed from the post of chairman of the Supreme Soviet's Council of the Republic after the August 1991 putsch and later became one of the leaders of the National Salvation Front. The committee prepared a set of constitutional amendments intended to turn the president into a figurehead.[15] Had these amendments been passed, executive power would have become concentrated in the hands of the government, and the government, in turn, would have been completely dependent on the Supreme Soviet. An open skirmish neared that both sides wanted and encouraged.

The Presidential Draft, the Constitutional Assembly, and the 1993 Constitution

Launching the game preemptively, the president presented the new draft constitution immediately after his victory in the referendum.[16] This was a significant move. As the chairman of the Constitutional Commission, the president disavowed the draft that the commission's working group had prepared and the Congress's conservative majority had amended, and produced a new draft. A successive series of decrees and executive orders established a new procedure for drafting the constitution.[17] The entire process was diverted from the Congress, the Supreme Soviet, and the Constitutional Commission, and was given to a newly established institution: the Constitutional Assembly. This entity was subdivided into five groups that were to include representatives from federal government bodies, including members of the Constitutional Commission; regional government bodies; and local administrations, political parties, trade unions and other public organizations, religious organizations, manufacturers, and entrepreneurs. Anatoly Sobchak and I were ordered to coordinate the work of the group that included representatives of political parties and social organizations.

A new draft of the constitution had to deal with both the old, broken constitution, which still remained as the country's basic law, and the working group's draft. The latter was in much worse form than its original version and had little chance of being approved by the obsolete quasi parliament. The assembly's draft was prepared by a group of well-known lawyers and published in the newspaper *Izvestiya* in the president's name on April 30, 1993.

This "presidential" draft was distinguished by a series of positive changes. Its formulations were shorter and legally precise, presenting clear decisions on a series of disputed issues. It established private ownership of land, banned internal customs between regions, and clearly delimited the roles of the two houses of parliament. Overall, however, the draft was no better than that of the Constitutional Commission. While it corrected some of the latter's flaws and unnecessary compromises, it contained its own serious defects.

If the April 30, 1993, Constitutional Assembly draft had become a law, the overwhelming share of the limited power that the draft gave to parliament would have been concentrated in the upper house, the Federation Council. The Federation Council would have appointed the premier upon nomination by the president, held votes of confidence or no confidence in the government, and determined the government's members. Half of the seats in the Federation Council would have been taken by representatives of the republics, autonomous *oblasts*, and autonomous *okrugs*, in which only 14 percent of the population lived, therefore only half of the Federation Council's members would have represented the remaining 86 percent of the population. This suggestion was the result of an aggressive onslaught by the representatives of the national-territorial autonomous regions that the CPD had also been subjected to. The Constitutional Commission also gave in to regional elites, having incorporated the federal treaties with their appendixes into its final draft.

According to the April 30 draft, the State Duma and the Federation Council would have participated in the appointment of the chair of the state bank, but would play no role in the appointment or removal of the chair and auditors of either the Accounting Chamber or the Human Rights Ombudsman's Office, which the draft did not even mention. The parliament as a whole would have become somewhat powerless because not only the state budget, but also all draft legislation regarding taxes, loans, and the state's financial obligations, could only have been introduced for parliamentary review by the president or the government.

By contrast, the April 30 draft would have given colossal power to the president. This would have included the power to disband both houses of parliament on the basis of such hazy formulations as "when a crisis of state power cannot be resolved on the basis of procedures established by the Constitution,"[18] although these formulations excluded disagreement over the appointment of the premier and the government. The president's decrees and executive orders would not have been required to conform to the constitution or to law, a notion introduced by the Constitutional Assembly. Finally, the draft created a kind of judicial monster—a superstructure on top of the entire judicial system—that was to contain the leaders of the three highest courts (the Constitutional Court, the Supreme Court, and the Arbitration Court) and three persons appointed by the president.

In addition, because of the pressure exerted by regional forces noted earlier, the full text of the treaties that delimited the powers and competencies of the federation's regions was squeezed into the body of this constitution even though this violated all the canons of constitutional law-making. Thus this constitution set up a three-tiered federal state structure: a hierarchy in which, in Orwellian fashion, some subjects of the federation would be designated as more equal than others. By the summer of 1993, under pressure from the Council of the Republics in which the heads of republics exerted inordinate influence, a memorandum on the republics as sovereign states appeared.[19]

The Constitutional Assembly played a positive role by removing or diluting certain aforementioned defects of the previous drafts. The assembly initially made a constructive decision to base its work on both the president's April 30 draft and the draft presented by the Constitutional Commission. In particular, it created a detailed section on citizens' human rights and freedoms, a topic omitted from the April 30 draft.

Some Constitutional Assembly members also presented a draft of a new election law that introduced a mixed majoritarian-proportional representation system for parliamentary elections. Approval of this text occurred outside the assembly's formal framework, but the concept of conducting elections to the Duma through a majoritarian, single-seat electoral district system was absent in the original draft of the constitution. This opened the way for the current electoral system, which has facilitated the establishment of political parties.[20]

Initially the assembly was to submit its draft to the Constitutional Commission and the Supreme Soviet in mid-July; however, the work of the Constitutional Assembly dragged on. Its interim draft was confirmed in mid-July and finalized only after the events of September and October 1993.

Yeltsin's forceful victory over the Congress in the autumn of 1993 created a new balance of political forces in Moscow, one that was entirely in the president's favor. It was these events that produced the December 1993 constitution and Russia's super-presidential system.

Assessing the 1993 Russian Constitution

American and Russian scholars such as Peter Reddaway and Dmitri Glinski categorically conclude that the 1993 Russian Constitution is a "partisan constitution" that "remains a major stumbling block to national reconciliation and democratic development."[21] Despite being a critic of both the process of adoption of this constitution and its content, as a participant in the events I nevertheless believe that considering the situation in 1993, what resulted was far from the worst possible scenario, and the outcome may perhaps be considered as the best possible outcome under the circumstances. As the years have passed it has become clear that the adoption of the constitution diverted the danger of a civil war and prevented a scenario similar to what happened in the former Yugoslavia.

Furthermore, the constitution created a set of rules that all the main actors have followed, willingly or unwillingly. The constitution has established separation of powers, political and ideological pluralism, democracy, and private ownership, including that of land; prohibited the incitement of social hostility; and established the priority of citizens' civil and political rights over the interests of the state. The last issue is the most important. All Soviet constitutions placed the state in the center of constitutional order, whereas the main framework in the new Russia is anthropocentric. Chapters 1 and 2 of the 1993 constitution—"The Fundamentals of the Constitutional System" and "Rights and Liberties of Man and Citizen"—are on the level of modern democratic standards, inferior in some cases, but superior in others.

Critics of the Russian Constitution claim that its many appealing principles remain entirely declarative. American researcher Thomas Remington notes

[T]hree…weaknesses in the capacity of the law and legal institutions to restrain the arbitrary exercise of power by the state: the extralegal powers of the successor bodies to the KGB, the prevalence of sub-legal administrative rules and regulations issued by executive bodies; and the inclination of the president to wield his decree power in order to circumvent constitutional limits on executive powers.[22]

Other commentators define eleven illiberal features of Russian democracy, including the following:

Governmental decision making is often closed to the public…Representative institutions in Russia, especially the legislatures, exert much less influence over government policies and budgets than do executive and administrative bodies…The Russian courts remain backward and cannot offer individuals reliable protection against the arbitrary acts of governments…Corruption is widespread within governmental agencies.[23]

Most experts would agree with Remington's assessment. Nevertheless, the question that remains unanswered is to what degree are these distortions of democracy a product of the constitution and its defects or are they from other sources?

Contradictions between formal and real constitutions are not new and do not only appear in Russia. Lawyers have long scrutinized the problem of book law versus street law. Comparing Russia with other Eastern European countries on the subject of constitutional law, political specialist George Urban quotes Aristotle: "Constitutions are worthless unless they are grounded in the customs and conventions of the people."[24] No constitution exists solely by itself. It functions in a complex context of a nation's mentality, customs, traditions, political and general culture, and value systems.

Is the government system created by the Russian Constitution what makes many of the constitution's proclaimed civil rights fictitious (as did all Soviet constitutions) or pernicious? Or do the roots of the problems of Russia's democratic transformation lie primarily in long-established social conventions and the age-old Russian tradition of living by unwritten rules rather than by laws? The question is not an academic one. If the former is true, the constitution needs a complete overhaul. If the latter holds true, then Russia will have to address a much more difficult challenge.

To understand how the constitution works (or fails to work) in real life, the organization and functioning of power in modern Russia can be separated into four clusters as follows: (1) the separation of powers and jurisdictions at the federal level, (2) the concept of federalism, (3) the organization of local self-government, and (4) the judiciary.

The Separation of Powers and Jurisdictions at the Federal Level

A main argument of the constitution's critics, especially the opposition, is that the constitution establishes a super-presidential political system. For example, documents of the Communist Party of the Russian Federation repeatedly refer to "the anti-popular constitution of presidential absolutism" and the "parliament without power."[25] A number of Russian and Western scholars share this assessment. Reddaway and Glinski, for example, maintain that "Yeltsin's and Putin's presidential powers have exceeded those of

American and French presidencies combined, and approximate the powers of Tsar Nicolas II under the 1905 quasi-constitutional system."[26] Remington provides a more balanced assessment: "Using a typology proposed by political scientists Matthew Shugart and John Carey, we can call the Russian system 'presidential-parliamentary.'"[27]

On this issue, however, just as on all others, we need to distinguish between the formal and real constitutions. In my opinion, the structure of governance as set out by the law deserves to be called insufficiently parliamentary rather than super-presidential. The excesses of presidential rule under Yeltsin and Vladimir Putin derive not only from the excessive powers the current constitution gives the president, but from the fact that there are virtually no working limitations on presidential power or on the power of officials appointed by the president.

The powers vested in the president by the constitution break the balance of the separation of powers. Clearly the president should not be the only "guarantor of the Constitution of the Russian Federation."[28] This is a dangerous stipulation, because it is open to vast variations in interpretation. Based on this article, the Constitutional Court refused to find unconstitutional the December 1994 presidential decree that started a wide-scale war in Chechnya without the declaration of a state of emergency and without parliamentary sanction. Democratic experience around the world shows conclusively that the entire system of checks and balances, including nongovernmental institutions, must serve as guarantor of the constitutional system. Accordingly, the president should not have exclusive power to "define the basic domestic and foreign policy guidelines of the state" and to "endorse the military doctrine."[29] However, the tools the constitution gives to the president to implement such functions are not excessive in comparison with other presidential and semi-presidential democracies. In the United States, the administration is an extension of the president. In Russia, the constitution—leaving aside the question of everyday practice—assigns an independent role for the government as well as appropriate powers for the administration.

A justified criticism points to the disproportionate role in the Russian system of numerous advisers; consultants; personal presidential representatives; and institutions created at the president's will, such as the Presidential Administration, the Security Council, and the Defense Council (created to serve obscure staffing purposes and then forgotten). However, this power imbalance is not the constitution's fault. The United States has a number of influential but noninstitutionalized political posts that are filled through presidential choice rather than through constitutional imperative. For example, presidential aid Henry Kissinger was a more important person than the secretary of state before he himself took the office. Similarly, Harry Hopkins did a great deal to help Franklin Roosevelt overcome Congress's stubborn isolationism before World War II.[30]

As a rule, presidents or prime ministers of those states whose parliaments are entitled to bring down governments through votes of no confidence may in turn dissolve parliament. This procedure is not restricted by additional measures. For example, British prime ministers can call for new parliamentary elections not only on the basis of a no confidence vote, but on their political calculations that new elections may give their party an electoral advantage. In Russia, dissolution of the State Duma is limited by a strict time frame and a number of conditions. Should the president want to exercise pressure by threatening to dissolve the parliament, the Duma may even respond by implementing impeachment procedures.[31] Presidential participation in the legislative process and the president's veto power are not Russian inventions. As elsewhere, in Russia's short constitutional history the presidential veto has blocked rational parliamentary initiatives, but it has also blocked populist gambits and dangerous initiatives of the Duma majority, especially in the field of foreign policy.[32] The real problem here is that the presidential veto can only be overridden by an extraordinary two-thirds majority vote in both the lower and upper houses.

The real weakness of the parliament is its lack of oversight authority. It does have certain control functions: approving the president's nominee for prime minister, approving the federal budget, and monitoring the use of expenditure funds through the Auditing Chamber. However, the Duma has no power to call on government officials to show up at parliamentary hearings or to secure the documents from executive officials needed to make independent inquiries into the executive branch's activities. As a member of the parliamentary commission investigating the Chechen war, I witnessed how a number of high-ranking state officials simply ignored Duma requests to testify at hearings. The Duma has similarly proven ineffectual in its efforts to amend the constitution, only once passing an amendment at a first reading and never getting to a second.

Another flaw of the constitutional system is the formation of the Federation Council. In 1993 the population elected its members, but the night before the publication of the constitution, a presidential aide amended the draft to include one representative from the legislative branch per one representative from each member region's state executive branch in the Federation Council.[33] This formulation makes popular election of senators not an obligation, but a matter of choice for the political elite. Thus this clause sharply limits the construction of a powerful senate.

Initially, regional governors and legislative chairs replaced the elected senators on the basis of this clause, becoming ex officio members of the Federation Council by virtue of their regional offices, though at least these officials had once been elected to their offices. However, a real monster was born in 2000–2001, when Putin decided that the upper chamber of the highest representative body of state power in each region was no longer to be elected, but to be appointed by each region's executive and legislative branches. Members of the Federation Council, not supported by the voters' mandate, became a pliable object of manipulation for both federal and regional authorities. This reorganization of the Federal Council raises the following question: If the authority of the chamber is diminished, should it not be deprived of some of its powers under the constitution?[34] Alternatively, should this institution be abolished altogether and replaced by the new State Council, an informal, advisory assembly of republican presidents and governors established in the wake of the Federation Council's reorganization as compensation for the loss of their seats in the Federation Council?

Unfortunately, analysis of the formal constitution and of other laws does not provide foolproof solutions to these problems. While oversight functions should be returned to the parliament, there are no guarantees that the parliament, dominated as it is now by the pro-Kremlin centrist bloc of factions led by Unity, would take advantage of this authority. The Federation Council, currently filled with unelected bureaucrats, should be replaced by a council composed of senators elected directly by citizens to prevent its manipulation by the Kremlin.

Thus the problem of strengthening the legislative branch is not so much one of correcting the constitution, as it is one of building a strong civil society able to oppose the regime of "managed democracy" and establishing a genuine political party system. This requires cultivating a middle class and rewriting numerous laws. Election laws should be improved and properly enforced to put an end to fraud, violations of campaign law, and to curtail the use of administrative resources. Duma and Federation Council rules need to be rewritten to forestall backroom deals. In March 2002, the committees in the State Duma were redistributed among the factions. The Kremlin demonstrated once again that it could punish the opposition by changing the inner configuration of the parliament. In theory, the new distribution is more just because it upholds the rights of factions that were violated in the 2000 collusion between the party of power and the communists, but in reality, both acts were political scandals that could have been avoided by clear rules providing for a more representative distribution of committee chairmanships. In sum, much work remains to be done below the level of the constitution.

Federalism

Russian federalism is a controversial issue. Article 5 of the constitution declares at the same time that all subjects of the federation are equal in rights and that only the republics can have their own constitution. As the English diplomat Martin Nicholson states:

> [T]he constitutional basis of post-Soviet Russia evolved as a series of compromises reached amid continuous political crisis, and as a result contains two underlying weaknesses. First, the country's asymmetrical structure is unstable because it perpetuates the distortions of the Soviet system. Second, the division of powers between the center and the regions is vaguely defined. These deficiencies underlie much of the maneuvering and bargaining that bedevils the economic and political relations between the center and regions.[35]

The constitutions enacted in a number of republics deepened the asymmetric structure of the federation. Moreover, the agreements on the distribution of power that were signed in the early 1990s between the central government and some regional governments are an exotic feature of Russia's constitutional and federal system. During the period of institutional decay after the collapse of the Soviet regime and state, these agreements played a stabilizing role. Yet these agreements gave some subjects authority that was not supposed to be granted to them under the constitution. Indeed, a large portion of federal-regional relations is regulated simultaneously by federal laws and other legal acts and by regional laws. Even a superficial comparison of federal and regional laws made by the Office of the Prosecutor General in 2000–2001 disclosed thousands of contradictions and differences, primarily between the federal constitution and the republics' constitutions. In short, the degree of asymmetry and autonomy some regions enjoy is characteristic of an asymmetric, treaty-based federation with strong elements of a confederation.[36]

Putin said that in 2000, about 20 percent of local legal acts contradicted the constitution and federal laws.[37] Bashkortostan, Kabardino-Balkaria, Komi, Tuva, and Yakutia give local constitutions supremacy over the federal constitution. In Adygei, Buryatia, Ingushetia, and Kalmykia, constitutions allow the regional governments to introduce a state of emergency. Bashkortostan and Komi provide special privileges for representatives of the main ethnic groups.

Aside from Chechnya, Tatarstan has the greatest sovereignty among the republics. In 1992, before the adoption of the federal constitution, Tatarstan adopted one of its own. Its authors believed that after the collapse of the USSR, the Russian Federation would follow, thus the constitution defined the republic not as subject to Russian law, but as subject to international law. It positioned Tatarstan as a sovereign state "associated" with Russia on an inter-state basis. In addition, the regional constitution tried to distinguish Tatarstan from Russia on the basis of ethnicity rather than solely on the basis of territoriality. Such an approach is dangerous. Russia has almost no mono-ethnic territories, and at least formally, the federal constitution considers the rights of nations to be equivalent to human rights.

A 1994 agreement on the delegation of authority and separate jurisdictions reduced, but did not eliminate, the contradictions between the two constitutions. Meanwhile, the place of Tatarstan in Russian governance became defined by informal relations between Yeltsin and Mintimer Shaimiyev, Tatarstan's president. When Putin became president, the lack of conformity between regional constitutions and laws and the federal constitution and laws became an important issue. Tatarstan and other regions, especially the national republics, were forced to prepare new constitutions and to amend laws that the courts found were in violation of federal norms.[38] What will result from this process is as yet unknown.

Certainly, contradictory laws create bizarre legal collisions and unnecessary political conflicts. Such a conflict occurred in 2001 on the subject of a third term for Yakutia's president. Federal authorities referred to the absence of allowance for a third presidential term in Yakutia's constitution, while the local political clan pointed to a federal law that seemed to allow it. For several months the entire republic was kept under pressure before an agreement was finally reached behind the scenes. Yakutia's president gave up his aspirations for a third term and received a seat on the Federation Council as compensation.

In fall 2000, regional laws began to be brought into conformity with federal legislation. By February 2002, nine out of forty-two existing agreements with subjects of the Russian Federation had been canceled and ten more were prepared for cancellation. This is a positive process. Federal laws have been amended to restrict the immunity of governors (but not of presidents of republics). Yet federal authorities, unable to use legislative measures to discipline regional bosses with many ties in their regions and in the central government, intervened in 2000 with a sort of work-around. They built executive power structures on top of or alongside regional ones, short-circuiting ineffective legislative procedures. They created seven macro-regions or federal districts headed by seven governor generals appointed by the president. Eminent politicians then began to recommend the appointment rather than the election of local governors. Should this happen, one of the fundamental principles of the constitution—the election of executive and legislative authorities—will be violated.[39] The equality of the federation's subjects will be damaged as well, because some subjects will be represented by appointed governors and others by elected presidents.[40]

Local Self-Government

The situation is even worse with local self-government, whose development is at best in an embryonic state. The idea of local legislatures exists in the constitution: local self-governments are autonomous within their jurisdictions and do not form part of the system of government organs. This principle is beyond reproach and should be left untouched. Local self-government is one of the most important institutions in democratic countries, yet in this respect Russia is behind even prerevolutionary Russia, where local self-government was gaining momentum before 1917.

Local self-government has been hampered in three ways: by a lack of material and financial resources in the face of large responsibilities, by pressure from state bodies, and by low prestige. In the eyes of the populace, local self-government is just another branch of the bureaucracy. Low turnout figures for local elections often lead to the invalidation of elections. In 2000–2001 the Law on Local Self-government was amended. Governors are now entitled to fire heads of municipalities. This is a dangerous change, because the vertical power structure that is so attractive to many politicians undermines the constitutional principle of local government autonomy. On the positive side, Putin has ordered a reform of local self-government that attempts to increase the powers and financial resources at this level of government.

The Judiciary

Understanding the basis of the Russian constitutional system and the role of the constitution is impossible without considering the Constitutional Court. The creation of an independent court whose decisions are binding and cannot be appealed was one of the major accomplishments of Russia's new constitutionalists. The history or, more precisely, the prehistory of Russian constitutional jurisprudence in the present era, begins with the USSR Constitutional Oversight Committee (KKN). The KKN, elected at the December 1989 and April 1990 USSR CPDs, was not a full fledged court. It could make recommendations only to government bodies that had, in its opinion, issued anticonstitutional acts. Moreover, only decisions about human and citizens' rights were final and not subject to appeal. Out of approximately thirty decisions the KKN adopted during its existence, the most significant focused on the defense of rights, including recognition of the unconstitutionality of the internal residence registration and passport system and of coercive commitment to substance abuse clinics. The KKN also made the publication of all legal acts concerning citizens' rights and freedoms obligatory.

However, the KKN played a minimal role in the critical conflict between the Union and republican authorities during perestroika. The republics simply ignored its decisions about the conformance of republican legal acts with Union law. The Baltic republics refused to send representatives to the KKN from the outset, and after August 1991 other republics recalled their representatives. During the August 1991 putsch, the KKN could not gather a quorum, and an appeal about the failure to observe required legislative norms in the removal of Mikhail Gorbachev from office was issued only by the chairman, Sergei Alekseev, and four other members.

Formally, the USSR KKN was never dissolved. In December 1991, when Union state bodies lost authority, it was simply forgotten. The operation of analogous committees in the autonomous republics, stipulated by the Union law on the KKN, was never implemented. The republics, having declared their sovereignty and then their independence, created their own constitutional courts without referring to Union law and the experience of the KKN.

The Russian Constitutional Court was introduced into the system of government through amendments to the RSFSR Constitution, adopted by the Fifth RSFSR CPD in December 1991. The RSFSR CPD adopted the Law on the RSFSR Constitutional Court in July 1991, and thirteen of the fifteen required judges were elected to the court at the same Fifth Congress in October.[41] Deputies' groups and Supreme Soviet committees put forward candidates for the Constitutional Court. The nominees of nine deputies' groups and several committees on human rights and freedom of conscience were elected. At the court's first session Valery Zorkin, professor of juridical correspondence at the school of the Ministry of Internal Affairs and leader of the Constitutional Commission's groups of experts, was elected its chairman.

The Constitutional Court has made decisions to protect legal principles, such as the supremacy of the constitution over laws that contradict it. The court's first decision was issued in January 1992 and concerned Yeltsin's decree on the creation of a unified Ministry of Security and Internal Affairs. It ruled that the president had exceeded his authority and struck down the decree as unconstitutional. After the events of October 3–4, 1993, Yeltsin's Decree Number 1607 terminated the court's activity until the adoption of a new constitution. During this period the political situation was defined by a destructive struggle between Yeltsin and the people's deputies. Because the Constitutional Court's decisions had seriously influenced the balance of power among the conflicting sides, it was embroiled at the center of this conflict. At several junctures, Chairman Zorkin took political initiatives to resolve particularly sharp collisions. During the Seventh Congress in December 1992 Zorkin acted as a mediator between the president and the Congress deputies, helping them to arrive at a compromise supported by the Congressional resolution On the Stabilization of the Constitutional Order in the Russian Federation. One of the points of the agreement dealt with the court. The deputies agreed to the president's proposal not to elect judges to the two remaining seats on the court until the adoption of a new constitution. With the election of these two judges, the court's antipresidential mindset would have become overwhelming.

The court's role in the 1992–1993 confrontation between the executive and legislative branches is ambiguous. The termination of its activity by decree confirmed that it had been turned into a political weapon and presented a threat to the state. Two court findings on March 30, 1993, and

October 21, 1993, confirm the impression that the court clearly opposed the president in this conflict. Both were adopted immediately after the president's televised declarations to the people, when he suggested resolving the prolonged conflict by referendum and limiting the activity of the people's deputies. The court found the president's actions to be unconstitutional. Both the March and October findings were adopted upon the court's own initiative—that is, without an appeal from one of the conflicting parties or a third party—a possibility permitted by a 1991 law. In September 1993, when the Plotnikov amendment had already been written into the constitution,[42] the court's findings gave the Supreme Soviet a basis for declaring that Yeltsin was no longer in power and electing an alternative acting president. As a result, a dual power structure began to emerge.

A review of all twenty-seven resolutions the Constitutional Court adopted during this period of constitutional crisis in 1993 gives no basis for concluding that the court harbored antipresidential inclinations. Half of the court's decisions dealt with the constitutional confrontation and almost all found violations of constitutional norms and repealed the disputed documents. At the same time, the court's partial satisfaction of inquiries doubting the decisions of the Congress and Supreme Soviet was more common than that of inquiries opposed to the president's acts.

An example of a carefully balanced decision regarding an acutely polarized issue was the court's conclusion about the rules for determining the results of the April 1993 referendum, made four days before the referendum. Regarding the first two referendum questions about trust in the president and his socioeconomic policies, the court decided that because of the referendum's "opinion inquiry character" and lack of "juridical consequences," a simple majority of votes would be sufficient for a positive answer in support of the pro-presidential side. Regarding the third and fourth questions about mid-term elections of the president and the people's deputies, the court left in force the Congress's requirement of a majority of registered voters for the answer to be considered positive. Note, however, that neither the president nor the leadership of the Supreme Soviet turned to the Constitutional Court for decisions on these questions. The inquiries were made by groups of people's deputies from various factions supporting one side or the other in the conflict.

During this pivotal period the following themes occupied a relatively less significant place in the court's activity: appeals by citizens and labor collectives disputing old norms in USSR and RSFSR law or recent government decisions (seven resolutions), disputes between Russian federal and regional authorities (four decisions), and internal regional conflicts (four decisions). The CPSU case, the review of which stretched out for about six months, occupied a special place. The decision, adopted in November 1992, turned out to be a balanced compromise. The court ruled that the decision to disband the CPSU's quasi-state structures was essentially constitutional, but it handed over decisions regarding the disbanding of primary party organizations in places of residence and disputes about the party's property to courts of general jurisdiction.

Yet separating judicial disputes simultaneously by type and administrative level is quite difficult, and political and legal debates in the center and the regions intersected closely with each other. Conflicts between government bodies of the Republic of Mordovia and Chelyabinsk Oblast, for example, in many respects replicated the conflict between the president and the deputies at the center. Thus the Constitutional Court reviewed not only normative regional acts, but also decrees the regions adopted on the basis of decisions by the president and the Supreme Soviet. Two Constitutional Court decisions were devoted to Moscow's conflict between the city council and the mayor, and in both cases the issues to be adjudicated were related to decisions by Russian federal authorities. The authors of the inquiries were groups of people's deputies, in one case allies of the mayor and the president, in the other their opponents.

In general, the work of the Constitutional Court is disappointing despite the court's vital role during the early period of Russian democratization and its often balanced approach to decision making. This is partially due to limitations imposed on it by the constitution. To begin with, the court doesn't adjudicate on its own initiative, but must wait for a request or complaint from people who believe their rights have been violated.[43] The legislature imposed this limitation in response to the Constitutional Court's intervention in the 1993 constitutional crisis between Yeltsin and the executive branch on the one hand, and the Russian legislature and the CPD on the other. The court is also limited by having only nineteen justices and by its heavy workload. On average, the court takes six to eight months to resolve a complaint, but more important, even the decisions of the Constitutional Court are sometimes guided by actual practice as opposed to the formal constitution. An outstanding example of this was the 1995 ruling that struck down a challenge to Yeltsin's right to start the war in Chechnya without the constitutionally required approval of the Federation Council. This was perhaps the court's darkest hour. Finally, no implementation mechanism exists to enforce decisions. Both the legislative and executive authorities are experienced in bypassing, or simply ignoring, the court's decisions.

In comparison with the Constitutional Court, the general and arbitrage courts are perhaps plagued by even more deficiencies. Through many formal and informal links, the courts are subordinate to executive power and often obey orders received directly from the executive. For example, courts became the main tool in the unlawful suppression of independent media in 2001–2002 and are used to stage intelligence operations against scholars and journalists. Against all expectations, common sense, and the law, the Pacific Fleet Military Court condemned and sentenced military journalist Grigory Pasko on the basis of obscure, secret instructions by the Ministry of Defense ruled nonbinding by the Supreme Court. Pasko remained in prison until January 2003. For the secret services, the driving motivation behind this and similar decisions was to return to the time when fear limited Russian citizens' contacts with foreigners. The courts may also act to protect the military's interests. For example, the Nizhny Novgorod Court ruled that local authorities had breached the law by allowing young people to participate in alternative military service. While this possibility is established by the constitution, it has not been operationalized by a federal law. In addition, the courts have been unable to challenge the widespread use of torture by police during investigations.

Moreover, the judicial legislation of 2000–2002 is restricted and contradictory. Some of the decisions actually decrease the independence of the judiciary, destabilizing the law-based state. First, each judge now has to serve for three years before getting tenure. Second, disciplinary measures have been restored, including the removal of judges by decision of the qualification collegium. Third, chairs of the courts and their deputies, appointed for six-year terms, can now serve for two successive terms. According to Yuri Sidorenko, chairman of the Council of Judges of the Russian Federation:

[T]he position of the Supreme Court is simple and unanimous. We consider that the legislation aims to lower the most important guarantees of the independence and immunity of judges and their legal protection, and we believe that its adoption can lead to a loss of independence of the third branch of power…Thanks to the new legislation, real opportunities have emerged for the firing of judges and the application of various other measures of punishment for purely formal reasons, and the procedure for charging judges with criminal responsibility is being simplified, creating powerful levers for pressuring [judges].[44]

Moreover, the procuracy and other law enforcement organs have successfully delayed the establishment of judicial institutions dictated by the constitution, such as jury trials and court-sanctioned arrest. Most judges, the main actors in the judicial process, still come from the Soviet education system, which was alien to rule-of-law thinking. Moreover, some judges are former prosecutors, militia staff members, or secretaries of courts with great experience in falsifying legal documents. They remember well the time when decisions were made after a call from party officials, and even now their careers and welfare depend largely on the benevolence of high-ranking officials. The courts also need more staff and resources to boost their effectiveness and prestige. Finally, court decisions should be given more weight. Enforcement is lax, because the bailiff system is just getting on its feet. Consequently, two jurisdictions exist side by side: a neo-inquisitional, Soviet-style system in effect in the great majority of the general jurisdiction courts, and a plaintiff-oriented system that functions only in the few courts based on a jury system.

Problems in Amending the Constitution

The constitution and other legislation have many weak points that should be eliminated. The questions are when and how this should be done. Both supporters and opponents of changing the constitution have backing in society. According to an opinion survey conducted by a reputable Russian polling and research center, the All-Russian Center for Public Opinion Research, in January 2001, 35.8 percent of the population supports changing the constitution and 43.4 percent accepts leaving it as it is now.[45] However, the Public Opinion Foundation obtained different survey results in December 2001. Participants were asked the question, "The issue of the introduction of various amendments in Russia's constitution is now widely discussed...In your opinion, should the constitution be reconsidered and amendments introduced into it or not?" Of the respondents, 67 percent answered that amendments should be made, only 8 percent were opposed, and 24 percent were undecided. The same question has been asked each year starting in early 1997, and the share of opponents to amending the constitution oscillated from 15 percent in 1997 to 17 percent in 1998, 11 percent in 1999, and 16 percent in 2000.

Another question was, "How do you grade our constitution as a whole? Is it, in your opinion, good or bad?" In response 28 percent answered that the constitution was good, 38 percent answered that it was bad, and 34 percent could not answer either way. The vast majority of citizens have only a vague idea of the constitution's content. In the Public Opinion Foundation survey, when respondents were asked if they knew the basic content and clauses of the constitution, only 36 percent answered that they did, 55 percent answered that they did not, and 9 percent could not answer. Asked whether they concurred with the view that the constitution defines life in Russian society or whether it is a purely formal document that does not define Russian life, 41 percent agreed with the former position, 47 percent with the latter, and 12 percent could not answer.[46] Thus constitutional change seems to be of interest to elite groups, not to society as a whole.

The position of the Yabloko faction, stated publicly numerous times, has been that the 1993 constitution needs a few corrections. Yabloko holds that the "external" chapters (chapters 1, 2, and 9) concerning the bases of the constitutional regime, rights and liberties, and conditions for changing the constitution require no changes, but that some corrections have to be made to the clauses regarding the political system. In 1996–1998, Yabloko prepared several amendments clarifying the rights of the president, expanding the parliament's powers (especially its oversight power), specifying the government's relationship with the president and the parliament, removing the amendment that does not require the election of senators to the Federation Council (though in my opinion, this amendment could be made without changing the constitution), and including a detailed description of the presidential impeachment process.[47]

In the late 1990s, a window of opportunity would have permitted the introduction of changes to certain articles of the constitution with the help of several political groups. Law and order could have been strengthened without weakening the main achievements of the anticommunist revolution of the late 1980s and early 1990s. The passage of such amendments was not certain, but could have succeeded if carried out correctly. Indeed, during Yevgeny Primakov's term as prime minister opportunities existed to change the constitution with the help of the parliamentary majority, not de jure, but de facto. However, following Primakov's ouster as prime minister, the situation has changed, and now the introduction of such changes to the constitution is considerably more problematic. Considering the balance of power in both houses of parliament, any attempt to amend the constitution is likely to fail unless the president introduces it. Moreover, with Putin's election the system of checks and balances has been further weakened, and the danger of managed democracy and limited civil rights has become more real.

In the new situation, opening up the issue of constitutional design could lead to a constitution that is worse than the existing one. Based on the words and actions of certain Russian politicians, the changes that would take place would likely be the restriction of civil rights, or at least a weakening of civil rights; the strengthening of the state and an increase in the prerogatives of quasi-civil structures created by means of guarantees; the transfer of too much power to the president of Belarus within the Union of Russia and Belarus; the weakening of the separation of church and state to the benefit of the Russian Orthodox Church; the introduction of ideological unification for the sake of the so-called "national idea"; and the weakening of the constitution's ninth section, which is a self-defense mechanism that complicates the amendment process.

Precursors to such changes have been evident. In early 2002, the Unity faction drafted a clearly anticonstitutional bill under which the state was to give several charters to so-called traditional confessions, which include first and foremost the Russian Orthodox Church, as well as Muslim, Jewish, and Buddhist faiths, but no others. In late 2001, the newly elected chairman of the Federation Council, Sergei Mironov, proposed extending the presidential term of office from four to seven years. Although the president rejected the idea, high-ranking politicians and some governors strongly supported the extension. The realization of such ideas would lead to the destruction of the law-governed state and set the regime on a course toward an authoritarian form of rule. In this situation Russian democrats, Yabloko in particular, see the current constitution as an obstacle to backsliding from democracy to authoritarianism.

The constitution now contains two ways of amending it. The first is the convocation of a constitutional convention to make corrections to the main chapters of the constitution or to work out a new draft. The convention can then either approve its changes or call a referendum to do so. The second way is to introduce a few amendments that do not contradict the basis of the constitutional regime, the sections on human and civil rights and liberties, and the system of changing the constitution. Such amendments need an extraordinary two-thirds majority vote in both chambers of the Federal Assembly and then ratification by two-thirds of the eighty-nine subjects of the federation.

The first method is long and complex and therefore unlikely to be undertaken. Although many impatient politicians are eager to change the constitution, the final result of this procedure could be quite contrary to their expectations. The bases of the constitutional regime and civil rights contained in the constitution should not become the subject of political games. The balance of political power in a constitutional convention formed in the present political and social environment could result in authoritarian measures. Thus the freeze put on the adoption of a law on constitutional conventions was the correct decision. None of the drafts of this law introduced in the Duma has been satisfactory. The only reasonable way to change the constitution in the midterm and long term is to add amendments gradually as has been done in the United States.

Moreover, the state structure can be changed without tampering with the constitution. Vital questions such as reforming the Federation Council, adopting budget federalism, increasing the role of the government, and abolishing the departmental courts could be addressed by means of new federal laws and federal constitutional laws. While considering the constitutionality of certain laws in the Constitutional Court and the Supreme Court is appropriate on occasion, the role of these institutions in the current situation should not be overestimated.

The time for grand constitutional experiments has passed, but the time for establishing a permanent document has not yet arrived. The principle of not doing any harm should be supreme. Working toward the observance of existing constitutional and legal norms and leaving matters in their present—albeit far from perfect—state is better than opening a Pandora's box.

4

Legislative–Executive Relations

Andrei Ryabov

The separation of powers between the executive and legislative branches has been among the most important accomplishments of the grand program of reforms to sweep post-communist Russia during the past decade. The transition from a one-party state led by the Communist Party of the Soviet Union to a new political system based on interaction between legislative and executive institutions was a tortuous process punctuated by a number of conflicts, including an armed conflict between the president and the parliament in October 1993. Since this conflict, the relationship between the executive and legislative branches has stabilized. The quality of their interaction also has improved. Neither side has threatened to abolish the other by extra-constitutional means. Even confrontations allowed by the constitution have been rare. The president has never dissolved the parliament, and the parliament has only tried to begin impeachment proceedings once (in 1999), but without success. Most national policies of consequence derive from laws passed by both houses of parliament and signed by the president, and are enacted by presidential decree. Both branches of government respect the basic tenets of the constitution. Since 1993, elections for both branches of government have occurred as scheduled and according to law.

This stability in legislative-executive relations was the result of compromise reached by the two branches of government, albeit with one side compromising more than the other. In successful conversions to democracy, the rules of the game governing relations between different branches of government have to be negotiated during the transition period. The timing of elections, the organization (especially the division) of power within the state, and even the range of issues open to political contestation should be decided beforehand. However, in the Soviet Union and then in Russia, elites did not succeed in negotiating these basic rules in delineating the path from the old to the new during the transition. Instead, the chosen mode of transition left many of the rules of Russia's new polity ambiguous, uncodified, and subject to manipulation. Is the president the head of state or the true holder of executive power? Should the Communist Party be considered a political party or is it better viewed as a criminal organization? What mix of planned economy and market institutions govern or should govern the organization of the economy? What are the borders of the new state? These issues were only settled when one power—the president—succeeded in establishing hegemonic control over the parliament in the fall of 1993. At that time Boris Yeltsin used his power to dictate a new set of rules to govern executive-legislative relations. Faced with the choice of acquiescence or renewed conflict, his opponents agreed to Yeltsin's constitution, even though they did not like the balance of power that it established between the president and the parliament. The result has been stability, but at the cost of eliminating genuine checks and balances in the regime. Critics refer to Russia's super-presidency as its most antidemocratic feature.

This chapter explains the emergence and consequent consolidation of the super-presidency by tracing the evolution of legislative-executive relations over the last fifteen years.

The Gorbachev Era

Russia's present political framework and system of checks and balances first emerged during the Soviet perestroika period, taking root in the representative institutions that sprang up independently of the Party and government cadres. The development of these structures was central to the string of political reforms undertaken by Mikhail Gorbachev, whose goal was to weaken the power of the Party's political apparatus. However, Gorbachev's reluctance to abandon fundamental socialist ideology—he wanted an improved version of socialism—prevented the reformers from establishing new representative bodies, and thus compelled them to rely on the traditional vertical power structure of the soviets.

The soviets were not decision-making centers. Their function amounted to little more than formally rubber-stamping decisions made in advance by the Communist Party of the Soviet Union. It was the introduction of semi-competitive elections in 1989 and 1990 (see chapter 2) that allowed the creation of the institutional groundwork for consolidating the democratic opposition that had as its base the existing structure of the soviets. Such efforts were especially successful at the municipal level in cities such as Moscow and St. Petersburg. The transformed soviets subsequently played an important role in relieving the pressure of orthodox communist ideology on society and in mobilizing public support for democratic reform. At the same time, their experience with ruling in 1990–1991 demonstrated that the soviets—even those that were fundamentally oriented toward reforms— were unsuitable mechanisms for implementing market-based reforms or setting up new social institutions.

At the root of this ineffectiveness was the soviets' limited authority— inherent in their very nature.[1] Inspired by the Paris Commune and the Russian revolutions of 1905–1907 and 1917, Vladimir Lenin's idea of a "republic of soviets" was the prototype for a nationwide, public system of self-government meant to replace the centralized state machinery and its institutions. Therefore the concept of a republic of soviets negated the notion of a professional legislature by definition. This approach ensured that democratically elected deputies to soviets at all levels could perform their legislative and representative functions only through public service during short sessions, delegating implementation authority to executive committees elected from among the deputies. This system was intended to be a vehicle for local self-government by individual enterprises and small communities, and therefore proved ineffective as a government institution. Moreover, no separation of power existed between the executive and legislative branches of government.

Institutionally, the changes carried out under Gorbachev were meant to return the soviets to their constitutional role as decision-making and enforcement agencies. Gorbachev considered various ways of gearing the Soviet system toward this goal, from creating delegations of worker union members to restoring the multistage election system that had existed in the Soviet Union before 1936 and the congresses of soviets. The assumption was that such measures would alert deputies at all levels to their political responsibility, since many experts at the time believed that a small group could hold the deputy it delegated to the soviet accountable more easily than a disjointed constituency of a territorial electoral district.

Some of these approaches to the formation of the soviets were implemented during the course of Gorbachev's political reforms. In particular, the restoration of the Congress of People's Deputies (CPD), where elected representatives of the people met during short sessions, was intended to institutionalize the abstract idea of the people's sovereignty. The Congress was instructed to outline the nation's strategic policy direction on behalf of the people. The USSR's CPD still drew a third of its delegates from professional groups, including the Communist Party of the Soviet Union and its affiliated social organizations. The conservative party elite thought that this system would allow them to form a more loyal corps of deputies. Instead, it was precisely groups like these that nominated Andrei Sakharov, the leader of the human rights movement in the USSR, and many other well-known pro-democracy public figures and journalists to the Congress.

The return to the soviets' founding principles was insufficient to make them into genuine decision-making centers. Therefore Gorbachev borrowed from the parliamentary model the idea of a permanent legislature, one that would be formed from a subset of deputies from the Soviet Congress as a whole. As a result, a mixed system emerged at the top level of representative power: whereas the Congress of People's Deputies was concerned with drawing up a political strategy, the Supreme Soviet elected by the CPD did routine legislative work. That system was strongly reminiscent of the people's rule mechanism of government, suggested before the 1917 Bolshevik revolution by the Socialist Revolutionaries, which combined a standing parliament with periodically convened national congresses of people's representatives called the Council of All the Land.

The Russian Soviet Federative Socialist Republic (RSFSR), the largest constituent republic of the Soviet Union, adopted a new system of soviets in 1990, discarding the practice of delegating deputies from social groups. But in 1990, soon after the first elections to the Russian CPD and to regional and city soviets, the soviets' inefficacy as government institutions became obvious. The deputies, who following Lenin still regarded the soviets as an executive as well as a legislative institution, began to interfere actively in the day-to-day activities of the executive committees, usurping their authority. Often the deputies went so far as to attempt to take over executive functions, which created an atmosphere of legal and political chaos. In a situation where any decision about national or local problems was a subject of public debate, the pursuit of any sensible and consistent policy was difficult.

In this context, new institutions of executive government that were independent of the system of soviets were established to promote reform. In 1990, the presidency of the USSR was established, and a year later, the people voted in a referendum to create the presidency of the Russian Federation. Likewise, the position of mayor and the office of chief magistrate of a municipality were established by referenda in Moscow and St. Petersburg. Nevertheless, the division of powers between these new executives and their corresponding legislative bodies was still ambiguous. At the time, ideological differences fueled the clashes. These differences were suppressed only by a larger institutional struggle between the USSR and the RSFSR. More often, however, the struggle derived from ambiguous rules. The struggle for power between the USSR government and the government of the RSFSR compelled Yeltsin and the Supreme Soviet of Russia to join forces in their struggle against Gorbachev, who was backed by Union elites. Lurking behind that confrontation was a political conflict between two trends among elites in the late Soviet era, one supporting Gorbachev and his policy of gradual transformation of the communist system, and the other emphatically in favor of radical, market-based reform. Most analysts believe that the creation of the Russian presidency is explained not so much by institutional reasons, that is, the need to enhance the efficiency of the political system in which the soviets were playing a growing role, as by political considerations, namely, plans harbored by some Soviet elites to carry out radical social reform and to speed up the redistribution of public property.[2]

The "August" Republic, 1991–1993

At the end of 1991, after the breakup of the USSR and the collapse of the communist regime, the conflict between these two trends within the ruling class shifted to the core of the Russian power structure. The institutional conflict between the Russian president and the system of soviets assumed center stage. This divide played a key role in the country's political life from 1991 to 1993, during the so-called August Republic.

In the fall of 1991, Yeltsin had a political mandate to reconstitute the formal rules governing relations between the president and the parliament. While he took some important steps in other areas of political reform,

including the dramatic series of changes that produced the peaceful dissolution of the Soviet Union, Yeltsin decided against pursuing political reforms
that could have helped to clarify the relationship between the president
and the parliament within the Russian Federation. For instance, he failed to
pass a new constitution even though his own Constitutional Commission
within the Russian Supreme Soviet had already drafted one. He preserved
the institutional configuration in place at the time, that is, the system of soviets, and augmented it with a newly created presidential office with ill-
defined powers. He also did not try to take advantage of his then incredible
popularity to create a new balance of power within the parliament by convoking new elections. Yeltsin feared that having gained a majority in the
supreme legislative government body, the mass democratic movement
would make a serious bid for political leadership during the process of
reform. By preserving a conservatively-minded parliament, he held on to his
monopoly on political initiative, retained a substantial amount of autonomy
in relation to various centers of influence, and secured a vast domain for
maneuvering.[3] Nevertheless, Yeltsin and his new government associates
were also busy doing many other things, such as managing the peaceful dismantling of the world's largest empire and beginning the difficult process of
transforming Soviet communism into Russian capitalism.

The lack of clearly defined, universally recognized rules of the game governing relations between the parliament and the president had detrimental
consequences for economic reform, and eventually for political stability.
Yeltsin appointed Yegor Gaidar to head his economic reform team within the
government. Once Gaidar began to implement reforms, a majority in the
CPD crystallized against his policies. Polarization between parliament and
the president on the issue of economic reform in turn produced a constitutional crisis, because both claimed jurisdictional authority over the economic reform process. The constitution, an amended leftover from the
Soviet era, offered little guidance as to which branch of government should
be in charge, but generally favored the CPD. The Congress possessed not
only legislative powers, but also other extensive rights. For example, the
Congress had to agree to the president's choice of candidate for the vice presidency. Congress could also impeach the president by a qualified two-thirds
majority vote without appeal. Finally, the government was not an independent political institution in the First Russian Republic or August Republic.
On the one hand, it was formed by the president, but on the other hand, its
activities were under the Congress's and the Supreme Soviet's strict control.

Only over time did the president establish his hegemony over the government. Subsequently, each cabinet member had to meet two criteria: commitment to the idea of socioeconomic reform and personal loyalty to the president. The government took its policy instructions from the president rather than from Congress or the Supreme Soviet. Eager as they were to exert influence on the government's policy, the Congress and Supreme Soviet deputies never succeeded in doing so. Only in exceptional cases did Yeltsin reshuffle his cabinet under pressure from the deputies. Ambiguity about who was in charge of the government helped to inspire yet greater polarization between the president and parliament. As Vladimir Ryzhkov writes, both institutions were equally anxious to claim extensive powers not explicitly determined by the Constitution. The president and the Supreme Soviet adopted decisions on budget expenditures and issued binding instructions to the government and to ministries practically independently of one another, thereby creating chaos and rendering executive authorities incapable of pursuing any sensible policy.[4]

Seeking to counter the soviets' vertical power structure, in August 1991, Yeltsin decided to appoint heads of regional administrations (later known as governors), although the official line stated that he did this to prevent the disintegration of statehood after the breakup of the Soviet Union. Yet he realized that the heads of these subjects of the federation would further the interests of local elites. To strengthen the ties these government authorities had to the Kremlin, the president also installed presidential representatives in supervisory positions in every region as a way to exert federal executive influence in the regions. Some of these plenipotentiaries tried to take over executive powers in the regions, but failed because they lacked control over local administrative resources.

The establishment of two rival vertical power structures only aggravated the institutional conflict between the president and the Supreme Soviet. The confrontation between the legislative and executive branches of government during the August Republic period was essentially reproduced at the level of the federal districts. In most regions, fierce power struggles broke out between the soviets and the governors in a situation where only eight out of eighty-eight regional heads of administration had been elected by popular vote, the rest having been appointed by the president.[5] In a few regions where the governor and a majority in the regional soviet belonged to the same political camp, constructive cooperation occurred between the executive and representative institutions. For instance, in Yaroslavl Oblast, both legislative and executive government institutions backed Yeltsin, while in Bryansk Oblast the regional head of administration and the regional soviet sided firmly with the Russian CPD. In most regions polarization echoing the standoff in Moscow shaped local politics.

The conflict between the president and the Supreme Soviet developed into an implacable standoff that both regarded as a life or death political struggle. These rival groups failed to reach agreement on the adoption of the new national constitution, the key issue of the August Republic. As a result, Russia kept the 1978 constitution, which was poorly suited to the changing relationships among the branches of government.

With the multiparty system still embryonic, both rival governmental institutions were compelled to perform the functions of "super-parties" to seek direct popular support and to mobilize their followers. In this context, the question of their relative legitimacy assumed special importance for the contending parties, but no unambiguous answer to this question was forthcoming for some time. Both sides sought to mobilize the public directly in support of their cause. Over time, the Supreme Soviet lost standing in society as the balance of power within the Supreme Soviet shifted decidedly toward the pro-communist, retrogressive forces, while the influence of the reformist forces waned. Society's preferences were confirmed by the April 1993 referendum, which showed that the president and his policies commanded much more popular support than the Supreme Soviet. Russia's political culture, whereby executive bodies of power have always held much greater appeal to the masses than representative bodies, also played a role in giving the president more popular support. This cultural artifact was cleverly exploited by Yeltsin and his team, which through journalists loyal to them, leveled devastating criticism against both the Congress and the Supreme Soviet in the mass media.

The crisis came to climax during the summer of 1993, when each side prepared constitutional reforms to weaken the other. In preparing for the Tenth CPD in the fall, deputies drafted a series of constitutional amendments that would have liquidated Russia's presidential office altogether. Yeltsin preempted their plans by issuing Decree Number 1400, which dissolved the Congress and called for new elections for a newly revamped parliament. The Congress responded by calling this decree illegal and subsequently recognizing Vice President Aleksandr Rutskoi as the interim president. In a replay of the 1991 drama, Russia suddenly had two heads of state and two governments, each claiming sovereign authority over the other. After a standoff at the barricades that lasted several days, the conflict ultimately exploded into an armed clash between the president's and the Supreme Soviet's supporters on October 3–4, 1993. On the second day of fighting, the president's armed forces prevailed.

In retrospect, the tense institutional and political stalemate between the executive and representative branches of government in the August Republic could indeed probably have been broken only by the force of arms. This was due not only to the existence of an internally contradictory political system. Heterogeneous political systems made up of institutions belonging to different political eras existed in many states in transition. Outside Russia, the transformation of those systems was accompanied by conflicts that did not always end in bloodshed because, as political analyst Lilia Shevtsova has noted, "[I]n Eastern and Central Europe there was no such manifest gravitation toward monopoly over power on the part of two democratically elected institutions so as practically to rule out a peaceful outcome of confrontation."[6] Russia was different. Its political culture lacks a tradition of tolerance and compromise because of its history of a lengthy authoritarian rule that did not tolerate opposition and strived to suppress it. Influenced by these traditions, politicians were accustomed to perceiving power as an indivisible phenomenon that could have only one real decision-making center.[7] This widespread perception only exacerbated the confrontation between the president and the Supreme Soviet.

The Presidential Republic

Yeltsin and his supporters' victory paved the way for a political system new to Russia: a presidential republic in which the relationship between the executive and legislative branches of government assumed new content and institutional form. From a purely legal standpoint, the changeover from the mixed political system of the August Republic to the presidential system was a step toward further democratization. The new Russian Constitution, adopted following the December 1993 referendum, put into effect the principle of separation of powers. Also multiparty elections were introduced for the State Duma, the parliament's lower chamber. The new laws, however, were far from perfect. Even though the new constitution was intended to be a departure from the incongruities that the previous constitution had allowed, in practice it too created myriad contradictions, particularly evident in today's relationship between the executive and legislative branches.

The framers of the new political system set several tasks for themselves: to overcome the divided power of the August Republic period, to provide institutional conditions under which the president and the government would be able to carry out radical market reforms unhindered, and to counter the tendencies weakening the unity of the Russian Federation.[8] In addition to these considerations, the corporate interests of the leading actors in the political process played a decisive part in laying and implementing the legal groundwork for relations between the executive and legislative branches of government.

The Russian elites who supported early market reforms and the promotion of a proprietary class sought strong and centralized executive power, which they felt would protect their interests against protests from those disadvantaged by economic reform. Because of Yeltsin's victory in October, they got their way, and the 1993 constitution consolidated the imbalance of power in favor of the presidency.[9]

As stated in the constitution, the president is the head of state and the guarantor of the constitution. The president is vested with the powers of head of the executive branch of government, which entails certain executive and legislative functions. In particular, the president has the exclusive right to appoint the prime minister, the head of the government. The State Duma, the lower house of parliament reconstituted in December 1993, is given the power to approve or reject the president's nomination, but rejection comes at a high price. If the Duma rejects the president's candidate three times in a row, then the Duma is dissolved and new parliamentary elections are held. The prime minister names government ministers and these ministers do not need the Duma's approval. Ultimate power over the government resides with the president, since he can dismiss the prime minister at any time. This degree of unchecked presidential authority in effect assigns the power to appoint ministers to the president, not the prime minister. In addition, the president is given direct power of appointment of the so-called power ministers: the minister of defense, the minister of internal affairs, the minister of foreign affairs, and the head of the Federal Security Service (the former KGB). These ministers report directly to the president, not the prime minister. In addition, the new constitution eliminated the post of vice president, ensuring that no rivals to the president's power would arise within the executive branch.

The new constitution also gave the president the right of legislative initiative and the authority to issue decrees having the force of law until the adoption of corresponding legal acts. In other words, the president has the power to perform law-making functions alongside parliament. Between 1993 and 1994, the president promulgated more laws than parliament.[10] According to the new constitution, the president also assumed principal responsibility for setting military doctrine, drafting the state budget, and controlling the central bank.

Consequently, the logic of the constitution placed the president above the entire political system. He was to play the role of a coordinating power in the spirit of Benjamin Constant and to integrate the efforts made by other institutions and branches of government.[11] This archaic political-legal construct stressed the transitional character of the new political system, in which the social and political forces of change were supposedly still so weak that they needed support from a strong head of state vested with the full powers of government.

In addition, the constitution gave the president the right to create special bodies on which to rely for help in performing his constitutional duties. The result was the proliferation of bureaucratic organs that eventually turned into uncontrolled, exclusive, decision-making centers. The most prominent among these was the President's Administration, which promptly went from being a technical service to an important—and often irresponsible—political institution.

Nevertheless, not all Russian analysts believe that the contemporary Russian political system is a super-presidency. For instance, Alexei Salmin, when analyzing the formal law aspects of the presidency as established by the constitution, comes to the conclusion that "formally the Russian presidency as an institution is not stronger than the French."[12] In my opinion, however, this inference is not objective, because of the narrowness of the formal legal approach in understanding the nature of the Russian presidency. The informal role that the president plays in the Russian political process must also be taken into account.

Yeltsin's constitution reorganized the internal construction of the parliament by creating a bicameral national parliament. The upper house, the Federation Council, was constituted on a territorial basis and consists of 178 members, 2 each from the 89 regions of the Russian Federation.[13] The lower house of parliament, the State Duma, has 450 deputies.

The constitution drafted and ratified in 1993 did not specify the procedure whereby representatives to the Duma and the Federation Council were to be selected. As discussed in chapter 2, when the first elections to these legislative bodies were held in December 1993, Yeltsin issued presidential decrees regarding the electoral rules. The constitution specified that these first legislators were to serve for two years only.

The powers of the State Duma were markedly curtailed in comparison with those of the former Supreme Soviet. The Duma was authorized to draft and pass bills, but the constitution required that the upper house also approve bills and gave the president veto power. Most of the checks on power in the new system of law work in favor of the executive. The Duma's only powerful function is approving the budget. While in theory it has the power to approve or disapprove of the president's candidate for prime minister, in reality, its control functions in regard to the executive branch are minimal, especially when compared with the powers of the Supreme Soviet. The president is empowered to dissolve the State Duma if it rejects the president's candidate for prime minister or passes votes of no confidence in the government three times in succession.

At the same time, the procedure by which the 1993 constitution provides for the president's impeachment is too complicated ever to be carried out. Impeachment proceedings can be initiated only in instances of treason or high crimes and the Supreme Court—not the Duma—has the authority to determine what presidential acts qualify as treason or high crimes. Impeachment requires a two-thirds majority in both houses followed by a confirmation from both the Constitutional Court and the Supreme Court stating that the process is legal and that the charge is an impeachable offense. Because the president appoints the members of these courts, they are unlikely to exercise this power.

Nonconstitutional Factors Influencing Presidential-Parliamentary Relations

The 1993 constitution consolidated the president's power over the legislature. This outcome responded to the strategic interests of the new elites who wanted the president to arbitrate their conflicts among themselves concerning the distribution of formerly public property. Taking advantage of the president's protection from public control, big property owners lobbied for their interests and built up informal centers with a high degree of leverage over political decision making in the executive branch. In the late 1990s, these informal centers all but took over official political institutions in some important areas. At the same time, the domineering president fostered political irresponsibility at all levels of state government and administration, with most agents of the political process steadily losing incentives to act on their own.

Civil Society

Parliament's weakness in the political system after 1993 derived not only from the aspirations of new elites, but also from the weakness of civil society institutions (discussed in greater detail in chapter 6). A recent book by a group of Yeltsin's former advisers includes this unattributed statement:

> Let's face it, Russian society has developed neither the need, nor the aptitude for exerting systematic influence on the government; there are as yet no arrangements for exerting such influence, such as through stable and responsible parties espousing a clear-cut ideology and truly expressing public interests. Accordingly, the representative body has not become a force exerting any real influence on the affairs of the state.[14]

As discussed in chapter 5, political parties were also weak and could not contribute significantly to the formation of the executive branch of government. Only two, the Communist Party of the Russian Federation (CPRF) and Yabloko, ran presidential candidates of their own in 1996. The parties took no part in forming a government that would be accountable to parliaments at either the federal or local levels. A strong presidential party was unnecessary, because such a party could have tried to exercise control over the activities of the head of state. The executive authorities, both federal and local, preferred to put together stable support groups in the legislatures (the so-called parties of power) as vehicles for conducting their policies.[15]

The Ambiguous and Changing Power of the Government

Yeltsin's personal ambitions became an extremely important factor in the development of the relationship between the executive and legislative branches of government in the period following the adoption of the 1993 constitution. Having emerged victorious from the conflict with the Supreme Soviet, he was in full control of policy, and that was reflected in the new power structure. Many analysts concluded that the 1993 constitution had been tailor-made for Yeltsin. By the time the nation's system of law was adopted in December 1993, however, Yeltsin had likely begun to lose confidence in his capacity to make Russia a modern, rapidly growing, and prosperous power, which accounts for the priority he placed on political survival instead.

Another reason for his change of emphasis was Yeltsin's personal mistrust of the leading members of his political team following the events of 1993, when his former comrades-in-arms—Vice President Aleksandr Rutskoi and Supreme Soviet Chairman Ruslan Khasbulatov—led the Congress's mutiny against him. Yeltsin arranged his relationship with the government and parliament in such a way as to keep maximum executive powers concentrated in his hands and the bulk of political responsibility resting with the government and the State Duma. This logic made the government under the new constitution a buffer between the president and the State Duma. Because the government was part of the executive branch, it had no means of formulating its own political objectives; that was the prerogative of the president. At the same time, to a certain extent the government had to take the Duma's position into consideration. The president was therefore in a position to shift the blame for the executive's political setbacks to the government.

In cases where the broad powers of the president and his political irresponsibility were in apparent imbalance with the Duma's and the government's feelings of precariousness and vulnerability, the prime minister and his government and the parliament decided to forge relationships of constructive cooperation. Working together, they secured themselves against forced retirement or premature dissolution. This trend became increasingly pronounced in 1994 and culminated around 1997–1998, when the government secured a firm stronghold in the Duma and developed into a center of executive power alongside the presidency. This happened even though in 1997–1998 most of the State Duma members belonged to the opposition: the Communist Party and its allies. Institutional interests of common political survival outweighed political and ideological differences between the "red" Duma and the moderately reformist government headed by Prime Minister Viktor Chernomyrdin.

The increasingly closer relationship between the government and the Duma effectively strengthened the government's power, a development that Yeltsin did not like. This fear of the Chernomyrdin government becoming an autonomous decision maker is what led Yeltsin to fire the prime minister and his cabinet without warning in March 1998. Rivalry between two executive power centers recurred in the spring of 1999, when the Yevgeny Primakov government had also established a relationship of close cooperation with the Duma, thereby precipitating the government's demise in May 1999.

The relations between the president, the government, and the State Duma, set up by Yeltsin to address specific political problems, were ad hoc, informal, and often polarized between individuals within the executive branch and not between different branches of government. At the same time, agreeing with the point of view that the government is "one of the most inscrutable and inefficient elements of the new Russian political system" is difficult.[16] If the government were strong, it could play an influential role in contemporary Russian politics and in the decision-making process.

One cannot rule out the possibility that the conflict between the president and a Duma-backed prime minister may be replayed during the period of Vladimir Putin's presidency, especially considering that the government under Prime Minister Mikhail Kasyanov is becoming a strong institution supported by influential interest groups. Nevertheless, relations between the president and the government may avoid a deep conflict, for instance, if Putin prefers to concentrate his activity mainly on international policy, defense, and national safety issues, leaving the realization of social and economic policy to the government. This is roughly the distribution of spheres of activity that has been evolving between Putin and the government since 2002. Theoretically, it could lead to the transformation of the super-presidential political system into a mixed presidential-parliamentary republic, but the success of such a transformation will depend on so many factors that defining it now is difficult.

Consolidation of the New Russian Elites

Another important factor in determining the character of the relationship between the executive and legislative branches of government during the presidential republic was the gradual consolidation of the new Russian elites. After the tragic events of 1993, Yeltsin awoke to the danger that a split in the ruling class posed for the presidency. As a result, starting in 1994, he accelerated the integration of the conservative wings of the old party and Soviet upper crust into a free market system. He did this primarily through a privatization policy that drew a large section of the former managerial elite—the "red directors" of industrial and agricultural enterprises—into the process of dividing up public property. By getting the red directors involved in the privatization process, Yeltsin helped level off the difference in economic potential between the reform-minded and conservative groups of the emergent Russian elite. To further remove barriers to the consolidation process, Yeltsin reneged on his earlier decision to ban the CPRF and initiated the 1994 Public Accord Agreement, which has, however, proven to be an inconsequential initiative.

Why the conflict between the "red" Duma of 1995–1999 and the president never culminated in a serious political upheaval is now clear. Since the late 1990s, the CPRF's leadership has been steadily integrating into the new establishment. It has made strong contacts with big business, and after the gubernatorial elections of 1996–1997, in which CPRF nominees scored impressive successes, the party secured a firm foothold in the executive government bodies of the constituent federal entities. Even though Yeltsin and the communist-controlled Duma often came close to severing all relations during the power struggle, each side recognized certain rational limits to the feud, something that was not the case during the fall of 1993. A remarkable example of this occurred in March 1996, when Yeltsin ignored his aides' recommendation to dissolve the Duma and ban the Communist Party on the pretext that parliament had denounced the Belovezhka accords and in doing so had called the legitimacy of Russian statehood into question.[17]

Remarkably, during this later period, both Yeltsin and the Duma communists had an interest in maintaining a degree of tension, because such a relationship best served their interests at the mass politics level. Yeltsin, who had lost his former drive for social reform, had to continuously validate his legitimacy by invoking the myth that the nation was in imminent danger of a communist comeback. The CPRF supported this line of political confrontation, because even though the Communist Party had gradually adapted to the emergent market economy, it was still under pressure to impress its electorate with the rhetoric of heroic resistance against the anti-communist regime.

The fourth and final element in the balance between the executive and legislative branches was the new relationship between the federal and regional elites. As mentioned earlier, one of the purposes of the 1993 constitution was to discourage the growing trend toward self-rule in certain federal regions and to restore the Russian Federation to the centralized political and legal entity it had formerly been. However, Moscow lacked the financial and administrative resources to carry this out, and to strengthen his authority, Yeltsin was compelled to compromise with regional leaders. Seeking to prevent the restoration of a vertical legislative power structure and simultaneously to meet the regional elites halfway, Yeltsin granted the regions the right to establish their own systems of executive and legislative institutions that took into account local needs and specificities, on the grounds that their systems were based on the general principles of federal law. To legalize the nonconstitutional practice of delegating power to local authorities, starting in 1994 Yeltsin signed a series of special agreements on the separation of powers between the federal center and members of the federation. Regions like Tatarstan, Bashkortostan, and Sverdlovsk, which were stronger than others politically and economically, took advantage of the new arrangements to create areas in the realm of authority in which local legislation took precedence over federal laws. The recognition of the enhanced political role of the regional elites manifested itself in 1995, when the transitional articles of the constitution lost effect.[18] The articles had restricted membership in the Federation Council to only those members who represented the heads of the executive and legislative government branches of the federation's constituent entities.

The feudal principle of power separation between the center and the regions that Yeltsin introduced enhanced his political leverage. In exchange for the regions' increased economic and political independence, Yeltsin was assured of a social and economic policy that was relatively free of conflict with the Federation Council. The upper chamber served also as a reliable legislative filter, blocking those bills pushed by the Duma that disagreed with Yeltsin and his government's positions. The members of the Federation Council often leveled sharp criticism against the government's policy line, but when it came to decision making—on the national budget, in particular—they inevitably fell in line behind Yeltsin. Similarly, in the 1996 presidential elections an overwhelming majority of the Federation Council rendered powerful support to Yeltsin, tipping the balance for him in his reelection bid. The only fully independent decisions made by the upper chamber concerned executive appointments, and here too they approved a number of Yeltsin's chosen candidates, most notably the attorney general, high court judges, and members of the Auditing Chamber.

Despite this seemingly advantageous arrangement, in mid-1999 Yeltsin and the Federation Council clashed in earnest. Yeltsin's ill-conceived policies and his neglect of the need for political certainty among most elites drove him and his closest circle, the so-called family, into political isolation. Even then, the upper chamber's resistance was somewhat passive. The regional elites, who chiefly sought to consolidate their positions, were neither prepared for, nor capable of, assuming the responsibility of shaping a new national strategy. The State Duma deputies, even while mindful of the clash between the president and the Supreme Soviet in 1993 and fearing its recurrence, were unable to initiate impeachment proceedings against Yeltsin in May 1999. Despite the constructive cooperation that the legislative and executive branches of government had achieved, lacking the necessary powers and political initiative, the parliament failed to take a leading role in the process of further democratization.

The 1993 constitution granted Russia's regions the right to establish their own power structures, a right further endorsed by the 1996 Federal Law on the Basic Principles Underlying State Power Organization in the Constituent Entities of the Russian Federation. The constitutions of the constituent republics of the Russian Federation, as well as individual districts' self-approved regulations, finalized the legal creation of the system of local government authorities. A large group of federation members copied the power structure that had emerged in Moscow following the adoption of the 1993 constitution. Only a few regions introduced a mixed election system under which some of the deputies were to be elected from single-seat constituencies by majority vote; others used proportional representation from party tickets. Other regions shifted completely to the majority vote system. Political parties were weaker in the constituent entities of the federation than they were in Moscow, which suited the governors, who sought freedom from any form of public control. For the governors to get local parliaments consisting of individual deputies representing single-seat constituencies under their sway was much easier than influencing parliaments structured on the principle of party affiliation. Only a new federal law passed during the Putin era mandated that all regional legislatures must adopt a mixed electoral system.

The changes that have taken place since the early 1990s have led to the emergence of various types of executive-legislative relations in the regions. Yet executive power remained dominant in individual districts. In many cases, the nature of the relationship between governors and local legislative assemblies was largely determined by the specific features of each region's political regime. Despite this diversity, various analysts, including Vladimir

Gelman, have identified three main types of political regimes in Russia's regions today.[19] The first model is characterized by the monopolization of a region's political power and resources by one political figure in a winner takes all fashion. In such a system, the local parliament has no independent voice and is compelled to serve as a vehicle for conducting executive policy. This is the case in Moscow, Tatarstan, Bashkortostan, and Kalmykia. In the second model, the dominant figure is forced to negotiate with political rivals about the division of spheres of influence with the aid of informal institutions and compromise-based strategies. Within such a regime, local legislative assemblies act as partners and at the same time as counterweights to the executive, depending on the strength of the rivals' position. The third model, war within law, presupposes fierce competition between various elite groups. Their struggle is projected onto the public sphere and stimulates the development of a multiparty system as well as the strengthening of the role of the local parliament as a representative government institution. A good example of a region with this system is Sverdlovsk, where the multiparty system is among the most advanced and stable in the entire federation.

Prospects for Constitutional Change

Toward the end of his rule, Yeltsin's all-out efforts to keep himself in power, combined with the scandalous failures of the government's social and economic policy (punctuated by the default of August 1998) led many to believe that the constitution needed to be amended to give the parliament greater power and oversight. Proponents of constitutional reform argued that if allowed to persist, the existing legal framework would block any political, social, and economic reform. An executive who is above the scrutiny and influence of parliament, and hence of society, the argument goes, cannot adequately respond to new social challenges or devise realistic policy and is doomed to chronic conflicts with the other branches of government, especially the Duma. As a result, many predicted that the 1993 constitution would not outlive its maker. Also under discussion were different proposals for an effective separation of powers. The options considered ranged from a presidential-parliamentary system like that of the French Fifth Republic to the classical presidential republic of the United States.

Despite various pessimistic predictions, the mechanism for the separation of powers provided by the 1993 constitution has held and has demonstrated stability. This can be seen in Putin's democratic election in 2000 and his subsequent successful formation of a new political regime. Indeed, the issue of constitutional reform has receded into the background as the relationship between the president and the parliament has shifted from confrontation to partnership. Although the Duma has not become an equal partner of the president, the parliament has become a more stable and effective partner. A number of factors have contributed to this evolution.

The first and perhaps most decisive factor was the pressure that public opinion exerted in favor of cooperation. After a decade of chaos and injustice, during the election campaigns of 1999–2000 the public unambiguously declared a desire for order and stability as well as for an improved standard of living. The new elites who had acquired power and property under Yeltsin also wanted stability so that they could consolidate their fiefdoms more effectively. Both the public at large and the elites pinned great hopes on Putin. From Putin's point of view, this popularity helped to stifle opposition and created an environment of political legitimacy and stability. A similar trend could be observed in the Duma, where the communist opposition held no more than 25 percent of the vote and grew from the executive's active antagonist into a reliable junior partner. Under these circumstances, neither Putin nor his government experienced any difficulties in the lower chamber when it came to passing market reform bills. This was unambiguously signaled in 2000, when Putin's reform of federal relations, aimed at weakening the political and economic influence of the regional elites, had the Duma's resounding support.

The second factor enabling a transformation in executive-legislative relations was the formation of stable interest groups in the upper strata of Russian society. The importance of these groups grew as the parliament proved an increasingly useful tool for law-making. This trend actually stemmed from the mid-1990s, when through its legislative activity the Duma wrested legislative initiative from the president's hands.[20] The Duma's importance increased toward the late 1990s, when political parties began to gain strength, the party system stabilized, and large and medium business secured stable and effective means of lobbying for their interests in parliament. The Duma cannot be considered an equal to, or even a check on, the president, but during the 1990s, the parliament did gain status and power.

Yet even with such encouraging trends, the new relationship between the executive and legislative branches is still far from stable, and more dynamic reforms will probably be needed in the future. For one thing, the Duma will keep its political loyalty to Putin only for as long as the president commands tremendous authority in society. The moment his policy becomes a target of public criticism, the Duma will turn against him. The prospect of a new confrontation between the executive and the Duma cannot be ruled out.

A reorganization of power between the executive and legislative branches may also be triggered by tensions within the ruling elite. An example is the conflict that took place in the summer of 2003 between part of president Putin's entourage and the large oil company Yukos. The company's leadership enjoyed a strong lobby among Duma deputies. For the sake of greater political effectiveness, it supported the idea of forming the government according to a parliamentary majority, thereby making it politically accountable to the Duma. Implementation of this plan would lead to a greater role for the parliament, which Yukos sought because the president became increasingly slow in making important political decisions as time neared the elections of 2007–2008. The idea was packaged as the creation of a strong, accountable government to assist the president, and Yukos counted on its lobby in the Duma to exert considerable influence on the government. The president at first looked on this idea with favor, which he expressed in his address to the Federal Assembly on May 15, 2003. Yet he later reneged, evidently convinced by the St. Petersburg wing of his team that Yukos, and possibly some other large companies, were interested in weakening presidential power in favor of the government. Perhaps it was these political initiatives by Yukos that prompted the accusations of economic crimes soon lavished on the company by law enforcement organs.

Moreover, problems created by previous reforms of federal relations and of the vertical power structure persist. The reorganization of the Federation Council in 2002 changed its fundamental character from an assembly of regional leaders into a gathering of lobbyists engaged in promoting various projects in the interests of the constituent entities they represent. The contradiction between the council's high constitutional status and its real political weight will likely lead to further modifications of its character and orientation in the future in accordance with the overall alignment of political forces in the country.

The final issue that needs to be addressed is the imbalance of power in the government's regional branches. The ousting of governors and local presidents of Russia's constituent republics from the federal policy level and the institution of Moscow's executive plenipotentiary representatives in every member of the federation caused regional leaders to tighten their grip on Federation Council members, promoting authoritarian tendencies that undermine a constructive cooperation between the legislative and executive branches of government in the long run.

In the final analysis, the existence of these problems may cause a relapse into antagonism between the president and parliament, leading to further pressure for effective constitutional reform and a change in the balance of power between the executive and legislative branches. No matter what form the separation of powers takes, the improvement of relations between the executive and legislative branches of government must proceed toward two objectives: first, to find effective ways to attach political responsibility to presidential power; and second, to balance the distribution of authority between the two branches of government.

5

Political Parties

Michael McFaul

A party system is an essential attribute of a democratic regime: no parties, no democracy.[1] Despite the erosion of the influence of parties in old democracies and the difficulties of establishing parties from scratch in new democracies, theorists still agree that parties and a party system are necessary evils for the functioning of representative government.[2] In liberal democracies, parties perform several tasks. During elections they provide voters with distinct choices, be they ideological, social, or even ethnic. After elections, parties then represent the interests of their constituents in the formulation, and sometimes the implementation, of state policy. The degree of party penetration of state institutions need not correlate directly with a given party's power over policy outcomes. Empowered by expertise or connections to key decision makers, small parties can have assymetric influence over policy debates, while large parties may suffer the opposite: no expertise, no personal networks, and therefore little influence over policy. Yet some degree of representation within the state is usually necessary for a party to influence policy outcomes.

The crux of party power comes from participating in elections and then winning representation within the state. In consolidated democracies, parties are the most important groups in representative structures, aggregating societal interests and then representing those interests. The degree of party control over electoral choices and the subsequent party penetration of significant state bodies serve as good proxy measures for party development.[3]

Thus to influence policy making, successful parties and developed party systems must be able to influence the vote and then win representation within the state.

By this set of criteria, party development has a long way to go in Russia. Parties influence electoral choices in some elections, but not all. In elections in which parties play a central role, they do not enjoy a monopoly in structuring the vote. Consequently, parties have only limited representation within the state and even less influence on the state's actions. The one oasis of party development has been the State Duma, the lower house of parliament. Parties have played a central role in parliamentary elections, have won seats in the Duma, and have been able to translate their electoral successes into parliamentary power by organizing the internal operation of the Duma in ways that benefit parties. In every other part of the government, however, including the President's Administration, the federal government, the Federation Council, regional administrations, and regional parliaments, parties have played a marginal role in structuring votes and an even smaller role in penetrating or influencing these other government entities.

Why have parties succeeded in organizing and influencing the work of the State Duma, but enjoyed only limited success elsewhere? Why has party success within the Duma not stimulated party development elsewhere? Is the current weak party system a temporary outcome or a permanent feature of Russian politics?

This chapter argues that parties are weak because the most powerful politicians chose to make them weak. Cultural, historical, and socioeconomic factors impede party emergence, but individual decisions—especially decisions about institutional design—have been the more proximate and more salient causes of poor party development. At the same time, the privileged position of parties in the State Duma also resulted from individual choices about institutional design, even if these design choices had unintended consequences that did not represent the preferences of the most powerful.

To demonstrate the centrality of individual choices about institutional design in the making and unmaking of Russia's party system, this chapter starts by providing a rough estimate of party development and of party penetration into the main political institutions that are filled through popular election. The next section explains these results. The third section then pushes the causal arrow back one step and explains the origins of the institutions described in the previous section. These electoral institutions are not the product of socioeconomic cleavages.[4] The argument is that most of the institutional arrangements for choosing elected leaders reflect the preferences of Russia's most powerful actors, those who have not needed parties to remain in power. The one exception is the electoral law for the State Duma, that is, the one institution that has encouraged party consolidation. In several respects, this law was an accident of history.[5] The final section offers some speculations about the future of party development.

Measuring Party Development

Party development can be measured in many different ways. Some ways count members, some measure partisanship among voters,[6] and others trace party influence over policy outcomes. Each of these approaches has strengths and weaknesses. The first two approaches can be quantified, but only provide proxy measures for party development and party influence. The party with the largest membership does not always enjoy the greatest electoral success or the highest level of influence over policy outcomes. Conversely, low or declining levels of partisanship do not necessarily translate into a loss of party dominance at the polls or in policy making. The third measure—party influence over outcomes—is the most interesting, but also the most difficult to trace.[7]

A fourth approach for calibrating party development—measuring the electoral success and subsequent degree of party representation within state bodies—is used here. In the causal chain between party organization, party identification in society, electoral success and representation in the state, and ultimate influence over policy outcomes, this measure assesses the penultimate step.[8] Although many other factors intervene to dilute or enhance the influence of parties over policies after elections have occurred, some degree of success at the polls, and subsequently some degree of representation within the state, are necessary conditions for policy influence in most countries. Analysts of party development have also asserted that the party in government often precedes the development of extraparliamentary organizations or the party in the electorate, suggesting that the party in government is a good place to start tracing party development in a young democracy like Russia.[9] This stage in the chain can also be quantified much more easily than either earlier stages or the final stage.

The President and the Federal Government

As discussed in earlier chapters, the most powerful position in the Russian political system is the office of president.[10] Whoever captures this office plays a dominant role in policy making. To date, parties have played a marginal role in structuring presidential votes and have not had any success in gaining party representation within the President's Administration. Party leaders have participated in presidential elections. In the first presidential election in 1991, political parties had a minimal role. Only Vladimir Zhirinovsky, who finished third, had a real party affiliation. In the 1996 election, three of the top five finishers were party leaders and the leader of the Communist Party of the Russian Federation (CPRF), Gennady Zyuganov, advanced to the second round. In the 2000 election, party leaders again participated, but the winner, Vladimir Putin, was once again not a party member.

Parties have played some role in influencing the composition of the federal government through the Duma. Formally, the distribution of power among parties in the Duma does not directly influence the selection of the prime minister or other ministers in the federal government. This institutional arrangement severely weakens the role of parties in the formation of the government and therefore weakens the role of parties more generally.[11] After crises, however, parties in the Duma have managed to influence the choice of prime minister and the composition of the government. Following the December 1993 elections, Yegor Gaidar and Boris Fyodorov resigned from their posts in the government after their party, Russia's Choice, suffered a devastating defeat at the polls. Prime Minister Viktor Chernomyrdin subsequently invited representatives from the Agrarian and Communist parties to join his team as a way to partially reflect the will of the people within his government as expressed in the parliamentary election. After the August 1998 financial crash, opposition parties in the Duma demanded the resignation of the liberal Prime Minister Sergei Kiriyenko and appointed a left-of-center candidate, Yevgeny Primakov. Primakov then appointed CPRF leader Yuri Maslyukov as his first deputy prime minister.

In all these cases of party penetration of the government, however, the president and the prime minister were not obliged to bring in party members. When party members did join the government, they usually transferred their allegiance to the prime minister and drifted away from their party organizations. Boris Yeltsin also dismissed his party-backed prime minister, Primakov, without suffering any sanction from Primakov's party supporters. He replaced him with Sergei Stepashin, who at the time had no party affiliation or party ties. Stepashin's successor, Prime Minister Putin, had a similar nonpartisan background. Putin's prime minister, Mikhail Kasyanov, also has no party affiliation. To date, the composition of the government has not reflected the balance of forces within the Duma.

The Federation Council

The Federation Council, the upper house of the parliament, is another party-free state institution. Between 1993 and 1995, when senators were elected, only a handful of them had parties ties. Between 1995 and 1999, the upper house consisted of chief executives of regional governments and chairs of regional legislatures, who did not rely on party support or party identification to win their seats on the council. Today, regional executives and legislatures send envoys to represent them in this body, and few of these appointees have party memberships. Committees and regional associations, not party factions, organize the internal work of the council.

A number of Federation Council members adopted party affiliations in the run-up to the 1999 parliamentary elections.[12] Most important, nine regional executives joined forces to form the electoral bloc Fatherland-All Russia (OVR), but this coalition quickly fell apart after the 1999 vote. In addition, these regional leaders lost their seats in the Federation Council in 2000 when Putin changed how the upper house was to be constituted. Similarly, the pro-government electoral bloc, Unity, garnered the endorsement of dozens of Federation Council members during the 1999 parliamentary campaign, but only one of the regional leaders actually joined Unity. Note that none of the regional leaders joined these blocs to enhance their own electoral prospects.

The State Duma

Elections to the State Duma constitute the one arena in which parties have played a major role. Parties have also played a central role in the Duma's internal organization and directly influence Duma policy

The current electoral system for the State Duma accords parties a privileged position in relation to the selection of 50 percent (225) of Duma members. This allocation is divided proportionally among parties that receive at least 5 percent of the popular vote in a national election (for a single electoral district). Proportional representation has helped stimulate the development of interest-based or ideological parties within the Duma. After three parliamentary elections in the 1990s, the core of a multiparty system appeared to be consolidating at the end of the decade. Four national parties comprise this core: the CPRF, Yabloko, the Liberal Democratic Party of Russia (LDPR), and the Union of Right Forces (SPS).

These four parties share many attributes with parliamentary parties in other political systems. First, all these parties participated in every Duma vote in the 1990s.[13] The ability to field national party lists and candidates in three consecutive national elections suggests that these four parties have financial resources, brand names, and organizational capacities. Three of the four have enjoyed representation in all three parliaments that have served since 1993.

Second, all four parties have well-defined political orientations, loyal electorates, and notable leaders.[14] The CPRF now recognizes the legitimacy of private property and free markets, but nonetheless still advocates a major role for the state in the economy.[15] The CPRF's position on the economy is not its only unique platform plank. CPRF programs and policy documents also include a heavy dose of patriotic slogans, nationalistic proposals, and nostalgic conservatism. The party boasts an extremely loyal following that identifies with these issues, especially among older, poorer, and rural Russians. The head of the party, Zyuganov, has been a nationally recognized political figure in Russia for the last decade.

Yabloko has also developed a well-defined political niche (as the democratic opposition), a core electorate (the not-so-well-off intelligentsia and white-collar workers in large and medium cities), a national grassroots organization, and a well-known leader, Grigory Yavlinsky. Yabloko's identity is defined more by the kind of people who identify with the party and less by the kind of ideology the party advocates.[16] Yet this identity is well defined, and compared with the other parties Yabloko probably most closely approximates a genuinely post-Soviet political party.[17] In contrast with the CPRF, this party was created from scratch after the collapse of the Soviet Union.

In contrast with the Democratic Choice of Russia in 1995, the SPS modified its platform before the 1999 campaign.[18] Most important, while Democratic Choice of Russia had opposed the first war in Chechnya in 1995, the SPS supported the second war in 1999. The rest of the SPS's program, however, has remained consistent over the decade, that is, unabashedly liberal (in the European sense of the word). The demographics of its electorate are the polar opposite of those of the CPRF: young, wealthy, and urban. SPS leaders, including former prime ministers Kiriyenko and Gaidar and former first deputy prime ministers Boris Nemtsov and Anatoly Chubais, are some of the best known, if not the most notorious, political figures in Russia. For most voters, no amount of campaign advertising would change their firm opinions—some positive, but most negative—about these people. Organizationally, the SPS has only a skeletal organization outside Moscow, St. Petersburg, Samara, and Chelyabinsk, but other resources—including strong financial backing—compensate for this weakness.

Zhirinovsky's LDPR also has an identifiable ideological orientation: nationalism and imperialism, and populism. His relationships with those in power have varied over time. In 1993, he and his party were clearly in opposition to the Kremlin, but their antiregime militancy was less apparent in the 1999 elections. Nonetheless, Zhirinovsky's core voters—a fraction of his original support in 1993—have remained loyal to the LDPR throughout these twists and turns.

Third, as table 5.1 demonstrates, three of the four parties won roughly the same percentage of votes in the 1999 elections that they won in December 1995. The CPRF won almost exactly the same percentage, with a slight improvement in 1999. Yabloko lost a percentage point, a big blow to the party, but a small variation when compared with Yabloko totals in 1995, or even 1993. The SPS performed surprisingly well in 1999, but the percentage is similar to the total pool of votes cast for parties firmly identified as liberal in the 1995 contest. Zhirinovsky's LDPR suffered a sharp decline and lost nearly half its electoral support, suggesting that the LDPR may be the weakest of these four "old" parliamentary parties. Given all that happened in Russia between parliamentary elections—the 1996 presidential election, the August 1998 financial crash, the rotation of prime ministers, and the wars in Chechnya—what is most striking about these results is the stability, not the volatility, of aggregate support.[19]

No new ideologically based party has managed to challenge these established parties for their political niches. New nationalist, communist, and liberal parties have formed, but none captured more than 2 percent of the popular vote in the 1999 elections.

Fourth, all four parties have acted together to make the Duma a "party-centric" institution. In the first post-Soviet Duma, which convened in 1994, party leaders took the initiative in writing the internal rules of order for the Duma, which have survived to this day.[20] Because of the mixed electoral sys-

Table 5.1. Results of Party List Voting in Duma Elections, 1995 and 1999
(percentage of national proportional representation vote)

Political party or bloc	1995	1999
Communist Party of the Russian Federation	22.7	24.3
Yabloko	7.0	5.9
Union of Right Forces	N/A	8.5
Democratic Choice of Russia	3.9	N/A
All right-wing parties[a]	8.1	N/A
Liberal Democratic Party of Russia/Zhirinovsky bloc	11.4	6.0
Unity	N/A	23.3
Fatherland-All Russia	N/A	13.3
Our Home Is Russia	10.3	1.2
None of the above and parties below the 5 percent threshold	49.6	18.6

Source: Central Electoral Commission
a. Includes Democratic Choice of Russia (3.86 percent), Forward Russia! (1.94 percent), Pamfilova-Gurov-Lysenko (1.6 percent), and Common Cause (0.7 percent).

tem, more than half the Duma deputies had a party affiliation, because some party members won seats in the single-mandate races so leaders moved quickly to establish the primacy of party power.[21] The new parliament voted to give the status of faction to all parties that had received more than 5 percent of the popular vote on the party list ballot. Independent deputies (or deputies elected on party lists who then opted to quit their parties) had to collect thirty-five members to form a new faction. Committee chairs were allocated proportionally between party factions, and the Council of the Duma was established to organize the Duma's agenda. The Duma also approved a new rule that gave party factions control over speaking privileges on the floor. Finally, party leaders passed a resolution that gave party factions the power to allocate staff to individual faction members. These new rules quickly established parties and party leaders as the preeminent actors in the Duma and created incentives for nonpartisan deputies to align with a faction. Internal cohesion made the Duma a more formidable opponent to the president.[22]

The results of the 1999 parliamentary elections suggested that party dominance over such elections and parliamentary representation might have been declining, not increasing. In particular, two new electoral blocs competed on the party list ballot and succeeded in capturing a significant portion of the popular vote: OVR and Unity (Medved).[23] These two election blocs shared many similar qualities, but had little in common with the four parties discussed earlier. In contrast with these four parliamentary parties, the two coalitions were better understood as parties of power. Parties of power are coalitions forged before electoral cycles whose intent is to defend the interests of those already in power. Typically, members of the government are members of these parties of power. In 1993, the party of power was Russia's Choice, an electoral bloc headed by several government ministers. In 1995, the party of power was Our Home Is Russia, headed by then prime minister Chernomyrdin. The prelude to the 1999 campaign was unusual in that the first party of power to form—OVR—comprised government officials, most of whom were already in power at the regional level, but aspired to power at the federal level and were not in favor with the Kremlin. To prevent this party of power from coming to power, the Kremlin eventually responded by creating its own new party of power, Unity.

These competing parties of power had many similar features. First, Unity and OVR were created to influence the presidential race in 2000. Leaders in both coalitions considered the parliamentary contest as a stepping-stone along the way to capturing the bigger prize. Yuri Luzhkov, mayor of Moscow, created OVR to promote his presidential aspirations, while Primakov joined OVR to advance his presidential prospects. On behalf of Putin, the Kremlin created Unity to weaken Luzhkov and Primakov as presidential candidates and strengthen Putin's prospects.[24] After Putin's victory, OVR collapsed.

Second, both OVR and Unity had poorly defined identities among the electorate. OVR's program was bland, middle-of-the-road, and contradictory.[25] Some leaders of this coalition emphasized the need for greater state intervention in the economy while others advocated cutting taxes. Regional leaders, such as Tatarstan's President Mintimer Shaimiev, stressed the need for greater decentralization of political power and for strengthening federal institutions while others, including Primakov and Luzhkov, advocated strengthening the federal government. The coalition's position on Chechnya also wavered and waffled. Unity's program was even more mysterious. Eventually, Unity published a program, but its target audience appeared to be electoral analysts, not Russian voters.

Third, almost by definition, these new political organizations had new electorates, that is, people without a tradition of voting for these two new organizations. OVR enjoyed the support of loyal followers in cities and regions governed by their leaders, but this constituted only several regions. Not surprisingly, therefore, and in contrast to the stable levels of support expressed throughout the fall of 1999 for the four parliamentary parties, popular support for the two coalitions varied considerably throughout the 1999 parliamentary campaign period. OVR took a nosedive at the same time that Unity climbed in the polls.[26]

Finally, while the four parliamentary parties did not have serious presidential contenders within their ranks, both the coalitions boasted one or two serious candidates before the parliamentary campaign began—Primakov and Luzhkov from OVR and Putin from Unity. After the parliamentary campaign—which served as a presidential primary for the two coalitions—both Primakov and Luzhkov accepted their defeat and withdrew from the presidential race.

Though concerned primarily with influencing the presidential election, the two new electoral coalitions together captured more than a third of the popular vote on the party list in the December 1999 elections. Their participation on the party list ballot impeded the expansion of support for Russia's more established parties.

Elections in the Single-Mandate Districts

Parties have never played much of a role in influencing electoral choices in single-mandate races. The trend in these contests is an antiparty direction. Thus the failure of the established, ideologically-based parties to expand their success on the party list in 1999 meant that they suffered serious setbacks in producing winners in single-mandate districts (SMDs), which account for the other half of the Duma. Nonpartisan candidates assumed a more prominent role in the 1999 vote than in 1995, and nonpartisan actors—including regional elites—played a much more active role in influencing the outcome of these elections than in previous years.[27] In the aggregate, as table 5.2 shows, nonpartisans captured more SMD seats in 1999 than in 1995.

One pattern is especially striking: the declining role of the older parliamentary parties in determining electoral outcomes in SMDs. The CPRF won eleven fewer seats in 1999 than in 1995. Yabloko's share of single-mandate seats decreased from fourteen to four, and two of these seats were won by candidates with only a loose affiliation with Yabloko, Stepashin, a former prime minister, and Mikhail Zadornov, a former finance minister. In 1995,

Table 5.2. **Number of Deputies Elected with Political Party or Bloc Affiliations, State Duma Elections, 1995 and 1999**

Political party/bloc	1995			1999		
	Deputies from party list voting	Deputies from single-mandate races	Total	Deputies from party list voting	Deputies from single-mandate races	Total
Communist Party of the Russian Federation	99	58	157	67	47	114
Yabloko	31	14	45	16	4	20
Union of Right Forces	0	9[a]	9	24	5	29
Liberal Democratic Party of Russia/ Zhirinovsky bloc	50	1	51	17	0	17
Unity	N/A	N/A	N/A	64	9	73
Fatherland-All Russia	N/A	N/A	N/A	37	31	67
Our Home Is Russia	45	10	55	0	7	7
Agrarian Party of Russia	0	20	20	N/A	N/A	N/A
Independents, others	-	103	103	-	114	114
Unfilled seats				0	9	9

Source: Central Electoral Commission
a. Democratic Choice of Russia.

the Democratic Choice of Russia captured less than 4 percent of the popular vote but won nine single-mandate races. In 1999, the SPS more than doubled the Democratic Choice of Russia's party list showing, but managed to win only five single-mandate seats. Zhirinovsky's party won no single-mandate seats. Even the two new presidential coalitions did not dominate the single-mandate races. Unity won only nine seats. OVR won thirty-one seats, but the vast majority of these were in regions dominated by regional executives associated with this coalition. In other words, local parties of power, rather than a national party affiliation, delivered the wins.

Regional Heads of Administration and Regional Legislators

Political parties have played a limited role in regional politics. In some major metropolitan areas, such as St. Petersburg and Yekaterinburg, multiparty systems are beginning to take root, but in most regions, a state-based informal network dominated by the local ruling elite—the regional party of power—still dominates politics.

Throughout the 1990s, few executive leaders (presidents and governors) at the regional level had open party affiliations. During the cascade of elections of regional executives in the fall of 1996 and spring of 1997, political parties played only a marginal role in selecting and endorsing candidates.[28] The CPRF, through its affiliate the National Patriotic Union of Russia, was the only party that had any real influence on these elections as a political party, and even the CPRF usually chased candidates to endorse rather than selected candidates to run. At the beginning of the electoral cycle, the National Patriotic Union of Russia had endorsed only twelve candidates.[29] By the end of this cycle, the CPRF claimed to have won as many governorships, but several of these so-called red governors distanced themselves from the party leadership soon after their election victories. In the 1999–2001 electoral cycle for regional heads of administration, the role of parties was even less pronounced.

In all electoral cycles for governors, the Kremlin backed candidates and funded campaigns, but not through party organizations. Other parties, including regional parties and coalitions, figured only in individual races. Zhirinovsky's LDPR ran candidates in several races, but won only one, in Pskov, where Governor Eugeny Mikhailov may have been the only candidate who won because of his party affiliation. Mikhailov has since distanced himself from the LDPR and grown closer to the Kremlin. Yabloko endorsements played an important role in some races, and especially in St. Petersburg, but Yabloko party members did not win a single race. Only one candidate with open ties to Democratic Choice of Russia, Semen Zubakin in the Altai Republic, succeeded in winning a governor's race in the 1995–1997 electoral cycle.

Local parties of power with no ideological affiliations and strong ties to local executive heads also have dominated most regional legislatures. In her study of party representation in regional legislatures, Kathryn Stoner-Weiss reports that only 11.5 percent of all deputies in regional parliaments have national party affiliations, mostly—7.3 percent of the 11.5 percent—with the CPRF.[30] Clearly, party development in the national legislature has not stimulated a commensurate growth of party influence in regional legislatures.

Importance of Institutions

The causes of party weakness in Russia are many and diverse. Seventy years of Communist Party rule created a strong negative reaction within Russian society in relation to party politics. Because party organizations and activities dominated Soviet society, post-Soviet Russian leaders and citizens have had an allergic reaction to parties. After quitting the party in 1990, Yeltsin vowed never to join another party again, and many in Russia sympathize with his decision. While other East European countries were able to revive old parties from their precommunist past, Russia had only a modicum of experience with competitive party politics before the revolution, and thus had no party culture to resurrect. The Soviet system produced substantial social and organizational capital, which continue to form the basis of the largest organizations in the post-communist era, including first and foremost the CPRF. However, as these organizations served to control people, atomize society, and discourage participation in real politics,[31] this inheritance may serve more as a barrier to the growth of grassroots party development than as a base from which to develop new party organizations.

A variation of this legacy approach goes back even further, in that some argue that Russian history and culture, not just the Soviet period, are the main impediments to party development. This school explains weak party development as part of a more general phenomenon of the lack of democratic development.[32] According to this argument, Russians have not built strong parties because Russians are not democratic. Instead, they prefer strong, paternalistic leaders who develop a direct relationship with the people that is not mediated or distorted through parties. Proponents of this view cite Russia's hundreds of years of autocratic rule as evidence.

The scale of socioeconomic transformation in Russia has also impeded party development. Socioeconomic cleavages were important for party development in Western Europe.[33] In Russia, these cleavages are still poorly defined. If transitions to democracy in capitalist countries primarily involve changing the political system, successful post-communist transformations destroy old classes; create new interest groups; and confuse, at least temporarily, almost everyone living through the transition. The slow development of capitalism in Russia suggests that a similarly slow formation of market-based interest groups is likely.[34] Moreover, as in all capitalist societies, small groups with well-defined interests, like Russia's financial oligarchs, are more likely to solve collective action problems more efficiently and rapidly than mass-based groups such as small business associations or trade unions, which are more likely to articulate their interests through parties. The slow emergence of civil society, discussed in detail in the following chapter, severely limits the organizational, financial, and ideological resources necessary for party development. Russian parties, for their part, have had difficulty in situating themselves along programmatic or interest-based dimensions.[35] For instance, Russia has weak liberal parties because it has a small and ill-defined middle class. Under these circumstances, interest cleavages in the 1990s were fashioned more by general attitudes about the transition rather than by particular economic, or even ethnic, concerns.[36] Between 1990 and 1997, political situations and electoral choices were often polarized into two camps, those for change and those against.[37] More conventional cleavages that demarcate the contours of stable party systems in other countries may perhaps emerge now that this polarization has begun to recede.

These structural approaches offer important insights about party weakness in Russia, but the long shadow of an authoritarian past and an unstructured post-Soviet society cannot take all the blame for the lack of party emergence or development.[38] The role of parties in government differs from institution to institution, suggesting that more proximate variables are intervening to cause this variation. Institutions and individual choices in designing institutions must also be brought into the analysis.[39] Specifically, Russian political elites made choices about the timing of elections, the kind of electoral systems, the relationship between the president and parliament at the federal level, and the relationships among the heads of administration of local legislatures at the regional level, all of which have impeded party development. But elites also made a few choices about institutional design, including first and foremost the incorporation of proportional representation in the parliamentary electoral law, which have stimulated the emergence and development of political parties.

As a complement to structural or organic models of party development that highlight the reasons for the lack of party development in Russia, individual politicians and interest groups also play a role in the emergence of parties. Structural, cultural, and legacy factors cannot explain the emergence of the four parliamentary parties described earlier and cannot account for the variation of party strength in different state institutions, because all these point toward weak or no party development. Yet a core of a multiparty system has emerged within the parliament. Over time, these parties may wither and die, but even if they do fade from Russian politics as important forces, their short-lived emergence must still be explained.

A comprehensive explanation of party development must be able to account for the weak party penetration of most state institutions as well as the relatively strong degree of party development in the Duma. The seeds of a multiparty system and the barren environment surrounding these seeds both demand explanation. To account for both the emergence and the lack of a party system, individual actors, their preferences, their power, and their decisions (especially their decisions about institutions) must also be brought into the equation. In particular, the kinds of electoral laws and the types of rules governing executive-legislative relations chosen during the construction of Russia's new political system have had a direct impact on both party development in one arena, as well as on the lack of party development in other arenas.

Proportional Representation in the Duma as a Lifeline for Party Development

As party analysts predicted and party advocates promoted, proportional representation as a component of electoral law governing the Duma has stimulated the emergence and consolidation of four parties: the CPRF, Yabloko, the LDPR, and the SPS.[40] The requirement that 50 percent of all Duma deputies must acquire their seats through proportional representation in a national election has allowed these four parties to organize and survive. This particular percentage has also been critical in giving these parties the power to organize the internal rules of the Duma. If the figure were less than 50 percent, as many have advocated, then the Duma might not benefit parties, but instead might gravitate to a more committee-dominated form of internal organization.

Without proportional representation, three of these four parties (Yabloko, the SPS, and the LDPR) most likely would not exist today. Yabloko and the LDPR got their jumpstarts as national organizations from the proportional representation ballot in the 1993 parliamentary elections.[41] In the last three parliamentary votes, the LDPR has won 126 seats through the party list, but only 6 single-mandate seats, while Yabloko has won 67 seats through the party list, but only 25 single-mandate seats. As the party of power in 1993, Russia's Choice—the predecessor of the SPS—won almost as many seats from single-mandate victories as it did from proportional representation. In

1995, the Democratic Choice of Russia (the liberal core that remained after Russia's Choice disintegrated and its ties to the Kremlin frayed) won no seats from proportional representation, but did win nine single-mandate seats. In 1999, however, the SPS, the new liberal coalition that included Democratic Choice of Russia, benefited greatly from proportional representation, winning twenty-four seats from the party list vote, compared with only five seats in single-mandate races. Only the CPRF, the one party with an organizational inheritance from the Soviet period, could survive without proportional representation.

If proportional representation has been the lifesaver that has kept parties afloat, it was tossed to them after years of splashing in the ocean alone. Generally, parties assume center stage in transitions at the moment of first or founding elections, which tend to serve up the largest menu of choices to voters.[42] Over time, however, these numbers dwindle as parties that do not win representation disappear. Voters also learn what their parties stand for, making them less likely to waste votes on fringe or nonviable parties.[43] This learning period takes longer in post-communist transitions than in countries with already established market economies, as the traditional class-based identities in society are also in flux. While declining in number, parties tend to increase in importance after a democratic transition as they emerge to play the central role in mediating interests between the state and society.

In Russia's transition, however, parties organized only after the first two national elections: to the Soviet Congress of People's Deputies (CPD) in 1989 and to the Russian CPD in 1990.[44] As already mentioned, parties played a marginal role in the June 1991 presidential elections. During this period of struggle against the Soviet system, democrats placed a premium on preserving a united anticommunist front. Proto-parties formed, but they remained under the umbrella of Democratic Russia (the organization for Russia's anticommunist movement in 1990–1991), biding their time until the moment for multiparty politics was ripe. In the opinion of party leaders, this moment came in the fall of 1991. After the failed putsch in August 1991 and the dissolution of the Soviet Union a few months later, party organizers believed that Russia needed to convene its first post-communist election—a founding election—right away. Yeltsin, however, disagreed and did not convoke new elections in the fall of 1991.[45] Russia finally had its first multiparty elections two years after the dissolution of the Soviet Union.

Had Yeltsin convened elections soon after the collapse of the Soviet Union, political parties might have been able to step in and provide voters with programmatic choices. With the right electoral law, they might even have succeeded in monopolizing the process of selecting candidates. At the time, the entire range of European-style parties existed, including liberal, Christian-democratic, social democratic, and communist parties.[46] Yeltsin's decision to veto the idea of holding such a founding election left these new political parties to wallow for the next two years with no political role in the polity. By the time of the December 1993 elections, most parties created during the heyday of democratic mobilization in 1990–1991 had disappeared. Liberal parties were especially hurt by the postponement of new elections, because many voters associated the painful economic decline of 1991–1993 with the leaders and policies of these liberal parties.[47] In contrast, new protest groups such as the LDPR, as well as older communist opposition groups such as the CPRF and the Agrarian Party of Russia, performed well in these first elections. Yeltsin also sequenced elections so that parliamentary and presidential votes did not occur simultaneously, a situation that hampers party development.[48]

Despite these timing and sequencing decisions that impeded party emergence, the incorporation of proportional representation into the 1993, 1995, and 1999 electoral system for the State Duma helped to stimulate party emergence. The importance of electoral rules for party development is especially apparent when national and regional parliaments are compared.[49] Only a small handful of regional legislatures have mixed electoral systems, while to date most deploy only single-mandate systems. Stoner-Weiss reported that the five regions that have incorporated some degree of proportional representation showed a higher degree of party penetration than the national average.[50] For party advocates, proportional representation appears to be their best tool.

Others have made the opposite claim, positing that national parties created and sustained by proportional representation distort the emergence of two parties in SMDs for the Duma by running multiple candidates. From this same analysis, one would expect to see a proliferation of party candidates in every majoritarian kind of election, be it an SMD race for a regional parliament seat, a governor's election, or a presidential contest.

To date, however, finding evidence to support this latter claim is difficult. Party proliferation has not occurred in these arenas. In Russia's first presidential election in 1991, only two candidates were affiliated with parties and

one of them, Nikolai Ryzhkov, only loosely so. In 1996, the same two parties that had competed in 1991—the CPRF and the LDPR—ran candidates
and were joined by a third party candidate, Grigory Yavlinsky from
Yabloko.[51] The remaining seven candidates, however, and two of the top
three finishers—Yeltsin and Lebed—had no party affiliation. Similarly, parties have not generated the proliferation of candidates for gubernatorial
elections. In the SMD elections for the Duma, several candidates still contest these seats, but the vast majority of those competing are independents,
not candidates affiliated with national parties. The cause of the slow emergence of a two-party system does not appear to be the proliferation of parties generated by the Duma electoral system.

The Effect of Strong Executives and Weak Parliaments on Party Systems

After the inclusion of proportional representation in the Duma electoral
law, the next most important design decision of consequence for party
development concerns the presidential system. Around the world, presidential systems are less conducive to party development than parliamentary
systems.[52] Russia is no different.[53] This institutional constraint has been
especially pronounced in Russia, because parties do not control the formation of government or even structure the presidential vote. This institutional arrangement resembles what Guillermo O'Donnell has called a
delegative democracy, where "whoever wins election to the presidency is
thereby entitled to govern as he or she sees fit, constrained only by the hard
facts of existing power relations and by a constitutionally limited term of
office."[54] Organizations such as parties, which mediate interests between the
state and society or constrain the freedom of maneuver of the chief executive, are not needed in delegative democracies. The one arena of state power
that parties dominate—the State Duma—is also one of the least effective
institutions in the system. Empirical research on the actual exercise of presidential power in post-communist Russia suggests that the Kremlin occu-
pant may not be as omnipotent as is commonly perceived, while the Duma
has grown stronger over time.[55] Nevertheless, the center of power is still
firmly ensconced in the Kremlin.[56] A similar distribution of power between
executives and legislatures exists at the regional level.

The presence of a presidential system is not, however, sufficient to
explain Russia's weak party development. After all, many established democracies with strong presidents also have robust party systems. The salience of

this institutional dimension only becomes apparent when combined with the mixed electoral system of the State Duma. Russia's current electoral law for the Duma has stimulated the emergence of a multiparty system, but it is a system in which no single party has garnered more than a quarter of the vote in any parliamentary election. Party leaders can hope to take advantage of the runoff system in the presidential vote as a way to reach beyond their party's electoral base; however, such coalitions are difficult to pull together because of interparty rivalries. Such a strategy is also risky, since party candidates have to rely on the endorsement of other parties and the support of their electorates in a second round of voting, which occurs only two weeks after the first vote.[57] To date only one party candidate, Zyuganov, has advanced to the second round, and even he considered that he needed to downplay his Communist Party affiliation and hide behind a presidential "coalition"—the National Patriotic Union of Russia—which claimed to represent more than 100 organizations.[58] To piece together a majority in 1996, Yeltsin decided not to affiliate himself with any single party in the December 1995 parliamentary elections. This strategic move then allowed him to act as a focal point for a large nonpartisan, anticommunist coalition. Prime Minister Putin used the same strategy. He endorsed not one but two parties in the 1999 parliamentary vote: Unity and the SPS. After this election, he then called on all reform and centrist organizations to join his presidential coalition. Affiliating with a party too closely before or during the parliamentary vote would have limited his chances in the general election.

Former prime minister Primakov's alternative path is instructive. For him, the 1999 parliamentary elections served simply as a presidential primary, an opportunity to build momentum before the more important vote in 2000. Different advisers offered different strategies.[59] One team recommended that Primakov run in an SMD as an independent, win a landslide victory in that district, and then call upon all anti-Yeltsin parties, including even the CPRF, to endorse him as their presidential candidate. Another group argued that Primakov needed an organization, that is, a party, to run a presidential campaign. It recommended that Primakov join Luzhkov's new coalition, OVR, as a way to jumpstart his presidential bid.

Between Primakov's decision to join OVR and the Duma elections in December, many unexpected factors intervened to undermine OVR's popular support and thereby decrease Primakov's prospects as a presidential candidate.[60] Negative television coverage of Luzhkov and Primakov during the fall campaign, a poorly run OVR campaign, and Putin's skyrocketing popularity as a result of successes in the Chechnya war played a decisive role.[61] At the same time, Primakov's decision to participate in a multiparty national election to the parliament would have weakened his chances to be elected president even if none of these other factors had intervened. Even under the best of circumstances, OVR is unlikely to have won more than 28 percent of the popular vote (the highest polling number I could find for the coalition) in the parliamentary vote. With this minority share of the total electorate, Primakov would eventually have had to invite other parties to support him that may have had serious problems with endorsing a candidate from Luzhkov's party. Thus instead of serving as the focal point of a grand, multiparty coalition that Primakov might have headed as a nonpartisan, father of the nation figure (like Yeltsin in 1996), Primakov would have had to negotiate a partnership with other parties, which would have been especially difficult without positions like the vice presidency to trade for support. (Not surprisingly, Primakov endorsed the idea of creating the office of vice president.)

Given OVR's poor showing in the multiparty arena, Primakov opted not to run at all in the presidential election. Had he won a major victory in an SMD, he might have been better placed to form a large, anti-Putin coalition.

Mixed electoral systems for parliaments, which encourage several parties with a minority share of the electorate, and runoff majoritarian systems for presidents, which require successful candidates to win 50 percent of the electorate, do not mix well. Only if and when two political parties dominate all others will candidates seeking executive office have an incentive to seek a party affiliation.

Institutional Design

The previous section attempted to show the causal relationship between institutions and party development. The next question is, why did Russian political leaders select this particular set of institutions in the first place? This question is especially puzzling given the inchoate mix of institutions chosen. Mixed election systems with strong proportional representation components simply do not mesh well with presidential systems in which the chief executive is selected in a runoff majoritarian system.

In tracing the decision-making process that produced this set of institutions that shaped party development, the first argument is that actors design institutions that serve their interests.[62] Over time, institutions can develop an independent role or have an autonomous intervening influence on social outcomes.[63] Some institutions may even become so powerful that they dominate individuals' preferences, choices, and capabilities.[64] During periods of rapid and momentous change when old institutions are collapsing and new institutions are forming, however, assigning institutions such an independent causal role seems unreasonable. Rather, autonomous actors—driven by preferences and armed with power—must be brought into the equation. Institutions are endogenous to the political process itself, reflecting the preferences of those affected by their design. Under certain circumstances, actors can cooperate and coordinate their behavior to produce institutions that offer everyone an improvement over the status quo.[65] However, in the design of new political institutions, zero-sum distributional questions are often most salient. In these situations, the new institutional arrangement more often reflects the preferences of the more powerful or more successful actors in the game of institutional design.[66] When actors design new political institutions, they rarely act for the good of society and usually work for their own good.[67] This means that they will design institutions that promote party development only if they see party growth to be in their interest. To date, most in Russia have not.

A second argument is that institutional designers seeking to maximize their self-interest also make mistakes. Especially during periods of rapid revolutionary change when uncertainty clouds means-ends calculations, actors' choices about institutions may have unintended consequences. Once in place, institutions—even accidental institutions—can begin to reform and reshape preferences and power in ways that can sustain them by offering increasing returns to those who abide by them.[68] This set of simple arguments provides an analytical framework for explaining the emergence of institutions in Russia that have both impeded and stimulated party development.

The Politics That Produced Presidentialism

Decisions of self-interest made in an uncertain context produced Russia's presidential system. These choices initially had little or nothing to do with concerns about party development, but were all about obtaining, and then consolidating, political power through a process that did not require strong parties. Once in place, the presidential system has provided aspirants to the office a path to power that does not require a party affiliation.

Concentrated power in the hands of the president is not the result of some kind of Russian cultural authoritarianism or of a historical proclivity for strong, individual leaders.[69] The office of the presidency, and then the considerable powers of this presidential office, emerged directly from the transition process. Moreover, in contrast with many other presidential systems in the region, the old communist elite did not create the Russian presidency.[70] On the contrary, the creation of the presidential office was a strategy adopted to insulate the anticommunist movement from the power of the old elite.

The idea for the creation of a presidential office had begun to circulate in democratic circles soon after the first session of the Russian CPD in the spring of 1990. At the first meeting of this newly elected body, Russian "democrats" realized that they controlled a minority of seats in the new parliament.[71] In its first act of consequence in May 1990, the new Russian CPD elected Yeltsin as chairman, but only by a paltry margin of four votes after several ballots. The vote reflected the precarious balance of power within the Congress and probably within society as a whole. Democrats were a minority in this body. Yeltsin pieced together his slight majority only by emphasizing his support for Russian sovereignty. Over time, as other issues became more salient, Yeltsin's majority withered.

Given this precarious hold on power, Yeltsin and his allies saw the creation of a Russian presidential office as a way to insulate him from the increasingly conservative Congress. Polls indicated that Yeltsin was much more popular with the people than with the deputies. If he could secure a direct electoral mandate, he would be in a much stronger political position in relation to his opponents in the Russian Congress and in the Soviet government. The push to create a Russian presidency was in response to a concrete political situation and was not the result of a carefully plotted strategy or a philosophy about the need for a separation of powers or checks and balances.[72] Indeed, the referendum on the presidency went forward before the actual powers of the president had been spelled out and incorporated into the constitution.

The March 1991 referendum on the creation of the Russian presidency passed overwhelmingly: 69.9 percent of voters supported the creation of the post of president and only 28 percent were against the idea. Not surprisingly, three months later, Yeltsin won a decisive electoral victory to become Russia's first president. He did not need a party affiliation to win this office, which had been created to insulate Yeltsin personally from the Russian Congress. Yeltsin had cultivated an electoral base well before parties had come into existence.

At the time of Yeltsin's electoral victory, however, all did not seem lost for his opponents. Yeltsin had won election to an office with ill-defined powers. After the June 1991 presidential vote, the Congress had six months to clarify and codify the constitutional division of powers between the president and the parliament. Had events unfolded in an orderly fashion, this Congress might have been able to turn Yeltsin and his presidential office into a weak executive. In the interim, however, a dramatic and unexpected event radically altered the political situation: the August 1991 coup attempt that Yeltsin and his allies thwarted. During the period between the failed coup and the dissolution of the Soviet Union in December 1991, President Yeltsin played the pivotal role and his office—not the Russian CPD—assumed primary responsibility for all major institutional innovations and policy initiatives. The institution of the presidency began building organizational capacity and power to deal with crises, and this encompassed a shift in resources that included new staff, new bureaucracies, and greater executive control over the state budget.

Initially, this blooming of the presidential branch of government met little resistance.[73] As a demonstration of its support of Yeltsin's leadership, the Russian Congress voted in November 1991 to give the president extraordinary powers of decree. This honeymoon period ended, however, soon after the beginning of radical economic reform in January 1992. The sources of polarization between the Congress and the president eventually grew beyond disputes about economic issues and became a contest over which political institution was supreme, the Congress or the presidency. The stalemate eventually resulted in armed conflict between the two branches of government in October 1993. Yeltsin's victory created the conditions for putting a super-presidential constitution in place. Yeltsin took advantage of his October victory to write a new super-presidential constitution, and then succeeded in ratifying his basic law in a popular referendum in December 1993. After an initial period of hesitation, all political actors, including those that Yeltsin had squashed in the fall of 1993, acquiesced to this new institutional order and began adjusting their behavior accordingly.

The institutional design that emerged as a result of Yeltsin's struggle to survive and eventual imposition of a super-presidential constitution has impeded party emergence. Powerful actors making choices about institutions—not history, culture, or socioeconomic structures—erected this barrier to party development.

Once in office, Yeltsin used the largesse of the state and the alliance between the state and Russia's financial oligarchs as the resources for his reelection campaign in 1996. These resources alone were insufficient to win reelection,[74] but were more than enough to compensate for the lack of a party base. While the state continues to enjoy an enormous resource advantage over nonstate actors in the economy and society, control of the state is the best strategy for winning the presidential election. On December 31, 1999, Prime Minister Putin won the game of musical chairs by being the lucky person in the prime minister's chair on the day of Yeltsin's resignation. Had Primakov or Stepashin managed to survive as prime ministers a while longer, they might have enjoyed the same advantage.

The emergence of powerful executives at the regional level followed a similar path. Most regional leaders obtained executive power through presidential decree in the fall of 1991, when Yeltsin created the new position of head of administration at the *oblast* level. These governors replaced the executive committee chairs of the *oblast* soviets as the new local executives, reporting directly to the national executive rather than to the *oblast* soviets.[75] These governors then appointed new mayors in their *oblasts*, effectively creating a hierarchical system of executive authority from the president down to local mayors. Elections for these heads of administration were scheduled for December 8, 1991, but Yeltsin decided to postpone them and instead unilaterally appointed executive authorities. He removed several local leaders who supported the coup leaders, but in many regions he appointed former first and second secretaries of the Communist Party of the Soviet Union. Once in power, these regional executives then used the resources of the state, rather than the electoral resources of a political party, to seek election when elections for these posts finally occurred several years later. Similar to the national scene, close, parasitic relations between the state and regional oligarchs sustain this nonpartisan model of electoral politics for governors and presidents of the republics.[76]

Securing support from the state-oligarch nexus at the regional level is also the most rational strategy for winning a single-mandate seat in a national parliamentary race. Especially because these elections do not include a runoff, the resources of the local party of power are sufficient to win the needed plurality for victory. Ironically, local elites have an interest in party proliferation, because it helps lower the threshold for victory in the single-mandate races. If only two parties competed in these elections, a coalition opposing the party of power might be able to consolidate.[77] The presence of many candidates helps thwart such coordination.

As mentioned earlier, challengers to state candidates have been compelled to form parties and electoral coalitions to balance the power of the incumbent or the handpicked successor within the state. Primakov opted for OVR while many governors followed the example of Eduard Rossel in Yekaterinburg and formed regional parties. In the 1995–1997 electoral cycle, these outsiders enjoyed some success.[78] The trajectory, however, is toward the entrenchment of nonpartisan executives through elections with less competition and a declining role of parties. In 1999, only one party-affiliated candidate out of nine won a gubernatorial election.[79]

Proportional Representation as an Accident of History

The origins of proportional representation have a different lineage than presidentialism. Because electoral law influences the electoral outcome, rational actors choose electoral laws that maximize their ability to succeed in the electoral process. The outcome of struggles over the design of Russia's electoral law should therefore reflect the preferences of the powerful, but it does not, at least not precisely. Russia's mixed electoral system resulted from a miscalculation on the part of the Yeltsin administration, which then produced an institutional arrangement difficult to change. To be sure, this mistake occurred in an arena of institutional design of least importance to Yeltsin and his team: the Duma. If the mistake had affected a more important institution or if the Duma were more powerful, Yeltsin and his team might have deployed extraconstitutional means to correct the error. Over time, however, this mistake has produced some unintended consequences in relation to party development, and eventually it could even threaten the power of the actors who allowed the mistake to occur in the first place.

Yeltsin spelled out the electoral rules for the Duma in Decree Number 1557, which was issued on October 1, 1993.[80] While the constitution reflected Yeltsin's preferences, the decree did not, since Yeltsin himself did not have strong inclinations one way or the other regarding the Duma's electoral rules. In late September 1993, he was much more focused on the constitution and was dealing with the standoff with Congress. Yeltsin issued the decree only three days before military conflict broke out between his government and the Congress-appointed government. In this context,

Yeltsin had little time or proclivity to ponder the electoral effects of proportional representation versus first-past-the-post systems. Instead, those involved in earlier debates about the electoral law, including People's Deputy Viktor Sheinis, played a central role in writing this crucial set of rules.

Though not a member of a party at the time, Sheinis was committed to multiparty democracy. He believed that proportional representation could be deployed to stimulate the emergence of a multiparty system and would help consolidate democracy. Sheinis took advantage of the chaos in September and October 1993, as well as his colleagues' ignorance about the institutional effects of electoral laws, to craft a presidential decree that allocated 50 percent of all seats in the Duma through proportional representation. Sheinis prevailed in securing this decree over the advice of several key Yeltsin advisers, including Aleksandr Kotenkov, Georgy Satarov, and Mikhail Krasnov. In public statements, these Yeltsin aides supported a majoritarian system, because they believed that direct elections of individuals allowed for greater accountability of deputies. Privately, Yeltsin aides also intimated that they believed a parliament composed of deputies from SMDs would be more supportive of the president, and therefore easier to control.

Days before the signing of the decree, the aides managed to reduce the number of proportional representation seats to one-third of the total Duma. However, in a last-minute intervention with Yeltsin, Sheinis and his colleagues Sergei Alekseev and Sergei Kovalev succeeded in maintaining the number of proportional representation seats at 50 percent. In his meeting with Yeltsin, Sheinis first argued for the merits of the mixed system on ideological grounds, claiming that a mixed system would stimulate party development and thereby promote democratic consolidation. In Sheinis's own estimation, this first argument about the need for parties did little to sway the president. But when Sheinis argued that the pro-Yeltsin electoral bloc, Russia's Choice, would be the biggest beneficiary of this electoral system, Yeltsin became more interested. Like most others at the time, Sheinis, and probably Yeltsin, believed that Russia's Choice and the other reformist parties running in the election were capable of winning a majority of the popular vote. Given their lack of reach in the regions, however, they were unlikely to win a majority of the single-mandate seats.

This election did not go as planned by the scriptwriters. Zhirinovsky's neonationalist LDPR won almost one-quarter of the popular vote on the proportional representation ballot. Russia's Choice secured a paltry 15 percent, less than half of what it expected, while the other democratic parties all won less than 10 percent of the popular vote. The CPRF and its rural comrades, the Agrarians, combined for almost 20 percent of the vote, while new centrist groups combined for less than one-quarter of the vote. As expected, the proportional representation vote stimulated the formation of a party system at the national level in Russia, but from the perspective of the drafters, it stimulated the development of the wrong kind of parties.

Horrified by this electoral outcome, the administration spent the next two years trying to rewrite the electoral law. The president and his team wanted to get rid of proportional representation altogether and reshape Russia's political landscape into a two-party system. Working through parliamentary factions loyal to Yeltsin, the administration proposed a new mixed system in which 300 seats would be allocated through SMDs and only 150 seats would be allocated according to proportional representation.[81] When debated in the spring of 1995, however, this amendment to the electoral law failed to pass through the Duma.[82]

The majority in the Duma wanted to keep the existing system because 50 percent of the deputies owed their seats to proportional representation. In addition, more than seventy deputies who had won Duma seats through SMDs were members of parties that won seats through the proportional representation ballot, meaning that a solid majority supported the fifty-fifty formula. This support cut across ideological lines as liberal, nationalist, and communist parties all supported the status quo formulation. These deputies also realized that the difference between 225 and 150 was pivotal, since 225 proportional representation seats would guarantee that a majority would favor the existing formulation, whereas the presidential proposal did not. Within the Duma, the new electoral system in place from 1993 had reorganized political forces to create a new majority in favor of the status quo. The Kremlin's campaign to reduce proportional representation after the 1995 parliamentary election also failed. Thus Russia's electoral decree, and then law, that the State Duma passed did not neatly reflect the well-defined preferences of the powerful.

The Future of Parties in Russia

The current state of party development in Russia is not stable. The institutional tensions in the present system create strange incentives and ambiguous signals for political actors. In particular, the mixed electoral system for the parliament does not reflect the interests of the most powerful political actors in the polity. In the long term, two paths to a more stable outcome seem to be available: liquidating the presidency and developing a multiparty parliamentary system or liquidating proportional representation in the Duma as the first step toward developing a two-party presidential system.

The first path would be an engineered solution to address party weakness. Not surprisingly, the same people who drafted the original mixed electoral system also advocate the weakening of presidential powers. These advocates of multiparty development still believe that proportional representation has given parties a foothold in the national legislature. From this base, these parties might then begin to influence other electoral situations, including the SMD seats in the Duma, the presidential campaign, regional legislatures, and eventually even regional executives.

The prospects for this trajectory are still alive, but are not gaining momentum. The old parliamentary parties have not managed to expand beyond the Duma's walls. On the contrary, the trend indicates that their influence in other electoral arenas and state institutions is decreasing. Constitutional amendments limiting the powers of the president constitute the one institutional change that could stimulate party power by design from above. While a glimmer of hope for such an institutional change appeared after the August 1998 financial crash, such amendments seem unlikely, especially after Putin's electoral victory.

More likely is the elimination of proportional representation and a weakening of political parties, at least in the short run. The results of the 1999 parliamentary elections unexpectedly undermined the majority coalition in favor of proportional representation and the status quo rules. Unity, which captured almost one-quarter of the popular vote on the party list in the 1999 elections, has promised to eliminate proportional representation as a component of parliamentary election law. Before the 1999 vote, pro-party deputies always had a solid majority in the Duma, since parties won all the party list seats and added more deputies to their ranks by winning some single-mandate seats. In other words, the innovation in the electoral system first introduced in 1993 initially had little to do with the preferences of the powerful and occurred primarily by chance in the uncertain and chaotic context of the 1993 crisis. Once in place, however, the rule change seemed to manufacture a coalition in favor of perpetuating it, even if other important actors in the Russian polity did not support the mixed electoral system.

These rules in turn allowed for proto-parties to sprout even if they were not firmly rooted in socioeconomic cleavages of Russian society.

The results of the 1999 elections threatened to undermine this equilibrium. For the first time, an electoral bloc that rejected proportional representation won seats through proportional representation. Not surprisingly, this party—Unity—was created by the Presidential administration. Since the 1999 vote, another major winner from the party list, OVR, has crumbled. Most of its elements have joined forces with Unity to form a new party of power, Unified Russia. As a first step toward eliminating proportional representation altogether, this new pivotal party in the Duma attempted to raise the threshold on the party list to 12.5 percent. The idea did not capture a majority, but a majority compromised by opting to raise the threshold to 7 percent for the 2007 elections. Opinion polls suggest that only two parties, Unified Russia and the CPRF, have enough support from the electorate to gain more than 7 percent. If these two parties emerge from the 2003 elections with a majority of the seats, then the Duma could easily eliminate proportional representation, a rule change that would deal a blow to multiparty development, especially liberal party development.

A two-party system consisting of Unified Russia and the CPRF could easily degenerate into a hegemonic party system. Given the Communist Party's failure to secure 50 percent in any national vote over the last decade—a decade in which the economic conditions were ripe for Communist Party renewal—a new electoral law that institutionalized a two-party system would effectively guarantee Unified Russia's role as the ruling party for the foreseeable future. Minor parties might continue to exist, but one party—the party of power—would dominate all electoral processes of consequence. After a decade of weakly institutionalized multiparty politics, Russia could be heading back toward one-party rule.

Two optimistic caveats are in order however. First, in the past, parties of power always looked much stronger going into the next national election cycle than they did after the vote. Unified Russia has the organizational capacity and state support to be a major contender in future parliamentary elections. At the same time, the voters have not rated the performance of those in power favorably. Only one politician still enjoys solid support: Putin. If Putin over time does not identify firmly with Unified Russia, then the Party's future becomes more uncertain. So far, however, Putin has demonstrated a real commitment to Unified Russia's development.

Second, the Duma, Federation Council, and president collaborated in 2002 to pass a new law that requires regional parliaments to use a similar electoral law as that in place for the State Duma.[83] Fifty percent of these seats will be elected through proportional representation. Ironically, given their disdain for proportional representation in national elections, the Kremlin and its parliamentary allies supported this reform as a way to weaken executive authority at the regional level. This group foresees Unified Russia winning many seats at the regional level through the proportional representation system, thereby giving the Kremlin a new ally in regional politics. Whether the Kremlin's game plan will succeed is hard to predict. At the same time, however, this electoral system could have the same positive consequences for party development at the local level that it produced in the national parliament. Of course, the outcome at the national level is only a partial success, and regional parties stimulated by proportional representation would also control the local institutions with the least amount of power. Nonetheless, whether intended or not, the strengthening of political parties at the local level might create opportunities for the emergence of meaningful national coalitions of partisans. More than a decade after the collapse of one-party rule, the process of grassroots party development might finally begin to take root.

6

Civil Society

Michael McFaul and Elina Treyger

At the end of the Gorbachev era, a society reared by decades of totalitarian rule surprised the world with political activity of unprecedented and unexpected scope. Tens of thousands of people took to the streets to protest against the Soviet system repeatedly in 1990 and 1991, including the attempted coup in August 1991. An open, democratic opposition materialized where dissidence had been sparse and scattered; and a heretofore passive, deferential citizenry formed political organizations unassociated with the Soviet party-state. The proliferation of nonparty, nonstate civic groups, trade unions, political parties, and newspapers and the exponential rise in citizen participation fueled hope that a civil society was taking root, one capable of assisting the demise of the communist regime and assuring the survival and health of Russia's infant democracy.[1]

A decade later, Russian society has not abandoned nongovernmental activity: by one estimate, more than 200,000 nongovernmental organizations (NGOs) have formed since the collapse of communist rule.[2] However, the excitement over the country's societal awakening has subsided and yielded to pessimism, and the thousands of NGOs and their members do not appear to be contributing to the consolidation of democracy to the degree that they, their observers, and their supporters had hoped earlier in the decade. Ironically, civil society's capacity to influence political outcomes on a national scale seems to have been greater during the last years of the Soviet era than it is today. Russian civil society is weak, atomized, apolitical, and heavily dependent on Western assistance for support. It exerts little influence over state actions and policies and lacks the capacity to play a meaningful role in mediating state and individual interests, let alone resisting state encroachment on societal freedoms.

Why has civil society failed to fulfill its promise, which seemed so great on the eve of Soviet collapse? Can we even talk meaningfully about a "civil society" in post-communist Russia ? If so, what has impeded its development? The first part of this chapter argues that something similar to a Western concept of civil society has emerged in Russia. We suggest that to understand what has happened in Russia we cannot adhere to an doctrinaire view of civil society, but must instead stretch our notions of civil society developed from analysis of American and European democracies.

Subsequent parts of the chapter analyze the development of Soviet and post-Soviet society, focusing on those societal activities that demonstrate independence from rather than obedience to the state and action rather than passive acceptance of exogenously determined events. In explaining the slow emergence of civil society we highlight several interrelated factors. First, the Soviet legacy offered post-Soviet civil society little upon which to build. In addition to the standard list of barriers from the Soviet era, we examine an often ignored inherited impediment with deep roots in Soviet and Russian culture: the persistent disconnect between the elite and the masses, between the well-endowed organizations and grassroots activity, and between Moscow-based and peripheral forces. A second impediment to civil society development unique to the post-communist era has been the kind of capitalism that has taken hold in Russia. An economic system in which the country's resources are concentrated in the hands of a few people—oligarch capitalism as it is often called in Russia—offers few opportunities for the emergence of a civil society centered around and supported by a middle class. A third barrier is the institutional design of the state. A regime dominated by powerful executives does not foster civil society development. Finally, the specific policies of the president—President Vladimir Putin in particular—have also contributed to civil society's decline in recent years.

Defining Civil Society

During the recent conceptual resurgence and popularity of civil society in policy and academic discourse, the definition of the concept has itself been debated. Rather than undertaking a comprehensive review of a large literature pertaining to civil society, we highlight points of contention in the debate and offer our own broader perspective. In particular, we introduce some common conditions that authors have offered to define the limits to the civil society realm and suggest that these, while useful for other purposes, do not pertain to the Russian case.

Scholars generally agree that civil society is a space distinct from the state and the market, that is, between the private and the public spheres, where individuals and groups voluntarily organize to collectively pursue their interests or values. Beyond this loose consensus, scholars and practitioners diverge along numerous dimensions, two of which deserve special attention. The first concerns the identity of the actors, that is, who can be considered part of civil society. The second concerns the functions of the actors, namely, what do the actors have to do to be part of civil society.

With respect to the identity of the actors, NGOs—nongovernmental organizations—have generally been the focus of attention. Associations formed to protect human rights, the environment, and various disadvantaged groups would likely top everyone's list of model civic actors, but broad consensus is lacking even with respect to this corpus of ostensibly self-governing, voluntary, nonprofit associations autonomous of the state. Many have pointed out that the mere legal status of an NGO does not suffice. In addition, these entities must meet certain requirements, which are often formulated as such qualities as openness, respect for diversity and pluralism, or a shared set of norms.[3] The Ku Klux Klan, the Mafia, fanatical cults, and other extremist groups are examples of undemocratic, illiberal groups that scholars are loath to admit into the holistic embrace of their concept of civil society. Indeed, most authors rule them out. Civil society, they admit, is not a normatively neutral concept and ought not to be divorced from its Western liberal pedigree.[4]

The temptation to subtract blatantly illiberal elements from the civil sphere becomes stronger when one considers Weimar Germany. Sheri Berman's important analysis of pre-Nazi Germany cautions against equating thriving associational life with democratization or liberalization.[5] We ought to look carefully not merely at the form (that is, voluntary associations), but also the character (the values and goals) of public social life, before we call it civil and consider it a democracy-enhancing phenomenon.

Berman's and others' accounts of Weimar Germany also demonstrate that determining whether a group is illiberal, antidemocratic, or otherwise threatening is not always possible ahead of time. Weimar Germany boasted a large number and variety of associations, most of which did not resemble the Ku Klux Klan or other intolerant extremists. Indeed, many of these groups were engaged in cultural or recreational activities. Yet even the seemingly apolitical and harmless groups ultimately contributed to Hitler's rise and helped serve the fascist cause. We should at the very least suspect our ability to identify such problematic groups. This problem is particularly true in Russia, where multiple shades of nationalism complicate the landscape, and discerning whether organizations such as the new youth movement Walking Together or the nationalist Eurasia movement contradict the pluralist ethos or, on the contrary, embody it, is hard. The same can be said of many Soviet era organizations, which at one time served totalitarianism, but now seem to have made the leap to supporting pluralistic, market-oriented institutions.

Further uncertainty about the identity of civil society actors arises from more or less rigid distinctions between civil society and other public spheres.[6] Scholars often distinguish civil society from economic society and political society. In this tripartite typology, economic society refers to those agents and organizations concerned primarily with increasing their wealth, political society refers to those focused on political power, and civil society labels those seeking to pursue societal or group interests. Scholars also tend to think of the units of civil society as being grassroots organizations, whereas the main organizations in economic society and political society are elite-based groups, such as business associations and political parties. As Marc Morje Howard succinctly states, "[W]hile political society and economic society are comprised primarily of elite actors and institutions in the pursuit of power or profit, civil society is the realm of ordinary citizens, who join and participate in groups and associations because of their everyday interests, needs, and desires."[7] Others argue that civil society must be distinct from or in opposition to the state. Still others want to distinguish civil society from mass social movements.[8] Each of these distinctions generates ambiguous cases. Do we consider a professional association of business people to be part of civil society or economic society? Does a nonparty group organized to elect a specific legislator belong in the civil or the political sphere? Should an organization that receives funds from the state be considered a civil society actor? Does a mass protest organized by an NGO represent a manifestation of civic life or a social movement? Even though these cases are problematic in established democracies, they are ten times as complicated in a country like Russia after decades of a comprehensive fusion of party and state; party-state and society; and all political, economic, and civil activity.

Any distinctions between the political and civil realms are outright impossible before the collapse of the Soviet Union, and dubious at best since. All existing political parties that trace their beginnings to the last years of the Soviet era formed as nonparty organizations, given the formal Communist Party monopoly until the repeal of Article 6 of the constitution guaranteeing that monopoly in 1990, following the first partially free and contested elections.[9] To campaign for noncommunist candidates for the elections to the revitalized Congress of People's Deputies (CPD) in 1989, citizens formed "voters' clubs," that is, civic associations that performed the function parties perform in multiparty democracies. In the post-Soviet era, the proliferation of political parties and the dim electoral prospects of most of them results in confusion about which society they belong to: the political or the civil.[10] Excluding those political parties that took part in the struggle for power with some chance of winning representation in the 1990s from the ranks of the potential civil society is reasonable. Excluding other political organizations, even if legally registered as political parties, may be drawing the limits on the acceptable goals of actors in a civil society too narrowly.

Similarly, insisting on strict autonomy from the state would not be sensible. Because private sources of funding have been scarce, many organizations still receive funds from the government. Just as the anticommunist movement acquired supporters within both dissident circles and official communist organizations, a civil society of the Russian variety can grow up among groups sponsored by either the post-Soviet state or incubated under Soviet party tutelage. While some state-sponsored associations indeed do little more than serve as the mouthpieces and cheerleaders of the Kremlin or local governments, we cannot dispense with all state-backed societal organizations so readily. A good example is the new youth movement "Walking Together," which is rumored to enjoy backing from the Kremlin. The group attracted an astounding number of members within a short period, and conducted large-scale activities mostly in support of President Putin. Even if launched and sponsored by some in the Kremlin, the large number of voluntary joiners surely says something about the authentic interests of Russian youth in the organization and in Putin.

Yet another problematic sector that cuts across the economic, civil, and political realms is the media sector. In capitalist democracies, the media can be split up between economic society (private, profit-seeking outfits), and the state itself (state-run broadcasts and press). During the last years of the Soviet era, the "renegade" publications that chose to disregard party directives and publish on and for the democratic movement were a vital part of society's awakening and mobilization, yet most of these were fully funded by the state. The media may deserve examination in their own right, and may be simply an indispensable partner to civil society proper, but we should not prematurely close our eyes to the interactions between the media and other elements as activity outside the civil sphere.

One other way to define civil society, and another dimension of theoretical disagreement, is the specification of the functions, rather than the identity, of the actors. Focusing on the function of civil society brings out the reasons why civil society has become so desirable, specifically, why it has become desirable in the context of democratization. Scholars and policy makers alike have asserted that civil society is a vital ingredient in transitions to and consolidations of democracy.[11]

Arguments about civil society's functions can be divided into two kinds. The first kind of argument posits that civil society strengthens democracy horizontally, that is, it builds up trust and connections among citizens, resulting in a participatory civic ethos.[12] The second kind of argument explains how civil society strengthens democracy vertically by aggregating the preferences of its participants and establishing channels of influence whereby these preferences can be brought to bear on government policy.[13] In performing this second function, civil society actors must engage directly with the state, and usually with political parties during elections, to be effective.

At the horizontal level, in Robert Putnam's terms, the function of civil society is to build up "social capital."[14] The term refers to a spirit of "social connectedness" that ostensibly facilitates cooperation and coordination for the common good. Social connectedness makes for associational life that facilitates effective organization for common, public interests. Activities that build social capital also promote the virtues of democratic citizenship, such as participating in public life, understanding the rights and responsibilities of citizens in a democracy, and tolerating different opinions—the frequently invoked democratic "habits of the heart."[15] The prominence of democratic values in turn serves to bolster the effective functioning of democratic institutions. Scholars also maintain that this process also mitigates societal divisions by uniting people across social classes and ethnic divides. These horizontal dynamics build democracy from "the bottom."

At the vertical level, civil society has two functions: to represent and transmit people's interests to the government and to act as a constraint on the abuse and misuse of governmental power, holding the government accountable to democratic norms and the will of the people.[16] That is, civil society creates another channel of influence for the public via connections with local and national governments. Public associations represent those public interests that may not be adequately represented by political parties or economic interest groups. Moreover, public organizations monitor the state's activities and communicate information to other actors, thereby contributing to a general atmosphere of transparency. Faced with constant exposure and scrutiny, government officials are less likely to violate democratic rules of conduct. An active society is the necessary counterweight to overreaching state power, in that state leaders find that behaving in an authoritarian manner is harder when societal actors are easily mobilized to resist state incursions. Increased accountability and responsiveness to people's interests in turn legitimizes the government, rendering society more governable.[17]

If a mature civil society is supposed to perform these two kinds of functions, then Russia does not have a mature civil society. Russians exhibited one of the lowest rates of organizational membership in the 1990s. They appear to distrust one another, and effective representation of societal interests to the state has been notoriously lacking.[18] In concluding that Russian civil society does not meet the ideal type, however, we do not make the opposite claim that civil society does not exist in Russia. The organization of autonomous interest groups in post-communist Russia may not resemble that in American civil society, but it also does not resemble Soviet society of twenty years ago. Nor has civil society development in the late Soviet era and post-communist Russian era been linear.

To understand the changes from Soviet society and capture the dynamics of civil society development in Russia requires a broader definition of the term that dispenses with all but the most minimal requirements. This broader image comprises all forms of societal activity that can be seen as legitimate representations of citizens' common interests or values at any level of voluntary organization. We draw a solid line between private society and civil society. The former comprises individuals, families, and circles of friends pursuing purely private goals, while the latter comprises groups of citizens expressing, sharing, and pursuing common collective goals. Our lines between political society, economic society, and civil society are less solid. We exclude groups in economic society focused only on profit seeking and political parties from our analysis. We do, however, consider groups that have one foot in civil society and the other in either economic or political society, because organized behavior autonomous from the state is still so novel and so rare in post-communist Russia.

Moreover, our broad conception makes no a priori assumptions about what a civil society does: it may or may not contribute to the health of a democratic polity. Instead, our main concern is to explain the evolution of civil society, focusing on those events, institutions, and socioeconomic factors that contributed to the rise and decline of civil society in Russia in the last two decades.

The Soviet Legacy

No political system has ever been more hostile to civil society than the totalitarian communist regime erected by Stalin.[19] Although pre-Soviet Russia also privileged the state and limited arenas of autonomous social activity, even the czars, especially from 1861 on, allowed genuine NGOs to exist. Because Marxist theory predicted an end to all political and social conflict after the proletarian revolution, pluralism and organization for the sake of any particularistic interest had no place in a communist society. In keeping with ideological dictates, the Soviet state's most salient characteristic became the virtual destruction of the space between the individual and the state, the space that the building blocks of civil society would occupy: social networks, private businesses, public associations, clubs, religious groups, labor unions, and so on. These institutions were either rooted out altogether or subordinated to the sprawling state and Communist Party of the Soviet Union (CPSU) structures, so that all social exchanges were carried out under the guise of the party-state.

The destruction or absorption of most public nonstate activities appeared complete after Stalin's rise to power in the 1920s. The 1932 Law on Associations and Stalin's 1936 constitution firmly eradicated the principle of free association, and his reign of terror effectively discouraged any overly enterprising independent initiatives.[20] The relationship between society and the state established by the maturing communist regime became a one-way street of dictatorial "democratic centralism." Official institutions were extremely hierarchical, with union leaders, factory and collective directors, and other heads of organizations responding to the Communist Party-state, the sole determinant of the country's course. The Soviet system created myriad social organizations that mimicked civic organizations in name, but helped to control society in practice. Because nonstate organizations were illegal, this rigid hierarchy did not allow the official organizations and institutions to claim much autonomy from the state.[21]

Even the Stalinist state could not stifle private expressions of dissent, but state terror and strict indoctrination successfully prevented informal networks from publicly articulating opinions different from official doctrines, seeking sympathizers and allies, or constituting any significant force. All reform and change in the Soviet Union originated strictly from above and, as with Stalinist mass collectivization and industrialization, at great cost to society. The Soviet system intended to destroy all independent public life and nearly succeeded in doing so.

After Stalin's death, the constraints of the Soviet system loosened somewhat, allowing society to breathe again, albeit with short and shallow breaths. Alongside a change in leadership, the demographic and social changes from the 1950s to the 1980s transformed the passive and inarticulate peasant society of the pre-Stalin era into an industrial society with a more complex social structure and an educated, modernized population, especially in the expanding urban centers.[22] Even as early as the late 1940s, in the aftermath of World War II, an anti-Stalinist underground was born in the larger cities made up almost entirely of students and children of the repressed.[23] Similar informal groups of intellectuals, technical elites, and youth became more numerous and noticeable in the decades following Stalin's death. Beginning in the 1960s, the reduced readiness of the Soviet government to use force against its citizens, combined with an increased level of education, fostered independent initiatives all over the USSR, starting in the realm of religion and national identity and extending into areas of culture and ecology.[24] Some nationalities in the republics and minority ethnic groups scattered throughout the USSR began to express open dissatisfaction with the Soviet suppression of their national or ethnic cultures.

Some suggest that civil society began to reemerge during the "golden age" of Leonid Brezhnev's rule.[25] A small number of brave, dissident individuals and groups openly challenged the Soviet system, and informal intelligentsia groups composed of scientists, writers, and other professionals began to challenge Stalinist taboos, communicating their views primarily through *samizdat*, self-published critical literature on forbidden subjects. They did not explicitly call for the overthrow of the Soviet government, but strove to create an atmosphere of freer discussion and to protect the rights of those still persecuted by the party-state. To the extent that organized social groups did exist outside the family, they were atomized, apolitical, and purposely sought to avoid rather than to influence the state.[26]

Peter Reddaway has drawn a useful distinction between dissent and opposition. Whereas opposition implies "an aspiration to rule in place of existing rulers," dissent merely denotes objections to existing rules and rulers.[27] Thus Brezhnev era dissidents did not constitute an opposition, since their goals were not confrontational and their numbers were small. Whenever progressive or reformist initiatives were introduced from the top, they were "in large measure a function of elite politics and cleavage" and not of public pressure or opinion.[28] The state continued to harass and suppress proto-civil society groups. Reacting to the forbidding conditions created by the regime, dissidents focused more on creating a parallel or autonomous society rather than one engaged with and trying to influence the state.

The dissident movement was also an elite affair. The seeds of dissent sown as the rigid Stalinist structure began to crumble did not grow into full-scale democratic—or any other—opposition because of the divide between those who originated the dissenting ideas and those who had the numerical force to support and act on them. The semi-informal associations that began forming after Stalin's death were almost completely the products of a small section of urban intelligentsia. Key dissident figures such as Andrei Sakharov, Alexander Solzhenitsyn, and Roy Medvedev offered up manifestos of opposition through their writings, but showed no inclination to realize such opposition on a mass basis. Millions resisted passively, indirectly undermining the Soviet system, for instance, through petty corruption and the steady growth of the black market. Yet overt mass challenges to the state remained limited and sporadic even decades after Stalin's death. Except for a few spontaneous demonstrations and strikes, the urban and rural working classes did not try to establish unions independent of the Party or join forces with other societal groups to achieve change.[29] Evaluating the prospects of a democratic opposition from society in the mid-1970s, one of the most astute observers of Soviet dissident movements wrote, "[T]he mainstream liberals [the intelligentsia dissidents] are numerically weak and ... their values, taken as a whole, are unlikely ever to receive mass support in the USSR."[30]

The Gorbachev Years

Within six years of coming to power, Mikhail Gorbachev's reforms created the permissive conditions for the emergence of quasi-civil society within the Soviet Union. To generate new allies and launch his perestroika, Gorbachev initiated sweeping reform measures with the objective of liberalizing Soviet society. Glasnost permitted the publication and discussion of previously taboo subjects, changes in the Soviet criminal code no longer punished political assembly and demonstration, and partially free elections and the repeal of Article 6 officially ended the Communist Party's monopoly on power. Although Gorbachev's reforms allowed nonstate organizations to form, the structure of the Soviet economy and society could not deliver a real autonomous space or independent resources for these new entities, which therefore remained somewhat dependent on the state. Furthermore, Gorbachev's reforms established only partial and imperfect institutional channels for communicating societal demands to the state. New parliaments organized and quasi parties sprouted, but access to the Soviet state remained restricted. This inaccessible state gradually lost the capacity to respond to societal demands, revealing its own weakness and contradictions. The result was polarization between state and society and, eventually, revolution.

Responses from Below to Reform from Above

In the increasingly permissive climate of openness, Soviet society came alive through the formation of numerous voluntary and professional associations, independent trade unions, rights advocacy groups, young political parties, and spontaneous mass actions. Nonstate associations began to appear as early as 1985. Most of these first groups were relatively apolitical, devoted to culture, education, and social problems. The first organizations with openly political goals organized later and included such notable new groups as Memorial, dedicated to uncovering Stalin era horrors, and Democratic Perestroika, a political discussion group organized by the intelligentsia. Between 1988 and 1989, independent groups mushroomed, some forming networks, or as Steven Fish dubbed them, "parties-in-waiting."[31] Triggered by miners' strikes in Ukraine in 1989, a wave of labor activism also swept the Soviet Union, spawning independent unions and setting off mass labor strikes nationwide. By 1989, with the exception of business associations, many proto–civil society organizations could already be discerned, reflecting the decades of stifled demands from a sophisticated society shackled by an outdated Soviet regime.

Gorbachev's decision to permit partially free elections to the Soviet Congress of People's Deputies in 1989 provided the first opportunity for societal forces to try influencing politics directly. The electoral process produced an unprecedented whirl of societal mobilization. Media criticism exploded; electoral clubs sprouted; and noncommunist, pro-perestroika organizations convened. Loosely-based voter clubs organized around specific candidates, some of whom won seats to the Soviet Congress. Although the number of successful candidates produced from the grassroots was small, the experience of participation for this first generation of nonstate, non–Communist Party activists proved pivotal.

The same activist groups tested their mobilization skills a year later during elections for republic, *oblast*, city, and district soviets. During these elections, held primarily in the spring of 1990, the candidates supported by new civil society groups achieved greater electoral success than in 1989. In the Baltic republics, for instance, anticommunist forces captured solid majorities in the new parliaments. In Russia, a newly organized opposition movement, Democratic Russia, won hundreds of seats in the Russian Congress of People's Deputies and controlled majorities in the Moscow and Leningrad city soviets.[32] Boris Yeltsin, the perceived leader of the democratic opposition, won election as chairman of the Russian Congress. After a century of noninvolvement, Soviet society was playing a direct and powerful role in politics.

The rapid growth of NGOs continued throughout the last two years of the Gorbachev era. By 1990, tens of thousands of organizations had registered with the government.[33] After the repeal in 1990 of Article 6 of the Soviet Constitution, a few intelligentsia-led groups transformed themselves into political parties. The Social Democratic Party of Russia, the Constitutional Democratic Party, the Democratic Party of Russia, and several others were born in this way.[34] Even when some organizations began to call themselves parties, drawing a distinction between civil and political society would have been somewhat arbitrary at this juncture. That society began a life of its own, apart from close tutelage from the communist state, is unquestionable. Even if Western labels cannot adequately describe the forms of societal activity at the close of the Soviet era, proto-organizations existed that fit the conventional categories, including a political society (incipient parties and electoral campaigns), a civil society (NGOs), and economic society (legalized cooperatives and covert business ventures). At this moment, therefore, predicting that this flurry of activity would settle into functional emulations of these elements of a Western capitalist-democratic order was not unreasonable.

The Disconnect Between State and Society

Initially, the activated societal forces reinforced Gorbachev's reform program. The kind and pace of change demanded from below, however, soon exceeded Gorbachev's own reform agenda as societal actors bent on truly revolutionary change began to oppose the traditional ruling leaders and institutions of the Soviet state. Societal forces in the Baltic republics were the first to organize and successfully challenge Soviet rule. Beginning in the fall of 1990, Yeltsin and Democratic Russia followed the Baltic example and directly challenged Soviet sovereignty. This kind of societal organization was not a parallel to civil societies in Western democracies, or even to Poland's Solidarity. Instead of seeking to win recognition of societal interests through incipient representative channels (that is, new legislative bodies), Democratic Russia and popular fronts in other republics pressed for the destruction of the Soviet regime. Instead of dialogue between state and society, polarization and confrontation ensued.

Early in his tenure, Gorbachev appeared to reach out to the new, independent groups and budding parties, whom he increasingly saw as alternative allies for perestroika against the conservative, mid-level Communist Party bureaucracy. He sanctioned the appointment of progressive editors of several popular publications, who were encouraged to publish freely and to explore previously taboo subjects.[35] Gorbachev also made a conscious attempt to convey his openness to their ideas to the intellectual elites: in a grand gesture he telephoned Andrei Sakharov in exile and personally invited him to return to Moscow to continue his work. Gorbachev and his government also responded to issues presented through mass actions, including demands for increased wages for miners, calls for the creation of a Russian presidency, demonstrations to rescind Article 6 of the constitution, and pressures to grant the republics greater control over their territories.

The embrace of new societal activism by Gorbachev's government was not unequivocal. For instance, the KGB still forcibly repressed early public demonstrations orchestrated by Democratic Union, the first organization in

1988 to declare itself an alternative political party. While the state allowed many other organizations to develop unobstructed, officials actually created some to counteract those real nongovernmental groups that proved too progressive for the communist regime. For example, soon after the creation of a new independent lawyers' union, the Ministry of Justice launched the USSR Union of Lawyers, which had a clearly conservative, pro-communist agenda. The same happened after the creation of an autonomous, democratic cooperatives trade union.

The absence of an effective partnership between the state and society only spawned revolutionary events when society captured control over parts of the state—the republic-level governments—after the spring 1990 elections. This capture did not occur in all, or even most, of the fifteen republics of the Soviet Union, but it did occur where it mattered most—the Russian Federation. After Yeltsin's election as chairman of the Russian CPD, Russian society could choose engagement with two states in place of one, but whereas Yeltsin and his allies in the Russian Congress had strong ties to societal organizations such as Democratic Russia, nascent noncommunist political parties, and the independent trade unions, connections between the Soviet state and Russian society wore increasingly thin. The fact that Gorbachev never sought to base his leadership on a popular mandate also underscored the differences between the two competing states. By the time Yeltsin became Russia's first elected president in June 1991, it was his third electoral victory in as many years. Soviet state structures still controlled most coercive resources, but Yeltsin and the Russian Congress enjoyed the open and active support of a visibly mobilized population.

Throughout various confrontations between Soviet and Russian authorities in the fall of 1990 and spring of 1991, Democratic Russia and its allies proved capable of assembling hundreds of thousands of people in the streets of major urban centers. When the coal miners organized another series of debilitating strikes in the spring of 1991, they called for the intervention of the Russian government, believing that the Soviet government would not (or could no longer) meet their demands. In the final showdown between the Soviet and Russian states—the attempted coup in August 1991 by conservative forces within Gorbachev's government—societal mobilization proved decisive in securing victory for Yeltsin's side. The last year of the USSR marked the apogee of Russian civil society. At critical moments, actors from outside the Communist Party or the Soviet state were able to decisively influence the course of history.

The Yeltsin Era

The collapse of the Soviet Union meant mission accomplished for many in Russia's democratic movement. After the collapse of the Soviet Union, issues of economic transformation became most salient. On this set of issues, civil society previously mobilized in opposition to the Soviet regime had little role to play, at least from the perspective of those now sitting in the Kremlin.

The State's New Agenda

Even at the peak of societal involvement in the state's affairs, the most visible societal participation took spontaneous, noninstitutionalized forms—on the streets and down the mineshafts—rather than lobbying or voting. NGOs were still poor and inexperienced, and parties were just forming. During these revolutionary times, the most active, vocal, and confrontational expression of public demands received the most attention. Less turbulent forms of interest articulation, such as elections or grassroots petitions, were important symptoms of societal awakening, but direct, physical actions of protest or support trumped these incipient civic practices. In the most conspicuous contrast, a solid majority of Russian citizens voted for the preservation of the USSR in the spring of 1991. The following August, a small but vociferous minority in Moscow acted to block the coup attempt and legitimated Yeltsin's moves to dissolve the USSR in December 1991.[36]

After 1991, Russian society rarely spoke as loud or with as much determination as it did prior to the USSR's collapse. As attention turned to economic transformation in the winter of 1992, Yeltsin's government wanted to demobilize society. During the transition to market capitalism, the standard of living would have to fall in the short term for the vast majority of Russians. A mobilized society would actively resist and perhaps thwart reforms in response to economic hardships.[37] The objective of Yeltsin's government was therefore to create a more autonomous state, so that it could conduct radical market reforms protected from societal pressures. Some of his advisers even called for an interim dictatorship until the painful process of economic transformation had been completed.

Consequently, Yeltsin did not call for new elections after the collapse of the Soviet Union, and the first post-Soviet elections did not take place until December 1993. He wasted no time on building links with formal political society—a pro-reform, pro-presidential political party never materialized.

Instead, Yeltsin and his team devoted their energies to strengthening the executive branch of government at the federal and regional levels, a strategy that required open cooperation with regional leaders, who were previously considered to be conservative and antidemocratic. Yeltsin's general political strategy for economic reform involved co-opting elites and interest groups formed under the Soviet regime while at the same time promoting new elite interest groups. Yeltsin and his team refrained from encouraging or allying with grassroots, reformist constituencies within society, hoping instead that society as a whole would resume its familiar passive disengagement from the government's activity. In particular, Yeltsin gave little support to Democratic Russia, the very organization that had helped him come to power. Instead, at this stage, Yeltsin believed that co-opting so-called red directors and former CPSU bosses in the regions was more vital to his economic reform agenda.

To say that the aim of Yeltsin's policies was to demobilize society and insulate the state from societal pressures is not to imply that Yeltsin or his government also sought to suppress societal activity or re-subordinate it to the state. On the contrary, the 1993 constitution provided for the protection of basic civil liberties—the freedoms of speech, press, religion, association, and peaceful assembly—without which a civil society could not meaningfully exist.[38] In 1995, with presidential backing, the Duma passed three laws—the Law on Public Associations, the Law on Philanthropic Activities and Organizations, and the Law on Noncommercial Organizations—that secured the legal standing of independent groups, set the rules governing their activities, and outlined their rights.[39] These and other relevant laws were not masterpieces of jurisprudence, and have often proven to be discriminatory and obstructive to the proliferation of independent activity; however, they legally enabled society to act independently of, and even in opposition to, the state, radically breaking with the Soviet legacy.

Society's Response

The Soviet Party-state created and controlled the trade unions, women's organizations, and youth clubs and owned all enterprises. After the collapse of the communist system, many of these organizations survived. Some of the survivors also acquired autonomy from the state and began to resemble interest groups and civic organizations.[40] Western analysts frequently dismiss these as mere organizational vestiges of Soviet times, but complete dismissal is a mistake, or at least premature, because in the initial years after the collapse, these groups seemed to represent real interests of real people. Among those Soviet organizations that did not survive the collapse, the Komsomol, the once powerful and wide-reaching youth group created and controlled by the CPSU, lost nearly all its members and resources. Instead of working within this Soviet era organization to advance their interests, Komsomol leaders cashed in their contacts, privileges, and resources to make big money as business people in the quasi market.[41] Mikhail Khordokovsky, the richest man in Russia, acquired his starting capital from the Komsomol. The Soviet women's organization also dissolved and gave way to new women's groups. Those organizations that survived must have offered some incentives to their members that other avenues did not. Given their inheritance of organizational expertise and resources, the Soviet survivors proved much more effective in influencing the state than the new, often Western-supported NGOs, and for much of the 1990s they also crowded out new, more independent associations, organizations, and interest groups.[42]

As an example, privatization was one issue that greatly animated the communist-era civic groups in the early 1990s. As devised by Anatoly Chubais and his team at the State Committee on Property, Yeltsin's original privatization blueprint hoped to create American-style corporations in which outsiders would own the majority of shares and would trade them publicly on open stock markets. One step toward this ownership structure consisted of a universal distribution of vouchers, whereby every Russian could purchase shares in privatizing enterprises.

The directors' corps of Soviet enterprises disliked this plan and used its organizational resources to resist it and maintain their insider "ownership."[43] They consolidated ranks and allied with other societal elements. Because the mechanics of social welfare provision during the Soviet period tied the fortunes of the workers of these enterprises with those of the enterprise itself, the directors enjoyed the support of Soviet-era trade unions. The national coalition of trade unions, the Federation of Independent Trade Unions of Russia (FNPR), was as firmly committed to thwarting the state's plans for privatization as were enterprise managers. So was the Civic Union, a coalition of interest groups, political parties, and parliamentary factions associated with the expired Soviet order.[44] This coalition should not be thought of as a reactionary force mobilized to stop or reverse capitalist reform. Instead, its organization and goals were perfectly consistent with what the

West would refer to as economic society. The alliance of trade unions and a nongovernmental political movement (Civic Union) with a more traditional business association (the Russian Union of Industrialists and Entrepreneurs) is what makes this political and social mobilization in response to privatization seem like something in between economic and civil society.

Likewise, the coalition's limited success should be considered in part a victory for society rather than a setback to reformers in the state. Through its strong links to important factions in the Russian Congress of People's Deputies, the directors' corps and its allies succeeded in amending the privatization law to permit insider privatization. The outcome of this major battle in the reform war was not the preference of Yeltsin's liberal reformers, and most certainly was not the program that Chubais wanted to implement.[45] The state was not immune from organized societal pressure. Societal groups originally organized by the Soviet party-state, now adapting to the new economic and political institutions of the post-Soviet era, had successfully pressured the state for an outcome that took their interests into account. Their tactics and goals, if not their origins, certainly resembled the tactics and goals of paradigmatic civil society actors.

After achieving control of these enterprises, this same set of Soviet-era interest groups succeeded in obtaining government credits and subsidies for most of the 1990s, thwarting efforts at macroeconomic stabilization for several years.[46] It was only institutional change of the Russian state—the adoption of the 1993 constitution—that weakened the influence and power of these interest groups. Even though the first State Duma—the new parliamentary organ created by the constitution—proved to be no less sympathetic to the directors' corps and its allies than its disobedient predecessor, the new super-presidential constitution allowed the president to overpower the Duma and its allies on most contentious issues. For instance, in the next round of privatization of Russia's most profitable firms—the so-called loans-for-shares program—these interest groups played almost no role.[47]

Obstacles to the Development of a Western-Style Civil Society

If some Soviet era organizations and interest groups managed to reconstitute and press their agendas after the Soviet collapse, many of the new elements of proto-civil society that sprouted during the Gorbachev era did not. In sheer numbers, the NGO sector—the heart of the paradigmatic civil society—has grown significantly in post-Soviet Russia. According to U.S.

Agency for International Development statistics, the NGO sector "has grown dramatically" from only 30 to 40 registered organizations in 1987 to about 238,000 by the end of 1998.[48] However, most indicators of this sector's actual functions, reach, and influence remained uninspiring throughout the decade: a minute fraction of citizens became engaged in civic or associational life, the sector's financial resources were negligible, and the number of groups that established and maintained effective channels of influence on government structures amounted to no more than a handful. Surveys indicate that few people—one of the highest estimates is 8 percent of the population—participate in NGOs.[49] Other estimates indicate that fewer than 2 percent of the population were involved in public organizations by the end of Yeltsin's rule.[50]

The obstacles are perhaps obvious and not unexpected in a country undergoing extensive transformations, but they bear cataloguing, if only to appreciate the difficult landscape the enterprising citizen needs to brave to build a civil society. In addition to the Soviet legacy, which privileged some groups not traditionally identified under the rubric of civil society, the kind of capitalism and the kind of state to emerge in post-communist Russia are the two most salient factors. In addition, societal attitudes—some of them new, some of them old—have contributed to the problem.

The organization of the new economy, as well as its poor and volatile performance, has not been conducive to civil society development. The economic society that grew up under Yeltsin has been deeply inimical to new entrants into civic and political life apart from the dominant class of oligarchs, the only new social layer that acquired disproportionate resources and influence. Business groups always constitute the most organized sector of society in capitalist democracies.[51] In the first decade of Russia's post-Soviet existence, the imbalance between the power of these groups and all others was striking. The oligarchs' influence over the state was demonstrated most dramatically during the 1996 presidential election. Although divided in the past over both political issues and markets, they united to provide Yeltsin's campaign with virtually unlimited resources. In return for its support, the new oligarchic class was rewarded with considerable representation within the Russian state.[52] Together with the aforementioned Soviet era economic actors, the oligarchic layer overshadowed poorer and newer societal elements, especially in national politics. What politicians need the endorsement of a women's organization when they have the support of multibillionaires? What politicians endorsed by even the most influential NGO have a chance if they do not have the financial backing that accompanies endorsement by an oligarch?

The dearth of rules governing the financing of parties and political formations also has encouraged a blatant buying of candidates and parties by wealthy commercial interests. The World Bank's comparative investigation of state capture placed Russia at the top, even among other formerly communist countries, by the end of Yeltsin's tenure.

In addition to outdoing any capacity by other societal actors to influence the political process, the old dinosaurs and new tycoons also have been stifling the development of small businesses, that is, of the middle class that tends to support civil society in mature capitalist economies.[53] While Poland, a country with less than a quarter of Russia's population, boasted more than 2 million private enterprises (excluding agriculture) by 1996, Russia had roughly 900,000.[54]

The nascent, small-scale, entrepreneurial sector faced, and continues to face, multiple obstacles. The unclear government regulations, the exorbitant taxes, the lack of liberalization, and the quasi-feudal regimes at the local level were not welcoming to small and inexperienced entrepreneurs.[55] The Mafia networks and the consolidation of large financial-industrial groups created monopoly control over many markets, rendering them impenetrable, and downright dangerous, to the aspiring middle class. Finally, the absence of enterprise-supporting structures, such as a functioning banking, courts, or mortgage system, and the instability of the Russian economy have combined to create an unfriendly environment for the small business person.

Thus those intent on staying afloat on the waves of Russia's turbulent capitalism have had no spare time or resources to devote to civic activism. While Russia's middle class grew throughout the 1990s, the limited independent organization that it has endeavored to undertake has been mostly for the sake of protecting narrow interests and, in contrast with Soviet era economic groups, has been extremely depoliticized.[56] While the managers and workers of formerly state-owned enterprises have taken their interests into legislative politics and lobbying, middle-class economic actors prefer to protect their interests outside the realm of politics and without involving the state.[57]

Resources for nonessential activities were scarce for most of the population during the bulk of the 1990s as the country's economy endured a severe depression. People had neither the time nor the money to support public goods when the acquisition of private goods was such a struggle. It has

become a cliché—
for most people n⎡etheless applicable—to say that in the new Russia,
room for collective⎡vival is a full-time occupation that leaves little
Russia's socioec⎡ucture is probably the greatest handicap for
civil society. The o⎡of the state is also not conducive to greater
societal involvement of ⎡life. Yeltsin's imposition of a presidential system, followed by th⎡ng of executives at the regional level, has
limited opportunitie⎡and engagement by civic organizations.
Civic groups are con⎡ught to be more successful at collabo-
rating with parliame⎡xecutives.58 Although the parliament
elected in 1993 house⎡communists, and liberals, the president and his governn⎡latively autonomous from the legislative branch in de⎡nistering public policies. This
arrangement carried a⎡onstate actors: if a group sought
real influence over majo⎡needed to reach the executive
branch. Allying with m⎡ture, the natural partners of
societal actors, rarely pr⎡strategy. Yeltsin, along with
several governors and ma⎡"social chambers," allegedly
as compensation for weak⎡d meant to bridge the gap
between civic groups and⎡w exceptions, however,
these advisory councils ca⎡nded to, the persistent
divide between the state a⎡blish a reliably func-
In addition, the new Ru⎡ioning judicial sys-
tioning judiciary and law e⎡: nonstate actors
tem is one of the key supp⎡ear and enforce-
need the courts to serve as n⎡civil society has
able laws to provide stable ru⎡by a shortage
not had the luxury of either.⎡hotocopying
of funds, personnel, and bas⎡ght before
machines), resulting in long⎡lly insuf-
them. The salaries of judges ar⎡igh inci-
ficient, as they have been for l⎡uption
dence of bribe taking and corru⎡ctions
have made the courts unreliab⎡for
between federal and regional la⎡
citizens seeking legal resolution⎡

Whereas the super-presidenc⎡
state appear to be unresponsive,⎡

ineffectiveness made it appear incapable of any subst*response. Even*
if Yeltsin's government had been attuned to deman*than those of*
rent-seeking corporate groups, the post-Soviet sta*tus lacked the*
capacity to meet most demands. For most of the *e bureaucracy*
grew in size as persistently as federal tax revenue*and the capac-*
ity to provide public goods declined.[60] Tax colle*became a sym-*
bolic process. Basic services traditionally provid*viet state, such*
as security, welfare and education, virtually cea*lic goods. State*
employees had to negotiate and strike just to*work they had*
already completed. Contractual arrangement*lf-enforcing to*
succeed. Mafias, security firms, and private *major respon-*
sibilities for providing security, in essence c*ate's monopoly*
on the use of force. By the beginning of Y*rm, the Com-*
monwealth of Independent States ranke*d Bank's 1997*
World Development Report in the category*e of core func-*
tions, even lower than the underdevelop*haran Africa.[61]*

When the state lacks the capacity to*unctions, soci-*
etal pressure on that state is unlikely t*ults. The visi-*
ble decline in the state's capacities disc*from engaging*
government and turned them "inwar*overnment, all*
kinds of societal groups looked sime*ice and goods*
provision left by the unreformed *market. The*
average citizen became more likel*ven criminal,*
networks for solutions to proble*nt agencies—*
and much rather than to fledgling*ting to engage*
government agencies. *kness of polit-*

The underdevelopment of p*ing civil soci-*
ical parties, has constituted a *rginal role in*
ety. As discussed in chapter*ots. With the*
Russian politics. They also *m to represent*
possible exception of the C*national poli-*
broad societal interests or *federal level,*
tics. Regionally based par*n able to offer*
and "national" parties cr*to win Duma*
much to their members*and society as*
seats contributed to th*ve support for*
they became eligible fo
reelection and no lon

Neither parties nor NGOs of a liberal-democratic orientation succeeded in influencing electoral and policy outcomes in the 1990s, and therefore both justifiably perceive each other as weak and ineffective partners. Instead, parties have sought electoral resources from other outlets, such as the oligarchs and government insiders, while NGOs have tended to avoid the electoral process altogether. Civic organizations have seen little benefit from participating in the electoral process, while political parties have discerned no electoral benefit from catering to insignificant civic groups.

Economic and political structures alone do not account for the absence of a civically active citizenry. Russians themselves do their share. The first barrier in this regard is the demobilization effect common to all states undergoing radical transformation. When the old system falls, the raison d'être of the civic groups mobilized to achieve systemic change also disappears.[62] In Russia, Democratic Russia and its allies seemed to have fulfilled their mandate when communism collapsed. What united many of them in the last years of Gorbachev's tenure was their opposition to the Soviet regime, and not some positive agenda, thus their mission expired with the Soviet Union. Democratic Russia and groups like it had difficulty making the transition to "normal" politics in the post-Soviet era, as did their followers. Moreover, unmet expectations on the part of those who did demonstrate to bring down communism made people less willing to organize a second time in the post-communist era.

Second, the demobilization effect is reinforced by another Soviet legacy: ingrained mistrust among the population.[63] This mistrust is aimed primarily at officialdom, but also at all people and institutions outside people's own circle of intimates.[64] Public opinion surveys showed low levels of trust for all major state and nonstate institutions throughout the 1990s. Note that the political parties, the parliament, the regional and local governments, the trade unions, the courts, and the police enjoyed significantly lower levels of trust than the churches and the armed forces, yet it is these least trusted institutions that a civil society needs to engage.[65] Even compared with other post-communist societies, trust between citizens in Russia is comparatively low.[66] During seven decades of communism, all citizens were forced to participate in many kinds of party-mandated organizations, from the Komsomol to trade and professional unions and cultural and sports clubs. Thus it is not surprising that for many people freedom after the collapse came to signify not the freedom to participate in public organizations, but the freedom not to participate. Marc Morje Howard also finds evidence for a preference for small "friendship networks" rather than for formal, less personal organizations, a preference that is markedly stronger in Russia than in other post-communist countries.[67] Soviet citizens learned to trust no one and rely on no one outside these essentially private networks, and post-Soviet citizens are reluctant to give up support that has proven effective in the past.

In addition to these hindrances, another less obvious barrier may be at work: our own analytical lens. Russia's new societal actors may be performing functions that Westerners would not associate with civil society, but that are nonetheless vital to the sustainability of the new market and democratic order. The collapse of the Soviet welfare safety net and the new socioeconomic conditions opened up a huge gap between people's needs and the state's ability or willingness to address them. The market did not step in to fill that gap and citizens have had to fend for themselves. Thus new associations stepped in to cope with problems of immediate importance to ordinary citizens: nutrition, shelter, health and sanitation, poverty, basic human rights, and ecological disasters. Many of these organizations have sprung up almost on an ad hoc basis as problems of this nature arose to make life livable for communities.[68] Because groups concerned with welfare provision are mostly small and formed on a local grassroots basis, little reliable information is available about the extent of their activities or the magnitude of their impact.

Some research into this function of Russia's civil society suggests that public associations formed during the Yeltsin era are quite important to achieve "a climate of self-generated social welfare to replace the paternalistic model of state provision."[69] This focus on basic needs and urgent problems, rather than on interest representation or lobbying for policy change, may constitute a distinctly post-Soviet way for a society to assert its autonomy from the state. The state took full responsibility for basic welfare only in formerly communist and socialist regimes. In new democracies without the legacy of such extensive statism, populations have always had to ensure their own survival. Consequently, in previously communist countries we can justifiably regard organizing for social welfare provision as an assertion of greater independence and an expression of increasing societal activism. This function of the new, nongovernmental, grassroots society requires further empirical investigation to determine its scope and whether we have overstated its importance. Also in need of further investigation is the possibility that these welfare-enhancing organizations have evolved to mediate between the state and society, a function more in line with the normative expectations of civil society theorists.[70] In addition, Russian citizens have continued to rely on their extensive social networks to deal with economic hardship. Some have speculated that these social networks could become the bases of a more vibrant, Western type of civil society.[71]

The Putin Era

Since Putin became Russia's second post-communist president in the spring of 2000, none of the structural or institutional impediments to the development of civil society have weakened or changed fundamentally. What has seemed to change is the government's policy regarding civil society. Whereas Yeltsin showed benign neglect, Putin and his team have introduced new policies, regulations, and laws whose effect has been to restrict the power and reach of civil society even further. Putin's state has curbed the activity of nongovernmental actors in some areas, co-opted them in other spheres, and rendered the institutional environment less friendly to civic activism in general. In response, some re-mobilization can be seen at the elite level and less at the grassroots levels.

Threatening Civil Society

Putin has often made statements championing the development of civil society. Addressing his representatives in the newly created supra-federal districts on their first anniversary, Putin identified the "establishment of civil society structures in the regions" as one of their eight basic responsibilities.[72] In June 2000, he met with representatives from various organizations and emphasized the importance of a "positive dialogue between the state and civil society," as well as the former's responsibility to support the latter. Most dramatically, in November 2001, his staff organized the Civic Forum. This congress of civic groups held in the Kremlin brought together thousands of civic leaders with representatives of the state, including Putin. The spectacle of Putin on the same podium as human rights activist Lyudmila Alekseeva appeared to be a historic moment in Russian state-society relations.

Putin's concept of civil society, which if it involves societal activism and participation is of a state-supporting kind, is, however, far from the paradigmatic vision described earlier. Putin once told a group of Media-Most journalists that their job was to support the state. Similarly, a "positive dialogue" with the state requires public organizations to work toward the same goals as the state. He champions a fundamentally state-centric view, dividing activity in every sphere into pro-state and antistate; criticism or embarrassment of the state could only be the latter. In a typical expression of this view, Gleb Pavlovsky, Putin's one-time political adviser, accused those who were publicly critical of the Kremlin in connection with Gazprom's takeover of the private television station (NTV) of seeking to "shatter the Presidential Administration." In other words, Putin sees criticism not as an exercise of the freedom of speech, but as a blatant campaign of antistate activity.[73]

Sergei Markov, director of the Institute for Political Studies and one of the organizers of the Civic Forum, offers a fitting testament to Putin's views. Addressing alleged problems within the human rights movement, Markov wrote:

> In Soviet times, it was the State that was the main abuser of human rights. That is why the human rights movement in the USSR naturally crystallized in an atmosphere of profound mistrust of the Soviet State. However, in post-Soviet Russia the sources of human rights abuses changed, but the human rights movement retained its traditional Soviet era human rights ideology.[74]

Markov went on to identify powerful "interest" groups as the real abusers of human rights, noting that the way to battle these perpetrators is to side with the state, which is making an earnest effort to "bridle the 'interest' groups."

Sergei Karaganov, director of the Institute of Europe, has identified "overcoming opposition of society" as one of Putin's main current challenges.[75] The opposing "society" here applies not only to civil, but also to political and economic society. The strategy of Putin's government appears to be to eliminate as many opposing actors from the political playing field as possible and to create what some of his advisers call "managed democracy."

The NGO community has asserted generally that the government's treatment of civil society has worsened since Putin assumed the presidency. According to Lev Ponomarev, long-time human rights activist, "Every day under Putin, things get a little worse, and eventually, will be a lot worse."[76] Under Putin, Russia has seen increased harassment of NGOs and other independent entities by the police, the Federal Security Service (FSB), and the tax collecting authorities, which have now been subordinated to the FSB; denial of mandatory registrations to legitimate NGOs; arrests of and legal suits initiated against prominent activists; and assaults on media sources unfriendly to the Kremlin. Many of the tools the state agencies use to curb undesirable activities originated under Yeltsin; therefore placing all the blame for acts belligerent to civil society on Putin and his government would be misleading. Nevertheless, Putin's ascendancy to power has been accompanied by a perceptible change in atmosphere.

The most common tactic for curbing civic activity is for the Ministry of Justice to turn down registration and re-registration applications. According to the new law on public associations, those NGOs that were not registered by June 30, 1999, can be shut down by a court order at any time. The Glasnost Public Foundation, a human rights watchdog, asserts that "nearly half of non-governmental organizations" were "eradicated" before this deadline, citing official Ministry of Justice statistics that as of the deadline, only 58 percent of the previously registered number, had registered at the federal level.[77]

The registration process is deliberately complex. Among other requirements, organizations must prove the existence of office space and representation in at least forty-six of the eighty-nine regions, meaning that the government has plenty of "legal" reasons for denying registration to any given group. The re-registration process is not impartial: the government appears to have targeted organizations that could potentially be problematic for the state.[78] The Glasnost Public Foundation has identified human rights and environmental organizations and independent trade unions, the groups that have challenged government policies in the past, as prime targets. Prominent environmental activist Alexander Nikitin agrees, claiming that one-third of all ecological and human rights NGOs have ceased to be legal entities as a result, including some of the oldest NGOs, such as the Glasnost Defense Foundation, a group that defends independent media, which was denied registration all over the country. Several human rights NGOs, including Ecology and Human Rights, the Glasnost Defense Foundation, and Memorial, reported that when they tried to re-register, they were instructed to remove the "protection of citizens' rights" from their mission and goal statements on the grounds that protecting citizens' rights is the business of the state.[79]

Nontraditional religious groups have also come under attack. The 1997 Law on Freedom of Conscience and Religious Associations passed under

Yeltsin was already an exceptionally discriminatory law that left the status of religions other than Christianity, Judaism, Islam, and Buddhism to the whims of local officials. An amendment to the law signed by Putin made survival for the unwelcome religions even more difficult: the deadline for re-registration was extended to December 31, 2000, leaving those unregistered after the date subject to "liquidation" by court order. Although the amendment does not directly eliminate the undesirable forms of public life, it relegates them to the forces of local prejudices, of bureaucratic tyranny and incompetence, and of pressure from the powerful Russian Orthodox Church.

Local governments gladly stepped up to the challenge. One of the most notorious cases was Moscow's denial of registration for the Salvation Army under the pretext that it is a militarized organization whose staff wears uniforms and that confers military titles, and may therefore present a threat to the government. The administrators of justice in Kirov Oblast banned all activities by a Pentecostal community after viewing video footage of a Pentecostal liturgy taped by an Orthodox Russian priest. Experts concluded that such activity "might be detrimental to health," and no further investigations were carried out.[80] In Cheboksary, the authorities tried to ban another Pentecostal group, because it "offered up prayers for healing, although they did not hold a medical license."[81]

As of September 2000, only 9,000 of the 17,000 religious groups in Russia had been able to register.[82] According to more recent estimates, 6,000 local religious groups were denied registration—a full 30 percent of all religious groups operating on Russian territory.[83] These organizations are subject to liquidation at any time.

Troublesome organizations not stopped by denial of registration are harassed by what has become a favorite method in the Putin era: the selective enforcement of the rule of law. A number of environmental and human rights groups have reported harassment by the General Procuracy, the tax police (before this organization was dissolved), and the FSB. In August 2000, armed masked men accompanied by a uniformed police official raided the offices of the Glasnost Public Foundation, holding personnel at gunpoint for nearly an hour. Before being forced out of business, the newspaper *Obshchaya Gazeta* reported on several cases of independent youth groups targeted by the FSB.[84]

In addition to the aforementioned uses of the law to prevent or stunt the operations of public associations, the taxation of the nonprofit sector, especially the taxation of foreign assistance, has also encountered setbacks. According to one provision of the new Tax Code, grants made to individuals are subject to a weighty 35.9 percent tax, payable by the organization providing the grant. Pernicious effects are already evident. For example, George Soros, one of the most prominent foreign supporters of civil society in Russia, has suspended his educational grant program, which has contributed $80 million in grants to support poor students, teachers, and professors over the last decade. NGOs have formed a national coalition to lobby for a package that protects the nonprofit sector, but these issues are not at the top of the legislative agenda.[85]

The new Labor Code could deliver perhaps the heaviest legislative blow to independent public organizing. While the Soviet era code was obviously anachronistic, the new code greatly diminishes unions' power to protect the interests of their members. The new code eliminates union approval for firing workers, deprives unions of the right to maintain offices or personnel on factory premises, replaces collective bargaining with individual agreements, and gives company management the discretion to deal with or ignore unions.[86] Pro-union deputies introduced an alternative version, but it received a lukewarm response from most members of parliament.[87]

In one unique case, Putin's government exercised its property rights in a parastatal organization, the All-Russian Center for Public Opinion Research (VTsIOM), to compel it to privatize. This oldest of Russian polling firms had a reputation for publishing accurate data on people's attitudes, including attitudes about political parties and electoral preferences. Many, including Yuri Levada, its long-time director, have asserted that the requirement to privatize was intended to eliminate this valuable source of information about Russian politics.[88] Levada and his team avoided the muzzling tactic by reconstituting a new firm, VTsIOM-A, though the long-term future of this new organization is uncertain.

Finally, one of the defining features of the Putin regime is an increasing climate of fear, termed by some "the KGBization of the state." The harassment of activists, researchers, and journalists, initiated under Yeltsin and during Putin's FSB tenure and continued during Putin's presidency, has been communicating a clear message to those involved in independent activities. In July 1999, while serving as head of the FSB, Putin wrote in the military newspaper *Krasnaya Zvezda* that Russian environmentalists supported by Western funds could be considered spies.[89] If enterprising individuals choose to engage in activities that concern certain sensitive issues—the impact of military activity or the ecological consequences of federal policies, for instance—they should be aware that full-scale "legal" harassment campaigns will be unleashed against them. Putin has professed to harbor great respect for environmentalists, but his admiration seems to be directed toward those who protect wildlife habitats or clean up neighborhoods, not those who investigate the mishandling of nuclear waste by the military. The FSB has targeted prominent individuals with charges of espionage and treason, communicating to all those engaged in similar activities that no one is immune. Any individual deemed troublesome to the state can turn out to be one of these, vulnerable to persecution at any moment.[90]

The circumstances of these cases lend credibility to the assertion that Putin's FSB is trying to create a general climate of fear instead of simply addressing actual cases of espionage and other infractions of the law. The president pardoned Edmond Pope, the American businessman convicted of espionage, because of the state of his health. The conviction itself was crucial, not the actual crime or punishment, in communicating a clear warning to foreigners contemplating involvement with Russian military technology.

In 1997, the legal arm of Russia's Pacific Fleet sentenced Grigory Pasko to twenty months in jail for passing reports to a Japanese television channel on the mishandling of nuclear waste. Even though he was released under amnesty in November 2000, the Supreme Court ruled that his case could be sent back to a military tribunal for review. Even after the amnesty, Pasko can conceivably be imprisoned again. The warning in this case is clear: ecological ramifications of the military complex are still off limits to independent researchers.

Another example is that of Valentin Moiseev, accused of passing secret documents to South Korea, who was initially convicted in December 1999, and whose attempts to obtain a retrial have been drawn out with arbitrary obstructions. The deterrent is clear: even in cases in which the FSB cannot convict its targets of espionage, it can certainly draw out the proceedings long enough to make the relevant activities extremely costly for any individual.

A particularly noticeable component of the Putin administration is a degree of xenophobia harkening back to the Cold War era. Putin's administration and his executive agencies are deeply suspicious of any foreign involvement in internal activities. In November 1999, Igor Sutyagin, a scholar at the USA Canada Institute, was charged with espionage based on his work on civil-military relations funded by the Canadian Ministry of Defense and two Canadian universities and tried at a closed trial.[91] Human rights NGOs are convinced that the accusations are bogus and that the intent is to inhibit foreign-funded research of military or security matters.

In May 2001, the Academy of Sciences released a directive entitled "The Academy of Sciences plans to avoid any harm to the Russian state in the sphere of economic and scientific cooperation," which requires all Russian researchers and scientists to report their contacts with foreign individuals or organizations.[92] The following month, Putin proclaimed that there "is no honor" in Russian NGOs taking money from Western foundations.[93] Among other anti-Western moves, the Russian government has asked the Organization for Security and Cooperation in Europe to leave Chechnya; terminated its agreement with the American Peace Corps; and refused reentry into Russia to Irene Stevenson, director of Moscow's Solidarity Center of the American Federation of Labor and Congress of Industrial Organizations (AFL-CIO), who had worked in the country for fifteen years.

Co-opting Civil Society

In parallel with efforts to curb antistate activity, Putin's government has tried to recruit allies among societal actors as well as create new civic groups funded by the state.

Most ambitiously, the Foundation for Effective Technologies—a Kremlin-sponsored NGO—was instrumental in organizing the November 2001 Civic Forum. Putin and many other senior government officials participated in the meeting, inspiring hope among some NGO leaders,[94] although the most vocal critics of the Putin government did not participate.[95]

The Civic Forum was the most visible attempt to co-opt civil society, but not the only such initiative. Putin has demonstrated a proclivity for meeting with and endorsing organizations that support what he sees as traditional Russian values and are not enthusiastic about pluralistic ideas. These are apolitical groups that do not concern themselves with affairs of state or groups and are not in a position to significantly affect public opinion. For instance, Unity and then its successor, United Russia—the political party most closely affiliated with Putin—has launched a Komsomol-inspired youth movement, "Youth Unity," also referred to as "Pusomol" (Putin's Komsomol), to build up patriotic pride and instill the proper values in Russia's youth. Working Together is another youth group sponsored by the state.

In June 2001, Putin extended an offer of formal partnership to some elements of civil society. He met with representatives of more than thirty NGOs, proposing to create a charter of civil unions to unite nonpolitical public organizations. The organizations Putin chose to invite to the meeting, however, were far from the most influential NGOs, and included stamp collecting, gardening, educational, cultural, and sports organizations and only a few that could be considered even remotely political.[96]

Similarly, in November 2001 the Russian Press Institute's Vitaly Ignatenko, the National Association of Television and Radio Broadcasters' Eduard Sagalayev, and new Media Union head Aleksandr Lyubimov created a new journalists' union, *Mediasoyuz*, sanctioned by the Kremlin, to counterbalance the "oppositionist" Russian Journalists' Union. This new union consists of journalists working for state-owned or state-loyal mass media.[97] Independent environmental groups also claim that the Kremlin is creating and funding its own ecological organizations, ones that would cooperate with state structures rather than attempt to overturn presidential decrees.[98] Other rumors claim that the Kremlin is behind "Eurasia," a new nationalist movement dedicated to reviving traditional Russian values.[99]

Putin has also reached out to the Russian Orthodox Church, encouraging it to play a greater role in social and political affairs.[100] He asked Patriarch Aleksii II to bless his ascension to the presidency. The president also attends Orthodox services on major holidays, maintains contact with the church's leading personalities, and has honored Orthodox priests with awards "for contributions to the rebirth of spiritual and moral traditions" in Russia.[101] The Orthodox Church eagerly accepted Putin's invitation to engage in political issues, blessing troops on their way to Chechnya and even naming a patron saint of tax inspectors.

In the same spirit, when trade unions voiced their dissatisfaction with the draft Labor Code, Putin's government chose to reach out to the larger Soviet era FNPR rather than to the independent trade unions to work on the draft with state officials. Indeed, according to Duma Deputy Oleg Shein, the FNPR was the only union to advise its members not to participate in the May 17, 2000, protest against the code, one of the biggest collective worker actions in post-communist Russia.[102] The FNPR's participation yielded dividends, however, because the new Labor Code provided it with huge advantages over new independent unions.[103]

Societal Responses to the Putin Regime

Some elements of Russian society have responded to the actions of Putin's government in a manner reminiscent of a paradigmatic civil society. For instance, in January 2001, human rights activists organized the Congress in Defense of Human Rights in response to specific antidemocratic policies of Putin's government. This congress issued the first official statement of civic opposition to Putin's regime.[104] Organizers emphasized that it was an "extraordinary" congress, assessing the state of affairs in Russia to be a veritable emergency that requires a decisive response from the human rights community. This was one the largest public events dedicated to human rights in post-Soviet times, drawing more than 1,000 activists and representing more than 300 organizations and 65 regions.

Aside from the event itself, already a considerable achievement, the congress was significant for two main reasons. First, perhaps for the first time, the fragmented human rights community was able to unite and transcend its disagreements. The development of civil society has suffered because of poor cooperation among different organizations working in the same realm. The participation rate and the diversity of groups represented were unprecedented, the degree of consensus reached on major issues of concern was even more impressive. With near unanimity, the congress passed firm resolutions on such contentious issues as the threats to the constitutional order, the brutal campaign in Chechnya, the freedom of the press, and social and civil rights. There is some basis for hope that the consolidation of the human rights movement may continue. The participants recognized the need to institutionalize collaboration within the movement and set up working groups that will meet regularly to come up with a coherent position and concrete proposals on each issue of concern.

Second, the participants recognized that at least the upper-level segment of civil society is asserting an active role in dealing with human rights issues politically. One of the resolutions of the congress was to create a committee "For the Termination of War and Establishing Peace in the Chechen Republic," which was launched in March 2001. Committee membership bridged the divide between civil and political society, because it included several Duma deputies and the now former president of Ingushetia Ruslan Aushev alongside human rights activists and prominent intellectuals. The committee has called for peace talks between Putin and Chechnya's President Ruslan Maskhadov. Its plan of action included, perhaps too optimistically, uniting the mass media, politicians, public activists, and the general public in support of ending the war and the committee wrote open letters to both presidents, to which Maskhadov replied with approval. The human rights congress met again in October 2003 and passed resolutions on everything from a call to end the war in Chechnya to a demand to respect the constitutional rights of jailed billionaire Mikhail Khodurkovsky.

To date, however, the concrete achievements of the newly mobilized groups have been few. Judging from the numbers that attend antiwar demonstrations or have joined these groups recently, society at large still is not ready to mobilize for political causes.

Societal mobilization around NTV's takeover (see chapter 7) represented an equally mixed result. On the one hand, mass demonstrations on the streets of Moscow to defend the television company against seizure by proxies for the Putin government signaled that part of Russian society understood the importance of independent media. Since the collapse of the Soviet Union, such mass events from the liberal sector of Russian society have been rare. Vladimir Gusinsky, founder of NTV, and his team could claim to command public backing, because thousands of people (20,000 by NTV's liberal estimation) participated in the two street demonstrations in defense of NTV's independence. Likewise, Yabloko, Democratic Russia, and some members of the Union of Right Forces spoke out against the Kremlin's assault on the freedom of speech and the independent press and attended the rallies and protests in defense of NTV. In the eyes of many of the media elite, the attack on NTV was a KGB-style "covert operation launched by the Kremlin," signaling the "death of democracy" and the restoration of a "quasi-Soviet system."[105] In the face of adversity, some unity seemed to materialize between the media, the political parties, and the public.[106]

The protests did not last, however. The government seized NTV and the Russian majority fell silent. In April 2001, the Public Opinion Foundation reported that 43 percent of its respondents viewed the conflict as a financial matter, whereas only 30 percent attributed it to political motives. VTsIOM's results reveal that 35 percent agreed that the conflict was a "massive attack on the freedom of speech," while 43 percent disagreed. Polls by firms all suggest that the majority did not view NTV and Gusinsky's holding as a symbol of free speech.

The lack of public response to the closure of TV-6, another independent station to which many former NTV staff flocked after NTV's seizure, was even more pronounced. The public paid no attention at all to the campaign against TV-6. When asked about their reactions to the closing of TV-6, the largest share of respondents—38 percent—expressed indifference.[107] Realizing the dearth of public interest, TV-6 staff did not organize public appeals, demonstrations, or work-ins. Led by Evgeny Kiselev, NTV's core cast moved to a third station, TVS, which won the backing of several oligarchs and therefore seemed to be on a better financial footing than either NTV or TV-6 had enjoyed before. When TVS was closed down in the spring of 2003, society did not even seem to notice.

Another instance of notable societal mobilization also ended with uncertain results. On May 17, 2000, Presidential Decree Number 867 abolished the State Committee for Environmental Protection and the Federal Forestry Service, and entrusted the functions of these agencies to the Ministry of Natural Resources. At the same time, the Duma was scheduled to vote on a bill backed by the Atomic Energy Ministry that would allow the importation of spent nuclear material into Russia for ten to fifteen years for reprocessing. This restructuring consolidated environmental protection, monitoring, and "exploitation of natural resources in a single agency. Many outraged environmental activists and scientists described the new arrangement as appointing the wolf to watch the sheep. The Atomic Energy Ministry's plan to raise revenues by importing and reprocessing spent nuclear fuel from as many as fourteen countries would generate radioactive waste, creating a hazardous environmental situation in a state already beset by potentially catastrophic environmental problems.

Until June 14, 2000, those outraged by these reforms were, according to ecologist and activist Alexei Yablokov, "voices crying in the wilderness."[108] On that date, however, Russia's dispersed environmental movement transcended its differences, much as the human rights movement did the following January, to convene at the All-Russian Emergency Conference for Environmental Protection, where more than 450 delegates from 58 regions pressed the minister of natural resources to account for the reorganization.

The clear unanimity of dissent revealed at the conference prompted an extraordinary and decisive action. A group of environmentalists led by Greenpeace and the Socio-Ecological Union launched a petition calling for a nationwide referendum to restore the abolished agencies and preclude voting on the draft law on nuclear imports. According to the constitution, such a referendum must take place if 2 million citizen signatures are collected within a certain period. Several organizations—Greenpeace, the Socio-Ecological Union, and Ecojuris—and notable members of numerous research institutions and think tanks also filed suits in the Supreme Court, organized numerous petitions to Putin, and endorsed a letter to the World Bank calling for freezing loans to Russia until the cut agencies had been reestablished.[109]

The Supreme Court suit was unsuccessful. The petition to the World Bank produced partial results, as the Bank agreed to stall a $60 million forestry loan pending new arrangements that were consistent with the Bank's environmental standards. The greatest success and a real step forward, however, was the unprecedented scope of the signature collection campaign. The petition's organizers submitted 2.5 million signatures to the Central Electoral Commission. The commission ultimately disqualified enough of the signatures to bring the valid number under the required 2 million, thereby forestalling the referendum. Nonetheless, the campaign triggered a consolidation of the fragmented civil society and broke through the slumbering civic consciousness of many citizens. The elite research and activist community, which organized the drive, seemed to have finally accepted that grassroots public organizations must be drawn into the effort if they were to have any chance of success. Russia is a vast country, and collecting signatures across its eighty-nine regions made local initiatives absolutely essential. To accomplish the task, local environmental organizations set up headquarters in sixty-two regions, creating a rare link between the upper and lower levels of civil society. Leaders of grassroots NGOs such as the Movement for Nuclear Safety were able to work with expert environmental researchers and well-known activists for the first time.[110] The experience of the petition drive also helped to bring the environmental movement and the human rights movement closer. Even a political party, Yabloko, became increasingly interested in engaging with civil society leaders once party officials understood the potent mobilizing potential of this campaign.

The campaign united not only the various civil society institutions, but also the unorganized and passive citizenry, whose support and signatures were essential. As many participating activists pointed out, collecting signatures in post-Soviet Russia is not an easy task: most people still harbor strong Soviet era fears about challenging the authorities and, as mentioned earlier, continue to mistrust all organizations. This means that signature collectors had to approach many more than the final 2.5 million signatories; however, those who did sign exhibited some degree of civic consciousness and responsibility.

The movement to contest this government decision hinted that the potential for Russian society to acquire traits closer to the Western paradigm has not disappeared. The alliance of the organizational power and expertise of the environmental movement elite, the workers and local resources of the grassroots organizations, the active press coverage, and the general public's willingness to support civic initiatives brought life to a vision that inspired the resurgence of the concept of a mobilized society checking the state's exercise of power. [111]

Ultimately, the referendum did not change policy, at least not as of the time of writing, but the campaign clearly worried the Kremlin. In response to accusations of an irresponsible coupling of functions within one agency, the Ministry of Natural Resources and the Kremlin put much effort into justifying and explaining their behavior.[112] The ministry clearly signaled its intent to solve this issue in collaboration with the environmental movement. Ministry officials proposed holding a third conference of experts and NGOs, and agreed to the movement's proposal for a common council. Putin also met with a group of researchers, and at least rhetorically agreed to meet their calls for a national ecological doctrine,[113] and in a somewhat clumsy and naïve attempt, ten days after the campaign failed Putin revealed his "secret" dream to become an environmental activist, while his wife publicly donated $300 to the World Wildlife Fund.

The scope of activities of society at the grassroots has changed little from the Yeltsin years. As was the case throughout the 1990s, small local groups continue their efforts to provide social welfare and to address the problems arising from state policies. Whereas large-scale events orchestrated by prominent organizations and activists are intended to prevent, reverse, or push through specific federal policies, efforts by smaller organizations strive to minimize the negative impact of such policies, be they the transition to a market economy or simply new regulations harmful to some constituency. While the discriminatory law on religious associations claimed numerous victims across Russia, many threatened religious groups have been saved and their status restored through grassroots efforts. For instance, the Slavonic Legal Center initiated and won several cases, reinstating a Pentecostal group in Kirov, the Kostroma Christian Center, and the "Church of Grace."[114] In more publicized cases, NGO-backed legal challenges successfully contested the denial of legal status to Jehovah's Witnesses in the Supreme Court. Similar case-by-case attempts to mitigate the negative consequences of policies and circumstance remain the common fare of grass-roots society.

Conclusion

Neither Soviet nor post-Soviet society could be said to conform to the West-ern ideal of civil society. In the Soviet era, society was organized and dom-inated by the party-state, with hidden, private dissent as its only independent activity. Under Gorbachev's leadership, society aggressively asserted independence, but moved to destroy the regime rather than to reform or democratize it through engagement with the state. The vigorous activity during Gorbachev's tenure transcended, or rather amalgamated, the civil, political, and economic realms. Concluding whether the proliferation of independent groups and mass actions signaled a birth of a civil or a polit-ical society is difficult. After the collapse, elements of post-Soviet society have tried to emulate the practices of their counterparts in Western democ-racies, while at the same time defending Russia's weak democratic institu-tions from further erosion, but other forms of societal activity have often overshadowed these organizations, be they social groups left over from the Soviet era or new, oligarchic, collective actors created by Russia's particular kinds of market reforms. In addition, the structure of the economy and party system, the organization and low capacity of the state, the population's weariness of upheaval, and the lingering mistrust among the people will probably continue to frustrate these democratic elements in the near future.

If we approach post-Soviet Russia with a broader concept of civil society in mind, the impression is somewhat more hopeful. Some Soviet organiza-tions have adapted to the new conditions and are able to act effectively on behalf of their members. Rather than acting as enemies of civil society devel-opment, some of these groups must be considered as part of Russia's new, hybrid civil society. In addition, small grassroots associations, although weak and nearly invisible, have been mounting efforts to fill the gap in social welfare provision and respond to urgent problems in an ad hoc man-ner. Although such activity does not directly enhance democracy, it does something important, that is, it enables the population to weather the hard-ships of a new economic climate. Over the long haul, these social networks may help Russian society survive the storm of "transition" and thereby help put society in a position to be more civic minded as the economy improves.

Moreover, the role of civil society has not been constant over the last fifteen years. Centuries of passivity did not stop grassroots, autonomous groups from playing a central role in making and breaking state policies at the end of the Soviet period. More recently, civil society has been less engaged and less influential, but still present and unlikely to wither away completely. No "iron hand," be it Putin's or his successor's, is likely to ever have the capacity to suppress the independent life of Russian society completely. Today, this society seems content to allow Putin and his team a free hand in reinvigorating the power and reach of the state at the expense of democratic practices and personal liberties. Several years of economic growth after a decade of decline have increased the freedom to maneuver of those in the Kremlin. Two circumstances, however, could alter this situation. First, a sudden economic downturn could erode support for Putin and his policies and create opportunities for his opponents both in the state and society. How the current regime responds to such a crisis would reveal its true intentions regarding democratic consolidation. A regime too exposed as leaning toward dictatorship might be the very development that spurs Russian society back into action. Second, if economic growth does continue over a period of years, the beneficiaries of growth will eventually want to limit the discretionary power of the state and influence its policies. When this moment will come is impossible to predict. The first term of Putin's presidency makes the emergence of full-fledged civil society seem further away than it did at the beginning of the Putin era.

7

The Mass Media

Andrei Ryabov

Every definition of a liberal democracy includes independent media as a critical component. Theorists of democratic transitions have highlighted the critical role that liberalizing media can play in forcing the pace of democratization. Russia has been no exception. The development of independent mass media, even if a sporadic and unfinished process, played a key role in Russia's postcommunist political transition and democratization. Thus the history of their development over the past decade and the obstacles they encountered has generated intense interest among political scientists and analysts and has inspired a vast amount of literature, both in Russia and abroad.[1]

The media played a pivotal role in easing the hold of the omnipresent communist ideology on society in the late Soviet period and in mobilizing broad social support for democratic change. Throughout the 1990s, the media evolved and gradually transformed into an important tool of political struggle in the hands of Russia's leading political and business elites. Currently, the role of the mass media as a catalyst for democracy has become less influential. Why did this occur? What are the implications for the future of Russian democracy? To provide answers to these questions, this chapter traces the rise and fall of Russian media as a force for democratization.

The Troubled Birth of Russia's Democratic Media

Starting with Mikhail Gorbachev's perestroika program and the associated policy of glasnost, state control over the media was gradually lifted. The press was given greater freedom, and the media became a vital channel for public information on the views and objectives of various social, professional, and, later, political groups. This liberalization of the mass media helped to connect people both to each other and to the outside world, so long shut away from both by communism and the Iron Curtain. By lifting the taboo of open discussion about previously closed political topics, such as Soviet history or unpopular aspects of official government policy, the mass media took on a wholly new role, alien to their traditional function in Soviet society before Gorbachev. From their former subordinate role the mass media rose to become the engine of democratization. During the Gorbachev era, a new generation of independent-minded journalists and commentators at such papers as *Moscow News*, *Argumenty i Fakty*, *Ogonyok*, and *Izvestiya* was ahead of the political elite and civil society in leading the charge toward democratic reform.

During the Gorbachev era, liberalization did not mean privatization. The state still owned or subsidized most media outlets and all electronic media. During the early years of Gorbachev's perestroika, when the mass media seemed to be developing into something arguably resembling a "fourth estate," they were far from being independent either economically and politically. With no access to advertising or private investment markets, the media necessarily remained part of the traditional Soviet state economy. The only reason for the existence of objective, multisource news coverage in the late 1980s was that it was in the interests of the two most powerful groups: the reformist wing in the soviets and the leadership of the Communist Party of the Soviet Union (CPSU). The reasons for this apparently counterintuitive support will be explained later, but the key point here is that despite its eventual popularity among the public, glasnost did not develop spontaneously and most likely would not have prevailed had government authorities chosen to block it.[2]

Indeed, the media's pluralism during the first years of perestroika was largely propelled by the ideological and political splits within the ranks of the ruling elite, that is, between the conservative hard-liners and the new reform-minded elite. The intense struggle in the upper ranks of the party and Soviet echelons prompted both sides to appear supportive of objective mass media, which, in turn, created opportunities for gradual liberalization of the media that often went beyond even the CPSU reform wing's original intentions. Seeking to mobilize public support, reformers promoted mass media support of democratic changes and thereby indirectly gave the media greater freedom. In the republics, nationalist leaders were particularly active in securing independence from the federal government for local media. Conservatives, seeing how rapidly orthodox communist ideology was losing currency, promoted the development of media groups that focused on the traditionally-oriented sections of society who disapproved of Gorbachev's policy for nationalistic and protectionist reasons. Independent communist publications proliferated faster than democratic outlets.[3]

In 1990, this ideological split finally spilled onto national television. The new Russian television station, Russian Television and Radio (RTR), on channel two and created at the initiative of the reform-minded Chairman of the Supreme Soviet Boris Yeltsin, was intended to inform and to provide support for radical political and socioeconomic views and developments, and in so doing counterbalanced the first national television station (ORT), which took a more conservative stance.[4]

Alongside the permissive political conditions provided from above by Gorbachev, another important factor encouraging the mass media's increasingly bold push for increased freedom of information was pressure from below by an information-starved public eager to know more. Over time, Gorbachev's launch of glasnost fueled expectations among the general public for rapid, radical change. This gave rise to social and political activism in the late 1980s that made use of the media as an instrument for breaking the diverse political and administrative barriers to freedom of information. It is in this context that the mass media appeared in the eyes of many to have developed into a special kind of fourth estate. This development in the early stages of the transition did not come about as a result of deep-seated economic or institutional change. Instead, it was largely unintended and determined by a series of coincidences, thus the trend was short-lived and hard to sustain once official political backing was removed.

Despite their weak foundations, the new mass media succeeded in carving out an important political role for themselves during the first years of perestroika, a role that they still hold to some extent even today. For example, during perestroika the mass media were instrumental in facilitating the formation of the first independent social and political associations. The newly independent mass media actually built on the traditions of the pre-perestroika Soviet press of the late 1970s and early 1980s when, in accordance with official communist ideology, the printed media attempted to support public initiatives, primarily at the local level, and especially those relating to the environment.[5]

With their growing influence in society, one of the mass media's new functions became their influence in the creation of the emerging new political elite. In liberal democracies, political parties assume primary responsibility for this task. Russia's lack of political parties at that time eliminated that option and allowed the media to step in instead. Indeed, it is no accident that the first generation of democratic politicians, particularly deputies in the USSR Congress of People's Deputies elected in 1989 and the Russian Congress of People's Deputies elected in 1990, included many writers, journalists, social scientists, and film directors. Even just "one successful article on a current topic instantly made its author a national celebrity and opened his or her direct access to the political arena."[6]

The mass media's departure from straightforward information reporting and communication, which on the surface remained their main function, and their transformation into a political entity were deeply rooted in their historic self-perception. Above all, the media viewed themselves as an institution whose "task involved not only informing the public or creating an authentic picture of reality, but also enlightening, agitating, and organizing the masses in the name of true values and ideals."[7] By adopting the role of an actor on the political stage, the mass media filled a political vacuum. At a time when the country had no active civil society able to mount coordinated pro-democracy movements or set up public organizations or any real political parties, the media became the vanguard of Russia's initial steps toward democratization.

The Test of Freedom: Yeltsin and the Market

Following the collapse of the Soviet Union in 1991, the mass media were compelled to redefine their relationship with the state. The initial post-Soviet, postcommunist phase was euphoric for most of the press. Those leaders whom the democratic press had supported during the last years of communism were now in power. The communist system, the media's long-time adversary, had left the historical scene. With some justification, leaders of the democratic mass media could claim that they had played an instrumental role in bringing about this outcome.

The rewards of victory were bittersweet. On the one hand, Yeltsin and the government took all the right steps to provide legal guarantees for an independent media sector. The first step was taken as early as 1990 with the adoption of the Soviet Law on Mass Media (confirmed in the Russian Legal Code in 1991), which upheld the mass media's legal independence from state control.[8] Publicly Yeltsin also reiterated his firm commitment to an independent press.

On the other hand, the media's financial standing became much more complex in the postcommunist era. During the last two years of the Soviet Union, the media received generous contributions from the state, while glasnost increasingly relieved them of ideological pressure from the CPSU. The situation could not have been better. The media continued to enjoy the benefits of the Soviet economy, including fixed prices on printing services and paper, privileged rates on leases of long-term facilities, and a centralized system of press distribution, while also being increasingly able to tap into additional formerly inaccessible funds from commercial activities such as advertising.[9] At the same time, these media outlets were subject to little control or supervision from their owner, the state. This comfortable position gave many editors a false sense of security and an altogether wrong impression of the real nature of the changes that a transition to the market would bring to the media industry. No one realized that soon the media's position would become untenable. As Iosif Dzyaloshinsky noted in a 2001 study in one of a series of Carnegie Moscow Center reports, in 1991 and 1992, on the threshold of radical market reforms, cohesive understanding of how changes might affect media organizations was lacking and "few [media leaders] made any effort to restructure their organization's economic base or reform the management of editorial boards."[10]

Radical reforms did come. With market reforms under way in 1992 and 1993, the advantageous economic status enjoyed by the printed mass media disappeared, and chief editors at all major publications encountered serious economic difficulties. The reason for this was twofold. First, subsidies declined significantly and the costs of printing and distribution increased proportionally. Second, because of rampant inflation and declining real incomes, demand dropped to unprecedented low levels. These difficulties did not stop the mass media from claiming a leading role in the political process. The media community's awareness of its own key role in the popular victory over communism led it to continue to view its main mission as pushing for democracy. Its model was the libertarian ideal of unrestrained individual freedom; not altogether by chance, the diametric opposite of the extreme that had existed under the Soviet political system.[11]

Taking Sides

Despite their overt espousal of broadly libertarian ideals, however, the great majority of media institutions were not ready for economic independence under market conditions. After long years of state support, most of them were still too dependent on subsidies to be able to entirely disassociate themselves from the government. In the end, the government connection proved quite powerful and was reflected in the political roles that the media came to play in the early postcommunist years. For most major media outlets the abstract, normative commitment to democratization became fused with the concrete policy of saving Yeltsin. Over time, the media's alliance with Yeltsin overshadowed their democratization mission. The alliance between President Yeltsin and the mass media that took shape during the August Republic (August 1991–October 1993) coalesced as a result of a common enemy: the Russian Supreme Soviet and its pro-communist outside backers.

The alliance between the mass media and the administration was mutually beneficial. The president's backing gave courage to the media community, many members of which felt threatened by the actions of the Supreme Soviet. The threats were real, as the parliament gradually did try to reinstate administrative controls over the press and other channels of mass information. For his part, confronted with a divided and polarized society, Yeltsin needed the backing of the mass media to mobilize public support behind his agenda. The media's cooperation with the executive branch of government was also helpful in the form of several important economic concessions, notably, an extensive renewed system of fixed prices on paper and partial subsidies on other production expenses. The mass media's willingness to enter into such an arrangement shows the duality of their commitment to reform. The liberal media allied themselves with those pushing for radical market reforms while at the same time avoiding market forces in relation to their economic sector.

Regardless of its inconsistencies, the alliance between the media and Yeltsin at least had the outward appearance of being resilient, and came to be eyed jealously by the Supreme Soviet. Indeed, the Supreme Soviet's new concern about reasserting authority over the media led it to court national television stations, whose popularity and influence among the public had risen dramatically in the early 1990s in comparison with other mass media. Faced with offers of an alliance with a predominantly communist Supreme Soviet, most journalists hastened to make explicit their preference for Yeltsin and his radical reform line. This inadvertent choice between the two political sides crushed the timid attempts by the television networks to take an independent position on the issues of the day, even though the television stations perceived their role as that of impartial informers and assistants in the resolution of specific social and human problems. During the political crisis of March 1993 they were unable to disassociate themselves in equal measure from the two sides of the conflict. Indeed, by the time of the September–October 1993 clash between the president and the Supreme Soviet, all the television channels gave their unconditional support to Yeltsin.[12]

The alliance between Yeltsin and the mass media proved lasting. Despite a handful of isolated conflicts, the relationship was solid and was supported by common long-term interests. Yeltsin understood that in exchange for his material and political support to the media, he could count on a favorable image in the press and unequivocal support in times of trouble. Meanwhile the mass media saw in Yeltsin a guarantee of the freedom they had gained since 1991. The 1996 presidential election campaign was decisive in this respect. Throughout the 1996 campaign, most of the mass media, formally independent by this time, supported Yeltsin, not only because of the implicit promise of lucrative financial profits, but also because they genuinely saw him as the only political candidate capable of thwarting a communist comeback.

The only time that this alliance between Yeltsin and the mass media soured was during the first Chechen war (December 1994–April 1996). The competing goals of the two sides could not be reconciled. Yeltsin initially saw the war as a tool that he could use to demonstrate the strength and efficacy of his leadership, an image he needed to regain public support and strengthen the state. Stability was slowly eroding because of widespread disappointment with his socioeconomic reforms.[13] Most of the media community, however, saw the war from a different perspective, and to them it was unacceptable for two reasons. First, the media feared that after the various cabinet reshufflings accompanying the Chechnya campaign, the decision-making initiative had passed to a group of political actors, the so-called Korzhakov group, active from 1993 to 1996, that sought to establish an administrative police regime in Russia of the kind that the democratic media had battled against since perestroika.[14] Second, for the mass media the war signaled the return of the state, which once again was trying to force its will upon the people, in this case the Chechens.[15] This rift between the media and the president was considerable, but by the spring of 1996, with the end of the war and the official launch of the presidential election, the close alliance between Yeltsin and the mass media was quickly restored. Every major media outlet supported Yeltsin.

Naturally, because of its very nature the union between Yeltsin and the mass media could not be an alliance of equals. The president played the role of senior partner, a status acquired largely because of his political victories in 1991 and 1993, in which the mass media had played a much less visible role. In 1992 and 1993, the general public and the elite resisted the strategy of radical market reforms that most of the mass media supported, and consequently these reforms were not implemented. Even after the overthrow of the Supreme Soviet on October 3–4, 1993, Yeltsin opted for a course of partial reforms that modernized, but did not altogether do away with, the former Soviet *nomenklatura*, thereby indirectly rejecting the strategy proposed by the media. The gradual disappearance of the communist threat combined with Yeltsin's moderate course undermined the media's claim to be the vanguard of the liberal revolution.

Privatization and the Media

During the early years of postcommunist Russia, a second constraining condition on the media's role in politics also emerged: the market. Ironically, the key change that produced a less critical and democracy-promoting press was privatization, along with the emergence of new private media firms. Market reforms initially helped to stimulate the growth of new media and independent outlets. Of these new companies, Media-Most, with its flagship television station, NTV, started by Vladimir Gusinsky in 1993, was the largest and most important. This media group rose to prominence during the first Chechen war, when its editorial line was decidedly more critical than that of state-controlled and state-affiliated media. In addition to NTV, Gusinsky owned a daily newspaper, *Segodnya*; acquired a major stake in a popular radio station, Ekho Moskvy; and later started a weekly magazine, *Itogi*, published in partnership with *Newsweek*.

Russia's other oligarchs followed Gusinsky's foray into mass media, but instead of starting new companies, these other oligarchs took advantage of their close ties with the federal government to obtain control, and sometimes ownership, of state media assets. Most surprisingly, Boris Berezovsky, a close confidant of the Yeltsin inner circle, acquired partial ownership and complete control of ORT, Russia's largest television station. Other Russian oligarchs also obtained minor shares in ORT, but Berezovsky exercised genuine property rights. He did so not because of his ownership stake, but through the use of second, off-budget salaries to key employees paid directly in cash by Berezovsky himself. By skillfully maneuvering among the various groups of shareholders and slipping bribes into the pockets of the management elite at the right time, the business tycoon ended up calling the shots at the largest officially independent public news corporation. Berezovsky also took control of another minor station, TV-6.

Nevertheless, the state continued to maintain major assets in television. The federal government retained RTR, while Yuri Luzhkov, the mayor of Moscow, and his quasi-private, quasi-state financial group, Sistema, founded TV-Center. Yet even the state channels served private interests. For instance, the advertising company Video International exercised strong influence over RTR's information policy through monopoly control over the channel's advertising time. Again, at the root of this arrangement was the media's economic dependence. The station's chronic underfunding from the government meant that the advertising revenues offered by Video International were RTR's only means for staying afloat, something that its management, understandably, valued above political independence. By the mid-1990s this trend became even more pronounced at the local level, where business control ranged from direct administrative subordination to indirect influence on editorial policy.

Russia's small group of financial houses and oil and gas companies also gobbled up most of the leading national newspapers. Specifically, the biggest Russian oil company, LUKoil, together with ONEXIM-Bank, gained control over *Izvestiya*, and ONEXIM-Bank acquired *Komsomolskaya Pravda*. The powerful national gas monopoly, Gazprom, bought the daily papers *Trud* and *Rabochaya Tribuna* and the magazine *Profil'*.[16]

Once in private hands, media outlets served a new set of purposes. The topics and style of media coverage were no longer determined primarily by journalists but by the media's new owners and, to a lesser extent, by various government institutions reasserting editorial control over their media holdings. The replacement of the media's democratizing mission with the more narrow goal of supporting Yeltsin, compounded by their economic dependence in the new market economy, explains their notable decline from the early transition period. The dual dependence of the democratic mass media—economic and ideological—explains why they did not develop into a fourth estate during the initial years of Yeltsin's presidency. Some tried but failed. For instance, Vitaly Tretyakov and his team established the *Nezavisimaya Gazeta* (Independent Newspaper). The intent was that the newspaper would be based on principles of pluralistic and inclusive editorial opinion and would be independent from government influence and even from pressures within the media industry. After a long and dramatic struggle to stay afloat, the newspaper fell under Berezovsky's control and became a tool for his political maneuvers.[17]

The erosion of the media's brief period of political independence and economic freedom had a negative impact on the basic freedom of information in society. A 1999 report, *The Anatomy of Free Speech: An Expert Study*, published by a group of Russian NGOs that included the Union of Russian Journalists, the Center on Law and the Mass Media, and the Union of Distributors of Press Productions and Titles, cited hundreds of instances in which freedom of expression in the media had been violated. The cases ranged from explicit prohibitions on the work of journalists in local regulatory laws to arbitrary administrative restrictions on reporters' access to information.[18]

At the same time, corruption among the mass media became an increasingly prevalent fact of life. Practices such as latent advertising (advertisements disguised as business or economic reporting) and so-called black public relations (the publication of commissioned articles against political rivals) became widespread in the media after the 1995–1996 national electoral cycle. More recently, the corruption of journalists has facilitated various media wars between oligarchic clans and other interest groups. Public relations specialists and political consultants now understand that media corruption is an important facet of working with the press.[19]

The Political Function of Media Controlled by the Oligarchs

The oligarchs acquired media assets to make money, but not in the traditional way. They were not seeking to maximize profits through advertising on popular programs. Given the depressed economy and accompanying limited consumer demand, media that relied on advertising could not be profitable. Rather, they acquired media assets to influence politics in a way that would produce economic payoffs via government connections.

Electoral Politics

A precondition for the oligarchs to make money through government contacts was to ensure that government leaders favorable to them stayed in power. By the mid-1990s Yeltsin had more or less rejected the path of radical political and socioeconomic reforms and instead focused on preserving the institutions and mechanisms already in place. Yeltsin's private convictions contradicted his public statements, which promised to maintain a rapid pace of reform and were intended to boost his image as an active reformer in the eyes of the business community and the public. As time went on, Yeltsin needed the media not to help him pursue economic or political change, but simply to stay in power. One of his most impressive attempts at feeding the illusion of reform to the public at the national level was in 1996, the year he threw in his bid for a second term in what would be a tough presidential campaign. At that time, Russia's ruling class supported Yeltsin as the best and only candidate worthy of the job, but his ratings in public opinion polls were mired in the single digits. Neither Yeltsin's campaign platform on Russia's future nor his past achievements in the socioeconomic realm were particularly impressive.

At this juncture, the value of Yeltsin's alliance with the media became apparent. His election headquarters orchestrated how the media portrayed Yeltsin's campaign, creating the illusion among a broad spectrum of voters that the president had an agenda for social reform and raising popular expectations for such an outcome. This was the pivotal point in the "mediazation" of Russian politics. Its essence was the creation of a parallel political reality that had little in common with the actual political process. Because all the major television channels supported Yeltsin, no independent source of information was available that could call into question the virtual world created by these television networks.

The specific mechanisms for generating information aimed at manipulating public opinion were diverse and were influential at a number of levels. The main techniques included the publication of reports about various initiatives by leading political actors and the targeted use of frequently fabricated leaks from government institutions that attributed fictitious statements to political figures refuted later in a lengthy, and hence highly publicized, series of investigative reports.[20]

Compensating for the lack of genuine political initiatives from the executive branch of government, the media dutifully fabricated sensational conflicts to detract public attention from the actual agenda and help Yeltsin at least maintain the Potemkin facade of successful reform. In 1996, for instance, the media constructed and immediately exposed two alleged conspiracies involving high-ranking government authorities who happened to be at odds with the president at the time. The first case implicated Defense Minister Pavel Grachev and the second targeted Security Council Secretary Aleksandr Lebed. Both instances involved alarmist stories about the threat these figures posed to democratization and economic reform in conjunction with their exposure either as revenge-seeking communists or major business magnates. In each case the mass media went out of their way to present the president as the guarantor of public order and stability and as the person who had resolutely thwarted the generals' dangerous, antidemocratic plots.

Justifying the use of such ethically dubious mechanisms Gleb Pavlovsky, a media representative who worked closely with the Kremlin, noted that their use was purely pragmatic. A president who did not possess reliable political or administrative structures was justified in resorting to the alternative, information-based form of influence that could target all levels of society.

Shaping Policy and the Government

The oligarchs promised to put the full weight of their media empires behind Yeltsin's reelection campaign in return for ownership of some of the country's most profitable companies. Yeltsin delivered the biggest reward during the 1996 presidential election, when Berezovsky acquired the Siberian oil company Sibneft in return for backing Yeltsin on ORT.

The oligarch wars that ensued after the 1996 election originated largely as a result of disputes about who received which promised assets. Gusinsky believed that he had been promised the rights to acquire the telecommunications company Svyazinvest as a reward for NTV's support of Yeltsin's campaign. When Gusinsky lost his bid to obtain this company, he retaliated by unleashing his media outlets on the new government. At that time, Berezovsky was his partner in putting together the failed bid for Svyazinvest. Thus two of the three largest television networks turned against the government.

The most successful intervention into the political sphere by Berezovsky's and Gusinsky's media outlets was the so-called case of the writers. The press accused a group of young reformers headed by Anatoly Chubais, Yeltsin's chief of staff, of receiving $100,000 for a small book about the history of Russia's privatization. These accusations received wide public attention. As a result of this scandal, Yeltsin was compelled to fire Chubais and several other young reformers from his government. This crisis spawned an almost permanent media war with the government.

Later in the year, the Korzhakov group used news reports especially selected from RTR broadcasts to convince Yeltsin to dismiss Oleg Poptsov, director of the Russian Television and Radio Company (the umbrella entity for RTR) on the grounds of disloyalty to the president. In the summer of 1998, by providing broad coverage of miners' protests at the government building in Moscow, the mass media successfully influenced Yeltsin's policy in relation to Prime Minister Sergei Kiriyenko. Perceiving Kiriyenko's policies as a threat to their business interests, the media stressed the weakness of the minister's government and the public's lack of confidence in him and convinced Yeltsin to withdraw his support for Kiriyenko.

Over time, the media also began to target the most powerful actor in the political system: the president. The Russian Constitution gives the president tremendous power and the office dominates the decision-making process. During his first years as president, Yeltsin made active use of a variety of democratic channels for deliberation and decision making, including consulting with experts in the Presidential Council. After the armed conflict with the Supreme Soviet in October 1993, Yeltsin's circle of contacts narrowed dramatically and he became less accessible. This trend continued into the late 1990s, and as a result the only way to reach the president was through the electronic media, which Yeltsin allegedly watched frequently, to the extent that media analyst and political adviser Pavlovsky openly noted in 1997 that the Russian mass media worked for one reader, viewer, and listener, namely, the president.[21]

The Restructuring of the Mass Media and the Impact on Society

The balance of influence wielded by different media outlets changed dramatically in the 1990s. Most important, the role and influence of the print media declined dramatically at the same time as the role and influence of television grew. Russia went from a "nation of readers" to a "nation of television-watchers."[22] From an economic perspective, the destruction of the centralized state system of press distribution and the resulting higher cost of distribution services, which often exceeded subscription revenues, accounted for the abrupt drop in consumer demand for printed material. At that time the advertising market could not compensate for the losses incurred by the inability to continue the low-price sales made possible by government subsidies. The resulting dramatic drop in readership drove down production and resulted in the virtual disappearance of the national press. As the number of political newspapers and magazines declined and the number and circulation of entertainment publications rose, television replaced print media as the most widespread source of information among the public.[23]

Another change to hit the media after perestroika pertained to its composition and intellectual orientation. Toward the end of the 1980s, the printed media served as society's intellectual inspiration, drawing much of their work from academic institutions, primarily theoretical and applied science institutes, as well as from the humanistic elite. But during the 1990s, when Russia stood at the crossroads of social development with its accompanying economic, political, and cultural implications, the intellectual elite largely lost its authority among the public.[24] Over the course of several years, all the respected print media essentially switched from providing information for the general public to being a source of information for the political and business elite, whose readership they ensured by launching political and business publications geared specifically at decision makers. Papers such as *Kommersant-Daily, Nezavisimaya Gazeta,* and *Izvestia,* and later *Segodnya, Russky Telegraph,* and *Gazeta,* became such "papers of influence."[25]

The demise of the national press for financial reasons, the drop in public interest in the political strategy for Russia's development, and the marginalization of the intellectual elite that had once served as the generator of new ideas resulted in changes in the structure of the print media market. A key change was an increase in the demand for local press, which in many ways became more relevant to people's daily lives. Yet these gains in influence by the local printed press at the expense of national publications pales in comparison with the rising influence of national television. Indeed, the transformation of television into the main source of news, along with its decisive influence on the public's political orientation and understanding of social processes, is indisputably one of the most notable features of contemporary Russian culture. Because of its continuous world news updates and viewers' feelings of personal involvement in broadcast events, live broadcasting holds a particular appeal to mass audiences that the press cannot match.

One of the by-products of increased television viewing was that passive watching not only replaced active public participation in politics, but also in many other forms of civic participation, such as support for various interest groups, associations, unions, and recreational organizations. People found in television an easy escape from the tough reality around them as well as a glimpse into a different, alien, but nevertheless more appealing life.[26] A national public opinion poll conducted by the Russian Independent Institute of Social and Nationalities Problems in 1997 showed that despite the tempestuous political events that had taken place in Russia that year, most Russians cited the death of Princess Diana as the most significant event, and did so even though they knew little about Diana's work compared with the Western public or about the reasons for her popularity in the United Kingdom and the United States.

The fundamentally changed relationship between the printed mass media and television compelled a certain adaptation by both. The former increasingly turned into a source of commentaries and new ideas while the latter became their popular distributor. This symbiotic relationship became particularly apparent among the leading media holdings.

While the influential new role that television came to play in Russia in the 1990s generally mirrored the broader world trend, by many standards Russia's case was the most striking. The reason for this was the persistent decline in popular political participation in Russia over the decade because of the general public disillusionment with reforms and the alienation of the political elite from society. The decline of the public's interest in politics and people's growing belief that they had no avenues for influencing government policy were important factors that pushed the public into politically passive activities, such as television watching. The elites' apparent transformation into a closed caste that, from the public's point of view, lived by their own laws was yet another factor in individuals distancing themselves from active politics. Thus the enthusiasm for television compensated for the public's lack of participation in politics.

In this light, a comparison between Russia and developed democracies would be inappropriate. In the latter case, society actively participates in politics, primarily by means of various civic initiatives and efficient systems of local self-government. The popularity of television in developed democracies is less a reflection of the public's political passivity than of the media's complementary role in political matters. The opposite is true of the Russian public. As Yuri Levada justly notes, "[T]rust in the effects and heralds of the mass media in Russia is inversely proportional to the individual's understanding of social phenomena or the opportunities that exist for influencing these."[27] The overbearing influence of television on Russia's contemporary society and culture is an indication of the underdevelopment of that society and not a sign of progress.[28]

The Mass Media Under Putin

The departure of Yeltsin and the election of Vladimir Putin as president created a new sociopolitical environment for the mass media. The new president came into office with the confidence and solid support not only of the political elite, but also of the majority of Russians, who were tired of the chaos and injustice that had marked Yeltsin's presidency. They saw the new president as a guarantor of effective social reform and stability. In response to these expectations, Putin began reshaping the political system with two important goals in mind: first, strengthening the vertical power structure, and second, restricting voices critical of the system, especially of the executive branch. To this end, the government introduced national regulations to limit freedom of information, including the Information Security Doctrine, a document approved by the Russian Security Council, a body headed and controlled by the president. Putin also criticized the media's unpatriotic role, for example, in publicizing information about the sinking of the *Kursk*.

By far the most widely publicized case of government restrictions on the media involved Gusinsky's Media-Most. Because of NTV's critical coverage of the second Chechen war, Putin was particularly disdainful of Gusinsky and his media empire. The company's financial problems made Media-Most—and especially NTV—vulnerable to state intervention. The Kremlin did not overtly shut down Media-Most, but instead used the courts to threaten Gusinsky with criminal charges. When that did not work (Gusinsky eventually fled the country), the government leaned on NTV's other major shareholder to install new management at the television station. Eventually, an entirely new team took over at NTV and at Gusinsky's magazine *Itogi*, while his newspaper *Segodnya* was shut down.

The conflict surrounding the takeover of the popular television station stirred up a nationwide debate on the freedom of speech. Gusinsky's supporters agreed with his claim that the confiscation of his stock holdings and denial of freedom of speech were illegal and politically motivated, and were not based on legal and economic reasons as the authorities claimed, citing Gusinsky's heavy debts. The opponents of this view maintained that the freedom of speech argument was irrelevant and that its loudest proponents were self-interested parties, namely Gusinsky's employees, who had a vested financial interest in defending their boss.

What this debate ultimately showed was not the rightness of one side or the other, but the weakness of civil society at that time. Talking about freedom of speech as such would not have made sense. Those arguing the case in the name of democracy were few, and they could not provide a counterweight to the state authorities.

This was an extremely important precedent because later, when most of the NTV journalists who had opposed the government's policies had switched to TV-6, another national television company, the government renewed its attempts to close those stations that were not to its liking with help from its loyal supporters in the courts and among shareholders loyal to the government and not Gusinsky. As a result of these efforts, a court verdict shut down TV-6. Later several groups of oligarchs loyal to the Kremlin created a new company, TVS, out of the remnants of TV-6. Those TV-6 journalists who went to work for TVS were forced to take the political line of the new owners into account and to soften their criticisms of Putin and his policies.

Yet the government viewed even soft criticism as an annoyance. Seeking complete control over the national information and news channels, the government played on the conflicts among TVS shareholders belonging to different interest groups and closed the channel under the guise of financial failure.

Most Western and Russian analysts take a negative stance on the new conditions in relation to the media, seeing them as a retreat from the pluralism of media organizations during Yeltsin's presidency and a sign of increasingly autocratic government pressure on the press. This pressure is applied in different ways: from direct administrative coercion to indirect influence (under the pretext of financial aid) on the editorial policy of those television stations, newspapers, or magazines that are out of line with the government's wishes.

As grossly undemocratic as this new system may appear at first sight, claiming that the status of the mass media has deteriorated because Putin's approach is more authoritarian than Yeltsin's would be an exaggeration. The issue is much more complicated and multifaceted than it appears and requires closer consideration of the mechanisms shaping the new environment in which the media operate and the media's adaptation to the challenges that have arisen under Putin's presidency.

Those factors that gave rise to the mediazation of Russian politics in the second half of the 1990s have either lost their significance or disappeared entirely. First, the government's use of the media to provide an illusion of political action so noticeable during Yeltsin's last years has decreased significantly under Putin. During the first year of his presidency, for the most part Putin kept to a policy line that was in step with that of the previous administration. The president frequently appeared on television in various situations and before diverse audiences. His messages to various social, professional, and political groups were clearly intended to address the high social expectations of the great majority of the populace. The rhetoric, as before, diverged with reality. With the exception of laws adopted in the summer of 2000 on federal reform that ran counter to the popular expectations accompanying Putin's arrival in office, no real decisions on socioeconomic and intragovernmental reforms were ever made. In the spring of 2001, however, when Putin, with parliament's support, embarked on a program of dynamic market reforms, the media's role as fabricator of fictitious political stories abruptly diminished.

This change was pivotal in reducing the ruling elite's interest in the media as a tool for deceiving the public. The elite once again began to view the media as an honest mechanism for delivering news about government decisions. In theory, the media were free from government and big business influence and were not a propaganda arm for either, a status the media tried hard to assert, gradually carving out the role of an impartial information source, critic, and channel for communication between society and the government. While the mass media continue to hold on to this goal, its existence does not ensure its realization. The media still have neither the economic independence nor the drive to effect such a dramatic turnaround in their political role. A related problem is that some members of the elite still nurture the idea of using the mass media as a tool for shaping policy, but their success in using the media for this purpose in the future is becoming less likely.

The second important change in the media's identity under Putin concerns the structure of the decision-making mechanism. In the new political environment the courts, the public prosecutor's office, and the tax police have become the coercive institutions and the only channels through which pressure groups can defend their interests in political and economic conflicts. The special role that the media once played no longer has the same importance. This means that media magnates like Berezovsky and Gusinsky, who tried to preserve the old ways of decision making that emphasized the media's status, did not fit into the new political order and ultimately found themselves outside influential circles. However, it also heralds a sharp decline in the prestige and significance of the mass media, transforming them from active participants in the decision-making process into ordinary information tools for leading political actors. The resulting politicized media are no longer ideological companions of politicized capital and business elites, but mercenary entities for sale to the highest bidder. Indeed, in describing the new attitude of the business elite toward the media, Lazareva noted that "no one wants to throw money at journalists any more…it is enough to keep them on minimal rations and to remind them from time to time that if they don't like their ration they don't have to eat it."[29]

The media's failure to retain a central role in conflicts between elites had an important consequence beyond stimulating changes in journalists' view of their purpose. The new situation forced media company shareholders to consider ways of turning these previously subsidized entities into commercially viable, profitable enterprises. Efforts in this direction have already been made and, at least in principle, this is a welcome development that could help make the media financially, and hence politically, more independent. This would bring them more closely in line with their Western counterparts.

The third change during the post-Yeltsin era was the public's perception of the mass media. Trust in the media was high at the end of Yeltsin's presidency, when the authorities' popularity was at a low ebb. People listened to the mass media when they exposed the "truth" about the corruption and injustice of some political authorities. But when Putin arrived in the Kremlin on a wave of popular hope and belief in the advent of peace and order, the mass media's critical articles were no longer needed and the public perceived them as unnecessary irritants. This skeptical attitude put the media in a highly vulnerable position and made them vulnerable to outside pressure, mainly from the government.

This vulnerability was compounded by a new orientation among the elites, including those in leading media corporations. After the tumultuous and uncertain times under Yeltsin, like society at large, the elite groups sought order and stability. In support of their goal of retaining the exclusive status that they had inherited from Yeltsin's time in office, they sought to restrict competition and understood the importance of the media in helping them accomplish that objective. This desire on the part of the elite to preserve the status quo was what pressured many media outlets to take a relatively neutral stance on the government's confiscation of Gusinsky's media holdings.

Compared with the confident, messianic role they assumed in the late 1980s and early 1990s, today's mass media are much more cautious. Self-censorship has again become widespread in the press, just as in Soviet times. Reports that might appear provocative or that could arouse negative reactions among the public and political and business elites now appear first on the Internet, from which they can be quickly and inconspicuously removed if necessary. Only after such test runs for adverse reaction are they allowed to appear in print or on television.

The move toward self-censorship became obvious after the seizure of hostages at Moscow's Theater Center on Dubrovka by Chechen terrorists in October 2002. Government officials accused some media of spreading panic and risking the lives of both the special forces and the hostages by live broadcasting of the beginning of the rescue assault on the Theater Center. As a result the State Duma adopted an amendment to the Law on Mass Media to limit the media's freedom to report and interpret terrorist crises. However, the president, who would like to represent himself in the West as a liberal politician, vetoed the amendment. In its place, journalists' associations agreed to work out self-limiting rules that would be oriented toward encouraging reporting standards, internal industry supervision, and self-censorship.

Nevertheless, the future for the media does not look altogether bleak. Indeed, arguing that the media's pluralism has completely disappeared in the new political era would be doing the media an injustice. Pluralism still exists under Putin, just as it did during the Yeltsin years. The difference now is that the media are driven less by democratic forces than by competition among the ruling elite.

The conflict that has split Putin's team since the earliest days of his presidency—between those people he retained from the old Yeltsin elite and those he brought to Moscow from St. Petersburg—is a good case in point. The media's evaluation of events is characterized by dramatically differing reports from leading media organizations, with some of the media taking a stance close to the views of the old Yeltsin family (for example, the television company TVS shut down in June 2003 and the daily newspaper *Vremya-MN*), and others that show unequivocal sympathy for the St. Petersburg group (for instance, TV-Center and the popular tabloid *Moskovsky Komsomolets*). In this battle, however, the latter is winning, which is a bad sign for pluralism in the media in the long run.

Conclusion

During the last fifteen years the mass media have undergone a series of challenging metamorphoses, changing from their role as spokespeople for democratic change under perestroika to tools in internal power struggles among the political and business elite in the latter part of the 1990s. Currently the media have for the most part reverted to one of the roles they played under the Soviet communist regime: the government's propaganda apparatus. Most of the mass media remain far from a genuinely free, democratic fourth estate. Many of the necessary preconditions for this are still missing, including economic independence and a developed civil society capable of lobbying for more access to information and for freedom of speech. The mass media stand a real chance of moving closer to Western media standards only with an open market economy and political democracy.

8

The Rule of Law

Mikhail Krasnov

Soviet jurisprudence theory did not recognize the concept of a law-governed state (meaning the control of law over power), classifying such a concept as a category of bourgeois law. The influential four-volume work *The Marxist-Leninist General Theory of the State and Law*, published at the beginning of the 1970s, states plainly: "The idea that law, whether understood as a supra-class norm of obligation, as an abstract, comprehensive kind of justice, or as a natural right of man, rules *over* the state and *over* the political authority, binding and limiting it, is by its nature a disguise for class dictatorship."[1]

This view was not surprising. Marxist doctrine not only defines the state as "a machine for the subjugation of one class by another," but also views law as "the will of the ruling class, expressed in statute."[2] In other words, Marxism-Leninism sees the value of law only insofar as it serves the interests of those in power. Such a view clearly directly contradicts the meaning of a law-governed state, and its legacy complicates Russia's ability to construct a law-governed state.

Mikhail Gorbachev's liberalization of the communist regime, known as perestroika, naturally influenced traditional Soviet legal thought. Many legal scholars had long harbored doubts about the communist system, but had kept their thoughts under wraps for fear of losing their jobs or their freedom; however, with the weakening of ideological restrictions they were able to make their concerns more public. Academics in educational and research institutes began to discuss openly the distinction between the concepts of statute law and general law, as well as the idea that the rights of man could be genuinely guaranteed only in a law-governed state.[3]

These debates in the academic community penetrated the ideological structures of the central organs of the Communist Party of the Soviet Union (CPSU). Indeed, orders that were worded as virtual demands for fresh ideas were handed down from CPSU's Central Committee to academic establishments, primarily the Institute of Law and Order of the USSR Academy of Sciences. On the one hand, these requests probed the state of mind of the academic intelligentsia; on the other hand, they indicated that the CPSU's leadership, which was, after all, the country's leadership as well, was experiencing an intellectual famine. The fact that the ideological apparatus of the CPSU was suffering from a dearth of unconventional and innovative ideas was not surprising, since its goal for many years had been complete conformity of thought in the struggle against bourgeois tendencies. Even though the thinking of certain individuals in the CPSU, such as Aleksandr Yakovlev, Georgy Shakhnazarov, and Fyodor Burlatsky, was a great deal more progressive than that of the average party bureaucrat, they too demanded another intellectual—or, more precisely, conceptual—source of nourishment.

Thus the idea of a law-governed state gradually made its way into the party apparatus in 1987 and 1988, but could not be substantively adopted at that time. In early 1988, Soviet leaders did not yet envision the social and governmental establishments undergoing sweeping radical change. The extent of innovation permitted by reformers was what Gorbachev called "socialism with a human face," that is modernization within the framework of the communist system. Given this constraint, the proclamation by the Nineteenth All-Union Party Conference of the CPSU—an event that played a key role in the liberalization of the regime—merely announcing an abstract course toward a "socialist, law-governed state" is not surprising. The conference resolution states,

> The Conference considers the creation of a socialist law-governed state, as a way of organizing the political authority fully in accordance with socialism, to be a matter of the highest importance. The performance of this task is inseparably linked to guaranteeing the rights and liberties of Soviet man to the maximum, to the responsibility of the state before the citizen and the citizen before the state, to raising the authority of the law and its strict observance by all Party and

government organs, public organizations, collectives and individual citizens, *and to the efficient work of law-enforcement agencies*. The radical restructuring of these agencies' activities ought to become *the core of judicial reform*, which the Conference considers expeditious to accomplish in a comparatively short period of time.[4]

Note that the adjective "socialist" in the resolution changes the essence of the concept of a law-governed state in the same way that the essence of the term democracy is radically changed when it is used, according to Lenin's doctrine of class democracy, only in the collocation "socialist democracy."

The wording in the resolution indicates that the communist leadership was reviewing its conceptual and doctrinal mechanisms and was in the process of turning away from the Marxist-Leninist view of a law-governed state as one entirely hostile to communist theory. The appearance of completely new thinking within the CPSU was an ideological signal to the party apparatus nationwide that led orthodox communists to view the party as sliding into revisionism, or even social democracy.

The resolution also introduced the idea of a law-governed state into more mainstream discourse. Unlike the term democracy, which had been common among the masses, the term law-governed state had traditionally belonged to the vocabulary of the elite. Therefore the public saw its entry into more widespread discourse as a major turning point, if not directly in politics, then at least in the attitudes of the ruling elite.

That these shifts would have a lasting influence was by no means assured, however. Had events developed otherwise, for example, had the conservative, orthodox forces in the CPSU leadership undergone a resurgence or had hard-liners triumphed in the August 1991 putsch, the term socialist law-governed state might have passed into obscurity. This was especially likely since the 1988 party conference had linked the idea mainly to the radical restructuring of law enforcement agencies.

Fortunately, this did not happen. The process of liberalization that gradually encompassed all spheres of life, from the spiritual to the economic, favorably conditioned public opinion to the concept of a law-governed state. Society, though not especially interested in its underlying political foundation, instinctively seized upon the law-governed state as an idea and popularized it. During this time—approximately 1989–1992—many prominent Russian jurists came forward with explanations of the meaning of a law-governed state. Their explanations finally corresponded with the classical definitions.

However, the general perception of a law-governed state has differed from its academic definition. The 1997 legal encyclopedia calls the law-governed state

> a type of state in which a regime of constitutional law operates, and a developed and uniform legal system and effective judicial authority exist, while there is at the same time a true separation of powers, under which the branches effectively interact and exercise control over one another while remaining accountable to the society in regard to political policy and authority.[5]

Some might argue that many of these features describe a democratic system rather than a law-governed state; however, the concepts of democracy and the law-governed state are so closely intertwined that for the aims of this analysis, this distinction is unnecessary.

The Soviet critique of the law-governed state performed a positive service by defining the law-governed state in terms of the rule of law *over* the state. The problem is that the law should not be viewed simply as an aggregate of statutes and other legislative acts, but rather as possessing natural worth, being of profound importance to civilization, even prior to the ascension of formal law. This distinction remains particularly difficult for many people, including politicians, to grasp. The following is a striking illustration. The original text of a public speech written for President Boris Yeltsin contained a statement that the state should be bound by law. The president quickly presented his own corrected text, in which the phrase was amended to appear as "the state should be bound *with* the law." Clearly, this small preposition radically altered the definition of a law-governed state, implying that the law reflects the tendencies of the state and is used to justify its actions instead of acting as an independent restraint. Nevertheless, the former is precisely the way in which many Russians envision a law-governed state.

Not long ago, for example, the newspaper *Trud* published a reader's letter that illustrates this widely held opinion. The reader wrote that "all states are 'governed by law,' even slave-owning states, since the law is a system of commonly-binding social norms protected by the power of the state."[6] This letter to the editor illustrates a serious problem. Do Russia's citizens really understand the concept of a law-governed state? If so, how accurate is their understanding? Is the government doing anything to educate the populace? While a democratic state should not promote ideology, the authorities do have means of enlightening the public at their disposal, for example, through official policy statements and programs or through support of legal education programs by nongovernmental organizations.

Moreover, high-ranking officials' use of political slogans and catchphrases that misrepresent the meaning of a law-governed state, such as "dictatorship of the law," clearly hinders the concept of a law-governed state from developing into a collectively shared idea. Such catchphrases only promote an inaccurate concept of the law as an aggregation of rules originating from those in power.

This chapter now attempts to outline the development of Russia's struggle for a law-governed state. In the last ten years, how far has Russia progressed on its way to becoming a law-governed state and is it really following that path?

The Struggle for a Law-Governed State

In 1990–1991, a revolution took place in Russia that resulted in a massive change in the social and governmental order and in the country's way of life. Yet official documents and contemporary history textbooks remain silent about this revolution for several reasons.

First, by the end of the 1980s, the thesis that Russia had reached its revolutionary limits became popular, and a negative attitude toward the word revolution, and toward the phenomenon itself, had become widespread in Russia. The Bolshevik revolution of 1917 had brought the country a bloody civil war, the destruction of the 1,000-year-old Russian state, the execution of millions of the country's own citizens, and the drastic attempts to eradicate basic human instincts and needs. Thus the idea of a new revolution aroused no romantic associations among former Soviet citizens.

Second, an appropriate political analysis of the revolution as such was impossible, because the usual attributes of a revolution were lacking. What happened in Russia had not been premeditated. The revolution had no academic foundation, no revolutionary political organization, and, at the beginning, no clear leader. The unsteady evolution of Gorbachev's and Yeltsin's views in a democratic direction took place before the eyes of the public. The fact that Russia's leaders at the time held solid (even if incorrect) convictions about the future, further deprived the events of revolutionary characteristics.

Third, simply defining the character of the revolution is difficult. For example, can it be characterized as a bourgeois-democratic revolution if Russia lacked a bourgeois class?

Fourth, one cannot assign a singular date to this revolution. Did it begin in May 1989, when the USSR Congress of People's Deputies (CPD) opened, marking the appearance of official opposition to the CPSU? Or did it start on August 21, 1991, with the victory over the communist putschists? Or perhaps it originated on September 23, 1993, with the adoption of Decree Number 1400, or on December 12, 1993, when the new Russian Constitution was adopted? This four-year period of uncertainty further obscures the revolutionary spirit of the transition.

The focus on the characterization of this breakthrough period as a revolution arises from the fact that the public's perception has had a critical influence on Russia's development. Replacing the concept of revolution with the euphemism of reform has had a negative effect on the entire process of modernization.

To begin with, the great majority of people made the mistake of viewing the reform process simply as a transfer of power from one group of Moscow bureaucrats to another, and continued to rely on the state's paternalism. Because of the dramatic political changes, however, the usual triggers that had once prompted state action no longer existed to produce the meager, yet guaranteed, social benefits to which people were accustomed. Had people understood that a revolution was occurring, however, their expectations would have been radically different.

In addition, reference to these changes as reforms instead of a revolution affected the mindset and behavior of the ruling elite. The leaders of the post-communist overhaul, understanding that their own way of life and the nature of public relationships were changing drastically, nevertheless perceived themselves to be participants in a purely evolutionary process. They did not understand that change had ceased to be evolutionary and instead became revolutionary by the end of the Gorbachev era.

Such a revolutionary course of action would have required not just the introduction of economic and political liberties but a radical restructuring of the entire state mechanism. In the absence of a large middle class; a robust civil society; traditions of democracy; and civic responsibility, the burden of democratization would have to rest upon the state. In other words, as governance was moving from totalitarianism to rule by law, all government institutions should have been influenced by its momentum. Unfortunately, this did not occur.

Yeltsin could have said, "I have come to give you freedom!" However, he did not do this, preferring to remain a sporadic liberalizer rather than a conscious liberal. The public also did not realize the value of freedom, and still does not. Moral protest was more likely the leitmotif for the public's support first of Gorbachev and then of Yeltsin. That was why the idea of a law-governed state became so popular in late Soviet society in the first place. Above all, the public saw in the idea of a law-governed state an opportunity for governance to renew itself morally. The absence of such renewal relegated the concept of a law-governed state to the neglected orbits of public interest.

Consider what a law-governed state means. Russia's current political, historical, and philosophical discussions occasionally suggest two contradictory veins of thought: on the one hand, that a law-governed state is a construction that has outlived its usefulness for a postindustrial society, and on the other hand, that this idea is, in general, not in keeping with Russian traditions and mentality. Agreeing with either position is impossible.

First, the options are limited, and so in rejecting the idea of a law-governed state (rather than any concrete institution embodying the idea), society inevitably establishes the opposite, that is, a legal state in which written law is not based on natural law and is dominated by power. In this postindustrial, information age a sensible approach is to consider modifications of traditional constitutional democracy in terms of its ability to provide equal treatment of interests, protect rights and liberties, and assure social stability. But a law-governed state is in itself an achievement that is not to be reconsidered or discarded. It is one of the rare contemporary ideas that hold civilization together.

Second, throughout its changes of government, the Russian state has maintained a paternalistic relationship with its citizens. Thus the spirit of a law-governed state has never existed in Russia, and the idea of obedience to the law is still not particularly popular. From this, many analysts conclude that a natural legal nihilism is manifest among Russia's citizens and that striving for a law-governed state is hopeless. I disagree with such conclusions.

While recognizing the value of positive law, the doctrine of a law-governed state nevertheless finds far greater value in natural law. As the Russian legal thinker Ivan Ilyin wrote:

[T]he value that lies at the heart of natural law is a dignified, internally independent and externally free life for the entire multitude of individual souls that make up mankind. Such a life is possible only if it takes the form of peaceful and organized equality for all subjective, competing groups; a balance that guarantees everyone the same opportunity for a spiritually dignified life, and therefore violates this equality only on the side of justice.[7]

This is one of the most comprehensive and precise definitions of the natural law approach to the rule of law.

So why has obedience to the law taken root so poorly in Russia? This has occurred because the political regime has never had a sense of responsibility to the public, and so could promulgate unjust and nonsensical laws without fear of punishment. Meanwhile, the population remained outwardly patient while silently bearing and adapting to all sorts of state and bureaucratic tyranny. This passivity does not, however, signify blind obedience. People's adaptation to the contemporary political environment has always been of a situational nature. They developed their own system of values within the existing positive law—toward which, as a rule, they were extremely hostile—and played games with the state, cheating it every step of the way. Russians have always had and continue to have their own opinions about every official act affecting their interests because they have the ability to distinguish justice from legality.

This sense of justice, as distinct from written statutes, is the concentrated expression of the Russian people's awareness of natural law. A popular Russian saying illustrates the intellectual separation of the two: "Judge according to the law or according to the conscience." Ilyin again offers a valuable insight:

A developed awareness of the law always knows how to decide where the law begins and ends, and where arbitrariness rears its head; and, having decided this question, it always knows how to make the appropriate practical conclusions: where it is appropriate to recognize and obey the law, and where it is appropriate to oppose tyranny and crude force with all the might of legitimate and consistent, to the point of heroism, disobedience.[8]

I do not assert that the Russian people have a developed awareness of the law, if only because such awareness presupposes high-level moral development. The following is clear, however: reconciling positive law with the people's natural understanding of law is a viable path for Russia, even though it demands many institutional and functional changes in government and public life. I am optimistic about the prospects for a law-governed state in Russia because the need for one is deeply felt. People may reject exaggerated slogans, but they do not reject the underlying issues of freedom and democracy. According to survey data, ten years after the start of reforms the largest number of respondents, 54 percent, ranked the equality of all citizens before the law first in the hierarchy of democratic values.[9] This highlights the extent to which Russians' sense of law equates law not only with freedom, but also with egalitarianism and justice, and repudiates the conclusion that trying to uphold the law in Russia is hopeless.

One of the fundamental strategic mistakes embedded in Russia's reform was its false paradigm. Reforms were intended not to reorganize the state, but only to liberate it—from the command administrative system; from censorship; and from political, spiritual, and economic prohibitions. At that time, both the elite and the public believed that economic and political liberalization and the privatization of national property could transform the country; however, the true transformation of a traditional society into a democratic one required more complex reform than mere liberation from administrative hindrances and fear.

A law-governed state develops not from a simple set of certain technological and institutional transformations, but from a change in the essence of the relationships between the state and the individual and between the authorities and society. However, the post-Soviet authorities and the democratic political elite viewed the idea of a law-governed state primarily as propaganda, or in any case, as an idea of secondary importance. By contrast, the post-Soviet Russian public instinctively awaited a greater change, and the fact that it never materialized became the decisive reason for the public's dissatisfaction with what has taken place. In other words, the method of reform did not allow the people to perceive the reforms as their own or as furthering their vested interests. The Soviet model of distant relations between the authorities and the public was completely preserved, and the individual remained in the same servile condition as a subject of the state instead of a citizen.

The lack of a compelling idea that could mobilize public involvement also made itself felt psychologically. Clearly, the concepts of democracy and the free market could not have a motivating effect because they were not, after all, ideals; yet reformers were unable to offer other alternatives. The Bolsheviks, for example, succeeded not because of their brutality, but because they were able to put lofty ideas into action and inspire the masses. The collapse of the communist ideal can be explained in a similar way: it is more attributable to the loss of social activism and ideological motivation than to the economic crisis of the 1970s, itself a consequence of the motivation shortfall.

Furthermore, the process of reform was accompanied by the process of opening Russia to the outside world and the outside world to Russia. This was facilitated by the heightened informational connectivity of the 1990s, which allowed Russians to evaluate their standard of living in comparison with that in the West. Russians still could not believe the huge gap in standards of living between Russia and the developed West. Highly and moderately qualified working people, such as university instructors, medical personnel, and engineers, were especially sensitive to the apparent gap. Reforms increasingly proved unjust. In the absence of a large middle class, Russian society resembled and continues to resemble an hourglass, albeit one whose upper end is significantly smaller than its lower end.[10]

Finally, the lack of focus on the institutional construction of the law-governed state negatively affected another segment of the reform process. Criminals, swindlers, and extortionists rushed into the newly created business sphere hoping to capitalize on its vacuum. Their visible presence and ostentatious, nouveau riche lifestyle engendered contempt and indignation. This had a particularly significant effect on the psychology of society: in the public's eyes, economic freedom began to seem like freedom reserved exclusively for unscrupulous individuals.

By 1995 or thereabouts, frustration with these processes led to a public outcry for order. Unsurprisingly, those running for president in the 1996 elections, including Yeltsin, seized upon this need, championing neither democracy nor freedom, but order.

The yearning for order can also be classified as a motivational idea or an ideal, but the lack of order—which can also be construed as the public authorities' inability to execute their basic functions effectively—gives rise to longings that are removed from the values of freedom. In the absence of legal order, the public demands any kind of order, and the idea of order becomes an alternative to the idea of a law-governed state. This is an extremely dangerous state of affairs for a democratic country. In post-Soviet

Russia, the notion of a law-governed state met the fate of other concepts such as democracy, freedom, and human rights, slogans on which society had instinctively pinned its hopes, but which brought about no fundamental changes in the way power was wielded.

The Soviet system had been propped up with repressive methods that guaranteed unlimited power to the ruling elite, employed harsh forms of centralization, did not recognize the private sphere, and assured the system's inviolability. Fear was omnipresent in relations between the authorities and their subjects. Self-protection mechanisms developed under this system were not legalistic, but were relatively effective.

A democratic system, by contrast, presupposes subordination to legal norms by the people as well as by the authorities, and governance is implemented not in a personalized, but in a legal manner. No longer motivated by the fear of a repressive party-state machine or of illegitimate governmental force, the authorities failed to replace it with another motivation: if not respect for, then at least a kind of fear of the operation of the law. Of course, one cannot say that the first reformers attached no significance to the building of a democratic state. To the contrary, they started with this ideal in mind.

Why did communists and democrats support the first major act of the Russian CPD: Russia's declaration of sovereignty from the USSR? They did so because the former saw this as a way to distance themselves from Gorbachev's policies, while the latter saw it as an opportunity to declare new principles of statehood and to create a constitutional order, that is, a regime based on constitutional law, one of the guarantees of a law-governed state.

Other major projects and resolutions from that initial state-building period of reform are also noteworthy. The concept of judicial reform, whose implementation was intended to rid society of inquisitional justice, was approved in 1991 by the Russian congress. The KGB, one of the pillars of the totalitarian edifice, was broken up following the putsch of August 1991, albeit somewhat formally and mechanically. That allowed Yeltsin to issue a decree soon afterward creating a new super-agency, the Ministry of Security and Internal Affairs, although the Constitutional Court of the Russian Soviet Federative Socialist Republic (RSFSR) later declared the establishment of this agency to be unconstitutional. In addition, the system of executive power agencies began to change. Because of the privatization of certain economic sectors, new corporations appeared in place of some ministries. This is how the super-corporation Gazprom came about. Gosplan, Gossnab, and

Goskomtsen, bureaus of the state-run economy, were eliminated altogether. The new economic relationships demanded that the functions of many ministries and agencies be changed, and many ceased to manage state enterprises directly. Furthermore, a system of agencies for local self-government began to take shape.

Yet all of this was macro-state building, or in other words, an endeavor to realize general ideas and put new institutions in place. The authorities were much less concerned with how these institutions were going to function, who would carry out the new judicial policies, and most important, who would supervise the transformation of the new Russian state into a law-governed state and how.

All this nascent work was impeded by the political conflict between the president and the legislative branch (the RSFSR CPD and the Supreme Soviet of the RSFSR), which became public after the start of radical economic liberalization in 1992. At the same time, the conflict itself was brought about in large measure by the elites' unwillingness to see the political and socioeconomic changes that were taking place in society as revolutionary.

No revolution pledges to observe the fundamental laws of the regime against which it has been waged. As Ferdinand LaSalle wrote: "Although law should undoubtedly take precedence over force, in reality force always precedes law, and will continue to take precedence over it so long as the law has not gathered adequate strength to break the power of lawlessness."[11]

Nevertheless, the political elites' unwillingness to perceive what was happening as a revolution was what led to the public misunderstanding of Yeltsin's actions. This was his own fault, since after the victory in the communist putsch in August 1991, neither he nor anyone in his immediate circle took the necessary, consistent steps to bring about a legitimate change in the essence of state power. The Soviet governmental structure, somewhat modernized during perestroika, was preserved intact.

In a legal sense, Yeltsin was right to use his Decree Number 1400 of September 21, 1993, to declare the RSFSR Constitution of 1978 invalid and to shut down the semi-Soviet CPD and the Supreme Court of the Russian Federation. Strictly speaking, in the post-Soviet political context, one cannot speak of violation of the constitution when one means the RSFSR Constitution of 1978, nor can one bemoan the illegal dissolution of parliament—something that the Congress never was—since both had retained the hallmarks of Soviet-style government, including the absolute power of the soviets and the vertical structure of the representative organs.

Nevertheless, the technical model of constitutional transition in Russia could have been different from the one undertaken in the fall of 1993. Yeltsin's mistake was again to reject the need to make such a transition within a revolutionary paradigm, which under the circumstances of 1991 he could have achieved without violence and would have helped to avoid violence in 1993. Such a paradigm would have called for the convocation of a constituent assembly or a constitutional convention, and maintaining the link with Soviet Russia through the extension of the RSFSR Constitution of 1978 would have been unacceptable. The Bolsheviks had created—and officially proclaimed—a completely new state. The period of Bolshevik rule therefore cannot be considered simply the government of a different ideology. It promulgated a different concept of statehood. In trying to perpetuate a dual role both as Soviet heirs and new democrats, the post-Soviet authorities disoriented themselves, the Russian people, and the entire world.

Thus the failure to comprehend the changes in Russia as a revolution adversely affected the entire transformation process. More than that, it influenced the results of the transformation and society's current situation. The main flaw in the state-building reforms was their reactive character. They did not follow a systematically developed plan. In the absence of an established program to which to adhere, events were often dictated by power struggles: initially the reformers were an instrument of the Russian government's conflict with the Union, then they became a tool of the president of the Russian Federation in his battle against the CPD. Thus as soon as a tangible opponent disappeared in 1991, and again in 1993 (although the main opponent always remained the system itself), the desire to carry out further reforms diminished.

Yet despite its internal inconsistencies, the reform process has nevertheless led to the creation of the democratic Russian Constitution. At the same time, today the constitution is essentially flapping in the wind, since it lacks the backing of a developed civil society that rightfully considers the constitution to be a social contract equally binding on all parties. Moreover, observing the letter of the constitution does not always mean that its spirit is observed as well. In many ways, the constitution stifles its democratic spirit itself through the imbalance of authority distributed among the main power triangle of president, parliament, and government.

Another reason also accounts for why none of the government's major military, administrative, judicial, or political reforms were ever carried out in full. Simply put, Yeltsin and his government gave priority to economic reforms at the expense of governmental and legal reforms. Without a doubt, the economic situation at the beginning of the 1990s was such that without radical liberalization a catastrophe would have occurred. However, the economic bloc within the new government quickly became dominant and started pursuing its own priorities. Privatization and the creation of a property owning class took precedence on its agenda, while it viewed the state primarily as an instrument that should help (or at least not hinder) these processes. State institutions such as the army, the police, and the courts, which were not directly related to the division of property, were treated as ordinary budgetary items. Thus the very concept of reform de facto came to refer primarily to economic reforms.

This attitude is evident in the history of the president's annual message to the Federal Assembly (the equivalent of the president's State of the Union message in the United States). Even though virtually all of Yeltsin's messages, beginning with the first in 1994, dealt directly with the publicly popular topic of strengthening the new state, his speeches proved ineffective. They failed because the policy recommendations outlined in these speeches were not linked to state budgets. Moreover, a failure to execute presidential directives went unpunished, allowing legislators to pursue their own agendas. Finally, Yeltsin himself soon ceased counting on these messages' effectiveness and shifted his attention to more customary instruments of power, such as personnel appointments.

New hopes for the consistent implementation of state-building reforms arose after the presidential elections of 1996, but Yeltsin's deteriorating health, as well as such alternative priorities on the part of his new inner circle such as image making, prevented judicial and administrative reform projects from taking on a new life.

The Outcome

By the end of the 1990s, the record of achievement has been mixed regarding the creating of rule of law.

First, in judicial terms the Russian Constitution is of high quality. Yet while it undoubtedly accords some stability, it cannot take the place of a transparent and comprehensible political system. Society cannot discern which political force is responsible for governing. As a result, no clear opposition force can emerge. Moreover, in a country that has constitutionally proclaimed itself to be a democratic and law-governed state, an entirely abnormal state of affairs persists: the left flank of the political spectrum is controlled by a party whose neocommunist platform runs completely counter to the values of a law-governed state. To make matters worse, Russian politics continue to be plagued by *ad hominem* declamations. Thus elections in all the branches of government are often stripped of meaning and are becoming criminalized.

Second, even today an effective system for the protection of rights has not been thoroughly established. The 1991 concept of judicial reform was at least partially realized during Yeltsin's administration. Trial by jury was introduced in nine constituent entities of the Russian Federation. According to the official explanation, extending it to the rest of the country was impossible for budgetary reasons. Criminal and civil proceedings were somewhat amended. Courts spun out of the purview of the Ministry of Justice to become more independent and arbitration courts were introduced. Bailiffs were introduced as physical protectors for those involved in court cases. The judicial branch was becoming specialized in constitutional, general, arbitration, and administrative law.

Despite such advances, Russia does not yet have an accessible, genuinely independent, and effective system of justice that includes modern civil and criminal procedures that presume the equality of the parties involved and their right to contest. Nor does Russia have a comprehensive legal framework that encompasses fully fledged appellate courts, the circuit principle of court jurisdiction, and the diminished weight of publicity. The country is dominated by a repressive, militarized, Stalinist era law enforcement system.

Under President Vladimir Putin, the legal system has undoubtedly been refined. New procedural codes, the Criminal Code, and the Civil Code finally replaced the slightly amended Soviet era codes; a law on the legal profession and amendments to the legislation on the status of judges were passed; a law on administrative courts (courts specializing in civil suits against the authorities) is being developed; the institution of justices of the peace is being created; and the financing of the court system is growing, which has finally allowed the jury system to be extended to the entire country. In addition to these reforms, attention is shifting to the sphere of administrative reform, for instance, reform of the internal affairs organs has been announced.

Yet these changes cannot be called anything more than refinements—they are not attempts at deep reform of the legal system. The latter requires trust in the abilities of the individual, and while sociological studies show that about 60 percent of the population are striving to free themselves from the philosophy of state paternalism, government practice and the methodology of state reform lack that impulse. Meanwhile, a law-governed state cannot be constructed without this philosophical component. Whether the legal institutions and procedures that accompany reforms are able to stimulate people's abilities, creativity, and civic consciousness depends on the sociopolitical environment in which the reforms begin, and at this time the quality of that environment does not seem to be conducive to any significant changes in the direction of a law-governed state.

Two instances of the current sociopolitical atmosphere can be cited. One is that the general weakness of the executive system has transformed the public drive for democracy and freedom into a drive for order (see chapter 11). This reaction to the unraveling of the state is reasonable, since this unraveling was anarchic, unsystematic, and chaotic rather than liberal. Indeed, the untrained "Russian liberalism" discredited the concept of liberalism by failing to make the economy independent and simultaneously left it open to unregulated opportunism. While the concept of order is not inimical to that of freedom, in Russia's circumstances both the authorities and society generally understand order as a component of a hierarchical and not of a democratic system.

Not only phrases such as the vertical power structure and the dictatorship of the law that have been voiced by the political elite, but also actual political practice, indicate that the strengthening of the state is thought of specifically in bureaucratic terms. In this kind of environment, few take seriously words about developing civil society and awkward government attempts to show its respect of nongovernmental organizations, for instance, by organizing the Civic Forum (see chapter 6). All this involuntarily fosters a pyramidal philosophy in which fear plays a key motivational role.

The other instance is that the political system as it is now is more appropriate for a personality-driven regime than a self-regulated system. It rejects the principle of responsibility, in which modern democracy and the development of a law-governed state are rooted. Its very constitutional construction stands in the way of the system becoming a normal party system, instead producing a clannish, oligarchic one. That is why current reform, whether in the administrative, judicial, or law enforcement area, is unlikely to produce the desired effect. The construction of a law-governed state will remain unlikely until the political system itself is reformed through constitutional reform.

Third, Russia still lacks a system for the thoroughgoing defense of liberty. As was true for most of the twentieth century, anything personal and private automatically seems to be suspicious; anything communal is ennobled. This is a perpetuation of Soviet paternalism. For example, according to the federal Law on the Office of the Prosecutor General of the Russian Federation, part of the notorious common jurisdiction of the Office of the Prosecutor General is

> ensuring the observance of human and civil rights and freedoms by federal ministries, state committees, services, and other federal executive agencies, representative (legislative) and executive organs of the constituent entities of the Russian Federation, organs of local self-government, organs of military command, organs of control, their officials, and the organs of management and heads of commercial and non-commercial organizations.

The prosecutor general has indeed begun to act in accordance with this, however, not only upon the request of individual citizens, but on his own initiative as well, under the pretext of preventing violations of human rights. The problem is that even when substantiating evidence of the alleged violation is lacking, the prosecutor general either informs the accused transgressor or goes to court. The Office of the Prosecutor General also gets a kind of commission from legal entities: 10 percent of the funds an enterprise or organization receives as a result of the prosecutor general's initiative. In this way the state discourages individual citizens from acting independently in the judicial defense of their violated rights. As in Soviet times, citizens are encouraged to submit their complaints through administrative channels.

This practice also applies to the problem of regional legislation that is not in accordance with federal legislation. The federal government spends an enormous amount of time and effort trying to overcome these inconsistencies. As a result, sharp political conflicts often arise. However, these legislative acts, most of which violate the rights of particular constituencies, could simply be appealed by individual citizens in court, but instead, an administrative logic usually prevails: let the constituent entities of the Russian Federation bring their own legislation in line with federal laws or risk the wrath of Moscow.

Fourth, the system of relations between the Russian Federation and its constituent entities and between the latter and organs of local self-government remains confused. Disdain for such legal concepts as competence plays a substantial role in the perpetuation of confusion. The system of relations between federal and regional entities assumes the presence of strict, clear, and operable mechanisms of responsibility, as well as effectively functioning institutions of control and the enforcement of responsibility. All this demands an understanding of the political significance of lawful methods of governance and a host of qualified judges and jurists. While command methods have not made a comeback, bureaucrats' expectations are still linked to them.

Fifth, Russia still lacks a rational system of institutions within the executive branch, of which it has no fewer than seven different types. Moreover, primary and secondary institutions have been created and the latter are striving to elevate their status. As concerns the functioning of these institutions, conflicts of interest often arise, such that the same agency both sets the rules of the game and issues the licenses and certificates, grants accreditation, and performs the services. In addition, under the current system, ministers are unable to set the strategy for development within their areas of interest and bear no political responsibility. This is largely because they have vice premiers superior to them keeping an eye on things, and also because of the operation of filters, that is, the departments of the government apparatus.

Sixth, Russia has still not undergone a bureaucratic revolution, that is, reform of the civil service. Thus the bureaucracy remains based on Soviet-era *nomenklatura* principles. For the people, this means that bureaucrats still serve their supervisors rather than the public good.

However, these incomplete reforms are less important than the tragic stagnation of the direction of state transformation. The public, as before, has no sense of the urgent need that governmental and legal reform be directed toward changing the way power is exercised, toward transforming the governmental apparatus into a system that serves the shared public interest, and toward making institutions conducive to free creativity and solidarity.

The power of a law-governed state lies not in its institutional content, but in its ability to transform the philosophy of public life. The basis of this philosophy is trust in the individual and the individual's independence. The actual practice of power, including the methodology of reforms, ought to foster freedom, not paternalism.

9

Federalism

Nikolai Petrov

Along with the regular holding of elections, the creation of Russia's federal system was perhaps the greatest achievement of the first decade of post-Soviet Russia. What is called federalism in Russia is a mixture of federal features along with a weak, centralized, unitary state, in which the central is opposed by quasi-democratic, semi-authoritarian, regional elites. Like Russian democracy, Russian federalism has many elements that are decorative rather than substantive and that appear similar to their Western analogues but have a different essence. Russian federalism serves as a ritual rather than as a function. Consequently, the current situation is unstable. If not accompanied by further development of federalism, strengthening and re-centralizing the state could lead toward the restoration of a type of federalism akin to that which characterized the Soviet state.

Origins of Federalism in Russia

The roots of Russian federalism can be traced as far back as the eleventh and twelfth centuries to the Kievan Rus of the Rurik dynasty, which rotated the leadership among the thrones of different principalities. Under the rule of the Golden Horde in the thirteenth and fourteenth centuries, the Great Rus was a very loose confederation of eleven large Russian principalities, divided into twenty smaller appanage principalities. The *zemsky sobor* of the sixteenth century (deliberative assemblies with elections and representation determined according to estates), and the gradual introduction of the *zemstvo* system challenge the widespread view that traditions of local self-rule, federalism, and grassroots democracy were totally absent before the present period.[1] Moreover, these measures of decentralization occurred in the heterogeneous Russian Empire, where vastly diverse territories ranged from Finland, with its own constitution and parliament, to the Central Asian khanates. Given such diversity, the state developed a vertical power structure, a variety of political institutions, and a number of forms of regional autonomy.

Arguing that Russia's contemporary regional borders are relatively new, artificial, and are simply a by-product of Joseph Stalin's red pencil is an exaggeration. The argument is especially misleading with regard to the European part of the country, where three-quarters of the federation's population and two-thirds of its regions are located. After the experiment with regional enlargement in the 1920s and early 1930s, the Soviets returned to the old *gubernia*-like pattern. Indeed, many subjects of the federation recently marked bicentennial anniversaries harkening back to the administrative reforms of Catherine the Great.

The real Soviet innovation was combining ethnic and territorial principles into the state's administrative territorial structure. National-territorial administrative units emerged during the civil war and later during the construction of the socialist state.[2] The Bolsheviks' use of national-territorial administrative units in building the Soviet state reflected both their co-optation and manipulation of ethnic movements in their struggle for domestic political power and their plans for spreading communism.[3] They considered not only regional, but also national, borders to be of minor importance on the eve of the expected world revolution, and believed that their shape could be manipulated to win allies, seemingly without consequence, once the postrevolution withering away of states and national differences occurred. After the revolution succeeded in Russia but failed internationally, Stalin's 1936 constitution codified a highly centralized authoritarian state with certain decorative elements mimicking ethnic federalism.

The Russian Soviet Federative Socialist Republic (RSFSR), itself a pseudo federation inside another pseudo federation (the USSR), employed the "raisins in a loaf" model for about a dozen first-tier ethnic units and about a dozen more second-tier ethnic units inside the "ordinary" regions. This arrangement was in many ways similar to that in modern China, meaning that Russian federalism at that time did not exist in any real sense.[4] It was only in the early 1990s that some elements of federalism appeared in Russia.

The Russian Federation has replicated the federal-unitary ethnic-territorial structure of the USSR. Until 1990, the Russian Federation was made up of eighty-eight administrative units: seventy-three primary and fifteen secondary (with the latter being subordinated to the former).[5] All the secondary units—five autonomous *oblasts* and ten autonomous or *rayons*—as well as sixteen primary units (autonomous republics), were considered to be ethnic homelands for some four dozen indigenous ethnic groups. The remaining fifty-seven regions were simple territorial or "proper Russian" units, and consisted of six *krais*, forty-nine *oblasts*, and the cities of Moscow and Leningrad. The fifteen secondary units were inherited from the hierarchical, *matroshka* doll-like structure of the Soviet state, with autonomous *oblasts* within *krais* and autonomous *okrugs* within *krais* and *oblasts*.

The end of communism was accompanied by the "republicanization" of Russia. All the former autonomous republics and four of the five autonomous *oblasts* declared themselves republics, and most of the autonomous *okrugs* declared sovereignty, freeing themselves from the control of their corresponding *oblast* or *krai* and becoming members or subjects of the federation in their own right.[6] Under the 1993 constitution, the Russian Federation consists of twenty-one republics, one autonomous *oblast*, ten autonomous *okrugs*, forty-nine *oblasts*, six *krais,* and the cities of Moscow and St. Petersburg, a total of eighty-nine federal components.[7] To further complicate the picture, even though one autonomous *okrug*, Chukotka, is a completely independent subject of the federation, the other nine *okrugs* are still considered parts of *krais* and *oblasts* as well as subjects of the federation themselves. This contradiction is another legacy of the Soviet constitution.

In 2001, the Federal Assembly passed a law on bringing new regions into the Russian Federation. The law allows not only for expanding the federation's membership, but also for enlarging its existing regions through the consolidation of federal components. Despite the long discussions about combining Moscow and St. Petersburg with their adjacent *oblasts* and uniting the Kemerovo, Tomsk, and Altai *krais* in southern Siberia, the most probable scenario is including autonomous *okrugs* into their mother regions, except perhaps for Tyumen Oblast's two northern oil and gas *okrugs*. In the case of the Irkutsk and Ust-Orda autonomous *okrugs*, some progress toward a merger agreement has already been made.

Dynamics of Federalism in Post-Communist Russia

Russian federalism—young, immature, and unique—must be understood in the context of the country's recent political history and climate. The Russian Federation is a product of the political instability of the past decade and a half. Put another way, the dirty secret of Russian federalism is that Russia lacks federalism. This system instead consists of the temporarily weakened federal center, where reforms have lingered too long, and the regional centers, where old elites have quickly regained control, if they ever lost it at all.

Despite being more virtual than real, the idea of Russian federalism has shaped both elite and public opinion in a positive manner and put on the agenda those questions that need to be answered to fill out the institutional infrastructure of genuine federalism. Weakly rooted in society, the design of Russian federalism largely reflects the balance of power between central and regional political elites during the period of political instability of the late Soviet and post-Soviet revolutionary period. Russian federalism emerged as a result of a temporary weakening of the center and a relative strengthening of the regional elites.

Elections

Elections are the key to understanding the first phase of the federalization process: the so-called parade of sovereignties, which took place in 1990–1991. Without elections federalism in its present form would not exist at all. The semi-elections of deputies to the new RSFSR Congress of People's Deputies (CPD) and to the regional soviets in March 1990 provided the impetus for the nationwide federalization of the early 1990s. The simultaneous election of these independently legitimate and ambitious legislatures and the emergence of opposition within the soviets nearly paralyzed the government. The situation was resolved first by the creation of parliamentary-presidential systems and then by the dissolution of the soviets in 1993.

The strength of opposition groups in the soviets at various levels in 1991 raised the issue of the source and delegation (downward or upward) of sovereignty. This problem was resolved on a first come, first served basis. Regional elites picked up a number of powers that the federal center had dropped, yet attempts by local elites to display initiative and grab something for themselves were mostly thwarted. As a result, the intermediate regional level came to occupy the dominant position. It delegated a portion of its authority upward to the federal center and another portion downward to cities and *rayons*.

Elections continue to be perhaps the most important component of federalism. The electoral process sets in motion the mechanism encouraging political bargaining between the central, regional, and local elites and acts as a catalyst for all other political processes. The boundaries of election constituencies coincide with those of regions. Only during the 1989 elections did large, national, territorial election districts incorporate several regions. Moreover, each region is entitled to at least one State Duma seat regardless of the number of voters living there.

The power struggle at the center, especially during electoral campaigns, compelled federal elites to seek the support of regional elites, which ultimately promoted decentralization. Until recently all elections, local or federal, have worked against the power of the central government. This posed such a problem that the center would even support certain gubernatorial candidates who engaged in populist, anti-Moscow rhetoric. Such rhetoric allowed candidates who were actually loyal to Moscow to assume the image of regional patriots and strengthen their position against opponents more hostile to the center.[8] Moreover, after the elections, especially when regional leaders had changed, the center would agree to various concessions to establish better relations with newly elected governors. Mostly such arrangements included replacing presidential representatives and other federal officials with individuals more acceptable to the new governors.

The center also had to agree to concessions and shower gifts and promises on regional leaders to secure their support in federal elections. During the 1996 presidential campaign, when Boris Yeltsin toured two dozen regions, he distributed gifts and money everywhere and signed decrees on new regional development programs. He also endorsed a salvo of bilateral agreements with a dozen regions that gave them greater control over their natural and financial resources.

The 1999–2000 election cycle was an exception. In this electoral cycle, some regional elites attempted to organize against the Kremlin. The attempt by regional elites under the electoral alliance Fatherland-All Russia, led by Moscow Mayor Yuri Luzhkov, St. Petersburg Governor Vladimir Yakovlev, and Tatarstan President Mintimer Shaimiyev, to consolidate and take an active part in the power struggle at the center was foiled. Instead, as discussed in chapter 2, the Kremlin's own creation, Unity, emerged victorious. Consequently, the center was able to continue its offensive against governors' rights and privileges. Anticipating the loss of their freedoms and eager to assure their preservation, regional elites rallied in support of Unity even before the rise of Vladimir Putin. Since Putin has become president, regional elites have cooperated and coordinated with the Kremlin on election-related issues.

The Instability of Asymmetries

The Soviet legacy has had a profound influence on Russia's unique form of asymmetrical federalism. Some aspects of the Soviet system, such as its ethno-territorial structure, were inherited directly without fundamental changes. In other respects, however, the collapse of the USSR had a profound effect, resulting in a series of both legal and institutional asymmetries. These peculiarities have contributed to the instability of the post-Soviet Russian federal state.

The cascade of declarations of sovereignty among Russia's autonomous regions can be seen as a legacy of the late Soviet era's period of state disintegration and a continuation of what happened with the republics of the Soviet Union.[9] Northern Ossetia was the first autonomous republic to issue a declaration of sovereignty a year after similar declarations by the Baltic republics, a month after Russia's declaration, and only four days after Ukraine's declaration. The chain reaction continued when Karelia, Komi, and Tatarstan declared sovereignty and Udmurtia, Yakutia, and Chukotka followed. The parade resulted from the epic power struggle between Mikhail Gorbachev and Boris Yeltsin. Gorbachev attempted to bypass Russia's leadership and invited the leaders of some of the Russian autonomous republics to sign the new Union Treaty with the leaders of the Union republics.[10] Yeltsin, in turn, appealed to the autonomous republics to seize as much sovereignty as they could handle.

Opportunities to accept sovereignty differed in each republic. Varying political climates also led to different results. Thus after the dust of the Soviet Union's collapse had settled and republics were signing Yeltsin's new Federal Treaty in March 1992, designed after Gorbachev's aborted Union Treaty, the republics of Tatarstan and Chechnya refused to sign.[11] Several other republics, such as Bashkortostan and Yakutia, signed the treaty with special conditions attached. Nevertheless, this agreement marked a giant step toward genuine federalism and the process of holding the federation together. Not only did the Federal Treaty provide the legal basis for the Russian Federation, but to some extent it diminished differences in status between regions, thereby weakening the ethnic character of Russian federalism.

This latter change was important because of the rise of ethnic sentiments and nationalist movements in the ethnic republics. Such mobilization along ethnic lines was reflected in the rapid strengthening of national cultural movements, the increasing proportion of local ethnic groups in local leadership, and the rising ethnic unrest. National groups held their own congresses in 1990–1992, creating leadership bodies for each nation, including its diasporas. The bodies established included the Tatar World Congress, the Mary-El Council, the World Chuvash Council, and the All-National Congress of the Chechen People. Regional authorities later stopped or, as in Tatarstan and Bashkortostan, co-opted these nationalist movements. Many regional authorities came to power on the wave of nationalist movements, but then distanced themselves from national radicals and took control of national congresses. Only in Checheno-Ingushetia, which was a united republic until 1991, did such a congress, the All-National Congress of the Chechen People, take power. It declared the Chechen Republic independent and elected its leader, General Jokhar Dudayev, as president. As a result, the Chechen-Ingush republic became the only republic to split in two. Similar attempts in Kabardino-Balkaria and Karachaevo-Cherkessia failed.

The new Russian Constitution, adopted in 1993 after the end of an intense power struggle in the center, also broke with the Soviet past and introduced the norms and institutions of a real federation. It did not, however, include the federal treaties, which would have given the ethnic republics the same status as *oblasts* and *krais* by making all 89 regions "subjects of the federation." Republic presidents were not happy with the draft constitution, and the failure of the December 1993 referendum on the constitution to win even a simple majority in many republics was not surprising. Some republics, like Tatarstan and Chechnya, refused even to hold the referendum vote.[12]

Rebellion Against the Center: The Tatar and Chechen Models

Both Tatarstan and Chechnya, Muslim republics with populations of 3.6 million and 1.3 million, respectively, refused to sign the Federal Treaty in

1992. Neither participated in the March 1991 referendum on the creation of the Russian presidency or in the elections of the president three months later. They did elect their own presidents in an effort to present a more united front in their confrontations with Moscow. While Tatarstan and Chechnya have much in common, how they treated the center and how the center treated them differed significantly.[13] One of the most important differences was the rise in Chechnya of unskilled radical leaders amid military and tribal traditions and plentiful weapons.[14] Refusing to compromise on the issue of secession, Chechnya's conflict with Moscow immediately escalated into violence and war. Tatarstan's former communist leadership used different tactics, seeking compromise while insisting on broad sovereignty in "association with" the Federation.

Chechnya and Tatarstan played an important role in Russian politics at the federal level. Both the 1994 and 1999 wars in Chechnya started on the eve of Russian elections, and therefore became as much about who would hold power in Russia as about who would lead. In the first instance, Yeltsin needed a little victorious war to restore his image as a decisive leader and an effective guarantor of the constitution. The second war was intended to facilitate the smooth transfer of power from Yeltsin to a handpicked successor. Yeltsin's inner circle or "family" selected an almost unknown person, Vladimir Putin, the idea being that he would position himself as a strong leader and the consolidator of the nation.

In 1994, Yeltsin decided that he needed to take urgent surgical action with regard to Chechnya. Things might have gone as well as they had for Gorbachev in Baku, Azerbaijan, in 1990 had Yeltsin possessed the appropriate surgical instruments and had the opponent been unarmed (as in Baku). Instead, Yeltsin became a butcher rather than a surgeon, and Chechnya became an armed warrior rather than a sedated patient. Once begun, the ongoing war in Chechnya became a key and permanent factor in Russian politics ever since.

The war in Chechnya has all the negative characteristics of the typical civil war: (1) atrocities and a huge death toll, both military and civilian; (2) large-scale destruction and the loss of large amounts of material and financial resources (amid conditions of an already weak economy); and (3) exacerbation of ethnic hatreds and the emergence of a nation at war mentality that can only undermine democracy and federalism.[15]

In sum, Tatarstan serves as a positive model for settling differences about the structure of Russian federalism, while Chechnya serves as a negative model, demonstrating how failure to compromise can be dangerous not only for Moscow and Grozny, but for the stability of the federal state as a whole. At the same time, the war in Chechnya prevents the center from attempting to reestablish hyper-centralized rule first, because it has been rendered too weak to accomplish the task, and second, because it forces Moscow to seek compromise with other regions to avoid another crisis that could lead to two simultaneous civil wars. Ingushetia's free economic zone, which existed until the end of the first war, serves as a good example of such compromise. Although Chechnya could become the tomb of Russian federalism in the future, at present it is preventing backsliding toward unitary rule.

Separate Negotiations: The Federal Treaty

The parade of sovereignties of 1990–1991 was followed by the parade of bilateral treaties between the center and individual regions that concluded in 1994–1998. These treaties were used to define the boundaries of authorities between Moscow and regional governments. After the first bilateral treaty on the division of power and competences between the chief executives of a region and Moscow was signed with Tatarstan in February 1994, forty-five more regions signed similar agreements with Moscow during the next four years. This process made some regions "more equal" than others, rendering the federation asymmetrical. This asymmetry has attracted a good deal of attention from scholars and other analysts.[16]

Several points are important in connection with the treaties. First, in effect the long parade of treaties constituted the signing of a new federal treaty in a more drawn out form. Several regions rejoined the federation, each on a different basis that reflected the balance of power between the region and the center. Second, the treaties or, more precisely, the intergovernmental agreements that followed them, varied depending on the different weights of each region and the types of powers extended. Thus treaties with Tatarstan, Bashkortostan, and Yakutia gave these powerful regions a single-channel taxation system, direct participation in foreign politics, and control over their natural resources and property, while other regions got far less.

As the political balance has shifted to favor the center under Putin, the process of abrogating and rewriting the treaties has also got under way. In 2001, federal and regional commissions were established to delimit powers and competences between the federal organs of state power, the organs of state power in the regions, and the organs of local self-administration. By the end of 2002, thirty regions had agreed to renounce their treaties with the center under strong pressure from federal authorities. The speed of treaty abrogation with *oblasts* and *krais* has been striking, although none of the treaties with major autonomous republics have been eliminated. The treaty between Russia and its capital is also still on the books.

One of the main incongruities in Russia's territorial and state structure is the existence of two tiers of regions and their autonomous *okrugs*. Seven *krais* and *oblasts* incorporate ten autonomous *okrugs* that are subjects of the Russian Federation in their own right. This is both unique and peculiar. During the movement for sovereignty in the early 1990s, autonomous entities made an attempt to break free from their mother regions and acquire independence. The autonomous *oblasts* succeeded and became subordinated directly to Moscow. The Jewish Autonomous Oblast was the only one to retain its old name—all the others became republics—but the Jewish Autonomous Oblast is no longer part of Khabarovsk Krai. Of the ten autonomous *okrugs*, only the Chukotka Autonomous Okrug managed to separate itself from its mother region, although it was never the biggest, richest, or most outstanding of *okrugs*. The others had to reconcile themselves with the status quo.

Now that social activism has slackened, the problem of the status of autonomous *okrugs* has ceased to concern the public and remains an issue only among political and economic elites. This is not the case during elections, however, when the masses are inevitably drawn into struggles for independence. The main instruments of this game include sabotage and ignoring the results of elections that bring irreconcilable opponents of the Kremlin to power in a regional or provincial capital. *Oblast* and *krai* authorities were confronted by the first signs of disobedience in 1994 during the elections to regional legislatures, when, for instance, Koryak Okrug simply refused to elect deputies to the Kamchatka Oblast Duma. Taimyrsky and Nenetsky *okrugs* experienced similar problems.

The situation worsened during the 1996 gubernatorial elections, when problems with Kamchatka's Koryak Okrug and Arkhangelsk's okrug reemerged. The problem of North Tyumen's rich and populous *okrugs* reached an unprecedented level. The first thing that the *okrug* governments did was to separate local and *oblast*-wide elections, making the sabotage of regional election outcomes easier. The Khanty-Mansiisky Okrug legislature went further, adopting the Law on Elections of the Tyumen Oblast Governor on the Territory of the Khanty-Mansiisky Okrug, which stipulated that to win the Tyumen gubernatorial election a candidate had to win 50 percent plus one vote with a minimum turnout rate of 25 percent within the *okrug*. Under this rule, the *oblast* could have elected one *oblast* governor while its constituent *okrug* elected a different one.

With political culture underdeveloped and no mechanisms for representing minority interests, the winner takes all elections have the potential to undermine stability in the multiethnic republics of the north Caucasus, where the situation is already tense. One example is the 1999 elections in Karachaevo-Cherkessia, which activated the dormant conflict between the republic's ethnic Karachai and Cherkess groups. The fears of worsening the ethnic conflict explain why three times in the past few years Dagestan has refused to introduce direct popular election of the head of the republic.

Itself a composite ethnic federation, Dagestan has become a testing ground for ethnic federalism. Dagestan uses two-tier, indirect elections of its top leader, the head of the State Council, which is made up of members of the Constitutional Assembly. Specifically, half of the Constitutional Assembly consists of parliamentary deputies and the other half of delegates from subregional units elected by local councils. The Constitutional Assembly elects members to the fourteen-seat State Council, with each seat held by a representative of each of the republic's fourteen main ethnic groups. The State Council elects a chair, who becomes the republic's highest official. Originally, the plan was to rotate the chair among State Council members every two years, similar to the system in the former Yugoslavia under Tito; however, the first elected chair has been in power since 1994. Dagestan also uses ethnic electoral districts to establish ethnic quotas for the distribution of seats in the republic's legislative People's Assembly as well as in local and town assemblies.[17] This method appears to have helped Dagestan avoid ethnic clashes similar to those that occurred in Karachaevo-Cherkessia during elections. Moreover, a mechanism is in place that allows a particular ethnic group to veto a decision that affects its immediate interests and prevents other ethnic groups from overriding the veto. Russia's federal system lacks such consociation mechanisms for harmonizing interethnic competition in relations between the center and the regions.

The Center in the Regions and the Regions in the Center

An understanding of the fragile and unstable nature of federalism in Russia requires looking at the institutions that permit interaction between the central and regional levels. Bicameralism, that is, the existence of a federative chamber that represents the regions in federal lawmaking, is one of the most important features of any federal state. It existed in the USSR, although not in the RSFSR,[18] after the adoption of Stalin's constitution in 1936. However, given the totalitarian nature, and therefore the purely decorative character, of any legislature under the Soviet system, bicameralism was only formally consociational to the extent that Soviet federalism was only formally federalist.[19]

The RSFSR Supreme Soviet, formed in 1990, was the first transitional Russian parliament and consisted of two chambers: the Council of Nationalities and the Council of the Republics, which were formally equal in powers and had 126 deputies each.[20] Deputy groups, rather than political parties, formed the basic organizational units of the Russian Congress. At the first Congress, six of the twenty-four deputies' groups were regionally based. After the disintegration of the USSR, Yeltsin established consultative bodies under his chairmanship: the Council of Heads of Republics in 1992 and the Council of Heads of Administration in 1993, which were the predecessors of the Federation Council. Figure 9.1 illustrates the evolution of these and other governmental bodies.

The 1993 constitution established genuine bicameralism in Russia's legislature. The concept of the Federation Council, made up of heads of the constituent territories of the federation, had been proposed several times under Gorbachev and Yeltsin. Under the 1993 Constitution, the Federation Council consisted of two deputies from each of the eighty-nine regions, and thus became a proper upper house of the Federal Assembly. The constitution delegates vast powers to the Federation Council, and some scholars even refer to it as one of the most powerful upper houses among federal states.[21] In reality, however, the power of the upper house is much more limited than similar bodies in other federal states.

Three episodes from different periods in Russia's post-Soviet development illustrate this point. First, in 1994 Yeltsin began the war in Chechnya without consulting the Federal Assembly and despite senators' opposition to the war. Even though the Federation Council has the prerogative to confirm presidential decrees regarding martial law and states of emergency, the Constitutional Court ruled that Yeltsin had not violated the constitution.

Second, in 1994–1995 and 1999–2000 Yeltsin used guards to prevent the acting prosecutors general from entering their offices, despite the Federation Council's strong opposition to the president's decision to replace the prosecutor general and notwithstanding the constitution's stipulation

Figure 9.1. Representations of Regions at the Federal Level, 1989–2004

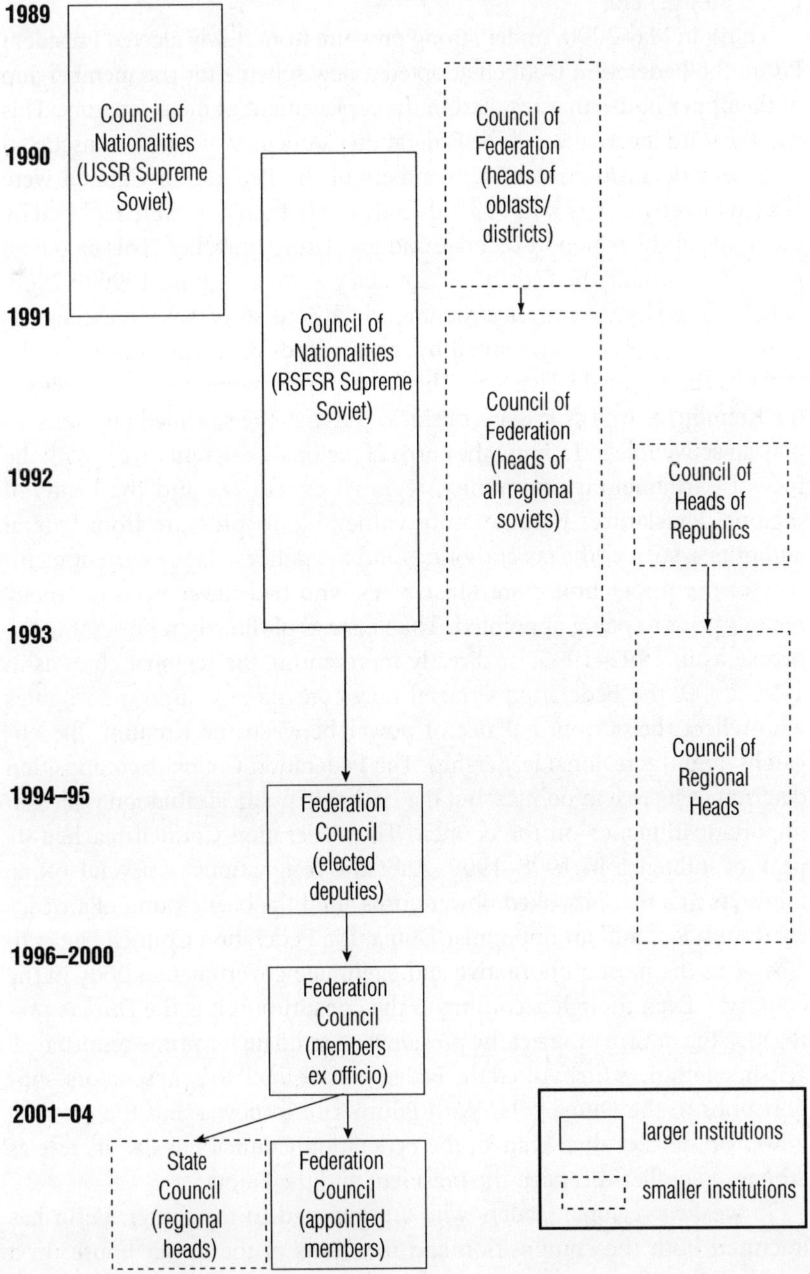

1989

1990

Council of Nationalities (USSR Supreme Soviet)

Council of Federation (heads of oblasts/ districts)

1991

Council of Nationalities (RSFSR Supreme Soviet)

Council of Federation (heads of all regional soviets)

1992

Council of Heads of Republics

1993

Council of Regional Heads

1994–95

Federation Council (elected deputies)

1996–2000

Federation Council (members ex officio)

2001–04

State Council (regional heads)

Federation Council (appointed members)

larger institutions

smaller institutions

that the upper house be responsible for both appointing and removing the prosecutor general.

Third, in May 2000, under strong pressure from newly elected President Putin, the Federation Council adopted a new scheme for the membership of the upper house that resulted in the replacement of most senators. This was the third incarnation of the Federation Council's structure. As discussed in greater detail in chapter 2, members of the Federation Council were elected directly in 1993. In 1995, directly elected senators were replaced by the heads of the regions' executive and legislature branches. This ex officio method of forming the Federation Council was in place from 1996 to 2000, to be replaced by the current structure, which consists of two representatives from each region, one appointed by the governor or the president and the other by the regional legislature. This method of appointing senators allows the Kremlin, as well as Russia's business tycoons, the so-called oligarchs, to play an active role in forming the corps of regional representatives. With the loss of parliamentary immunity, regional executives and the heads of regional legislatures became more vulnerable to pressure from federal authorities, such as the tax authorities and the police.[22] Many current members of the upper house are Muscovites who had never been to "their" regions prior to being appointed. Thus instead of directly representing the people as in 1993–1995, or directly representing the regional elites as in 1996–2000, the Federation Council now consists of compromise figures who reflect the current balance of power between the Kremlin, the oligarchs, and the regional leadership. The Federation Council's composition determines its role in politics, but the changing political situation is also an important influence on the council. The Federation Council reached its peak of influence in 1998–1999. After the resignations of several prime ministers in a row provoked power crises amid the background of a weakened president and an unpopular Duma, the Federation Council began to emerge as the most authoritative and legitimate governmental body in the country.[23] Even though according to the constitution it is the Duma's prerogative to confirm or reject the president's candidate for prime minister, all Yeltsin's nominees first visited the Federation Council to gain senators' support prior to the Duma vote. With Putin's rise to power and the growing power of the executive branch, the Federation Council has lost its role as arbiter in conflicts between the president and the Duma.

To weaken regional leaders who are opposed to the center, Putin has fractured both the composition and functions of the upper house. In a sense, the Federation Council has two clones. One, with the same name but a very different composition, inherited its formal functions. The other, which consists of the same regional leaders who once sat on the Federation Council, is called the State Council and to some extent retains the informal role of its predecessor: a governors' club providing a forum for contact between the regional and federal elites. The State Council meets four times a year to discuss such key issues as economic strategy, land reform, and municipal reform. Between meetings, the State Council Presidium holds monthly meetings with the president.

The Presidium consists of seven regional leaders who represent each federal district and who the president replaces twice a year. Presidium members often lead working groups that prepare programs on specific issues on the agendas of Presidium or State Council meetings, but their role is strictly advisory. Putin and his government have rarely used their reports. Presidium members can, however, initiate discussions, articulate opposition to or support for government programs under consideration, and work out program modifications in cooperation with the government. The main purposes of the State Council and its presidium seem to be to help fashion compromises between the federal and regional elites, to train top executive officials at the federal and regional levels who participate in the presidium meetings, and to diversify the sources of information available to the president.

Putin's Antifederal Reform

The administrative changes Putin adopted, in particular, the creation of seven federal districts, could be viewed as an effort to reclaim federal powers that were illicitly grabbed by the regions and to flesh out the constitutional provisions needed to create a normal, functioning, federal system. A more accurate interpretation is that Putin is aggressively pursuing an antifederal policy designed to take away or circumscribe most powers exercised by regional leaders. The purpose appears to be the establishment of a unitary state under the guise of restoring "effective interaction between various levels of state power" and a unitary executive power or "vertical" to use Putin's own word.[24] In keeping with Putin's background in the KGB, the main emphasis is on discipline, order, and hierarchy. His approach represents a rejection of federalism—which is still very much a work in progress—and an attempt at re-centralization. Whether Putin's institutional and personnel choices will achieve the desired result is not clear. Neither is it evident that re-centralization will be an effective administrative strategy in post-Soviet Russia.

The August 1998 financial meltdown and subsequent political crises in Moscow radically weakened the center's position. By early 1999, the process of decentralization had gone so far that a risk emerged that the system might shift from a weakly institutionalized, asymmetrical, federal system to a disintegrating confederal system. Further decentralization seemed inevitable, despite its dangers, in light of the imminent start of another major election cycle. May–September 1999 was the most difficult time for the Kremlin and the Russian government, which were both perceived as being in their last months, and a mass exodus of top officials and bureaucrats became a real threat. The regional elite already perceived the authority of the center as having declined sharply, and the growing incompetence of the civil service added to such perceptions.

With Putin in office, the center regained its initiative, made a show of the use of military force in Dagestan and Chechnya, and secured the active cooperation of the Federal Security Service (FSB). The process of decentralization was reversed. Contrary to conventional political logic and the lessons of previous Russian elections, the center started to strengthen its position.[25] This effort was stimulated by further growth in international oil prices and increased budgetary revenues, which allowed the government to pay its wage and pension arrears. These revenues also allowed greater use of financial carrots and sticks funneled through government-controlled oligarchic structures such as Gazprom, RAO Unified Energy Systems, and the Ministry of Railways. This strengthening would not have succeeded if the center had not consolidated and demonstrated political will.

The onset of the second war in Chechnya was the main factor in the political developments that brought Putin to the presidency. Chechnya was both evidence of and an aid to further consolidation of the center's strengthening position. The war enabled the Kremlin to transfer presidential powers to its chosen heir, who became acting president upon Yeltsin's resignation on December 31, 2000. Subsequent elections confirmed that transfer in March 2000. However, the war's side effects and its long-term negative implications for Russian federalism and the Russian state may prove to be very serious.

Beginning in the fall of 1999, the center moved to strengthen its relations with the regions in several areas. In the personnel sphere, the trend was to strengthen the heads of federal institutions in the regions, primarily presidential representatives and heads of power structures.[26] Other measures included efforts to weaken regional leaders' control over federal civil servants in the regions. To put pressure on regional leaders, compromising materials were gathered during so-called anticorruption campaigns in the regions and used to force governors to leave such opposition blocs as Fatherland-All Russia on the eve of Duma elections and to join Unity, the new pro-Kremlin party of power.[27]

In the financial sector, the center tightened control over the use of federal budgetary resources in the regions, channeling funds through regional branches of the federal treasury. In 2000, in a number of the most subsidized regions, such as Dagestan, all payments were affected through the treasury's city- and *rayon*-level branches on a pilot basis.[28]

In the legal sphere, two fundamental laws were adopted on the delineation of power among the various levels of government and on the fundamental organizing principles of state power in the regions, which unified the rules of the game regulating interactions between the center and the regions. The practice of shaping regional legislation into conformity with federal legislation was expanded to the strongest and most obstinate regions, such as Bashkortostan and Tatarstan.

In the media sector, the development of the All-Russia State Television and Radio Company continued, incorporating all state-owned regional television and radio companies.

After the 2000 presidential elections, the Kremlin acted with unprecedented speed and energy to strengthen the center at the expense of the regions. Soon after winning the elections, Putin issued decrees abolishing regional decisions, which encroached on the powers of several regions. In Ingushetia, Bryansk Oblast, and other regions, regional authorities tried to intervene in the work of law enforcement agencies, to introduce illegal taxes, and to regulate imports and exports of some goods to and from their regions.

The next step occurred on May 13, 2000, when the president issued a decree that created seven federal districts or super-regions headed by presidential envoys, five of whom were generals (one of whom has since been replaced with a civilian). These federal districts were created to increase the federal government's presence and power in the regions. In particular, the new presidential plenipotentiaries have moved to take control of federal agencies located in the regions—such as the FSB, the tax police (later abolished in March 2003), and the regional branches of national television stations—that had drifted under the authority of regional heads of administration. The Security Council—an organ of the Kremlin—designed the federal districts and drew their borders to match the districts used by Ministry of Internal Affairs troops. These seven regions do not match up neatly with Russia's eleven economic regions or its eight inter-regional economic cooperation associations.[29] A contest appears to have arisen within the Putin administration between civilian and military proposals, which the military won.[30]

The construction of a new, intermediate level of government between the federal and regional governments could lead either to more centralization if powers are transferred formally and informally from the regional level to the federal district level, or to decentralization if the federal government devolves some of its powers to the federal districts. Putin's goal is clearly centralization, though some elements of decentralization are evident in conflicts between presidential envoys and federal ministries. Presidential envoys are elements of a new vertical power structure, with both the Presidential administration and the Security Council at the top. The envoys are members of the Security Council. As such, they are a conduit for bypassing both the Russian government and the governors. The establishment of federal districts is the third attempt in recent history to enlarge Russia's regions. The first two—one in the late 1920s and early 1930s and the second in the late 1950s and early 1960s—failed.

Putin has pushed a new law through the parliament that allows the president to remove governors and dismiss regional parliaments (which would require State Duma approval). In addition, the new Tax Code changes inter-budgetary relations by increasing the share of taxes going to the center and gives the federal government greater control over tax receipts and expenditures.

Less formally, Putin has introduced a more subtle federal reform: the rise of St. Petersburg and the commensurate weakening of Moscow. Paradoxically, while the center is becoming stronger, the capital is weakening. Moscow is a unique subject of the federation. It accounts for a little less than one-fifteenth of Russia's population. It is not only far more populous than any other city in the country, but it is far more populous than any other subject of the federation. Not surprisingly, the city dominates Russia's political and economic life. Putin has tried to undermine this hegemony by strengthening Russia's other major city, his hometown of St. Petersburg. Putin is the first of the country's Soviet or post-Soviet leaders who was born and raised in St. Petersburg, Russia's imperial capital, rather than coming from a far-flung province. Moreover, unlike his predecessors, Putin did not spend a lengthy period of time in Moscow prior to becoming president. As a result, he has maintained good connections with his hometown. This has had two major consequences. First, a significant flow of elites has taken place from St. Petersburg to Moscow. Reportedly, on Monday mornings a traffic jam of limousines waits outside the railway station in Moscow to pick up officials returning from weekends with their families in St. Petersburg. Second, some capital city functions have shifted from Moscow to St. Petersburg. Putin himself visits the city often, and the Constantine Palace is being restored as an official presidential residence. Serious discussions have taken place about moving the capital, or at least some of its functions, to St. Petersburg.

St. Petersburg's growing clout can be considered, at least in part, to be an outcome of Putin's reliance on his former colleagues from the city's FSB. This group's imprint on the federal government is significant, and includes Nikolai Patrushev, FSB director; Sergei Ivanov, defense minister; Viktor Ivanov, deputy head of the President's Administration in charge of personnel; Igor Sechin, Putin's chief secretary and deputy head of the presidential administration; Viktor Cherkesov, presidential plenipotentiary; Georgy Poltavchenko, presidential plenipotentiary; and Viktor Zubkov, chairman of the Financial Monitoring Committee of the Ministry of Finance. In addition, Putin has access to at least three other sources for recruiting St. Petersburg elite: lawyers and former colleagues from Mayor Anatoly Sobchak's administration,[31] liberal economists,[32] and so-called unallied individuals.[33]

One explanation for the dominance of the St. Petersburg group is Putin's need to fill key posts with people he trusts and who have demonstrated their loyalty to him. Another factor is a desire to systematically dismantle the old Moscow-based bureaucratic machine. Following long-standing practice, officials from St. Petersburg tend to bring their own subordinates with them, thus the number of midlevel officials from St. Petersburg has also increased enormously.

While officials flow from St. Petersburg to Moscow, the Kremlin is sending money in the opposite direction. For example, it allocated $1.5 billion in federal investment to celebrate the city's 300th anniversary in 2003. Coverage of St. Petersburg is increasing in the national media, and visiting foreign dignitaries are often taken to there as part of their official itineraries.

With the completion of these centralizing reforms in 2002, Russia ceased to be an emerging federation and was transformed into a unitary state with

Figure 9.2. Configuration of the Center regarding Regions, as of the End of 1998

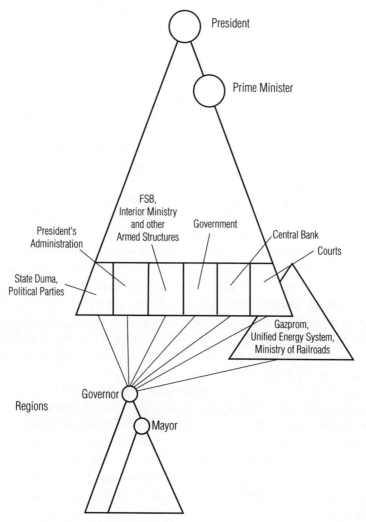

some regional and ethno-regional elements. Figure 9.2 shows the overall political configuration of the center—and the regions at the end of 1998. This configuration has since changed dramatically.

The most importance change is that the level of internal diversity in the center and the coordination among various federal structures in the regions (which has sometimes disintegrated into competition) have been improved by a corresponding reduction in the size and ambiguity of the base of the center's power pyramid in the regions. The role of these federal institutions, which feature better command and control than other government entities and are coordinated by the Security Council, has grown. Confrontation between the president and the prime minister, and between the President's Administration and the government have decreased considerably. In addition, infrastructure monopolies have started to work in tandem with the authorities. Consequently, the center has become considerably more monolithic and better organized than the regions. In the regions, the recent monopolistic position of regional leaders, even in relation to federal institutions working at the regional level, has started to weaken. This is a result of the center's clearer and stronger political will backed by more disciplined use of financial resources. This trend is shown as the breaking off of some federal structures from the regional pyramids.[34]

Figure 9.3 illustrates the changes in relations taking place between the center and the regions. What distinguishes this trend from previous trends goes beyond the emergence of an intermediate tier represented by federal districts headed by presidential envoys. Considerable changes have taken place at the pinnacle of the federal pyramid—the Presidential Administration, the government, and the Security Council, the triumvirate of executive power under the president—and at its base. The roles of the former have been expanded at the expense of the latter. At the base, the roles of the Federal Assembly, and especially of the Federation Council, have been diminished, while the roles of the more centralized judiciary and prosecutorial systems have grown. This was accomplished by creating twenty-one inter-regional, administrative, judicial *okrugs*; a corresponding collegium under the Supreme Court; and branches of the federal procuracy in the federal districts. The independence of the old oligarchs and of the infrastructure monopolies has also eroded. At the same time, regional leaders have been losing their monopoly on power.

The strengthening of the center at the end of 1999 and the beginning of 2000 was not a sudden or unplanned development, but a process that developed along lines mapped out in 1997 and 1998. It was only by 1999, however, that the consolidation of the elites in the center and the changed social, economic, and political situation enabled full-scale implementation of the earlier plans to strengthen the state.

In the context of contemporary Russian politics, a certain degree of centralization might be beneficial for the following reasons. First, an effective

Figure 9.3. Configuration of the Center regarding Regions, as of the end of 2000

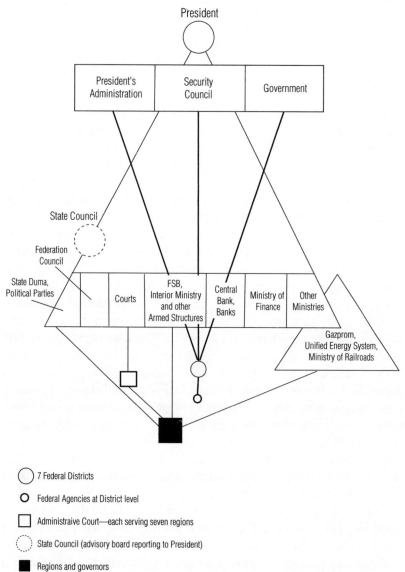

civil society is impossible to build on the basis of small, subnational units whose political development is drifting in different directions. Second, in their present form, Russia's regions are still too fragmented, and many are too small, for the purposes of federalization. Some of the regions do not have enough capacity to be subjects of the federation and perform the appropriate functions, while other regions can only be federal territories. Third, strong federal power promotes second-tier decentralization, that is, a redistribution of power from the regional to local levels of government. Fourth, the preservation and development of a unified political space will facilitate the separation of economic activities from politics: the segregation of political and economic power will turn governors from feudal lords into top corporate managers.

As the decentralization-centralization pendulum swings, a critical problem is finding the optimal balance between short-term and long-term prospects and between unitary-centralist and federalist components. However, the optimal situation cannot be reached at once and is always shifting as political and economic conditions change. Hope that the political debris will be cleared out of the way first and that only then will a normal federation be created is even more naive. Rather, the process of federalization is developing simultaneously with other processes, reflecting all the difficulties and vicissitudes of the Russian political landscape.

Prospects for the Future

Relations between the center and the regions are still in flux. The ongoing transition to a new state may become more gradual and more radical, depending on the nature of political developments. At various stages of the transition, federalism may become the quintessence of the political process, or it may find itself on the periphery, having been turned into a facade as is the case today. Hardly anything will change until the development of civil society generates conditions for new transformations whose objective will be a more sophisticated system of power that combines a clear delineation of authority with the delegation of authority to lower levels of government.

Changes will affect both the country's state-territorial administrative division and the system of ties between government institutions, both vertically between levels and horizontally across levels. Regions will almost inevitably become larger because of purely political reasons rather than because of any abstract self-sufficiency and management considerations. Enlargement has both advantages and disadvantages. The main disadvantage is the stronger threat of separatism caused by an increase in the political and economic resources available to the few newly elected regional leaders. Yet every time federal authorities come up with the idea of regional enlargement, they insist that it is intended to counter separatist sentiments. Clearly, the main advantage would be replacing the current system of hyper-centralism with a multicenter, multipolar economic and political system that would result from having fewer, larger, and therefore more politically substantial regional governments.

Will re-centralization and the attempt to recreate a unitary system be effective in today's Russia? The first years of experience with the system of federal districts provide contradictory evidence. On the one hand, the new policies do seem to be removing gubernatorial control over the military, police, and federal agencies that rightfully belong under federal jurisdiction. On the other hand, Putin's advisers do not seem to recognize that this could go too far or that excessive centralization was one of the weaknesses of the failed Soviet system. Putin's statements on restoring the vertical power hierarchy clearly indicate that his main point of reference is the USSR. To someone who is a product of the Soviet system, checks and balances are worth sacrificing to increase the manageability and effectiveness of the political system. This trade-off may be worthwhile in the short run, but it entails a huge risk. A highly centralized system runs the risk of collapsing in the face of changing conditions or circumstances. Like a dinosaur, it takes too long for any signal to reach the brain, and thus for feedback to produce a reaction. Such an encumbered system simply functions too slowly to respond to the numerous and different reactions that can be needed for different parts of a huge structure. In general, the bigger and more centralized a system is, the greater the difficulty with which it accommodates changing conditions.

Putin's top aides and presidential representatives have only a hazy notion of what constitutes federalism. To an extent, this parallels Soviet era misunderstandings about the nature of democracy and a market economy. The absence of a planned or command system for allocating resources was equated with chaos and anarchy. Similarly, the absence of a clear chain of command in the political and administrative sphere is viewed as disorder or as a situation that is bound to spin out of control. The idea that certain important decisions could actually be made in the regions without a directive from the center is alien to this mindset. The same desire for order will likely focus on the subregional level as well, that is, the cities and towns. Yeltsin's declared policy of creating autonomous local government institutions was an important affirmation of federalist principles. Putin's plans are not likely to increase the effective powers exercised at the local level, and may result in the direct subordination of mayors to governors.

Putin's policies threaten not only the development of a federal system, but also democratization. Democratization, federalization, and popular elections are an unbreakable triad. Despite all the rhetoric to the contrary, until recently the situation could be described as one of weak state-weak society and weak regions-weaker center. Power is not about the extent of authority, but about how much of that authority can be effectively implemented.[35] At present, neither the center nor the regions can exercise their authority effectively. As the state becomes stronger, the elements of democracy generated by a weak state rather than a strong society will inevitably be reduced or eliminated. As for the regions, the strengthening of the state and the center means the weakening or withering away of a number of elements of Russia's pseudo-federalism. The creation of new levels of administrative authority in the form of presidential representatives and federal district offices of government agencies does nothing to facilitate Russia's political development. Ultimately, the political center of gravity should be in the regions. In the 1990s, the effectiveness of both state and societal political institutions and independent mass media was undermined by the disproportionate power wielded by governors and republic presidents.

Why are relations between the center and the regions so vitally important to the future of democracy in Russia? Since Yeltsin's victory over the parliament in 1993, the horizontal division of power has shifted in favor of the executive branch. The vertical division of powers between the center and the regions, despite its less than fully institutionalized form, compensated for the almost uncontrolled power of the executive in Moscow, allowing for another center of power: regional chief executives. Now, with the representative branch even weaker than it was under Yeltsin, regional leaders represent the last bastion of democracy.

If the center were to use its power to guarantee political freedoms and rights in the regions, it could encourage participation and democratization. Instead, Putin's policies are designed to create a new level of decision making above the regions, making policy less dependent on the governors. However, his centralizing policies also put important policy decisions out of the reach of citizens and nongovernmental organizations. Needless to say, virtually none of the latter are organized at the federal district level. The few regions that have shown some progress in democratization could easily see these gains disappear as the locus of power and policy moves upward.

Putin's policy toward political parties and elections in the regions illustrates this point. Rather than encourage pluralism and allow the bottom-up development of grassroots parties, Putin has pushed for the creation of a national super-party through the merger of two of the six parties represented in the Duma: Unity, and Fatherland-All Russia. This new entity, United Russia, is highly centralized under the control of Putin loyalists. As a result of the new 2001 law on political parties, regionally-based parties will not be allowed to register and compete in national elections. At the same time, the Kremlin is trying to change the rules on electing regional legislatures to require a mixed single-member and proportional representation (party list) system. This appears to be designed to allow United Russia to establish a foothold in regional legislatures and deprive governors of control over them. In addition, the presidential representatives have been mobilized to assist in party formation in their federal districts' regions, obviously to benefit United Russia.

Officials in the presidential administration have announced plans to establish a new organizational mechanism for election commissions, which would give the center greater control over the conduct of regional and local elections. The proposal is akin to the restoration of a Soviet-style system using a single party to provide a parallel chain of vertical authority that reaches from the top state bodies to the lowest level of society. Finally, the president may get additional rights to appoint regional chief executives if the Duma passes certain amendments to the Law on the Main Guarantees of Election Rights of the Citizens of the Russian Federation and the Right to Take Part in a Referendum. One proposal from pro-Kremlin factions supported by the Central Election Commission is to introduce the requirement of a minimal voter turnout of 50 percent in regional elections, with elections being held in two rounds if turnout is below that.[36] If elections are invalidated because of insufficient turnout in the second round, then the president will have the right to appoint governors for a term of two years upon agreement with regional parliaments.

Thus Putin's vision for Russia appears to be one of strong vertical chains of command: his own administrative chain based on federal districts and presidential representatives; a national police system with a strong presence in the regions; a vertical political party; and a vertical electoral commission. If implemented fully, the result would be a vertically integrated but horizontally fractured state.

10

Regional Models of
Democratic Development

Nikolai Petrov

Those discussing the fate of democracy in Russia often focus on ostensibly nationwide phenomena, such as the separation of powers, the relationships between various political institutions, the freedom of the press,
and the activity of nongovernmental organizations. Yet observers often erro-
neously deduce trends from developments solely at the federal level of government. The reality is that the situation in Moscow and its adjacent regions
(Moskovskaya Oblast), diverges fundamentally from the situation of each of
the eighty-seven other subjects of the federation. A full and accurate picture
of the state of affairs in Russia with regard to democratization or any other
aspect of the complex and troubled transformation from communist rule
requires a close analysis of the situation at the regional level.

Few comparative studies of Russia's cross-regional political trends by
either Russian or Western analysts are available,[1] despite the popularity of
such research and the analysis of comparative cross-national trends. This is
somewhat surprising, given that Russia's transition has now been under
way for more than a decade and that many regions are larger than some
Central European and Latin American countries in terms of both territory
and population. A comprehensive analysis of the post-Soviet political transition in the regions is badly needed, primarily to enable researchers to
develop a more complete picture of the country's political development and
the process of democratization.

The process of democratization, one of the main goals of Russia's post-Soviet development, varies widely from region to region. This chapter seeks to capture this variation systematically by examining the extent of democratization in the regions, establishing a scale of the dynamics of democratization, and then explaining these dynamics.

The Dynamics of Regional Democratization

Rankings of levels of democracy are useful not so much because they permit an assessment of the processes in the different regions, but because they permit comparisons of regions and tracking of their development. In other words, looking at variations in the rating or index of the level of democracy across space and time is far more important than simply preparing an index. In addition, any imperfections in the methodology have less of an effect if the method is applied repeatedly and the results aggregated.

In trying to assess levels of democracy, researchers run up against the universal problem of assessing different aspects of democracy together across space and time. Given the limited availability of data, the period covered is less than ideal. In addition, Chechnya has not been included in the analysis because of the ongoing war. In any case, political life in the regions does not change so much that ratings are needed for every region every year. However, if ratings are calculated only once every four or five years, then the work takes a more historiographical approach and is deprived of any political significance.

Given these issues, the authors of the new ratings and rankings of Russia's regions according to their respective levels of democracy have proposed a compromise solution. The base rating is calculated from a large number of factors during the last few years. Partial indicators that are part of the overall rating are then recalculated on a yearly basis, but only when sufficient data are available for such a recalculation, such as elections, important changes in local legislation, or political conflict. Ratings are preserved without change until new data necessitate a new assessment. A detailed evaluation once every four years with the completion of an election cycle seems to be the optimum timing. The completion of an election cycle is an appropriate cutoff point, because elections are the most important and revealing indicator of the state of a regional polity, and also because they flush out all of a local democracy's dark corners and expose the secrets of local politics.

What and How to Count

For many years the independent political research institute and democracy watchdog Freedom House has produced its own evaluations and ratings of the state of democracy across the world. It usually assigns number grades for the state of democracy as reflected by both political and civil rights on a seven-point scale, with a ranking of 1 indicating maximum freedom and of 7 indicating minimum freedom. Freedom House applied a much more detailed grading to post-Soviet and post-communist countries in transition. This separate rating system is referred to as the nations in transit ranking.[2] It uses twelve individual ratings calculated to two decimal places to come up with the final rating. The individual rankings measure (1) the nature of the political process, (2) the development of civil society, (3) the extent of media freedom, (4) the system of administration, (5) the legislative and judicial systems, (6) the extent of corruption, (7) the degree of privatization, (8) the condition of macroeconomic policy, (9) the condition of microeconomic policy, (10) the extent of democratization, (11) the rule of law, and (12) the amount of economic liberalization. For the last few years, Freedom House has rated Russia as a partially free state and as one of the top ranked countries of the Commonwealth of Independent States. Among all the former Soviet republics, it only lags behind the Baltic states.

Comparative analyses make frequent use of this rating system, but have applied it to Russia without substantial adaptations. Given its transitional nature, Russia requires detailed monitoring in real time and a wealth of insider information that is often difficult to access. Politics in the regions are typically neither public nor transparent. The hypertrophy of executive power, the weak extent of institutionalization, and the underdevelopment of civil society together with the observation of formal democratic procedures is creating a pseudo democracy. As the experience of Freedom House shows, the usual instruments of analysis cannot be applied in such a situation. Such instruments endow most regions with the same results and smooth over variations between them. The way to correct this is by supplementing general analyses with specific ones tailored to conditions in Russia.

Expert Evaluations of Democracy in the Regions

Thus the goals and the task posed are clear: obtaining a base rating plus annual adjustments. However, a caveat exists with regard to the base rating in that it can be calculated in two ways: Freedom House's method of assessments by experts and an "instrumental" mark. In the first case, the advantage is a more complete evaluation of the entire spectrum of interconnected factors that define the level of democracy, while the second method provides an opportunity for interim recalibration. The expert evaluation will be considered first.

The level of democracy is an integral expression of the overall political climate. It is not momentary or narrow and cannot be directly observed and assigned a numeric code. Indeed, it is not easily measured and can only be assessed on the basis of a series of observations. Subjectivity is inevitable. One way to reduce the level of subjectivity is to bring in a number of experts to do the calculation. We took this path in 1997 and 1999 to assess the extent of democracy in fifty-seven *oblasts* and two federal cities (Moscow and St. Petersburg).[3] What complicates this approach is that experts do not have an equally well-informed understanding of all the relevant regions, particularly in the context of the stormy political life of post-Soviet Russia. At best, qualified experts have personally visited a few regions recently and are well informed about the situation in a number of other regions, but their opinion about most regions will be based on indirect, and at best secondary, sources. Two erroneous notions emerge from this approach: analysis is often reduced to the ideas that a region is democratic if it votes for so-called democrats and if power is in the hands of a democratic regional governor or republican president.

The second approach can help avoid systematic mistakes conditioned by the mass media and public awareness. This alternative approach lies in detailing the scores for levels of democracy and breaking them down into individual components. Such an approach is labor intensive, and requires going through a voluminous amount of raw data from each of the regions. At the same time, it is justified for two reasons. First, it ensures relative uniformity of the evaluation method in each region. Second, because the grade is assessed not once but each year, it highlights the dynamics of the transition. The data compiled by the Carnegie Moscow Center's project on sociopolitical monitoring of the regions from 1995 to 2002 offers an opportunity to trace the level of democratization in Russia's regions by region and over time along the lines of the Freedom House surveys of democracy of other countries around the world.[4]

The overall rating of the democracy level is calculated on the basis of scores for ten separate political spheres: (1) the openness of political life (the extent of transparency and of public involvement in political life); (2) the level of democracy in federal, regional, and local elections held in the regions (the existence of free and fair elections for posts at all levels, their competitiveness, the use of so-called administrative resources, including direct interference by the authorities or the courts, and the limitations to realizing political rights); (3) the extent of political pluralism (the existence of stable parties, factions in the legislative assembly, and coalitions during elections and afterward); (4) the degree of media freedom and independence; (5) the extent of economic liberalization, including privatization (through regional legislation and in practice); (6) the development of civil society (nongovernmental organizations, referenda, various forms of public activity, demonstrations, pickets, and strikes not sanctioned by the authorities); (7) the region's political regime (the balance of power, the number of elected versus appointed officials, the independence of the judiciary and law enforcement agencies, and the extent of citizens' rights); (8) the quality, perpetuation, and turnover of political elites (changes of leaders implemented by means of elections that do not lead to a dismantling of the whole system, varied nature of the elites, and vitality of mechanisms for compromises between competing interests); (9) the degree of corruption (the merging of political and economic elites and corruption scandals); and (10) the amount of local self-administration (the existence of elected bodies of local government and their level of activity and influence). Each region is assessed on a five-point scale in each of the ten spheres. The higher the number, the more democracy. The overall rating is tallied by adding up the individual ratings, with the highest score possible being 50 and the lowest possible score being 10 (table 10.1).[5]

Despite the large variation between the highest and the lowest ratings of democracy—from 45 for St. Petersburg to 14 for Kalmykia—the contrasts are not as great as might be expected. Five regions stand out for their high level of urbanization and democracy: St. Petersburg (45), Sverdlovsk Oblast (43), the Republic of Karelia (41), Perm Oblast (41), and Nizhny Novgorod Oblast (40). Following the five leading democratic regions is a group of five moderately democratic regions all rated at 37. Ten regions score less than 20. These authoritarian regions—all national autonomies—include

Table 10.1. Ratings of Democracy in Russian Regions Based on Expert Evaluation, 1991–2001

Rating	Region	Openness	Free and fair elections	Political pluralism	Independent mass-media	Economic liberalization	Civil Society	Political regime	Elites	Corruption	Local self-government	Total
1	St. Petersburg	5	5	5	5	4	5	5	5	3	3	45
2	Sverdlovskaya	5	5	5	5	4	4	5	3	2	5	43
3	Karelia	4	5	4	5	4	4	4	4	3	4	41
4	Permskaya	4	4	4	4	5	4	4	4	4	4	41
5	Nizhegorodskaya	5	3	4	5	4	4	4	4	3	4	40
6	Arkhangelskaya	4	5	4	3	4	3	4	4	3	3	37
7	Irkutskaya	4	4	4	4	3	4	3	4	3	4	37
8	Novosibirskaya	4	4	4	3	3	4	4	4	3	4	37
9	Samarskaya	5	3	4	3	4	4	4	4	2	4	37
10	Yaroslavskaya	4	4	4	4	4	3	4	3	4	3	37
11	Volgogradskaya	4	3	4	3	3	3	3	4	3	4	34
12	Kaliningradskaya	4	4	4	3	4	3	4	3	1	4	34
13	Chelyabinskaya	3	4	4	3	3	3	4	3	3	4	34
14	Udmurtia	3	4	4	4	3	3	3	2	3	4	33
15	Krasnoyarsky	4	4	3	4	3	3	4	3	2	3	33
16	Sakhalinskaya	4	3	4	3	4	3	3	3	3	3	33
17	Vologodskaya	4	3	3	3	3	3	3	4	3	3	32
18	Leningradskaya	4	4	3	2	4	3	3	3	3	3	32
19	Khanty-Mansiisky	4	3	3	3	4	3	3	2	3	4	32
20	Chuvashia	4	3	3	2	3	3	4	3	3	3	31
21	Kostromskaya	3	4	3	3	3	3	3	3	3	3	31
22	Buryatia	3	3	3	3	3	3	3	3	3	3	30
23	Moskovskaya	3	3	3	2	3	3	3	3	2	5	30

Table 10.1. Ratings of Democracy in Russian Regions Based on Expert Evaluation, 1991–2001 (continued)

Rating	Region	Openness	Free and fair elections	Political pluralism	Independent mass-media	Economic liberalization	Civil Society	Political regime	Elites	Corruption	Local self-government	Total
24	Murmanskaya	3	3	3	3	3	3	3	3	3	3	30
25	Novgorodskaya	4	2	2	2	5	2	2	2	5	4	30
26	Tyumenskaya	4	3	3	3	3	3	3	3	2	3	30
27	Moscow	3	4	3	3	4	4	2	2	2	2	29
28	Khakassia	3	3	3	3	3	2	2	3	3	4	29
29	Vladimirskaya	3	3	3	3	3	2	3	3	3	3	29
30	Ivanovskaya	3	3	3	3	3	2	3	3	3	3	29
31	Kaluzhskaya	2	3	3	3	3	3	3	3	3	3	29
32	Kamchatskaya	2	4	3	2	3	3	3	3	3	3	29
33	Kirovskaya	3	3	3	3	3	2	3	3	3	3	29
34	Omskaya	3	3	3	3	3	3	3	2	3	3	29
35	Tomskaya	3	3	3	3	3	3	3	2	3	3	29
36	Altai	3	3	3	2	3	2	3	3	3	3	28
37	Marii El	3	3	2	3	3	2	3	3	3	3	28
38	Astrakhanskaya	3	3	3	3	3	2	3	2	3	3	28
39	Belgorodskaya	3	3	3	2	3	2	3	3	3	3	28
40	Bryanskaya	3	3	3	3	2	2	3	3	3	3	28
41	Kemerovskaya	3	2	2	3	3	4	3	3	2	3	28
42	Tverskaya	3	3	3	3	3	2	3	3	2	3	28
43	Yamalo-Nenetsky	3	3	3	3	3	2	3	2	3	3	28
44	Komi	4	3	3	3	3	3	2	2	2	2	27
45	Lipetskaya	3	3	3	2	2	2	3	3	3	3	27
46	Pskovskaya	3	3	3	3	3	2	2	3	2	3	27

Table 10.1. Ratings of Democracy in Russian Regions Based on Expert Evaluation, 1991–2001 (continued)

Rating	Region	Openness	Free and fair elections	Political pluralism	Independent mass-media	Economic liberalization	Civil Society	Political regime	Elites	Corruption	Local self-government	Total
47	Ryazanskaya	3	3	3	2	2	2	3	3	3	3	27
48	Smolenskaya	3	3	3	2	3	2	3	3	2	3	27
49	Krasnodarsky	2	3	3	2	3	2	3	2	2	4	26
50	Amurskaya	2	3	2	3	2	2	3	3	3	3	26
51	Magadanskaya	2	3	2	2	3	3	3	3	2	3	26
52	Orenburgskaya	3	3	2	2	2	2	3	3	3	3	26
53	Saratovskaya	3	2	3	2	3	3	3	2	2	3	26
54	Tambovskaya	2	3	3	2	2	2	3	3	3	3	26
55	Tulskaya	3	3	3	2	2	2	3	3	2	3	26
56	Komi-Permyatsky	3	3	3	2	2	2	3	3	3	2	26
57	Altaysky	2	3	3	2	2	2	3	3	2	3	25
58	Stavropolsky	2	3	3	3	2	2	2	3	3	3	25
59	Khabarovsky	2	3	2	3	2	2	3	2	3	3	25
60	Voronezhskaya	3	3	2	2	2	3	2	3	2	3	25
61	Penzenskaya	2	2	2	3	2	2	3	3	3	3	25
62	Chitinskaya	2	3	2	2	2	2	3	3	3	3	25
63	Daghestan	3	2	3	2	2	3	3	1	1	4	24
64	Karachaevo-Cherkessia	3	2	2	2	2	2	3	3	2	3	24
65	Kurganskaya	2	3	2	2	2	2	3	2	3	3	24
66	Rostovskaya	3	2	2	2	2	3	3	2	2	3	24
67	Koryaksky	2	3	3	1	2	2	3	3	3	2	24
68	Taymyrsky	2	2	3	2	3	2	3	3	2	2	24

Table 10.1. Ratings of Democracy in Russian Regions Based on Expert Evaluation, 1991–2001 (continued)

Rating	Region	Openness	Free and fair elections	Political pluralism	Independent mass-media	Economic liberalization	Civil Society	Political regime	Elites	Corruption	Local self-government	Total
69	Tatarstan	2	2	2	2	3	3	2	1	4	2	23
70	Primorsky	4	2	2	2	3	3	2	2	1	2	23
71	Jewish Autonomous	2	2	2	2	2	2	3	2	3	3	23
72	Nenetsky	2	2	2	2	2	3	3	2	3	2	23
73	Adygeya	3	2	3	2	2	2	2	1	2	3	22
74	Ulyanovskaya	3	3	2	2	1	2	2	2	3	4	22
75	Mordovia	2	2	2	3	2	2	2	2	2	2	21
76	Yakutia	2	2	2	2	3	2	2	1	2	3	21
77	Kurskaya	2	2	2	2	2	2	2	2	2	2	21
78	Orlovskaya	2	2	2	2	3	2	2	2	3	2	21
79	Northern Ossetia	2	2	2	2	2	2	2	2	1	2	19
80	Tuva	1	2	2	2	1	2	2	2	2	3	19
81	Ust-Ordynsky	2	2	2	2	2	1	2	3	2	1	19
82	Evenkiisky	2	2	2	1	2	1	2	2	3	2	19
83	Bashkortostan	1	1	2	2	2	2	2	1	4	1	18
84	Aginsky Buryatsky	2	2	2	1	2	1	2	2	3	1	18
85	Kabardino-Balkaria	2	1	2	1	2	2	2	1	2	2	17
86	Chukotsky	2	2	1	1	2	1	2	2	2	2	17
87	Ingushetia	2	1	1	1	2	2	1	2	2	1	15
88	Kalmykia	1	1	1	2	2	1	1	2	2	1	14

Source: Calculations by Nikolai Petrov and Alexei Titkov.

the republics of North Ossetia and Tuva and the national *okrugs* of Ust-Orda, Buryatia, and Evenkia (all rated at 19); the Republic of Bashkortostan (18); Aga-Buryatsky Okrug (18); the Republic of Kabardino-Balkaria (17); Chukotsky Okrug (17); the Republic of Ingushetia (15); and the Republic of Kalmykia (14). The remaining regions fall between these two extremes. The city of Moscow falls roughly in the middle with a rating of 29. Almost half of the regions score between 25 and 30. The city of Moscow is closer to the democratic group of regions than Kemerovo, Buryatia, Saratov, and many regions of the pro-communist "red belt."

To complete the analysis, we add the temporal dimension to the regional rating system to register shifts in the relative values of selected indicators during 1991–2001. Despite initial expectations, grades for the level of democracy in individual regions during this period fall within a narrow range and significant movement was found in only a few cases. Three regions moved toward greater democracy: the republics of Altai (in 1997), Karachaevo-Cherkessia (in 1999), and Chuvashia (in 1993). Four regions moved toward more authoritarian rule: Mordovia (in 1993), Primorsky Krai (in 1993), Kemerov Oblast (in 1997), and Saratovskaya Oblast (in 1996). All these regions fall in the middle of the ranking ladder in table 10.1. The position of democratic leaders and authoritarian outsiders was stable.

Such remarkable stability indicates either that essential features give rise to the specific level of democracy in each region, such as the dominant political culture, or that all development stems from the initial push. The dominant political culture is in turn a composite of many factors, such as the history of the region's society, its composition, its structure, and so on. The initial push theory sees political development as a consequence of the establishment and reproduction phases. The most important innovations appear during the establishment phase, when the sociopolitical system passes through a point of bifurcation and the trajectory of further development is defined. It is during this phase that different regions choose different trajectories, which they can modify only slightly during the following reproduction phase. Both models of development can coexist, contributing to regional political development in parallel.

Plotting regions according to their level of democracy follows a normal distribution with most regions falling in the middle range and smaller numbers of regions at the top (the ten regions that comprise the two groups of leaders) and the bottom (the ten authoritarian outsiders). The top group, led by St. Petersburg, consists of large urban regions, and indeed, includes all cities with more than a million residents except Moscow. The outsider group consists entirely of national republics and *okrugs*. A look at all the regions that scored less than 23 still incorporates only a few of the so-called Russian regions (*krais* and *oblasts*): Orlovskaya (21), Kurskaya (21), and Ulyanovskaya (22) *oblasts*. The Republic of Karelia, tied in third place with Permskaya Oblast, is the only national republic among the top ten democratic leaders. The next highest rated republics are Udmurtia (with a rating of 33 that lags behind only 13 of Russia's regions) and Chuvashia (with a rating of 31, behind only 19 regions). The Muslim republic, Tatarstan, falls outside the group of authoritarian outsiders but well below the average Russian region with a rating of 23, ranking behind 68 regions.

Aside from the urbanized nature of the top-ranked democracies and the authoritarian nature of the republics, no other obvious pattern is visible. Even the two factors cited are subject to exceptions: as noted earlier, the Republic of Karelia sits among the leaders and Russia's most urban city, Moscow, is ranked behind 26 regions, many of them rural.

Regional Elections as a Barometer of Democratization

As an institution representative of direct democracy, elections offer researchers an unique opportunity to assess the state of democracy not only at the national level, but also at the regional level. Elections highlight a great variety of key features that need to be examined to assess the level of democracy in any particular polity, including the level of public political awareness, the level of civil society's vitality and social activism, the role of the elite and of political parties, the degree of improper administrative control exercised by incumbents, the separation of executive and legislative power, and the overall state of the rule of law. A special advantage of elections from the point of view of monitoring democratic development is that they are usually conducted simultaneously across the country, thereby allowing a regional comparison.[6]

From the variety of possible electoral indicators, the authors selected a few to use in appraising democracy levels in the regions, namely: the level of voter participation (turnout) in federal and regional elections, the competitiveness and intensity of the races, the instances of voting against all candidates and parties (negativism), and the violations of electoral law. Our initial hypothesis was based on the assumption that the transition from the

Soviet administrative command model of elections to the normal democratic model was almost complete in the regions. An overview of our assessment of the state of Russian regional democracy along these six parameters follows.

Voter Participation in the 1999 Parliamentary and 2000 Presidential Federal Elections

In accordance with our heuristic assumption, two patterns of turnout variation should have emerged from the study of electoral process in the different regions. The first would include a small group of regions, primarily national republics, that have made few gains in democratization. There the old model of nearly total population turnout driven by the administrative mobilization of voters from state farms and enterprises should still prevail. A second group would comprise most of the remaining regions, the Russian regions, where democratization should have progressed considerably further than in the national republics and *okrugs*.[7] In this second group of regions, the turnout distribution should be electorally motivated, and thus relatively normal even by Western standards, with higher turnout reflecting higher levels of political activism among citizens.

The actual data point to a fundamentally different pattern of variation, one that is much closer to the old post-Soviet model initially observed in the first relatively free elections of 1989, in which no correlation is apparent between a higher turnout and a higher level of democratization. Indeed, the greater the degree of reform and democratization before the 1989 USSR Congress of People's Deputies elections, the lower the turnout, as less reformed regions and republics continued to mobilize turnout through the still intact party-state apparatus that extended into state farms and enterprises.[8] Thus according to this model, higher turnout can be attributed to a higher level of administrative mobilization of participation in elections and a relatively lower level of freedom and institutionalized democracy.

To avoid the confusing influence of subjective and accidental factors— specific political situation, differences between parliamentary and presidential campaigns, interconnections between federal and some local elections, or seasonal variations—a statistical mean was taken for the turnout in the two most recent federal elections: the December 1999 State Duma election and the March 2000 Russian presidential election. The correlation between turnout ratings and the model's expectations is high: 0.75. Regional variation in turnout is high as well. In some regions, like

Ingushetia, Kabardino-Balkaria, and Dagestan, the turnout for presidential elections exceeded 80 percent. In others, such as the Evenki Autonomous Okrug, it was less than 60 percent. Therefore the resulting rankings of turnout at the federal elections varied from a high of 10 in Evenki Autonomous Okrug to a low of 1 in seventeen regions, with fairly even distribution in between. For various reasons—mainly Russia's super-presidentialism and the significant tilt in the balance of power between the executive and legislative branches in favor of the former—presidential elections spark much more public interest than parliamentary elections. Furthermore, the difference in public interest in presidential rather than State Duma elections seems to be getting wider. The turnout for the 2000 presidential elections exceeded the turnout for the December 1999 Duma elections by an average of 6.8 percent in the regions. The average difference between the July 1996 presidential elections and the December 1995 Duma elections had been lower by 5.3 percentage points.

A comparison of individual regions shows that relative public interest in elections varied greatly. For instance, in Ingushetia turnout for the 2000 presidential elections was almost 25 percentage points higher than that for the 1999 Duma elections, but the reverse was true in the Altai Republic, where the presidential elections attracted 2.5 percent fewer voters than the Duma elections. In St. Petersburg, apparent deviations from the general trend can be explained by the distorting effect that interest in the political future of one of the city's own probably had on turnout. In other cases, diverse turnout reflects the active use of administrative resources. Because of obvious distortions in several cases, we gave additional penalty points to regions with the largest deviations: 2 points for deviations above 10 percent and 1 point for deviations between 6.8 and 10 percent. We gave thirty-one regions 1 additional point and nine regions (Ingushetia, Kabardino-Balkaria, North Ossetia, Chuvashia, Irkutskaya, Kaliningradskaya, Leningradskaya, Sverdlovskaya, and Tomskaya *oblasts*) 2 additional points.

A Comparison of Turnout for National and Regional Elections

National and local elections often follow different patterns. This is especially true for regions that have a high degree of administrative control. In such regions turnout can vary greatly either because of a lack of interest in federal affairs, which results in a low turnout, or, conversely, regional leaders inflate turnout using administrative resources and mobilization to demonstrate their usefulness and support of the center. For Russia as a whole, turnout for regional elections is, on average, 12 percent lower than for federal elections.[9] This average difference served as a base value for assessing electoral democracy in regional versus federal elections: deviations in either direction were taken as indications of lowered democracy levels. We considered a lower value or difference in a regional election as a sign of the old model of administrative interference and mobilization of local political activity. We viewed a higher difference in turnout as indicating a lack of interest in local elections, and lack of interest is either a cause or a consequence of less democracy in the region.

Gubernatorial elections are the more telling among regional elections, and so we used them for rating analysis in preference to other elections. In cases of simultaneous gubernatorial and federal elections, we sometimes used elections to regional legislative assemblies with an appropriate corrective coefficient.[10] Despite these and other statistical techniques, we could only measure or evaluate electoral turnout in gubernatorial elections in seventy-five regions because federal or local electoral data were missing for the remaining thirteen regions (and Chechnya).

Negative Voting

Like voter absenteeism, voting against all candidates and parties is a traditional form of electoral protest. As such, it may be considered a sign of health in a democracy. Voters show that they are not afraid to register their displeasure with the candidates or the system publicly, and that they are willing to turn out at the polls to register that displeasure, thereby displaying their interest and concern in their country's democracy.[11] Variation from region to region in the extent of negative voting has been high for all four elections we selected and ranked: two for the 1999 State Duma (one for the party list vote and one for single-mandate district voting), one for the Russian president, and one for regional heads.

These four elections deal with two fundamentally different phenomena. On the one hand, in presidential and Duma party list voting, the electorate exhibits different reactions to similar situations: the situation countrywide, the candidates' and parties' programs, and the voters' perceptions of candidates' abilities to carry out the programs appropriately. On the other hand, in gubernatorial and Duma single-mandate district voting, differences exist with regard to the specific regional situation and therefore in the electorate's reaction to it.

In the latter two types of elections, the average regional negative voting level is taken as a norm. Deviation in either direction in a given region is taken to indicate a lower level of democracy. We adopted this method under the assumption that an unusually low share of votes against all candidates suggests the presence of excessive administrative control over the electoral process. Conversely, a larger percentage of negative voting is taken to indicate voters' negative reaction to various violations of election laws and norms regarding fair play by candidates, parties, and their election staffs. Presidential and Duma party elections with the same candidates and parties competing nationally, and not regionally, are an exception to this rule. In these, negative voting is considered proportionately, hence reflecting public activism on the part of the electorate.

Taking into account the various methodological challenges and solutions and keeping in mind that the levels of democracy in a region can vary greatly in regional and federal elections, we found that at the extremes, the difference in the frequency of recourse to negativism by voters is more than tenfold in case of national elections (both the presidential and Duma party list votes) and in single-mandate districts, and more than seventy-fold in gubernatorial elections. The latter result in particular reflects the broad range of democracy levels across the regions, as well as the widely divergent levels in the violations of electoral laws and norms, the use of administrative resources, and the prevalence of dirty election campaign techniques (the use of false editions of newspapers, candidate doubles, and the like). The correlation between all the indicators of negativism is statistically insignificant, suggesting that different phenomena lie behind each indicator and that they should not be interpreted reductively to indicate some general level of protest.

Electoral Competition and Political Pluralism

The level of electoral competition is an important indicator of the level of democracy, since it reflects the overall level of political pluralism. At a minimum it reflects the number of competitive elite groupings that can viably fight for power in the election process. At a maximum, it may reflect the strength of truly grassroots political parties and the autonomy and power of civil society. We used three indicators to measure the degree of political pluralism, electoral competition, and intensity of competition: the effective number of parties in the 1999 Duma elections,[12] the effective number of candidates in gubernatorial elections,[13] and election victors' winning margins.

The average "effective" number of parties in each region was 6.8 in 1999. Variation across the regions ranged from the low and undemocratic number of 1.3 parties in Ingushetia and 2 in Tuva to highs of 9.3 in Perm Oblast and 9.7 in Nenetsky Autonomous Okrug. Clearly having two or more effective political parties meets the standard of the most advanced liberal democracies. Some might consider a large number of effective parties as a counterintuitive indicator of an immature democratic system that has still not combined its political forces into cohesive mediating organizations (whether for institutional or strategic reasons) and that remains a highly fractured, and even polarized, polity. Indeed, Nenetsky Autonomous Okrug rated dismally on most parameters and finished ahead of only sixteen regions, tying with several others, in the overall level of democratization. At the same time, Perm's high rankings not only of electoral, but of other institutional aspects of democracy, and its first place ranking among all the regions in the overall level of democratization (which includes all electoral and nonelectoral parameters), suggest that a large number of parties can also be a sign of a healthy, vibrant democracy.[14]

The average effective number of gubernatorial election candidates was 3, which suggests a reasonably good level of candidate choice for voters overall; however, for individual regions this figure varied from a low of 1.2 to 1.3 in Kabardino-Balkaria, Kalmykia, Mordovia, Khabarovsky Krai, Kemerovskaya, Murmanskaya, Novgorodskaya, and Orlovskaya *oblasts* and Aga-Buryatsky, Khanty-Mansiysky, Chukotksky, and Yamal-Nenetsky autonomous *okrugs* to a high of 7.1 in Primorsky Krai and Novosibirsk Oblast. Again, having fewer than two effective candidates clearly reflects a limited degree of political pluralism that does not meet a liberal democratic standard.

The third parameter for assessing electoral competition turns on elections' actual results, that is, the victors' winning margin. In the seventy-two regions where gubernatorial elections took place in 1999–2002, the average margin of victory was 40.2 percentage points. This compares unfavorably with general patterns observed in liberal democratic systems, where competition tends to drive winners' margins down to much lower figures. Variation in the Russian regions is enormous and ranges from differences of

90 percentage points in some regions such as Kemerovskaya and Orlovskaya *oblasts*, and a zero or even negative value in cases where the second round winner finished second in the first round.[15]

Removal of Incumbents

While election victors' winning margins are important for assessing the democratic nature of election results, an even more significant statistic is the rate of removal or turnover of incumbents through the election process, which is a good indicator of the vibrancy of electoral, if not liberal, democracy. It is particularly relevant to the debate about a particular democracy's level of consolidation, because one standard that has often been used to define a consolidated democracy that has gone beyond the mere process of elections is the turnover of power from one group of officials to another, preferably an opposition group. Although elections are considered a minimalist sign of democratization or transition to democracy, they cannot be regarded as a sign of a democracy's consolidation, but power changing hands from one group to another through elections can be considered a minimal criterion for democratic consolidation.[16] This is especially important in Russia, since many political leaders from the ancien regime have remained in power in numerous regions, particularly in the presidencies of the national republics. These are often former Communist Party first secretaries and other regional, or even federal-level, officials from the late Soviet era.[17]

On a scale of 1–10, the regions broke down into the following five groups as regards leadership turnover: (1) those without any instances of a regional chief executive being replaced by means of elections (9–10 points); (2) those without any replacement of the regional chief executive in the last elections, but a completed replacement in other elections (7–8 points); (3) those where the replacement occurred by nonelectoral succession, such as retirement, resignation, or appointment to another post (5–6 points); (4) those where the replacement by election of a regional head by a representative of the regional or federal establishment occurred (3–4 points); and (5) those where the replacement by election of a regional head by a politician not representing the establishment occurred (1–2 points). A little variation within each grade made precise adjustments possible that took into account all region-specific circumstances. For example, if a challenger representing genuine opposition wins the race in a particular region, then the region receives a 1, but if the incumbent governor is replaced by a representative of the ruling elite who is either the regional center mayor or a former governor, the region gets a 2.

Rule of Law in Elections

A single, universal indicator for evaluating all possible violations of the law during elections does not exist. Indeed, such an indicator could never feasibly exist for the simple reason that such violations are so numerous, so hard to track, and so open to different interpretations as to their illegality. One possible approximate universal indicator may be data from strictly enforced examinations of sample ballots in each region, a system offered by one of the first versions of the Law on Public Control, but one not yet in existence. A method that is more realistic at this time is the indirect evaluation of violations through observation of various deviations from electoral behavior both across time and in space: between different elections, between different regions, and between subregions. Another possibility is the use of expert evaluations based on information about various scandals connected with federal and local authorities' interference in elections. For the maximal accuracy, objectivity, and usefulness we used both approaches along with our own third evaluative approach.

The sources of evaluation were intentionally varied as well. In our study of federal elections, we used the Mercator Group's three-grade rating of freedom of elections to calculate major parameters of electoral behavior by region and lower-level territorial electoral commissions.[18] Specifically, we converted the Mercator rating to a 10-point scale to obtain aggregated indexes for the stability of electoral preferences and the level of voting in favor of the government or party in power. We compared the results generated by the Mercator studies against a base of electoral violation data created earlier by the regional program of the Carnegie Moscow Center.[19] In addition, we conducted a separate expert evaluation of violations based on regional monitoring in the 1999–2002 gubernatorial elections.

One curious observation to have come out of the study, substantiated by all three separate evaluations, is that while correlation between the statistics on electoral violations in federal and regional elections is generally relatively good, evaluations for these separate levels in some cases diverge quite sharply in either direction. A few good examples of the latter are the regions of St. Petersburg, Yakutia, Karachai-Cherkessia, Krasnodar Krai, and Tyumen Oblast and Kurskaya Oblast, where violations have been significant in local elections and much less pronounced in federal elections. A departure from this general pattern was seen in Astrakhan Oblast, the republics of Altai and Dagestan, and the Ust-Ordinsky-Buryatsky Autonomous Okrug, where the most notable violations are in the Duma and presidential federal elections. In general, however, violations are more prevalent in regional elections.

The Composite Picture

As shown in table 10.2, the composite democracy rating for each region is an arithmetic mean of the ratings in all eleven subcategories of regional elections' level of democracy: (1) turnout for the Duma and presidential elections, (2) turnout for regional chief executives' (gubernatorial and national republic presidential) elections; (3) competition in Duma party list votes assessed by effective number of parties, (4) competition in gubernatorial elections assessed by effective number of candidates; (5) competition in the elections of regional chief executives as assessed by victors' winning margins, (6) competition in the elections of regional chief executives assessed in terms of their rate of replacement by election or another method of replacement, (7) votes against all in elections of regional chief executives, (8) votes against all in Duma party list votes and federal presidential elections, (9) votes against all in Duma elections in single-mandate district voting, (10) violations of the law in regional elections, and (11) violations of the law in federal elections in the regions.

The ratings varied from 2.4 in Permskaya Oblast to 8.3 in Kabardino-Balkaria in a fashion that resembles a normal distribution skewed slightly toward the democratic end. Although overall variation is more than threefold, the majority of regions are concentrated near the mean: 40 are located within an interval of 3.5 to 4.5 points. The most notable lack of coherence in the distribution separates the ten least democratic regions from the rest. Novgorodskaya Oblast, which in recent years gained the reputation of being a region of exemplar reforms, is located in the bottom dozen, together with a number of northern Caucasian republics. Many other regions with well-known leaders are found in the bottom half of the table, ranking near the more authoritarian republics such as Tatarstan, Bashkortostan and Kalmykia. These include Yegor Stroyev's Orel Oblast, Dmitri Ayatskov's Saratov

Table 10.2. Index of Democracy in Russian Regions Based on 1999–2002 Elections

Rating	Region	Integral evaluation	Turnout: Duma and presidential elections	Turnout: Gubernatorial	Competitiveness: Duma elections by party lists	Competitiveness: Duma elections by SMDs	Competitiveness: Gubernatorial	Competitiveness: Gubernatorial	Negativism: Duma (by party lists) and presidential	Negativism: Duma elections (by SMDs)	Replacement of regional head	Violations: Regional elections	Violations: Federal elections
1	Permskaya	2.4	3	1	1	2	5	3	3	1	2	3	2
2	Moskovskaya	2.5	2	2	4	2	1	1	1	5	2	4	3
3	Nizhegorodskaya	2.5	2	5	3	4	2	2	3	1	2	1	2
4	Novosibirskaya	2.5	3	–	4	3	1	2	4	3	2	2	1
5	Kamchatskaya	2.5	2	1	4	1	1	6	1	4	2	4	2
6	Tambovskaya	2.6	3	1	5	2	2	4	5	1	2	2	2
7	Ivanovskaya	3.0	4	3	4	3	5	2	3	2	1	4	2
8	Leningradsky	3.1	1	4	4	2	2	1	4	1	7	3	5
9	Kaliningradsky	3.3	2	1	5	3	4	1	5	4	4	5	2
10	Ryazanskaya	3.3	4	4	5	2	3	1	4	1	7	3	2
11	Sakhalinskaya	3.3	1	2	4	2	6	1	2	3	9	4	2
12	Komi	3.4	3	2	4	2	6	1	5	2	4	4	4
13	Tumenskaya	3.4	3	1	4	4	6	1	5	2	4	6	1
14	Amurskaya	3.5	4	4	6	1	3	4	5	3	1	4	3
15	Orenburgskaya	3.5	4	2	5	4	3	1	7	3	3	2	4
16	Primorsky	3.5	2	2	4	3	1	2	4	5	2	8	6
17	Arkhangelskaya	3.5	4	4	3	1	5	6	3	2	7	2	2
18	Pskovskaya	3.5	5	1	6	2	2	1	6	2	7	4	3
19	Sverdlovskaya	3.5	1	3	2	3	4	2	4	7	7	3	3
20	St. Petersburg	3.6	2	2	2	2	8	3	2	3	8	6	2

Table 10.2. Index of Democracy in Russian Regions Based on 1999–2002 Elections (continued)

Rating	Region	Integral evaluation	Turnout		Competitiveness			Negativism			Replacement of regional head	Violations	
			Duma and presidential elections	Gubernatorial	Duma elections by party lists	Duma elections by SMDs	Gubernatorial	Gubernatorial	Duma (by party lists) and presidential	Duma elections (by SMDs)		Regional elections	Federal elections
69	Karachaevo-Cherkessia	5.3	4	9	4	5	3	5	4	8	4	9	3
70	Novgorodskaya	5.4	5	2	5	4	10	3	5	6	10	6	3
71	Altaysky	5.5	5	-	6	6	9	1	6	6	8	4	4
72	Adygeya	5.5	3	5	7	2	8	5	7	8	4	7	5
73	Northern Ossetia	5.5	3	2	7	2	6	4	8	6	8	7	8
74	Ust-Ordynsky	5.5	5	1	6	7	6	1	8	9	7	4	7
75	Chukotsky	5.5	6	4	7	9	10	3	4	2	4	6	6
76	Kemerovskaya	5.6	2	1	6	10	10	3	6	5	10	6	3
77	Saratovskaya	5.7	6	2	5	4	8	10	4	1	10	8	5
78	Rostovskaya	5.8	5	4	6	5	9	6	6	2	10	6	5
79	Orlovskaya	6.5	7	4	7	10	10	4	5	5	10	4	5
80	Tatarstan	6.5	8	7	7	5	9	3	6	2	10	7	8
81	Kalmykia	6.6	4	9	6	2	10	5	6	5	8	10	8
82	Tuva	6.6	5	1	10	7	6	4	8	9	10	7	6
83	Aginsky Buryatsky	6.8	6	3	7	10	10	2	9	10	8	4	6
84	Mordovia	6.9	8	5	7	6	10	3	8	3	10	8	8
85	Bashkortostan	7.3	8	2	6	6	8	10	7	4	10	10	9
86	Ingushetia	7.3	9	4	10	7	2	6	10	10	4	8	10
87	Daghestan	7.8	9	-	8	6	-	6	10	5	10	6	10
88	Kabardino-Balkaria	8.3	10	5	7	10	10	5	9	7	10	9	9

Source: Calculations by Nikolai Petrov and Alexei Titkov.
SMD = single-mandate district.

Oblast, Aman Tuleyev's Kemerovo Oblast, and Mikhail Prusak's Novgorod Oblast.

The problem of both general and spatial contrasts arises here. Enormous regional diversity can be considered to pose a threat not only to democracy in Russia, but to its very existence as a unified state.[20] In 1990–1998 clear evidence indicated that political development was going in different directions within some of the ethnic republics and the rest of Russian regions. Because of their authoritarian regimes, the former were often compared with medieval khanates, with the country as a whole being referred to as "the federation of tyrannies."[21] The situation changed fundamentally in 1998–1999, first with the adoption of a number of important laws that established universal principles of state power organization in the regions, and then with the strengthening of the center, which permitted the introduction of all these universal schemes at the regional level in practice (for more details see chapter 9). Although a general northward gradient is apparent, with an increase in democratic development associated with movement from the more agrarian, rural, and paternalistic south to the more industrial, urban, and individualistic north, in many cases regions with opposite democracy rankings are close neighbors.

Comparing the correlations among components of the integrated index of democracy based on elections also provides interesting results (table 10.3). The fact that most of the binary correlations are not high and are statistically insignificant indicates that there is no collinearity between our different measures of democracy and the absence of double counting. Some exceptions are apparent, with the more prominent of these being the correlation between the number of effective parties and the level of popularity of negative voting, both at the parliamentary and the presidential elections (0.68), the intensity of competition at gubernatorial elections and the replacement of regional leaders (0.61), the turnout and the level of electoral violations at federal elections (0.59), and the magnitude of electoral violations and level of negative voting in federal elections (0.59). Yet despite the weakness of the statistical relationship between the great majority of partial evaluation indexes, most demonstrate a rather high correlation (0.5–0.7) with the composite democracy index. This correlation is especially high for the turnout rate in federal elections (0.73) and violations in federal elections (0.75). Thus the latter two parameters are the most useful in estimating the level of democracy in a region.

Table 10.3. Correlation Matrix of the Components of Democracy Index Based on 1999–2002 Elections

	Turnout		Competitiveness			Negativism				Violations		
	Duma and presidential elections	Gubernatorial elections	Duma elections by SMDs	Duma elections by party lists	Gubernatorial	Gubernatorial	Duma (party lists) and presidential elections	Duma (SMDs)	Replacement of regional head	Regional elections	Federal elections	Integral evaluation
Turnout: Duma and presidential elections	1.00											
Turnout: gubernatorial elections	0.19	1.00										
Competitiveness: Duma elections by SMDs	0.43	0.00	1.00									
Competitiveness: Duma elections by party lists	0.48	-0.08	0.30	1.00								
Competitiveness: gubernatorial	0.26	0.10	0.08	0.37	1.00							
Negativism: Gubernatorial	0.37	0.19	0.10	0.14	0.09	1.00						
Negativism: Duma (party lists) and presidential elections	0.51	-0.20	0.68	0.41	0.13	0.10	1.00					
Negativism: Duma (SMDs)	0.18	0.15	0.23	0.33	0.02	0.10	0.25	1.00				
Replacement of regional head	0.24	-0.06	0.11	0.30	0.61	0.05	0.22	-0.07	1.00			
Violations: Regional elections	0.41	0.22	0.36	0.26	0.27	0.37	0.34	0.36	0.15	1.00		
Violations: Federal elections	0.59	0.05	0.52	0.42	0.19	0.28	0.59	0.41	0.19	0.51	1.00	
Integral evaluation	0.73	0.25	0.57	0.65	0.58	0.43	0.62	0.47	0.51	0.66	0.75	1.00

Source: Calculations by Nikolai Petrov and Alexei Titkov.
SMD = single-mandate district.

As table 10.4 shows, in most cases the weighted evaluations differ little from the initial composite ratings. As expected, those regions that improved their position in comparison with the initial composite rating were those that had "heavyweight" factors like turnover of regional leaders and gubernatorial elections pushing them down. In a few cases a region's rank improved considerably as a result of weighting. For example, Moscow moved from its original fifth-seventh place to forty-fourth out of eighty-eight (Chechnya excluded). Similar changes in rank emerged for Tyumen Oblast and the Khanty-Mansiysky, and Yamalo-Nenetsky autonomous *okrugs*, as well as for Astrakhanskaya Oblast, where gubernatorial elections in particular appeared less democratic in the nonweighted composite ranking than in the weighted ranking. Among those regions whose rankings worsened after weighting were Primorye, Amur, Altai, Chita, and Krasnoyarsk. As a whole, however, the composite democracy ratings for the regions increased as a result of weighting, as eight out of eleven factors became heavier, while the variation remained almost the same. Note that those regions whose ratings changed were located in the center of the distribution.

The stability between the nonweighted and weighted rankings is apparent. The most democratic region, Permskaya Oblast, held its position, as did four of the authoritarian outsiders (Bashyortostan, Ingushetia, Dagestan, and Kabardino-Balkaria). The gap between these extremes and the other regions increased slightly. Furthermore, six regions kept their positions and sixteen moved up the scale by one place. Other evidence pointing to the essential similarity between the initial and weighted evaluations is that the top six regions and bottom ten regions are identical in both cases.[22]

Several patterns emerge in relation to those regions that lead in terms of the efficacy of their electoral democracy. The regions that fall into this category are Permskaya, Novosibirskaya, Moscovskaya, Nizhegorodskaya, Tambovskaya, Ivanovskaya, Leningradskaya, and Kaliningradskaya *oblasts* and Kamchatka and Sakhalin. Predictably, while the traditionally democratic European and Ural areas are represented here, the notoriously conservative south is not. At the same time, the central area, rather than being represented by the city of Moscow, is represented by the surrounding and less urban Moscow Oblast along with the economically depressed and opposition-oriented Ivanov and red belt Tambovskaya *oblasts*. Just as curiously, the Northwest Federal District is represented neither by Novgorodskaya Oblast, the showcase of reforms, nor by St. Petersburg, traditionally viewed as the bastion of democracy. Instead, the Northwest Federal District is rep-

Table 10.4. Nonweighted and Weighted Ratings of Democracy Based on 1999–2002 Elections

Region	Nonweighted ratings		Weighted ratings	
	Evaluation	Place	Evaluation	Place
Permskaya	2.4	1	2.7	1
Moskovskaya	2.5	2–5	2.9	2–3
Nizhegorodskaya	2.5	2–5	3.0	4
Novosibirskaya	2.5	2–5	2.9	2–3
Kamchatskaya	2.5	2–5	3.2	6
Tambovskaya	2.6	6	3.1	5
Ivanovskaya	3.0	7	3.5	8–9
Leningradskaya	3.1	8	3.5	8–9
Kaliningradskaya	3.3	9–11	3.6	10–12
Ryazanskaya	3.3	9–11	3.6	10–12
Sakhalinskaya	3.3	9–11	3.4	7
Komi	3.4	12–13	3.7	13–14
Tyumenskaya	3.4	12–13	3.6	10–12
Amurskaya	3.5	14–19	4.2	26–30
Orenburgskaya	3.5	14–19	3.9	16–20
Primorskiy	3.5	14–19	4.2	26–30
Arkhangelskaya	3.5	14–19	4.2	26–30
Pskovskaya	3.5	14–19	3.8	15
Sverdlovskaya	3.5	14–19	4.0	21–24
St. Petersburg	3.6	20–24	3.9	16–20
Stavropolskiy	3.6	20–24	4.0	21–24
Volgogradskaya	3.6	20–24	3.9	16–20
Voronezhskaya	3.6	20–24	4.0	21–24
Tulskaya	3.6	20–24	3.9	16–20
Chitinskaya	3.6	20–24	3.7	13–14
Karelia	3.7	26–28	3.9	16–20
Smolenskaya	3.7	26–28	4.4	33–34
Tomskaya	3.7	26–28	4.0	21–24
Irkutskaya	3.8	29–31	4.1	25
Tverskaya	3.8	29–31	4.3	31–32
Ulyanovskaya	3.8	29–31	4.2	26–30
Bryanskaya	3.9	32	4.2	26–30
Krasnoyarskiy	4.0	33	4.9	45–50
Kurganskaya	4.0	34–35	4.4	33–34
Taymyrskiy	4.0	34–35	4.8	41–44
Khabarovskiy	4.1	36–38	4.3	31–32
Vladimirskaya	4.1	36–38	4.8	41–44
Omskaya	4.1	36–38	4.5	35–38
Kaluzhskaya	4.2	39–40	4.9	45–50

Table 10.4. Nonweighted and Weighted Ratings of Democracy Based on 1999–2002 Elections (continued)

Region	Nonweighted ratings		Weighted ratings	
	Evaluation	Place	Evaluation	Place
Kostromskaya	4.2	39–40	4.8	41–44
Chelyabinskaya	4.2	39–40	4.6	39
Altai	4.3	42	5.2	56–58
Mariy El	4.3	43–46	5.0	51–52
Khakassia	4.3	43–46	4.5	35–38
Penzenskaya	4.3	43–46	4.7	40
Kirovskaya	4.3	43–46	4.5	35–38
Murmanskaya	4.4	47–49	4.8	41–44
Koryakskiy	4.4	47–49	5.2	56–58
Khanty–Mansiiskiy	4.4	47–49	4.5	36–38
Udmurtia	4.5	50–53	4.9	45–50
Yakutia	4.5	50–53	5.1	53–55
Kurskaya	4.5	50–53	5.3	59–62
Nenetskiy	4.5	50–53	5.4	63–65
Vologodskaya	4.6	54–56	5.1	53–55
Lipetskaya	4.6	54–56	5.3	59–62
Magadancskaya	4.6	54–56	5.1	53–55
Moscow	4.7	57–61	4.9	45–50
Yamalo–Nenetskiy	4.7	57–61	4.9	45–50
Buryatia	4.7	57–61	5.2	56–58
Astrakhanskaya	4.7	57–61	4.9	45–50
Evenkiiskiy	4.7	57–61	5.8	66–68
Yaroslavskaya	4.8	62–65	5.0	51–52
Chiuvashia	4.8	62–65	5.4	63–65
Samarskaya	4.8	62–65	5.3	59–62
Komi–Permyatskiy	4.8	62–65	6.0	70–71
Krasnodarskiy	4.9	66	5.3	59–62
Jewish Autonomous	5.0	67	5.4	63–65

resented by its surrounding region, Leningradskaya Oblast (although the latter has outbid or equaled the former in attracting foreign direct investment in recent years), and the corruption- and crime-ridden exclave of Kaliningradskaya Oblast.

Several common factors unite many of the most democratic regions. They include the absence of consolidated elites and concomitantly the presence of political conflicts, both in the present and in the recent past. Political conflict is prevalent in relations between local governors and mayors of

Table 10.4. Nonweighted and Weighted Ratings of Democracy Based on 1999–2002 Elections (continued)

Region	Nonweighted ratings		Weighted ratings	
	Evaluation	Place	Evaluation	Place
Belgorodskaya	5.2	68	5.9	69
Karachaevo–Cherkessia	5.3	69	6.6	77–78
Novgorodskaya	5.4	70	5.8	66–68
Altayskiy	5.5	71–75	5.8	66–68
Adygeya	5.5	71–75	6.5	75–76
Northern Ossetia	5.5	71–75	6.2	72–73
Ust–Ordynskiy Buratskiy	5.5	71–75	6.2	72–73
Chukotskiy	5.5	71–75	6.3	74
Kemerovskaya	5.6	76	6.0	70–71
Saratovskaya	5.7	77	6.6	77–78
Rostovskaya	5.8	78	6.5	75–76
Orlovskaya	6.5	79–80	7.2	79
Tatarstan	6.5	79–80	7.4	80–81
Kalmykia	6.6	81–82	7.7	83–84
Tyva	6.6	81–82	7.4	80–81
Aginskiy Buratskiy	6.8	83	7.6	82
Mordovia	6.9	84	7.7	83–84
Bashkortostan	7.3	85–86	8.4	85
Ingushetia	7.3	85–86	8.7	86
Daghestan	7.8	87	8.9	87
Kabardino–Balkaria	8.3	88	9.5	88

Source: Calculations by Nikolai Petrov and Alexei Titkov.

regional capitals. This is the case in Permskaya, Sakhalinskaya, Novosibirskaya, and Nizhegorodskaya *oblasts*. In Novosibirskaya and Permskaya *oblasts*, the mayors even competed against the governors in the gubernatorial elections in 2000 and won. Another type of conflict existent in these democratic regions is a clash between an elite group controlling the administration and legislature and an oppositional elite. This is the case in Tambov, Ivanov, and Kamchatka *oblasts*. Clashes also arise between the regional administration and the legislature as occurred, for example, in Kaliningrad and Kamchatka *oblasts*. This common trend may be explained in part by the fact that the governors in these regions have neither outstanding popularity ratings nor reputations as political heavyweights with the requisite authority or gravitas to firmly consolidate their hegemony over other political actors and forces. Moreover, three of the regions—Nizhny Novgorod, Ivanov, and

Kamchatka—are governed by communists, disproving the widespread assumption that a democratic region is a region led by a democrat.[23]

No expert would likely label all the regions singled out in the two previous paragraphs as among the country's most democratic—they are too different from most experts' expectations and analyses.[24] However, the unexpected nature of our findings in this regard perhaps illustrates the advantages, as well as the disadvantages, of our evaluative approach. To begin with, our approach virtually excludes the possibility of initial bias on the part of experts in their preliminary assessments. From another perspective, the fact that our evaluations diverge significantly from common views may invite the widespread disapproval of critics. On balance, the apparent counterintuitiveness of the evaluations concerning the most democratic regions is more useful than not, because it breaks stereotypes and drives forward the search and debate on the specific positioning of regions on the democratic scale.

The list of the ten least democratic regions is likely to be less controversial. Some of the regions included in that group are republics of the northern Caucasus (Ingushetia, Kabardino-Balkaria, and Northern Ossetia); the republics of Tatarstan and Bashkortostan, two regions that have led in forging ethno-national republic sovereignty; Kalmykia, Mordovia, and Tuva; the Aga-Buryatsky Autonomous Okrug; and Orlovskaya Oblast. These regions fall into the undemocratic category for a variety of reasons. One of them is the caution of regional leaders in the late Soviet era mold, such as Tatarstan's Mintimer Shaimiyev, Bashkortostan's Murtaza Rakhimov, and Orel's Stroyev or the rise to power of brash "new Russian," post-Soviet outsiders such as Kirsan Ilyumzhinov, in Kalmykia. Moreover, these leaders and those from other similar regions have stayed in office for extended periods of time, well beyond any democratically acceptable limit. Many of these are authoritarian, long-term survivors whose election generally proceeded in the Central Asian manner as a referendum on public trust in the "father of a nation." Paraphrasing Leo Tolstoy, while democratic regions are democratic in different ways, undemocratic regions are undemocratic in much the same way.

No less eloquent on the level of divergence from the usual assessments are the pairs of regions that are of geographical and socioeconomic proximity, but upon closer examination turn out to be very different. Some examples include the real, not virtual "bastion of democracy" and industry, Perm, and heavily industrial Sverdlov Oblast (ranked twenty-fourth);

Russia's second city and northern capital, St. Petersburg (seventeenth in the weighted list, twentieth in the nonweighted list) and Russia's first city and real capital, Moscow (forty-fifth and fifty-seventh, respectively); the north-western border regions Pskov Oblast (fifteenth and eighteenth) and Nov-gorod Oblast (sixty-sixth and seventieth); and the automotive Volga region Ulyanovsk (twenty-ninth and thirty-first), which until recently was consid-ered to be a bastion of socialism, and the democratic bastion of Samara Oblast (sixtieth and sixty-forth).

Two other groups seem not to correspond to previous expert analyses. One includes the conservative, communist, red belt region *oblasts* of Tam-bov (sixth), Ryazan (tenth), Amursk (fourteenth), Tula (twenty-fourth), Smolensk (twenty-seventh), and Bryansk (thirty-second), which are located in the top third of the ranking. The reverse case consists of a group of regions that had generally gained a reputation as national showcases of reform and includes the *oblasts* of Yaroslavl (sixty-second), Samara (sixty-fourth), and Novgorod (seventieth). Despite their reputations, the numbers clearly show this group of regions to be closer to the bottom of the democ-ratization scale. In general, conflicts, including those that lead to the replace-ment of a leader in elections, seem to play a greater role in the rating—and one hopes in the actual development of democracy—than the presence of democratically-oriented regional heads.

The comparison of the two different evaluations of democracy—the first based on expert assessments for 1991–2001 and the second, based on elec-toral statistics from the late 1990s to 2002—has produced informative results. The relatively high correlation between the results of the two sepa-rate evaluations of 0.61 not only upholds the accuracy and usefulness of expert evaluations, but also the completeness and multifaceted character of the statistical method using electoral results.[25] Another important deduction can be inferred from the similarity of results taken over a certain period. This concerns the actual political dynamics in the regions. Political change in each region progressed in proportion with that of the others, thereby keep-ing the democracy ratings of regions relatively unchanged over time.

11

Public Attitudes About Democracy

Vladimir Petukhov and Andrei Ryabov

During the 1990s, Russians endured one of the fastest and most far-reaching transformations in their country's political, social, and economic history. During this decade, Russia embarked on a painful transition from a centrally planned to a market economy, while simultaneously moving from a closed, totalitarian political regime to a more open and pluralistic system. By the mid-1990s, after years of formal government control, parts of the mass media became independent and began to play an important role in shaping public opinion. The fundamental principles of the former political system were revamped to promote the development of new, more democratic structures. These transformations in the organization of the economy and of the political system occurred in the wake of another spectacular change: the collapse of the Soviet Union and the rebirth of Russia as an independent state.

Despite this impressive list of changes, Russia remains a state in transition whose future evolution and commitment to liberal democratic reform are still uncertain. As discussed elsewhere in this book, scholars and analysts have identified many flaws in Russia's democracy. But what do the people of Russia think? A conclusive assessment of the country's successes and failures in creating a democratic regime must take into account the views of its citizens.

This chapter offers a broad overview of popular Russian attitudes about democracy based on research conducted by prominent Russian polling institutes between 1990 and 2001.[1] Ultimately, our analysis arrives at a somewhat paradoxical conclusion. While most Russians strongly endorse fundamental democratic values, they also have a high degree of tolerance for blatantly undemocratic phenomena, such as administrative lawlessness (at all levels of government); unpunished violations of human rights; and attempts to limit certain democratic freedoms, for instance, free access to information. This chapter explores several possible explanations for the origins of this striking inconsistency and its implications for democratization. The chapter will demonstrate that Russian citizens were frequently offered only two choices in the 1990s: either to leap toward advanced liberal democracy or to return to autocracy, with little or no middle ground.[2] Since 1991, three episodes have forced this kind of binary choice: Boris Yeltsin's political clash with the Supreme Soviet in 1993, the 1996 presidential elections, and the 2000 presidential elections. When offered only two options, most Russians select democracy. However, this binary, polarized menu does not allow people to express the full range of attitudes they have developed about the democratization process. When a larger range of options is explored, the commitment to democratic norms is not as deep as it appears when viewed only through the bipolar lens of dictatorship or democracy.

An Unusual Path Toward Democracy

Contemporary political science has proposed many theories to explain the unique set of factors characterizing Russia's transition.[3] The concept of democratic values figures prominently in this discourse. Comparative studies have shown that in Russia, unlike in the Central and Eastern European countries and the Baltic states, the initial push for transition was not accompanied by a "revolution in values."[4] Democratic values were part of popular consciousness in some of the former Eastern bloc countries long before they saw the formal collapse of communism. Therefore anticommunist revolutions in Central and Eastern Europe and in the Baltic states took on a primarily political, anti-Soviet nature and democratic values were bundled together with anti-Soviet views, including nationalism, anticolonialism, and, eventually, market liberalization. By contrast, such goals were not at the top of Russians' priority list.

The disintegration of the communist regime in Russia was determined by a completely different set of factors. The durability of the communist regime in the USSR—that is, its ability to successfully sustain itself for some seventy years—cannot be attributed solely to its impressive bureaucratic mechanisms or even to intimidation by the state. The authoritarian communist state developed public legitimacy through the government's constant appeals to the political myth of commitment to equality, especially with regard to the state's ability to provide the best variety of free, universal social services. Although often omitted from Anglo-American treatises, democracy and equality are closely related concepts for many people and certainly for Russians. Without a doubt, the myth of equality propagated by the Soviet government was sustainable only in a closed society that had no access to unbiased sources of information. Living behind the Iron Curtain, Russians simply knew no other system, and for a long time they believed that their own society epitomized the model of democracy. Only after objective information about life in the West became available to millions under Mikhail Gorbachev's glasnost was this myth dispelled. Evidence of a better standard of living in the West convinced the Russian public that Western political systems were more efficient than their own communist model. As people began to rethink the values that had been drummed into their minds from early childhood, they took the first step toward the de-legitimization of the Soviet regime and toward the country's democratic development. Note that the decisive factor for this switch in attitudes among the majority of the public was the West's palpable economic advantage, not its political organization. People saw democratic institutions and governing principles as a useful vehicle for attaining higher, Western standards of living, rather than as the preferred way to govern.

The basic awareness that the Western economic system was more successful had produced attitudinal shifts by the late 1980s and early 1990s and democratic values quickly began to replace communist ideology. Many Russians—especially the younger generations—embraced democratic norms not because of deep-seated ideological values, as was the case in Central and Eastern Europe, but because they saw democracy as a quick and easy way to improve their standard of living. One response to a sociological survey in the early 1990s captured this way of thinking particularly well. "Democracy," the respondent said, "is when I wake up and feel good."[5] Given the idealistic optimism with which many Russians embraced the transition in the early 1990s, the unexpected costs engendered by the reforms—including a quickly declining standard of living, rising crime, and increasing bureaucratic arbitrariness—clearly evoked disappointment. One of the defining factors of Russia's transition to democracy was that the disillusionment came almost as quickly as the euphoria. Citizens blamed not only the government, but also the democratic values themselves, for their economic hardship.

The second peculiarity of Russia's transition—closely related to the first—lies in the country's lack of strong democratic traditions. Before the 1990s, Russia had almost no experience with democratic governance.[6] This was true of Russia's pre-Soviet history, and it was equally true of the early transition period during perestroika, when an understanding of and active interest in advancing the cause of democracy was limited to small pockets of the population, such as the intelligentsia, the affluent strata of society (mostly modernized, pragmatic bureaucrats and the rising business elite), the various national minorities, and the young.[7] The historical absence of democratic practices meant, however, that even these groups saw no problem with the use of what Western observers would regard as undemocratic political tools. Indeed, according to a survey the Center for Sociological Research at Moscow State University conducted in the summer of 1990, only one-fifth of those who claimed to support democracy reported that they would be willing to actively contest the old system to pave the way for democratic reforms.[8]

Therefore the failure of many socioeconomic reforms in the 1990s rapidly eroded people's faith in democratic institutions, especially since their initial support had been so superficial. When the economy collapsed simultaneously with the Soviet Union's demise and then did not recover for years, the absence of stable democratic traditions fostered an ambiguous, skeptical attitude toward democracy among ordinary Russians. According to data from a March 2000 survey conducted by the Monitoring.ru sociological service, 68 percent of respondents believed that the political and economic reforms of the previous decade were "to the detriment of the people."[9] Attitudes about economic reform were the primary determinant of attitudes about democracy, but negative attitudes about the economy did not produce a complete breakdown of faith in democracy. However, Russians did not internalize democratic values, and as a result the demand for democratic reforms dwindled. Indeed, while recognizing the significance of democracy for Russia's future, many people believed that a large number of democratic structures were incompatible with the conditions in Russia at the time. Accordingly, the prevailing logic endorsed disregarding democracy to improve general social conditions.

Exaggerating how much energy and effort the public expended in the 1990s as it adapted to the country's new social and economic order would be impossible. The task for society was enormous, draining it of the time or energy to pursue other endeavors such as democratic development. As two respected Russian sociologists and pollsters, Lev Gudkov and Boris Dubin, noted:

> [T]he great majority of Russians in the second half of the 1990s expressed the view that they do not need anything beyond basic stability in their life and survival. Regardless of whether or not the present social and political system guaranteed better living conditions, people preferred to leave things as they were: *the one thing they explicitly do not want is change.*[10]

The burden of constant adaptation throughout the 1990s fostered a conservative backlash and many Russians yearned for a return of the old system—totalitarian, to be sure, but at least stable and predictable.

This conservatism and the corresponding decline in support for basic democratic institutions and rights is reflected in the public opinion data collected by the Russian Independent Institute for Social and Nationalities Problems (RIISNP). Table 11.1 summarizes the institute's findings.[11]

As table 11.1 shows, the importance the general public attached to various democratic institutions and rights declined by an average of 10 percentage points from 1997 to 2000. This does not mean, of course, that democratic values lost all currency. Indeed, the majority of Russians' recognition that most democratic structures—with the notable exception of a multiparty system and representative organizations—are an integral component of their country's political system confirms a certain normative triumph of democratic values.[12] Given the hard-hitting disappointment of the 1990s as a whole, these results can actually be interpreted as proof of a relatively robust popular democratic consciousness.

Normative Perceptions

The trends presented in table 11.1 might even appear encouraging if viewed within the context of Russia's turbulent changes. Most optimistically, the public at large has never questioned the need for transition toward a democratic system of government. Indeed, according to data from the All-Russian Center for Public Opinion Research (VTsIOM) a great majority of Russians

Table 11.1. Public Views of the Importance of Democratic Institutions and Rights, 1997 and 2000

Institution or right	1997 Important	1997 Not important	2000 Important	2000 Not important
Multiparty system	39.2	36.1	26.4	49.7
Representative organs of power (e.g., State Duma)	49.8	20.2	38.5	32.7
Free enterprise	62.6	15.7	56.9	21.8
Freedom of speech and of the mass media	85.8	5.1	77.3	9.9
Freedom to travel abroad	67.7	17.2	52.4	29.6
Electivity of all organs of power	75.6	9.2	64.2	15.2

Source: RIINP data.

consider democracy and political freedoms to be the only significant achievements of recent years despite the negative experiences that most tend to associate with the Yeltsin era (table 11.2).[13]

Regarding optimism about democracy, the first decade of the post-communist transition differed from any other period in Russia's history. According to RIISNP survey data, the majority of Russians (70 percent of polled respondents) associate the concept of civil and political liberties more with the 1990s than with any other decade in the twentieth century. By way of comparison, only 10 percent associated the presence of political and civil

Table 11.2. Popular Assessment of Achievements of the Yeltsin Era, 2000

Achievement	Percentage of respondents
Nothing good	45
Democracy and political freedoms	23
Overcoming of shortages, ration cards, lines	16
Reintroduction of private property	13
Freedom for private enterprise	12
Removal of communists from power	10
Destruction of the totalitarian system	7
Improved relations with the West	7
Hope for Russia's rebirth	5
Improvement in the quality of goods and services	4
Disappearance of the threat of another world war	3

Source: All-Russian Center for Public Opinion Research data.

Table 11.3. Popular Perceptions of the Essentials for Democracy

Essentials for democracy	Percentage of respondents
Equality of all citizens before the law	54.0
Freedom of the press	47.6
Independence of the courts	40.2
Free elections of the authorities	39.4
Opportunity to express one's political views freely	37.2
Direct election of the president by the people	25.9
Freedom of religion	23.7
Private property	23.0
Presence of an opposition capable of influencing the president and the government	20.6
Public participation in referenda on nationally important issues	17.8
Freedom to travel abroad	17.7
Freedom to choose one's profession	17.6
Small differences in people's levels of income	17.6
Freedom of movement within the country	16.8
Right to choose between several competing political parties	15.5
Worker participation in the management of enterprises	12.9
Right to strike	11.9
Self-sufficiency of the nation's regions	9.5
Free membership in a political party	3.8
Submission of the minority to decisions by the majority	3.0
Other	2.5

Source: Michael McFaul and Andrei Ryabov, eds., *Rossiyskoe obshestvo: stanovlenie demokraticheskikh tsennostey?* [Russian society: the formation of democratic values?] (Moscow: Moscow Carnegie Center, 1999), p. 211.

liberties with prerevolutionary Russia and a mere 15 percent with the Soviet Union under Leonid Brezhnev.[14]

These findings are complemented by the results of more specific survey questions as depicted in table 11.3. Russians seem to draw a clear distinction between those elements of democracy that were previously observed in Russia's political history and those that were not. Democratic features they believed to be completely new in the 1990s included free elections to organs of power; freedom of speech and of the press; freedom of movement, including the right to travel abroad; and entrepreneurial freedom.

To the question, "What is democracy?" most Russian respondents in various polls gave responses that parallel the findings of similar polls among Western publics. Yet despite these similar normative perceptions, important differences remain between Russian and Western understanding of democracy. Most important, Russians distinguish between the ideal set of democratic practices and values listed in table 11.3 and the set that is actually observed and practiced in Russia. Indeed, the Russian public is keenly aware of an intrinsic divergence between the normative ideal of democracy and the reality that took shape in the aftermath of perestroika. This is revealed in part by the fact that even though poll participants identified the same set of key democratic features as their Western counterparts, the relative values they attached to these were considerably different. Some stark examples include the relatively low ratings assigned to personal freedoms, democratic mechanisms at all levels of government, local self-government, worker participation in enterprise management, and the right to strike.

Fueled by economic hardship, disappointment with democratic reforms deepened in the mid-1990s when people realized that personal interests rather than normative convictions had shaped the ideologies of many leading reformers. A large number of so-called democrats had a financial stake in the substance and implementation of the reforms they advocated. Data from a 1995 Public Opinion Foundation poll confirms this public disillusionment. Two issues on which poll participants reached consensus were (1) that Russia's government structures were still far from democratic, and (2) that the ruling democratic leaders represented an impediment to the development of a true democracy.[15] Even though people understood that many of the government's antidemocratic features were inherent in its structures, they resented that the democrats in power exploited, rather than tried to change, these flaws. The public came to believe that the democrats were just as likely as the communists to seek personal gain through the use of corruption, the lack of transparency or professionalism, unpredictability, and the inability to establish a credible system of law and order.

As data from the RIISNP summarized in table 11.4 show, this general outlook has not changed significantly since 1995. People continue to desire further democratization even as they recognize that to date democracy has failed to materialize. Most Russians believe that current democratic shortcomings result from misguided policies pursued by bad leaders and not from Russian history or traditions.

As the vast majority of Russians understand democracy, it is a way of organizing society using a set of practical principles. The most important of these are (1) law and order, and (2) economic prosperity and social well-being. This ordering is clearly discernible in the results of a poll that asked

Table 11.4. Russian Attitudes Toward Democratic Procedures, Selected Years
(percentage of respondents)

Opinion	Agree			Disagree		
	1995	**1997**	**2000**	**1995**	**1997**	**2000**
Democratic procedures are a facade	73.1	74.4	74.5	13.3	12.9	11.8
Democratic procedures are indispensable	56.0	51.0	47.8	13.6	17.9	18.3
Public participation is important	23.4	18.8	23.8	52.5	59.9	60.7
Ordinary citizens have no role to play, only politicians do	66.1	70.3	66.4	20.0	17.7	21.8

Source: RIINP data.

respondents to rank the most important rights and freedoms available to individuals (rather than to society as a whole) in a democracy.[16] The findings were as follows:

1. equality before the law,
2. public safety and law and order,
3. right to a job,
4. right to education,
5. equality of opportunity,
6. right to privacy.

Once again, these results are an example of divergence between the normative popular perceptions of democracy that surfaced under Gorbachev and the actual quasi-democratic system that Russians have observed in their day-to-day lives since then. The source of their real disillusionment is not democratization itself, but the particular course political leaders adopted in the early 1990s. The popular mistrust and scorn of contemporary democratic institutions evident today is in no small measure the result of a general disappointment with Yeltsin's failed social and economic reforms.

This general disappointment may also be attributed to the overblown expectations for democracy at the outset of reforms. The public's lack of previous exposure to democratic mechanisms promoted idealized visions that ignored (1) the new system's imperfections; (2) the real difficulties of transitioning from the old totalitarian regime to a new democracy; and (3) the flaws in all democratic regimes, including the established liberal democra-

Table 11.5. Responses to the Question "Do You Agree That, During the Soviet Period, Russians Became Irrevocably Different?" 1994 and 2000
(percentage of respondents)

Response	1994: 2,000 people polled	2000: 1,600 people polled
Agree	54	68
Disagree	29	21
Difficult to say	17	11

Source: Leonid Gordon and Eduard Klopov, "Sovremennie obshestvenno-politicheskie preo-brazovaniya v masshtabe socialnogo vremeni" [Contemporary public and political transformations on the scale of social time] *Sotsis*, no. 1 (1998), p. 21.

cies in the West. Sociologists Leonid Gordon and Eduard Klopov conducted some of the most important work in this field of mass attitudes. In their research, they ascribed the public's unwillingness to embrace democratic principles and procedures to the mentality carried over from the Soviet era. According to Gordon and Klopov, seventy years of communism rooted out all understanding of democracy, the seeds of which had first begun to germinate in public consciousness in prerevolutionary Russia. At that time, emerging democratic notions included "principles of entrepreneurship, social structures, norms of social behavior, the role of courts and the law, private property, legislature, and various rights and liberties such as the freedom of speech."[17] Various sociological studies conducted throughout the 1990s provide indirect confirmation of Gordon and Klopov's study by revealing popular recognition of the distinct and irrevocable change in social psychology since 1917. Table 11.5 shows poll results on the question "Do you agree that, during the Soviet period, Russians became irrevocably different?"

Signals emanating from the West also influenced Russia's democratization efforts. Even though the Russian public was highly critical of the political practices of Yeltsin's administration, it received relatively high approval ratings by Western leaders and the Western press. This adversely affected ordinary Russians' perceptions of Western democracy. In addition, the deterioration of the economic and social situation in the mid-1990s contributed to increasing general dissatisfaction with the West, which appeared to have failed to aid Russia. Moreover, the Western model of democracy, offered to Russia as the best blueprint for rebuilding the polity, had done little to improve Russians' lives. Indeed, the Yeltsin era was so difficult that after his departure about one-third of the nation's population was firmly convinced that the values of individualism, liberalism, and Western democracy worked against Russia's long-term interests and needs. The same percentage believed that a strong Western influence on Russia's development was hindering the country rather than helping it cope with its problems. Moreover, almost 70 percent of Russians were certain that "Russia is a civilization of its own and would never be able to transplant a Western way of life."[18]

This disenchantment with the West was not unique to Russia. A similar phenomenon occurred in postunification Germany, where, according to a German sociological survey, only one-third of all Germans living in the region of the former East Germany were sufficiently satisfied with the democratic order that they would defend it at all costs.[19]

The Historical Roots of Popular Attitudes About Democracy

The identity crisis in which Russian society found itself in the 1990s can be explained largely by the hasty dismissal of its previous value system before a new set of values had taken root. Given the resulting ideological vacuum, that the only set of ideas the public had to fall back on was the long forgotten beliefs of the pre-1917 era is hardly surprising. These resurrected ideas had an important influence on society's perceptions of the theoretical and legal dimensions of democracy as well as on social and political behavior.

Above all, the return to essentially medieval ideals influenced the popular notion of freedom, democracy's most fundamental tenet. The traditional Russian understanding of freedom is escapist, grounded to a large extent in the country's historical, social, and political context, and representing liberation from something or somebody. The best example of this interpretation of freedom is characterized by the term *volya*, which means something close to liberty, and has for centuries expressed the longing to be free from oppression, be it from private landowners prior to the emancipation of serfs in 1861 or from the state. Traces of *volya* remain in contemporary understandings of freedom. Indeed, RIISNP studies demonstrate that more than 60 percent of all Russians believe that freedom is primarily "the ability to be one's own master." By contrast, only a quarter of respondents viewed freedom in the legal or political terms prevalent in the West.[20]

The traditional Russian idea of freedom made sense in 1991, as the collapse of the communist state seemed to promise an escape from oppression followed by self-determination. The realization of this traditional form of liberty, however, has faced two significant problems. First, the goal it endorsed was incredibly idealistic. Second, and most important, it failed to recognize that personal freedom entails personal responsibility for one's decisions. In many ways, this disconnect is an obvious hangover from Soviet times, when people had little incentive to assume individual responsibility and much incentive to pass it up the ranks instead, to their employers or, even better, to the state. This dependence on a paternalistic state directly contradicts the deep-seated escapist understanding of freedom noted earlier. In the end, however, Russians have chosen the easiest path, leaving the reins in the hands of the state, as shown by the declining popular interest in active political participation.

This preference for state responsibility remained consistent throughout the 1990s. RIISNP studies show that in 1995, approximately 40 percent of Russians believed that the average citizen was best off living under a strong state with a strong public sector, albeit a public sector that remained open to opportunities for private enterprise and grassroots participation in politics. Beyond this middle-of-the-road position, only 13 percent of the population considered a hands-off state policy with regard to the economy to be optimal, and, at the other extreme, only 15 percent opted for completely centralized state management of the economy.[21] These statistics closely parallel the results of a Monitoring.ru study conducted in May 2000. To the question "Which path of development would you have preferred for the nation during the past decade?" the majority of poll respondents (44 percent) replied that the government needed to "carry out reforms with social safeguards for the population."[22]

Some observers interpret such data as proof of Russian society's commitment to a socially oriented market economy or a social democratic model of development, which is not altogether inaccurate. Social democratic models of development accept the principle that citizens and the state share responsibility for any problems and achievements. In the eyes of the Russian public, however, responsibility rests solely with the state. As Vladimir Lapkin astutely remarks, this popular perception is a hybrid of two popular ideological models that have dominated Russia's political history and are deeply rooted in people's consciousness, that is, "a blend of the archaic principles of state paternalism and the [more recent] vision of a so-called 'socialist democracy.'"[23]

As a result, the political system most Russians prefer is utopian in nature. The birth of this ideal in the late 1980s, during the Gorbachev era, is no accident: at this time new optimism about pending reforms and the possibility of freedom blended with the reality of paternalistic social structures that dominated the contemporary Soviet system.[24] This model remains essentially unchanged to this day, despite the intervening institutions of free elections and other mechanisms requiring active public intervention in public policy. A good number of Russians (approximately 25 percent) fully support their country's current system, that is, a fundamentally paternalistic presidential republic, even if many democratically-oriented analysts deride it as an "elective monarchy" that discourages any public accountability to the electorate by the powerful head of state.[25]

Alongside this tradition of paternalism, pre-Soviet patterns of delegative rule also seem to have enjoyed a rebirth. [26] During the Middle Ages, peasants and craftsmen fleeing the oppression of the feudal state formed separate communities on the outskirts of Muscovy (now Moscow), where their locally elected governments centered on a single authoritarian elder. The regularly elected leaders in these societies were essentially free to govern as they saw fit and bore no obligation to their electorates.[27] The substantial, perhaps even decisive, influence of this system on Russians' perception of the optimal political system is clearly visible.

Democracy for the Elite?

Despite its apparent popularity, we believe that this system is not the best path for Russia's democratic development. The most vital component of a well-functioning democracy is active popular participation in and influence on policy making and not the delegation—and essentially the abdication—of power to the elite. Our model does not presuppose the participation of every individual, but it does extend the opportunity for involvement. Several preconditions support this opportunity. First is a solid, national, political infrastructure, including an efficient system of local self-government, social partnership, courts, trade unions, and local communities. Second is citizens' basic confidence in the efficacy and, above all, the usefulness, of these mechanisms. Third is political will among the electorate to employ existing mechanisms to solve pressing problems both locally and nationwide. Only when all these conditions are fulfilled, notes American sociologist Robert Inglehart, can the public transform from a mere voting crowd into a more assertive, politically active body. [28]

Table 11.6. People's Perceptions of Effective Ways to Influence State Authorities, Selected Years
(percentage of respondents)

Method of influence	1995	1997	2000	Employed it in 2000
Taking part in elections and referenda	22.4	21.4	22.2	46.5
Taking part in rallies and demonstrations	2.4	6.7	3.5	2.1
Taking part in strikes	4.3	5.9	2.7	1.4
Taking part in the activities of political parties	3.2	4.2	2.4	1.2
Taking part in the activities of public organizations	15.0	6.5	4.2	1.8
Appealing to the mass media	3.7	5.4	7.4	1.0
Appealing to government agencies	–	–	3.5	2.4
Taking independent action through personal contacts and acquaintances	4.2	4.6	4.4	3.3
Going to court	2.8	5.5	9.4	4.9
Effective means of influencing the authorities do not exist	42.0	53.4	56.7	N/A

Source: RIISNP.
N/A = Not applicable.

The institutions that have emerged over the past decade do not encourage democratic participation. The federal government continues to restrict the practice of local self-government, both formally and informally. Trade unions seem to engage more in publicity stunts than in building concrete social partnerships at the grassroots level. In the meantime, citizens' initiatives, such as ecological movements or committees of soldiers' mothers, are gradually pushed to the fringes of the political agenda. The net effect is the rapid depreciation of democratic participation and the reinforcement of widespread skepticism about democracy.

Quantitative data confirm this trend as presented in table 11.6. Disillusionment with the country's current political course, as well as with the lack of opportunities for active political involvement, is reflected by the growing numbers of Russians who believe that no effective means for influencing the authorities exist: an increase from 42 percent in 1995 to almost 57 percent in 2000. Only the utility of going to court has increased in public estimation, although this in itself is important, because it indicates that Russians no longer view the legal system as merely a punitive organ.

Sociological surveys also indicate that even though levels of popular participation in electoral activities are often relatively high, public interest is much lower in more active types of political participation. Table 11.6 illustrates this phenomenon, showing the low percentages of respondents who admitted having participated in any kind of political activity the previous year.

The low level of public participation in politics does not only reflect the low public value placed on these activities. The increasingly oligarchic and authoritarian tendencies of the ruling elite also play an important role in encouraging the public to maintain a distance from politics. In this connection, some of the most compelling evidence comes from analyst Herman Diligensky, whose study demonstrated that people tend to view political processes to be democratic if they perceive their architects and actors as being moral and as having an internalized obligation to serve the needs of ordinary citizens.[29]

If, as Diligensky's findings suggest, public faith is all that is required for democracy to function, why did it not work in Russia? The answer is that few Russians understand democracy as a way to communicate societal preferences to states authorities. By the mid-1990s, most Russians (80 percent) had become convinced that the authorities had little interest in the opinions of ordinary people.[30] This widespread disillusionment not only reveals the public's original expectations, but also explains its unwillingness to aid the democratization process once under way. As discussed earlier, participatory democracy works only if the general public recognizes and performs its vital role in the political process—particularly its indirect responsibility as a collection of voting individuals—to set the tone and direction for policy. Such an arrangement did not materialize in Russia, where public indifference to political decision making suggested the attitude was one of leave us alone, and we will leave you alone.[31]

Post-Soviet society adopted this posture of indifference in part because of the cautious approach to politics that prevailed during Soviet times. This hands-off attitude toward politics on the part of the public served the interests of the political and business elites. After the collapse of the Soviet Union, Russia's new political and economic elites wanted society to be demobilized so they could profit from the redistribution of former state property, an objective that required maximum cover from public scrutiny. Accordingly, the elites formulated a new twist on the traditional idea of escapist freedom: they released the public from most of its responsibilities

Table 11.7. Popular Expectations of Political Leaders, 1998
(percentage of respondents)

Expectation	Agree	Disagree	Undecided
Everyone should have an equal opportunity to influence government policies	54.5	12.6	19.3
The country ought to be governed by those with experience	94.9	0.5	3.0
Only leaders and experts can choose the correct path for our country in this complex world	71.5	7.5	14.7

Source: V. Mansurov, *Sovremennoe Rossiyskoe obshestvo: perehodniy period. Rezultati sociologicheskogo oprosa naselenia Rossii* (Issledovania Centra Socioexpress Instituta Sociologii RAN: 1998).

to the state and relieved the state of its burden to the public. This implied benefits for both parties. For example, the state stopped paying wages to public employees, but also ceased to collect taxes. In return, the public kept out of politics and the shady dealings of the authorities.

Under these conditions, the prospects for a well-functioning, participatory democracy became increasingly distant. After voting candidates into office, citizens delegated full powers to their allegedly democratic representatives without reserving any real checks on their behavior, creating the system that still persists. Furthermore, while many people remained critical of the "elitization" of politics engendered by this system, most Russians continued to hope that it would eventually facilitate the advent of wise leaders. Table 11.7 illustrates this contradiction.

Moreover, as table 11.8 shows, the elites' concerted attempts to alienate the public from politics resulted in political apathy and subdued public activism, even at the grassroots level. This indifference only deepened as the many hardships of the transition period relegated political and public activities secondary to more immediate needs. Concern for family and friends took precedence over collective action even given the opportunity to organize around common problems.

Social Stratification in Post-Communist Russia

The social alienation induced by the elites also points to another important issue in relation to public participation in the democratization process: Russia suffers from extreme social stratification and the lack of a middle

Table 11.8. Hierarchy of Personal and Public Values

Which of the following is most important for you?	Percentage of respondents
Responsibility for yourself and those close to you	49.9
Friendship	39.5
Social justice	37.8
Privacy	32.9
Individual freedom	26.0
Equal opportunity for all citizens	23.8
Opportunity to choose your residence	15.5
National identity	12.0
Solidarity with like-minded others	11.3
Patriotism	10.5
Responsibility for events in Russia	9.7
Readiness to participate in solving common problems	6.2
Independence from society and the state	4.9
Difficult to say	3.2

Source: V. Mansurov, *Sovremennoe Rossiyskoe obshestvo: perehodniy period. Rezultati sociologicheskogo oprosa naselenia Rossii* (Issledovania Centra Socioexpress Instituta Sociologii RAN: 1998).

class. Indeed, an important reason for the slow progress toward democracy lies in the incompleteness of Russia's post-communist social transformation. The failure to develop a middle class is particularly significant, as theories repeatedly emphasize that this class contributes most to the promotion of democracy. While Russia does have a middle class, it is still too small and too vaguely defined to influence the country's political course. The financial crisis of August 1998, which hit the socioeconomic interests of the middle class hardest of all, only aggravated this stunted development. [32] However, social classes are not static. This mobility is significant because, as mentioned earlier, sociological findings reveal a close, positive correlation between people's socioeconomic status and their degree of engagement in the democratic political process. In other words, the higher people's level of material well-being, the greater the value they attach to democratic ideals and mechanisms, as shown by survey results presented in table 11.9. [33]

Extremely wealthy people or oligarchs were an exception to the dominant pattern in that they had no interest in democratic institutions during the transition from communism to capitalism. Today, however, as rents and state-owned assets dwindle, even the oligarchic class has an interest in developing democratic institutions to constrain the state.

Table 11.9. Views About Democracy by Respondents' Social Class
(percentage of respondents)

Element of democracy	Middle-income strata		Low-income strata		Below the poverty line	
	Important	Unimportant	Important	Unimportant	Important	Unimportant
Multiparty system	31.8	42.9	25.9	51.0	20.9	56.1
Presence of representative organs of power (e.g., the State Duma)	43.6	28.8	39.0	33.3	33.1	35.5
Freedom of enterprise	71.7	12.8	55.3	23.6	40.9	31.1
Freedom of speech and of the mass media	85.7	5.0	76.9	10.7	66.2	15.5
Freedom to travel abroad	66.7	18.5	50.4	31.8	37.8	40.9
Electivity of all government bodies	68.2	11.0	63.7	16.5	61.8	16.9

Source: RIISNP.

High- and middle-income groups account for less than one quarter of the population (0.5 percent and 23 percent, respectively), while 57 percent of Russians are low income and 17 percent live below the poverty line. Given these statistics and our earlier discussion, the parallel patterns of elitization and widespread political alienation are not surprising. Recent empirical studies complement these findings: despite relatively high popular interest in following day-to-day politics (70 percent, on average), only a small percentage of people (less than 2 percent) said that they had participated directly in political activities. This figure approximates the size of Russia's political class, that is, those active in politics.

Threats to the Development of Democratic Culture

Analysts both in Russia and in the West hotly debate the future of democracy under Vladimir Putin.[34] One leading Russian scholar, Dmitri Furman, argues that Putin's election brought about a "peculiar elected monarchy."[35] Putin, as a predetermined heir, received the keys to the Kremlin from his old boss, Yeltsin, essentially to be legitimized by the popular ballot. Ironically, this resulted in the creation of an extraordinary, hybrid political animal that combines a revived, traditional, autocratic-monarchical system of government with conditions of free political activity and freedom of choice. In contrast to Furman's pessimism, other analysts suggest that Putin's inauguration as president began a new phase that would offer opportunities for the development of democracy, even the kind of democracy that would best fit Russia's historical and immediate political needs. Boris Kapustin, for example, argued that Putin's government would mark a positive departure from Yeltsin's old self-interested demagoguery and would pave the way for a transition to true freedom—liberty guaranteed by the state, not liberation from it.[36]

Most Russians do not view the latest change of leadership as a black-and-white transition from the democratic Yeltsin to the autocratic Putin. Few believe that the current leadership is attempting to establish a strictly authoritarian regime, a concern expressed by only 14 percent of Russians polled in 2000.[37] If anything, what most people feared was not an excessively strong government but, on the contrary, a weak one that, like Yeltsin's, could not restore order and stability following the disruptive reforms of the 1990s. This desire for order figured prominently in the federal elections of 1998–2000 and largely determined their results, demonstrating people's widespread concern. Furthermore, this popular preoccupation with stability and order somewhat confirms Furman's hypothesis that the Putin government is indeed an autocracy endorsed by the people.

A close look at Putin's track record further substantiates Furman's view. The wave of public sentiment that swept Putin into office formed long before the 2000 elections. It developed out of public frustration with the hardship and chaos that followed, among other things, the August 1998 default, and exposed a widespread desire to restore the government as a strong, effective social agent. The turmoil of the Yeltsin era only increased the appeal of a stronger government, discrediting the seemingly empty promises of the democratic values that had once underwritten both Yeltsin's legitimacy and his political platform. In 2000, 81 percent of those asked whether order or democracy was more important for Russia supported order. They even commented that, in pursuit of this priority, the violation of certain democratic principles and the restriction of individual liberties were fully acceptable. A mere 9 percent favored the preservation of democracy as being more important.[38]

The Continued Centrality of Leaders

In relation to Putin's impact on democratization, both optimists and pessimists agree on the importance of the president. While this universal preoccupation certainly captures an important truth about Russia's political system, the prospects for democracy clearly do not depend entirely on the will of a single person. The concentration of decision-making power in the hands of a small elite could lead to despotism in the absence of popular checks, while the underdevelopment of a public committed to the principles and practice of democracy creates conditions that permit democratic backsliding. Russian citizens need a greater appreciation of their unalienable democratic rights and the legitimate limits to government power. Only the strengthening of such attitudes can guarantee Russia's future democratic progress.

Even though Russia has taken several small steps toward democratization, the overall political environment still poses many notable impediments to democratic development. As already noted, some of these problems lie in the actions and behavior of the authorities themselves, others are rooted in society and its beliefs, and still others are attributable to Russia's sociocultural and historical peculiarities. Characterizations of the most recent stage of Russia's political development, a period of conservative retrenchment sometimes described as a "post-revolutionary Thermidor," fall into this last category.[39] Thus the question is whether Russia's historically centralized, top-heavy political system can ever become conducive to broad democratization and whether it can be supported by an effective and functional government structure.

The American political scientist Stephen Holmes offers a pessimistic answer to this question. In 1997 he noted that the contradiction between emergent liberalism on the one hand and a towering federal government on the other has pulled post-communist Russia in two irreconcilably different directions, laying the foundation for most of the country's major political difficulties since 1991.

> The spectacle of political disorder in post-communist Russia reminds one of the deep connections between liberalism and a functional state system. The idea of self-supporting individuals who are able to freely exercise their rights provided they are not bothered by the state finds alarmingly little reflection in Russia's reality...Russian society can be likened to an hourglass that does not work. Those at the top neither exploit nor oppress those on the bottom. They don't even govern them; they simply ignore them.[40]

Whether out of necessity or because of its inherent approach to politics, the public mirrors this arrangement perfectly in its sharply differentiated

Table 11.10. Moral Infractions
(percentage of respondents)

Action	Can never be justified	Is sometimes permissible	Should be handled leniently
Bribe giving or taking	67.4	25.3	7.3
Evading taxes	48.7	37.0	14.3
Evading the draft	38.0	46.8	15.2
Resisting the police	34.0	56.7	9.3

Source: *Rossiya na rubezhe vekov* [Russia on the brink of centuries] (Moscow: Russian Independent Institute of Social and Nationalities Problems and Russian Political Encyclopedia, 2000), p. 371.

ideas of state and government. Historically, the public has idealized the state while harboring negative feelings toward the government in power. One socio-psychological study found that 92 percent of Russians surveyed expressed a positive attitude toward the state while only half as many responded favorably to various references to the government.[41] This long-standing, bifurcated perception became particularly pronounced during the Yeltsin era, when, as discussed earlier, many Russians desired both a strong state to restore law and order and the freedom from the state that would allow them to avoid taxes or evade the very laws they championed. Table 11.10 illustrates this divergence between people's goals and their willingness to take appropriate measures to carry them through by revealing that the public's apparent disaffection with bribery contrasts with its approval of draft evasion and resistance to police penalties following civil offenses.

Various explanations for this paradox exist. So-called transitologists emphasize that the transitional nature of post-communist society promotes parochial attitudes discouraging civic morality and responsibility.[42] By contrast, traditionalists, most prominently philosopher Valentina Fedotova, believe that the government has failed to guide society and therefore deserves the full blame for the dearth of civic responsibility. The government's reluctance to involve itself in the difficult task of engaging the public to solve social problems means that the state has left the public to find its own solutions. This, the argument goes, widens the gap between the political elite and the people, removes all means of communication and feedback, and ultimately causes the political demobilization of society.[43]

Table 11.11. People's Views About the Motor of Social Transformation

Cause of social transformation	Percentage of respondents
President Vladimir Putin	45.4
Russian people as a whole	35.3
Market economy-oriented people	23.4
Entrepreneurs	13.8
Academics and teachers	12.3
The mass media	11.9
The middle class	10.7
The government	9.4
The Russian military	6.8
Creative intelligentsia	6.7
Political parties	3.1
The State Duma	1.8

Source: RIISNP (2000).
Notes: See also V. Petukhov, "Demokratiya v vospriyatii Rossiyskogo Obshestva," *Carnegie Moscow Center Bulletin* (July 2001), pp. 10–11 and V. Petukhov, "Democracy in the Opinions of the Russian Society," *Carnegie Moscow Center Bulletin* (March 2001), pp. 10–11.

The transitologists' view is reinforced by evidence of society's rising paternalism and conformism. A survey asking individuals to name the "engine of social transformation" found that the majority of Russians value the president above themselves as political actors (table 11.11). With next to no input from the public and little dialogue with generally accepted moral authorities (with the possible exceptions of Patriarch Alexei II or Aleksandr Solzhenitsyn), the Russian authorities today, just as before, are left to do essentially as they please.

Traditionalists, however, support their claims with reference to the public culture of passivity that was shaped by the Yeltsin and Putin administrations. Once directed at the Yeltsin elites and the clannish, oligarchic system of government in the wake of failed reforms and various political corruption scandals, public disaffection is increasingly directed toward those who oppose or criticize Putin. For the public, Putin embodied renewed hope. To preserve that powerful image, he has tarnished his opponents and distanced himself from the man who handpicked him for the presidency. Major changes in the public's attitude toward the role of the opposition serve as visible manifestations of this trend. In the mid-1990s, 80 percent of Russians considered the opposition to be necessary for a stable political system; now only 55 percent hold this view. Furthermore, people now see

Table 11.12. Public Readiness to Support Authoritarian Measures in Exchange for Leading the Country Out of Crisis, 1995 and 2000
(percentage of respondents)

Are these authoritarian measures acceptable in exchange for leading the country out of crisis?	Yes		No	
	1995	2000	1995	2000
Banning political associations and newspapers that speak out against the present government	10.6	12.3	68.4	63.0
Confiscating the fortunes illegally amassed by "new" Russians	45.2	62.6	35.6	20.2
Banning strikes and other collective actions	18.0	12.2	60.7	68.6
Restricting the freedom to travel abroad	10.3	12.5	74.5	70.3
Canceling all elections for the near future	12.4	19.6	62.7	57.7
Using military means to eliminate the conflicts that threaten Russia's territorial integrity	25.6	45.2	51.6	30.1
Suspending the parliament for the period of transition and concentrating all power in the hands of the president and the government	18.1	17.2	50.6	49.9

Source: RIISNP.

the opposition not as an instrument of criticism, but as a source of assistance to the authorities. Clearly, the traditional idea of political opposition as a whole has lost much currency in the eyes of the Russian public. This does not suggest that the opposition will disappear. It will probably transform into a body independent of the political system and will draw its legitimacy from its quasi democratic appearance in the eyes of the world community rather than from national public opinion or the party system. International approval will not, however, increase its influence domestically, and if Russian public opinion is a guide, the opposition will weaken significantly in the future.

As the foregoing theories and analyses indicate, many analysts have some reservations about the prospects for democratic development in Russia; however, the predictions that democracy will be rolled back upon the request of the working masses are unfounded. Most Russians are by no means fully satisfied with the course of reforms as they have developed thus far. At the same time, they value the rights and liberties gained over the last decade and understand that, despite all its imperfections, the current political system does provide some form of stability and protection against chaotic power struggles. As table 11.12 shows, the proposition that Russia stands on the brink of a choice between democracy and authoritarianism is rather far-fetched. What research data do show is that while Russians generally support a paternalistic form of government, they categorically oppose any extreme, authoritarian government.

Conclusion

Benign skepticism characterizes many assessments of the development of democracy in Russia. In general, optimists who foresee the future consolidation of democratic principles and laws outnumber pessimists who fear the establishment of an authoritarian regime. The phrasing of survey questions, however, often has a decisive impact on their results. When asked "What would most help the development of Russia in the twenty-first century?" 54 percent of the public surveyed looked to scientific and technological progress, 48 percent mentioned better enforcement of law and order, 35 percent stated the development of education, and a mere 10 percent saw the development of a genuine democracy as critical. In other words, most Russians believe that democratic values and institutions make sense only when included in the overall context of Russia's development for the common good.

A politically empowered public is essential to a developed democracy, yet the question remains whether Russia has a public whose opinion counts. On the one hand, the public clearly expresses its faith or disappointment in reforms and other developments, but on the other hand, the public is also vulnerable to political manipulation. This was evident during the first Chechen war and various election campaigns.

The debate concerning public opinion and democracy is ongoing, and the jury is still out on its attributes and accomplishments. A truly objective analysis must factor in the history and distinctive characteristics of Russia's transition seen in the context of global trends. In absolute terms, Russia's form of democracy is clearly underdeveloped if measured against the liberal, democratic standard of the West. In relative terms, however, the standard that Russia has achieved is certainly adequate, if not remarkable, for its current stage of development. The fact that most Russians want to see this new regime improve along a democratic trajectory might be the most hopeful sign of all.

12

Postscript:
The 2003 Parliamentary Elections and the Future of Russian Democracy

Michael McFaul, Nikolai Petrov, and Andrei Ryabov

The political system that President Vladimir Putin headed at the end of his first term as president differed qualitatively from the regime that President Boris Yeltsin had bequeathed to him. Yeltsin proved to be more able at destruction than construction. The first Russian president helped to guide the Soviet empire to a relatively peaceful collapse, dismantled the Communist Party of the Soviet Union, and destroyed the Soviet command economy. In the wake of this regime destruction, Yeltsin managed to build only weak political institutions of a democratic nature. Nor was his destruction of the ancien régime complete, as many powerful Soviet-era institutions, including the intelligence services, the military, and the procuracy, avoided reform in the 1990s. By the end of the decade, therefore, Russia's democracy had many flaws: a constitution that gave overweening power to the president; a fledgling party system; a weak and detached civil society; a media sector incapable of turning a profit, and therefore dependent on owners with political motivations; and corrupt and ineffective legal institutions. In his four years in office, Putin has done little to correct these flaws. Instead of seeking to improve the quality of Russia's democracy, Putin has devoted considerable time and energy to weakening what were already fragile democratic institutions. The Russian polity has considerably less pluralism in 2004 than it did in 2000. In addition, the human rights of individual citizens are less secure today than they were four years ago.

Nonetheless, public demand for more democracy and greater protection of human rights has not increased during the Putin era. Putin enjoys solid and stable support among both the elite and the masses. On the one hand, most of the post-Soviet elite who acquired power and property during the Yeltsin era seek to preserve their status and wealth, and therefore welcome a guarantor of stability and the status quo in the Kremlin. On the other hand, the people as a whole are tired of the chaos, uncertainty, and injustice that they associate with the Yeltsin era, and thus welcome a new era of calm and stability. This combination gives Putin a powerful social base and the capacity to make antidemocratic changes to the way that Russia is ruled.

Each chapter of this book has attempted to trace the development, or lack thereof, of Russia's democratic institutions since independence. Most chapters conclude by tracing the trajectory of democratic development during the Putin era, and most assessments of the individual components of a democratic polity have identified a negative trend for democracy in the last four years.

Pockets of positive change have occurred under Putin. The legal reforms that presidential aide Dmitri Kozak drafted and that the Duma passed into law have fueled hope that the rule of law may someday determine the way the Russian courts currently work. Russia's experiment with jury trials has produced some unexpected outcomes in which the will of ordinary citizens trumped the preferences of the state.[1] More generally, Putin and his government have strengthened the state after a decade of decay, quasi-anarchy, and obligation shirking, and everyone concurs that a functioning state is a necessary condition for effective democracy. Finally, Putin has not canceled elections or suspended the constitution. The formal institutions of Russian democracy remain in place.

The actual democratic content of these institutions has, however, eroded. Indeed, Putin has systematically weakened or destroyed every check on his power, while at the same time strengthening the state's ability to violate the constitutional rights of individual citizens.

This project began in Chechnya. For *derzhavniki*—those who desire a strong state—like Putin, the anarchy in Chechnya was the most embarrassing testament to Russia's weakness. When the fanatic Chechen commander, Shamil Basayev, moved into neighboring Dagestan in 1999 to liberate the Muslim people of the Caucuses, Putin had the perfect pretext for invading Chechnya. All states, after all, have the right to defend their borders against invading forces, and Russia was obligated to address the lawlessness that enveloped Chechnya after the Khasavyurt accord ended the first war in 1996. However, the way in which Putin's army has fought this war has demonstrated his weak commitment to defend the rights of Russian citizens. The rape, pillage, murder, and destruction of civilian property that has accompanied the war have revealed how little value Putin assigns to protecting individual human rights. Elections in Chechnya since the second war began have been a mockery of the democratic process.

Chechnya is not the only place where Russian citizens' rights are violated. Putin's former employer, the Federal Security Service, the successor to the KGB, has increased the number of arrests of Russians accused of treason and espionage. These alleged spies have been held for years without being notified of their alleged crimes or being tried.[2] The constitutional rights of Russian businesspeople considered disloyal to the Kremlin have also been violated when they have been charged and held for alleged crimes. In October 2003, Russian authorities arrested Russia's richest man, Mikhail Khodorkovsky, on charges of fraud and tax evasion. His lawyers have issued reports documenting how his and his associates' constitutional rights have been violated.[3] The state has refused to respond.

After Chechnya, television came next. When Putin came to power, only three television networks had the national reach to really count in politics: ORT, RTR, and NTV. By running Russian oligarch and former Putin sponsor Boris Berezovsky out of town, Putin effectively acquired control of Russia's largest television network, ORT. The state still owns 100 percent of RTR, so this network quickly became a loyal mouthpiece for Putin and his policies. The acquisition of the third channel, NTV, proved more difficult, because it was in private hands. But the anarchy of the early 1990s provided Putin and his lieutenants with a treasure chest of compromising material on anyone who was trying to do business back then. Charges were filed against NTV's principal owner, Vladimir Gusinsky, who eventually lost his property and then fled the country. NTV's original team of journalists tried to make a go of it at two other stations, but eventually failed. Today the Kremlin de facto controls all national television.

Next came the regional barons. In the 1990s, governors of *oblasts* and presidents of republics acquired genuine political autonomy when power in Moscow evaporated. To reassert Moscow's dominance, Putin started by creating seven new supraregional executive authorities whose mandate is to enforce Putin's policies at the regional level. He then emasculated the Federal Council, Russia's closest approximation to the U.S. Senate, by removing governors and heads of regional parliaments from this upper chamber. Formally, each regional executive appoints one representative to the Federal Council and each regional legislature appoints one representative to the upper house. Informally, the Kremlin has exercised considerable influence in shaping the selection of these representatives, effectively making this parliamentary body a rubber stamp for Kremlin policies. With exceptionally troublesome regional leaders, that is, those who resisted submission to Putin's authority, federal authorities have rigged elections to ensure their downfall. Disqualifying candidates from the ballot on some technicality became the weapon of choice. Putin's aides then resurrected "party" politics in the regions by inviting or coercing regional executives to join Putin's party, United Russia. This new party, built in no small measure on the remnants of the old Communist Party of the Soviet Union, is expected to provide the Kremlin with another institutional mechanism for controlling regional politics.

After Chechnya, the media, and the regional governors, the final two components to be tamed and weakened were the Duma and the independent political parties that worked within the lower house of parliament. After the 1999 parliamentary election, Putin enjoyed a majority of support within the Duma, but that was not good enough, because sometimes a coalition of dissenters in the previous Duma had blocked Putin's initiatives. To make the Duma more compliant, Putin and his administration took advantage of earlier successes in acquiring control of other political resources (such as NTV or the backing of governors) to push hard for a complete victory in the December 2003 parliamentary election. Of course, the Kremlin's greatest asset was Putin himself. Because he enjoyed an approval rating that hovered between 70 and 80 percent during the fall 2003 campaign, a presidential endorsement helped the electoral prospects of United Russia enormously.[4] Constant positive coverage of United Russia leaders and negative coverage of Communist Party officials on all the national television stations, overwhelming financial support from Russia's oligarchs, and near unanimous endorsement from regional leaders also contributed to United Russia's success.[5] In the 1999 parliamentary election, regional elites, oligarchs, and national television networks were divided, resulting in a real battle between Fatherland-All Russia and Unity.[6] In 2003, hardly any divisions occurred among these groups. Mikhail Khodorkovsky, the one oligarch who had pledged to support parties not loyal to the Kremlin, was sitting in jail on election day.

The final results of the 2003 election represented a major victory for the Kremlin. United Russia won 37.6 percent of the popular vote, while two nationalist parties loyal to the Kremlin—Vladimir Zhirinovsky's Liberal Democratic Party of Russia and the newly formed Rodina (Motherland), headed by Sergei Glaziev and Dmitry Rogozin—won 11.5 and 9.0 percent of the party list vote, respectively. United Russia also performed exceedingly well in the 225 single-mandate districts, winning more than 100 seats. When the new Duma first convened two weeks after the election, the United Russia faction boasted 300 members, only one vote short of the two-thirds majority needed to amend the constitution.

At the same time that parties loyal to Putin surged, those parties independent of the Kremlin faltered. The Communist Party of the Russian Federation (CPRF) won only 12.6 percent of the popular vote, half of its total in 1999. Equally important, CPRF incumbents lost in dozens of races in single-mandate districts, winning only 11 seats out of 225 contests. The 2003 election cut the CPRF faction in the Duma in half and eliminated the CPRF as a pivotal player in the legislature. Even more shocking was the dismal performance of Russia's two liberal democratic parties, Yabloko and the Union of Right Forces.[7] Neither crossed the 5 percent threshold needed to win seats through the system of proportional representation or fared well in the single-mandate contests (Yabloko won four seats, the Union of Right Forces won three seats).[8] For the first time since competitive elections began in Russia in 1990, the liberals will not have a faction in the parliament.

The results of the 2003 elections had two major negative consequences for democratic development in Russia. First, the new parliament will be totally loyal and subservient to the Kremlin. For most of the 1990s, the Duma represented a check—albeit a weak one—on presidential power. No more. Second, the 2003 election further weakened independent party development. The three big losers in the December 2003 election were all parties with long histories, support rooted in society, and ideological orientations that could be plotted on a traditional left-right scale. They formed the nucleus of a proto-party system. After the 2003 vote, the political orientations (especially along the traditional left-right spectrum) of Russia's party system have become less clear, while parties' dependence on the state for their survival has grown.

The 2003 vote also confirmed the obvious: the 2004 Russian presidential election will not be competitive. Putin's victory is assured, making the 2004 election a nonevent.

When observed in isolation, each of the outcomes that have occurred on Putin's watch can be interpreted as something other than democratic backsliding. The government in Chechnya did not work, terrorists did and do reside there; Berezovsky and Gusinsky have many skeletons in their closets; some of the regional barons that Putin has reigned in behaved like tyrants in their own fiefdoms; Khodorkovsky is no Sakharov; and Putin is popular, thus the results of the December 2003 parliamentary vote reflect the popular will. But when analyzed together, the thread uniting these events is clear, namely, the elimination or weakening of independent sources of political power.

In the long run, the forces of internal modernization and international integration will push Russia in a democratic direction. In the short run, however, the prospects for renewed democratization are uncertain. Putin now faces no serious opposition: not from governors, not from oligarchs, not from political parties, not from the media, and not from the upper or lower houses of parliament. Those willing to criticize the president—human rights activists, a handful of print journalists, and a smattering of individual politicians in the Duma and regional assemblies—have little or no power. The new balance of power within the polity offers Putin the possibility of ruling Russia for a long time. He can certainly amass the support needed to amend the constitution and extend his time in office, currently limited by the constitution to two terms. Under more dire circumstances, he probably has the power to suspend the constitution altogether.

The real question for the short term, therefore, is what kind of political system does Putin ultimately desire? To date he has demonstrated little tolerance for criticism or checks on his power. At the same time, he has shown no desire to resurrect full-blown dictatorship. He has not taken the more extreme steps of canceling elections or arresting hundreds of political opponents. Even during his persecution of dissident forces, he has used the law, not brute force. His is an arbitrary use of the law for political purposes, but it is not open defiance of the law or a complete disdain for democratic procedures. Putin has not articulated any alternative ideology or project in opposition to democracy. In this sense, he must be distinguished from those communists, fascists, and Islamists from the past and present who have openly challenged democracy as a political practice. However, whether Potemkin democracy or "managed democracy" (as Kremlin loyalists euphemistically call it), facilitates the future development of meaningful democratic practices or not is an open question. Today we know one thing for sure: that Putin, and Putin alone, gets to decide what kind of political regime Russia should have is a bad sign for the future of Russian democracy.

Notes

Acknowledgments

1. An earlier version of this chapter appeared as Michael McFaul, "Explaining Party Formation and Nonformation in Russia: Actors, Institutions, and Chance," *Comparative Political Studies*, vol. 34, no. 10 (December 2001) pp. 1159–87.

Chapter 1

1. Collier and Levitsky counted more than 500 subtypes of democracy alone and did not even tackle the various forms of autocracy. See David Collier and Steven Levitsky, "Democracy with Adjectives: Conceptual Innovation in Comparative Research," *World Politics*, vol. 49, no. 3 (April 1997), pp. 430–51.

2. For more skeptical assessments, see Vladimir Brovkin, "The Emperor's New Clothes: Continuities of Soviet Political Culture in Contemporary Russia," *Problems of Post-Communism*, vol. 43, no. 2 (March–April 1996), pp. 21–28; Peter Reddaway and Dmitri Glinsky, *Market Bolshevism: The Tragedy of Russia's Reforms* (Washington, D.C.: U.S. Institute of Peace, 1999); and Stephen Cohen, "Russian Studies Without Russia," *Post-Soviet Affairs*, vol. 15, no. 1 (January–March 1999), pp. 37–55.

3. Joseph Schumpeter, *Capitalism, Socialism and Democracy,* 3rd ed. (New York: Harper & Row, 1950), p. 269.

4. Adam Przeworski, *Democracy and the Market: Political and Economic Reforms in Eastern Europe and Latin America* (Cambridge, U.K.: Cambridge University Press, 1991), p. 14.

5. Larry Diamond, *Developing Democracy: Toward Consolidation* (Baltimore, Md.: Johns Hopkins University Press, 1999).

6. Terry Lynn Karl, "Imposing Consent? Electoralism Versus Democratization in El Salvador," in Paul Drake and Eduardo Silva, eds., *Elections and Democratization in Latin America, 1980–1985* (San Diego, Calif.: Center for Iberian and Latin American Studies, 1986), pp. 9–36; and Karl, "The Hybrid Regimes of Central America," *Journal of Democracy*, vol. 6, no. 3 (July 1995), pp. 72–86.

7. On the distinction between liberal and electoral democracy, see Diamond, *Developing Democracy*. On forms of autocracy, see Larry Diamond, "Thinking About Hybrid Regimes," *Journal of Democracy*, vol. 13, no. 2 (April 2002), pp. 21–35; Steven Levitsky and Lucan Way, "The Rise of Competitive Authoritarianism," *Journal of Democracy*, vol. 13, no. 2 (April 2002), pp. 51–65; and Philip Roeder, "Varieties of Post-Soviet Authoritarian Regimes," *Post-Soviet Affairs*, vol. 10, no. 1 (January–March 1994), pp. 61–101.

8. Diamond, *Developing Democracy*, pp. 11–12. The numbers have been added.

9. On the rise of the FSB in Russian state structures, see Olga Kryshtanovskaya, *Rezhim Putina: liberalnaya militokratiya?* [Putin's regime: a liberal militocracy?], unpublished manuscript, 2002.

10. Human Rights Watch, *Welcome to Hell: Arbitrary Detention, Torture, and Extortion in Chechnya* (New York: Human Rights Watch, 2000).

11. Few political regimes, including the American political system, would meet this standard. See Russell Hardin, *Transition to Corporate Democracy*, unpublished manuscript, 2003.

12. Przeworski, *Democracy and the Market*, p. 10.

13. For details, see Timothy Colton and Michael McFaul, *Popular Choice and Managed Democracy: The Russian Elections of 1999 and 2000* (Washington, D.C.: Brookings Institution Press, 2003).

14. Crane Brinton, *Anatomy of Revolution* (New York: Vintage Press, 1938).

15. Premature predictions of dictatorship in Russia have been plentiful. The forum for the *Journal of Democracy* on Russia's 1993 elections was called "Is Russian Democracy Doomed?" We believe, however, that the reemergence of autocracy is closer today than at any time since the collapse of the Soviet Union.

16. Way and Levitsky have identified a new category of regime type, "competitive authoritarianism," to describe such regimes. Diamond uses this category to rank most of the political systems in the world. Although sympathetic to the notion of making the category of dictatorship more nuanced, we do not agree that the Russian regime should be labeled as competitive authoritarianism in part because the Russian system has more democratic features than this label implies, and in part because this label puts Russia in the same category as regimes such as Iran, which to us seem to be more autocratic than Russia. That Russia is on the borderline between electoral democracy and competitive authoritarianism is without question. See Levistky and Way, "The Rise of Competitive Authoritarianism"; and Diamond, "Thinking About Hybrid Regimes."

17. Nevertheless, over time the kind of democracy varies, and changes in the quality of democracy occur within the set of countries ranked 1, 1.

18. Diamond, *Developing Democracy*, p. 20.

19. On why multiple types of regimes emerged following transitions from communist rule, see Michael McFaul, "The Fourth Wave of Democracy *and* Dictatorship: Noncooperative Transitions in the Post-communist World," *World Politics*, vol. 54, no. 2 (January 2002), pp. 212–44; Roeder, "Varieties of Post-Soviet Authoritarian Regimes"; and Valerie Bunce, "Rethinking Recent Democratization: Lessons from the Post-communist Experience, *World Politics*, vol. 55, no. 2 (January 2003), pp. 167–92. On getting stuck between dictatorship and democracy, see the forum on democratic consolidation in the *Journal of Democracy*, vol. 7, no. 2 (April 1996), pp. 3–143; and especially Guillermo O'Donnell, "Illusions About Consolidation," *Journal of Democracy*, vol. 7, no. 2 (April 1996), pp. 34–51. More recently, see Thomas Carothers, "The End of

the Transition Paradigm," *Journal of Democracy*, vol. 13, no. 1 (January 2002), pp. 5–21; and Fareed Zakaria, *The Future of Freedom: Illiberal Democracy at Home and Abroad* (New York: W. W. Norton, 2003).

20. Diamond, *Developing Democracy*, p. 22.

21. Samuel Huntington, *Political Order and Changing Societies* (New Haven, Conn.: Yale University Press, 1968).

22. Guillermo O'Donnell, "Illusions About Consolidation." In making this argument, O'Donnell has questioned the use of the term consolidation. See also Larry Diamond, Marc Plattner, Yun-han Chu, and Hung-mao Tien, eds., *Consolidating the Third Wave Democracies: Themes and Perspectives* (Baltimore, Md.: Johns Hopkins University Press, 1997), pp. 40–57.

23. Stephen Hanson, "Defining Democratic Consolidation," in Richard Anderson, M. Steven Fish, Stephen Hanson, and Philip Roeder, eds., *Post-communism and the Theory of Democracy* (Princeton, N.J.: Princeton University Press, 2001), p. 141, emphasis added.

24. Bunce provocatively suggests that Russia's democratic limits may actually have contributed to democracy's endurance in Russia, however imperfect. See Bunce, "Rethinking Recent Democratization."

25. This is the definition of an equilibrium. See Jack Knight, *Institutions and Social Conflict*, (Cambridge, U.K.: Cambridge University Press, 1992), p. 37.

26. On why, see chapter 9 of Michael McFaul, *Russia's Unfinished Revolution: Political Change from Gorbachev to Putin* (Ithaca, N.Y.: Cornell University Press, 2001).

27. Krasner makes a similar kind of argument about the institution of sovereignty in the international system in Stephen Krasner, *Sovereignty: Organized Hypocrisy* (Princeton, N.J.: Princeton University Press, 1999).

28. Vladimir Ryzhkov, "Constitution Under Fire." *Moscow Times*, December 11, 2002, p. 10.

29. Richard Rose and Neil Munro, *Elections Without Order: Russia's Challenge to Vladimir Putin* (Cambridge, U.K.: Cambridge University Press, 2002); and Timothy J. Colton and Michael McFaul, "Russian Democracy Under Putin," *Problems of Post-Communism*, vol. 50, no. 4 (July–August 2003), pp. 12–21.

30. www.nns.ru/Elect-99/chron99/1999/12/23.html.

31. Greater scholarly attention must be devoted to explaining these variations. For excellent first cuts, see Jeffrey Kopstein and David Reilly, "Geographic Diffusion and the Transformation of the Post-Communist World," *World Politics*, vol. 53, no. 1 (October 2000), pp. 1–37; M. Steven Fish, "The Dynamics of Democratic Erosion," in Richard Anderson, M. Steven Fish, Stephen Hanson, and Philip Roeder, eds., *Post-communism and the Theory of Democracy* (Princeton, N.J.: Princeton University Press, 2001), pp. 54–95; Philip Roeder, "Transitions from Communism: State-Centered Approaches," in Harry Eckstein, Frederic Fleron, Erik Hoffmann, and William Reisinger, eds., *Can Democracy Take Root in Post-Soviet Russia?* (Lanham, Md.: Roman and Littlefield, 1998), pp. 201–28; Valerie Bunce, "Regional Differences in Democratization: The East Versus the South," *Post-Soviet Affairs*, vol. 14, no. 3 (1998), pp. 87–211; and Valerie Bunce, "Comparative Democratization: Big and Bounded Generalizations," *Comparative Political Studies*, vol. 14, no. 6/7 (2000), pp. 703–34.

32. Philippe Schmitter and Terry Karl, "The Types of Democracy Emerging in Southern and Eastern Europe and South and Central America," in Peter Volten, ed., *Bound to Change: Consolidating Democracy in East Central Europe* (Boulder, Colo.: Westview Press, 1992), p. 43.

33. For discussions on the applicability of transitology in the post-Soviet context, see Bunce, "Regional Differences in Democratization"; Valerie Bunce, "Should Transitologists Be Grounded?" *Slavic Review*, vol. 54, no. 1 (Spring 1995), pp. 111–27; Philippe Schmitter with Terry Karl, "The Conceptual Travels of Transitologists and Consolidologists: How Far East Should They Go?" *Slavic Review*, vol. 53, no. 1 (Spring 1994), pp. 173–85; Roger Markwick, "A Discipline in Transition? From Sovietology to 'Transitology'," *Journal of Communist Studies and Transition Politics*, vol. 12, no. 3 (September 1996), pp. 255–76.

34. On path dependency, see Paul David, "Clio and the Economics of QWERTY," *American Economic Review*, vol. 75, no. 2 (1985), pp. 332–37; Douglass North, *Institutions, Institutional Change, and Economic Performance* (Cambridge, U.K.: Cambridge University Press, 1981); Sven Steinmo, Kathleen Thelen, and Frank Longstreth, *Structuring Politics: Historical Institutionalism in Comparative Perspective* (Cambridge, U.K.: Cambridge University Press, 1992); and Paul Pierson, "Increasing Returns, Path Dependency, and the Study of Politics, *American Political Science Review*, vol. 94, no. 2 (June 2000), pp. 251–68.

35. Guillermo O'Donnell, Philippe Schmitter, and Laurence Whitehead, *Transitions from Authoritarian Rule*, four volumes (Baltimore, Md.: Johns Hopkins University Press, 1986).

36. In discussions with McFaul, Valerie Bunce has noted that scholars of Eastern Europe were much more attuned to theoretical developments in comparative politics, yet Soviet experts dominated the field. If a university department was going to have only one communist specialist, it usually opted for an expert on the Soviet Union who then also covered Eastern Europe.

37. Samuel Huntington, *The Third Wave: Democratization in the Late Twentieth Century*, (Norman, Okla.: University of Oklahoma Press, 1991). For a critic of this conceptualization for post-communism, see McFaul, "The Fourth Wave of Democracy and Dictatorship."

38. Russell Bova, "Political Dynamics of the Post-Communist Transition," *World Politics*, vol. 44, no. 1 (October 1991), p. 113–38.

39. In addition to this list of three simultaneous transformations, one could add postindustrialization, the rise of postmodernization values in society, identity changes, Russia's integration into the West, and probably several more revolutionary changes.

40. Guillermo O'Donnell and Philippe Schmitter, *Transitions from Authoritarian Rule: Tentative Conclusions* (Baltimore, Md.: Johns Hopkins University Press, 1986), p. 69.

41. For elaboration, see McFaul, "The Fourth Wave of Democracy and Dictatorship."

42. In comparative terms, the level of violence in Russia's latest revolution is much lower than in the other great social revolutions, such as the French, Bolshevik, or Chinese revolutions. The basic mode of transition—confrontational rather than cooperative—is similar to that of these other revolutions.

43. Theda Skocpol, *States and Social Revolutions: A Comparative Analysis of France, Russia, and China* (Cambridge, U.K.: Cambridge University Press, 1979); and Barrington Moore, *Social Origins of Dictatorship and Democracy: Lord and Peasant in the Making of the Modern World* (Boston: Beacon Press, 1966).

44. For an overview, see Jack Goldstone, "Toward a Fourth Generation of Revolutionary Theory," *American Review of Political Science*, vol. 4, no. 3 (June 2001), pp. 139–87.

45. Notable exceptions include Charles Tilly, *European Revolutions, 1492–1992* (Oxford, U.K.: Blackwell Publishers, 1993); and Jack Goldstone, *Theories of Revolution and the Collapse of the U.S.S.R.*, unpublished manuscript, 1996. McFaul's own case for this lens can be found

in his "Revolutionary Transformations in Comparative Perspective: Defining a Post-Communist Research Agenda," in David Holloway and Norman Naimark, eds., *Reexamining the Soviet Experience: Essays in Honor of Alexander Dallin* (Boulder, Colo.: Westview Press, 1996), pp. 167–96.

46. The most comprehensive use of the analogy to help explain post-communist Russia is Irina Staradubrovskaya and Vladimir Mau, *Velikie revolyutsii: ot Kromvelya do Putina* [Great revolutions: from Cromwell to Putin] (Moscow: Vagrius, 2001).

47. See Dominic Lieven, *Empire: The Russian Empire and Its Rivals* (New Haven, Conn.: Yale University Press, 2000); and Karen Barkey and Mark Von Hagen, eds., *After Empire: Multiethnic Societies and Nation-Building* (Boulder, Colo.: Westview Press, 1997).

48. Lieven, *Empire*.

49. Anders Åslund, *How Russia Became a Market Economy* (Washington, D.C.: Brookings Institution Press, 1995).

50. How flawed is still hotly contested. For recent assessments, see Anders Åslund, *Building Capitalism: The Transformation of the Former Soviet Bloc* (Cambridge, U.K.: Cambridge University Press, 2002); Clifford Gaddy and Barry Ickes, *Russia's Virtual Economy* (Washington, D.C.: Brookings Institution Press, 2002); and Erik Berglof, Andrei Kounov, Julia Shvets, and Ksenia Yudaeva, *The New Political Economy of Russia* (Cambridge, Mass.: MIT Press, 2003).

51. In the multivolume study of transitions by O'Donnell and Schmitter, all case studies examined "had some of these rules and procedures [of democracy] in the past." Guillermo O'Donnell, Philippe Schmitter, and Laurence Whitehead, *Transitions from Authoritarian Rule*, four volumes (Baltimore, Md.: Johns Hopkins University Press, 1986), p. 8.

52. Some will quibble that the pre-Soviet period had traditions and organizations to resurrect, but we see few signs of resurrection from this period. On the dearth of democratic civil society in Russia at the beginning of the transition from communist rule, see M. Steven Fish, "Russia's Fourth Transition," *Journal of Democracy*, vol. 5, no. 3 (July 1994), pp. 31–42.

53. Some did attempt to invoke prerevolutionary parties such as the Cadets as a way to mobilize new party cadres. None of these parties succeeded. For an accounting, see Michael McFaul and Sergei Markov, *The Troubled Birth of Russian Democracy: Political Parties, Programs, and Profiles* (Stanford, Calif.: Hoover Institution Press, 1993).

54. Michael McFaul, "Russian Centrism and Revolutionary Transitions," *Post-Soviet Affairs*, vol. 9, no. 4 (July–September 1993), pp. 196–222.

55. Terry Lynn Karl, "Dilemmas of Democratization in Latin America," *Comparative Politics*, vol. 23, no. 1 (October 1990), pp. 1–22; Terry Lynn Karl and Philippe Schmitter, "Democratization Around the Globe: Opportunities and Risks," in Michael Klare and Daniel Thomas, eds., *World Security* (New York: St Martin's Press, 1994), pp. 43–62; Terry Lynn Karl and Philippe Schmitter, "Modes of Transition in Latin America, Southern and Eastern Europe," *International Social Science Journal*, vol. 128, no. 2 (May 1991), pp. 269–84.

56. O'Donnell and Schmitter, p. 72.

57. Roeder, "Transitions from Communism," p. 209.

58. Dankwart Rustow, "Transition to Democracy," *Comparative Politics*, vol. 2, no. 2 (April 1970), p. 352.

59. Daniel Levine, "Paradigm Lost: Dependence to Democracy," *World Politics*, vol. 40, no. 3 (April 1988), p. 379.

60. See Hardin's review and then rejection of this approach in Russell Hardin, *Liberalism, Constitutionalism, and Democracy* (Oxford, U.K.: Oxford University Press, 1999).

61. Przeworski, *Democracy and the Market*, p. 90.

62. Harry Eckstein, "Lessons for the 'Third Wave'," in Eckstein, Fleron, Hoffmann, and Reisinger, *Can Democracy Take Root in Post-Soviet Russia?* p. 264.

63. Levine, "Paradigm Lost," p. 392.

64. This argument is elaborated in McFaul, *Russia's Unfinished Revolution*.

65. M. Steven Fish, *Democracy from Scratch: Opposition and Regime in the New Russian Revolution* (Princeton, N.J.: Princeton University Press, 1995).

66. An official investigation reported that 147 people died in the conflict, although many estimate the actual number to be much higher.

67. On the negative consequences of presidentialism for democracy in the post-communist world more generally, see Fish, "The Dynamics of Democratic Erosion." Fish's finding confirms earlier arguments about the perils of presidentialism for new democracies in Alfred Stepan and Cindy Skach, "Constitutional Frameworks and Democratic Consolidation," *World Politics*, vol. 46, no. 1 (October 1993), pp. 1–22; and Juan Linz and Arturo Valenzuela, *The Failure of Presidential Democracy* (Baltimore, Md.: Johns Hopkins University Press, 1994).

68. On Russia's cultural proclivities for autocratic rulers, see Stephen White, *Political Culture and Soviet Politics* (New York: St. Martin's Press, 1979). A review of Russian cultural history also reveals proto-democratic institutional arrangements. See Nicolai Petro, *The Rebirth of Russian Democracy: An Interpretation of Political Culture* (Cambridge, Mass.: Harvard University Press, 1995); and the review of these debates in Russell Bova, "Political Culture, Authority Patterns, and the Architecture of the New Russian Democracy," in Eckstein, Fleron, Hoffmann, and Reisinger, *Can Democracy Take Root in Post-Soviet Russia?*

69. For details, see Michael McFaul, "Institutional Design, Uncertainty, and Path Dependency During Transitions: Cases from Russia," *Constitutional Political Economy*, vol. 10, no. 1 (March 1999), pp. 27–52.

70. Michael McFaul, "State Power, Institutional Change, and the Politics of Privatization in Russia," *World Politics*, vol. 47, no. 2 (January 1995), pp. 210–43; Andrei Shleifer and Daniel Treisman, *Without a Map: Political Tactics and Economic Reform in Russia* (Cambridge, Mass.: MIT Press, 2000); and Clifford Gaddy, *The Price of the Past: Russia's Struggle with the Legacy of a Militarized Economy* (Washington, D.C.: Brookings Institution Press, 1996).

71. David Hoffman, *The Oligarchs: Wealth and Power in the New Russia* (New York: Public Affairs, 2002).

72. Moore, *Social Origins of Dictatorship and Democracy*, p. 418.

73. On the positive role of labor in the process of democratization in Western Europe, see Dietrich Rueschemeyer, Evelyn Huber Stevens, and John D. Stephens, *Capitalist Development and Democracy* (Chicago: University of Chicago Press, 1992).

74. Adam Przeworski and Fernando Limongi, "Modernization: Theories and Facts," *World Politics*, vol. 49, no. 1 (January 1997), pp. 155–83.

75. Juan Linz and Alfred Stepan provide a comprehensive discussion of the relationship between state power and democracy in *Problems of Democratic Transition and Consolidation: Southern Europe, South America, and Post-Communist Europe* (Baltimore, Md.: Johns Hopkins University Press, 1996). See also Stephen Holmes, "Cultural Legacies or State Collapse?" in Michael Mandelbaum, ed., *Perspectives on Post-communism* (New York: Council on Foreign

Relations, 1996), pp. 22–76; Stephen Holmes, "What Russia Teaches Us Now," *American Prospect*, no. 33 (July–August 1997), pp. 30–39; and Thomas E. Graham, "Fragmentation of Russia," in Andrew Kuchins, ed., *Russia After the Fall* (Washington, D.C.: Carnegie Endowment for International Peace, 2002), pp. 39–61.

76. On the divides between the center and regions, see Daniel Treisman, *After the Deluge: Regional Crises and Political Consolidation in Russia* (Ann Arbor, Mich.: University of Michigan Press, 1999). On divisions within the federal government, see Eugene Huskey, *Presidential Power in Russia* (Armonk, N.Y.: M. E. Sharpe, 1999).

77. The Russian Congress altered the Russian Constitution (the amended Soviet Constitution of 1977) to include this phrase, thereby de jure subordinating the office of the president to the Congress.

78. Olga Kryshtanovskaya, *Rezhim Putina: liberalnaya militokratiya?* [Putin's regime: a liberal militocracy?], unpublished manuscript, 2002.

79. Theda Skocpol, "Social Revolutions and Mass Military Mobilization," *World Politics*, vol. 40, no. 2 (January 1988), pp. 147–68.

80. Timothy Frye and Andrei Shleifer tell a parallel story about an unconstrained Russian state preying on the economy in "The Invisible Hand and the Grabbing Hand," *American Economic Review*, vol. 87, no. 2 (May 1997), pp. 354–58. See also Joel Hellman, Geraint Jones, and Daniel Kaufmann, *Seize the State, Seize the Day: An Empirical Analysis of State Capture and Corruption in Transition Economies*, unpublished manuscript, 2000.

81. On the role of charismatic leaders in such settings, see Max Weber, *Economy and Society*, vol. 2, in Guenther Roth and Claus Wittich, eds. (Berkeley, Calif.: University of California Press, 1978).

82. The definitive biography of this important figure in Russian history is Leon Aron, *Yeltsin: A Revolutionary Life* (New York: St. Martin's Press, 2000). On the relationship between Yeltsin the individual and Russian democracy, see also Lilia Shevtsova, *Yeltsin's Russia* (Washington, D.C.: Carnegie Endowment for International Peace, 1999).

83. The first comprehensive evaluation of the man and his regime is Lilia Shevtsova, *Putin's Russia* (Washington, D.C.: Carnegie Endowment for International Peace, 2003).

84. On the differences between politically closed authoritarianism and competitive authoritarianism, see Diamond, "Thinking About Hybrid Regimes"; and Levitsky and Way, "The Rise of Competitive Authoritarianism."

Chapter 2

1. On the distinctions, see Larry Diamond, *Developing Democracy: Toward Consolidation* (Baltimore, Md.: Johns Hopkins University Press, 1999); David Collier and Steven Levitsky, "Democracy with Adjectives: Conceptual Innovation in Comparative Research," *World Politics*, vol. 49, no. 3 (April 1997), pp. 430–51; Larry Diamond, "Thinking About Hybrid Regimes," *Journal of Democracy*, vol. 13, no. 2 (April 2002), pp. 21–35; and Steven Levitsky and Lucan Way, "The Rise of Competitive Authoritarianism," *Journal of Democracy*, vol. 13, no. 2 (April 2002), pp. 51–65.

2. In 1996–1997, Freedom House scored Russia as a partly free democracy, giving the regime a score of 3 on a scale of 1 to 7 (with 1 being the most democratic and 7 the least democratic) for political rights and 4 for civil liberties. See Freedom House, *Freedom in the World: Annual Survey of Political Rights and Civil Liberties, 1996–1997* (New York: Transaction Books, 1997), p. 421.

3. Joseph Schumpeter, *Capitalism, Socialism, and Democracy, 2nd ed.* (New York: Harper, 1947), p. 269.

4. On why Russia may nonetheless still have too few elections, see Peter Ordeshook, "Russia's Party System: Is Russian Federalism Viable?" *Post-Soviet Affairs*, vol. 12, no. 3 (October–December 1996), pp. 195–217.

5. By resigning in December 1999, President Boris Yeltsin moved up the date of the presidential election by three months. He did not break the law in doing so, even if he did violate the spirit of competitive elections by giving his chosen successor an unfair advantage.

6. Diamond categorizes Russia as a competitive authoritarian regime. See Diamond, "Thinking About Hybrid Regimes," p. 21. Others have argued that Russia never was an electoral democracy. See Peter Reddaway and Dmitri Glinski, *The Tragedy of Russia's Reforms: Market Bolshevism Against Democracy* (Washington, D.C.: U.S. Institute of Peace, 2001).

7. Guillermo O'Donnell and Philippe Schmitter, *Transition from Authoritarian Rule: Tentative Conclusions About Uncertain Democracies*, vol. 4 (Baltimore, Md.: Johns Hopkins University Press, 1986), p. 27.

8. Daniel Friedman, "Bringing Society Back into Democratic Transition Theory After 1989: Pact Making and Regime Collapse," *East European Politics and Societies*, vol. 7, no. 3 (Fall 1993), pp. 482–512.

9. O'Donnell and Schmitter, *Tentative Conclusions*, p. 69. See also Adam Przeworski, "Problems in the Study of Transition to Democracy," in Guillermo O'Donnell, Philippe Schmitter, and Lawrence Whitehead, eds., *Transitions from Authoritarian Rule: Comparative Perspectives*, vol. 3 (Baltimore, Md.: Johns Hopkins University Press, 1986), pp. 47–63.

10. Dankwart Rustow, "Transition to Democracy: Toward a Dynamic Model," *Comparative Politics*, vol. 2, no. 3 (April 1970), pp. 337–63.

11. O'Donnell and Schmitter, *Tentative Conclusions*, p. 40.

12. Michael McFaul, *Russia's 1996 Presidential Election: The End of Polarized Politics* (Stanford, Calif.: Hoover Institution Press, 1997).

13. Anatoly Sobchak, *Khozhdenie vo vlast* [Voyage to power] (Moscow: Novosti, 1991).

14. Some of these social organizations' seats were contested internally, including the famous battle for Andrei Sakharov's election within the Soviet Academy of Sciences. The CPSU list, however, was not competitive. After considering competitive elections within the party, Gorbachev opted for the nomination of exactly 100 candidates to ensure that the party's leadership received seats in the Congress. See Georgy Shakhnazarov, *Tsena svobody* [The price of freedom] (Moscow: Rossika/Zevs, 1993), pp. 74–75.

15. See A. Berezkin, L. Smirnyagin, V. Kolosov, M. Pavlovskaya, and N. Petrov, "The Geography of the 1989 Elections of Peoples Deputies of the USSR," *Soviet Geography*, vol. 30, no. 8 (August 1989), pp. 607–34; and Vladimir Kolosov, Nikolai Petrov, and Leonid Smirnyagin, eds., *Vesna 89: geografiya i anatomiya parlamentskikh vyborov* [Spring of 89: a geography and anatomy of the parliamentary elections] (Moscow: Progress, 1990).

16. Stephen White, Richard Rose, and Ian McAllister, *How Russia Votes* (Chatham, N.J.: Chatham House Publishers, 1997), p. 29. Elections had occurred throughout most of Soviet history, but had no real meaning.

17. For details, see Michael McFaul and Nikolai Petrov, eds., *Politicheskii al'manakh Rossii 1995* [A political almanac of Russia 1995] (Moscow: Carnegie Moscow Center, 1997).

18. Vitaly Vorotnikov, *A bylo eto tak: iz dnevnika chlena Politburo TsK KPSS* [And that's how it was: from the diary of a CPSU central committee politburo member] (Moscow: Veterans of Publishing Union, SI-MAR, 1995), p. 253.

19. All the republics except Belarus and Kazakhstan eliminated these social lists.

20. See M. Steven Fish, *Democracy from Scratch: Opposition and Regime in the New Russian Revolution* (Princeton, N.J.: Princeton University Press, 1995); and Geoffrey Hosking, *The Awakening of the Soviet Union* (Cambridge, Mass.: Harvard University Press, 1991).

21. The number of deputies who identified with Democratic Russia changed over time, depending on the nature of the crisis.

22. Quoted in John Morrison, *Boris Yeltsin: From Bolshevik to Democrat* (New York: Dutton, 1991), p. 238.

23. Yeltsin captured 57.3 percent of the popular vote, compared with 16.8 percent for Nikolai Ryzhkov and a surprising 7.8 percent for Vladimir Zhirinovsky. Chechnya-Ingushetia, Tatarstan, and Tuva did not participate in the elections. See Michael Urban, "Boris Yeltsin, Democratic Russia, and the Campaign for the Russian Presidency," *Soviet Studies*, vol. 44, no. 2 (February 1992), pp. 187–208.

24. Several other republics refused to hold the referendum vote, meaning that the vote could not be considered free and fair.

25. For details, see Michael McFaul, "Institutional Design, Uncertainty, and Path Dependency During Transitions: Cases from Russia," *Constitutional Political Economy*, vol. 10, no. 1 (March 1999), pp. 27–52.

26. For a similar explanation of the American Constitution, see Bruce Cain and W. T. Jones, "Madison's Theory of Representation," in Bernard Grofman and Donald Wittman, eds., *The Federalist Papers and the New Institutionalism* (New York: Agathon Press, 1989), pp. 11–31.

27. The major reason why Yeltsin did not adopt the idea of new elections was because regional electoral commissions remained under the control of Soviet communist elites, and by rough estimates pro-Yeltsin forces would fail in three-quarters of the regions. Sharp conflicts between legislatures and elected mayors in Moscow and St. Petersburg played a role as well. Thus Yeltsin asked the Congress to establish a one-year moratorium on elections for regional heads (except in ethnic republics), which lasted until 1996.

28. Mikhail Gorshkov, Valerii Zhuravlev, Leonid Dobrohotov et al., eds., *Yeltsin-Khasbulatov: edinstvo, kopromiss, bor'ba* [Yeltsin-Khasbulatov: Unity, Compromise, Struggle] (Moscow: Terra, 1994).

29. For more details on the 1993 referendum, see Michael McFaul and Nikolai Petrov, eds., *Politicheskii al'manakh Rossii 1995* [A political almanac of Russia 1995], vol. 1 (Moscow: Carnegie Moscow Center, 1998), pp. 177–78.

30. In eight regions appointed governors met strong opposition from legislatures and gubernatorial elections took place in April 1993. In all but one case opposition candidates won and were later appointed by Yeltsin. In one of these regions, Chelyabinskaya Oblast, Yeltsin ini-

tially did not allow elections; however, they took place anyway. He did not recognize the results and left his appointee to govern.

31. For details, see chapter 4 in this volume and Eugene Huskey, *Presidential Power in Russia* (Armonk, N.Y.: M. E. Sharpe, 1999).

32. Decree Number 1400 did not specify that the Federation Council, the upper chamber of parliament, had to be elected. A later decree made this specification, but the concept of electing the upper chamber did not make it into the constitution.

33. On the consequences of these electoral rules, see Robert Moser, *Unexpected Outcomes: Electoral Systems, Political Parties, and Representation in Russia* (Pittsburgh, Pa.: University of Pittsburgh Press, 2001).

34. On why this particular mixed electoral system was adopted, see Michael McFaul, "Institutional Design, Uncertainty, and Path Dependency During Transitions." One of the authors of this book, Viktor Sheinis, was the principal author of the electoral decree and the subsequent law.

35. As discussed in chapter 5, a new law was passed in 2002 that would raise the threshold of the party list ballot to 7 percent for the 2007 parliamentary elections.

36. Aleksandr Sobyanin and Vladislav Sukhovolsky, *Demokratiya, ogranichennaya falsifikatsiyami: vybory i referendumy v Rossii v 1991–1993 gg.* [A democracy constrained by falsification: elections and referenda in Russia from 1991 to 1993] (Moscow: Evraziia, 1995). For a discussion of these issues, see also Mikhail Myagkov and Aleksander Sobyanin, "Irregularities in the 1993 Russian Elections," working paper (Pasadena: California Institute of Technology), 1995; and Mikhail Filippov and Peter Ordeshook, "Who Stole What in Russia's December 1993 Elections," *Demokratizatsiya*, vol. 5, no. 1 (Winter 1997), pp. 36–52.

37. The actual law governing referenda in place at that time and as used during the April 1993 referendum stated that support had to exceed 50 percent of all registered voters for the constitutional provision to be accepted. To lower this high threshold, Yeltsin called the vote on the constitution in his decree an all-nation vote. For this kind of vote to be valid, 50 percent plus one of all eligible voters had to participate. Of those participating, 50 percent plus one then had to support the referendum. This is a far smaller number than 50 percent of all eligible voters.

38. For detailed analysis of the 1993 elections, see Timothy Colton and Jerry Hough, eds., *Growing Pains: Russian Democracy and the Election of 1993* (Washington, D.C.: Brookings Institution Press, 1998); and Ralph Clem and Peter Craumer, "A Rayon-Level Analysis of the Russian Election and Constitution Plebiscite of December 1993," *Post-Soviet Geography*, vol. 34, no. 8 (October 1993), pp. 459–75.

39. Jerry Hough, "Institutional Rules and Party Formation," in Colton and Hough, eds., *Growing Pains*, pp. 52–53.

40. At one point in his negotiations with the Russian Congress, Yeltsin had agreed to move up the date of the presidential election to 1994. After October 1993, discussion of early presidential elections ended.

41. The new law did incorporate a few changes. It stipulated that candidates running in single-mandate districts could specify their party affiliation on the ballot. It also stated that parliamentary elections and presidential elections could not occur simultaneously. This meant that Yeltsin did not have to associate himself with any one electoral bloc competing in the parlia-

mentary vote. On the importance of electoral cycles, see Matthew Shugart and John Carey, *Presidents and Assemblies* (Cambridge, U.K.: Cambridge University Press, 1992), chapter 9.

42. On these debates, see Thomas Remington and Steven Smith, "Political Goals, Institutional Context, and the Choice of an Electoral System: The Russian Parliamentary Election Law," *American Journal of Political Science*, vol. 40, no. 4 (1996), pp. 1253–79.

43. For more on apportionment and districting, see McFaul and Petrov, eds., *Politicheskii al'manakh Rossii 1997* [A political almanac of Russia 1997], pp. 192–93.

44. For detailed accounts of the 1995 vote, see Michael McFaul, *Russia Between Elections: What the 1995 Parliamentary Elections Really Mean* (Washington, D.C.: Carnegie Endowment for International Peace, 1996); Laura Belin and Robert W. Orttung, *The Russian Parliamentary Elections of 1995* (Armonk, N.Y.: M. E. Sharpe, 1997); and Matthew Wyman, Stephen White, and Sarah Oates, *Elections and Voters in Post-Communist Russia* (Cheltenham, U.K.: Edward Elgar, 1998).

45. When framed through a bipolar lens, the 1995 vote actually appeared similar to previous elections. The Agrarians performed so poorly that they failed to cross the 5 percent threshold needed to win proportional representation seats. The combination of a communist surge, an Agrarian Party collapse, and Zhirinovsky's comparatively poorer showing meant that the total votes cast for opposition parties had changed only marginally in two years. The same stability of voter attitudes persisted on the other side of the ledger. In 1993, Gaidar's Russia's Choice, Yavlinsky's Yabloko, and the now defunct Russian Movement for Democratic Reforms combined to win 28 percent of the popular vote. In 1995, Chernomyrdin's Our Home Is Russia, Yabloko, and Russia's Choice together collected 21 percent of the vote, with an additional 7 percent of the vote divided between small reformist parties.

46. For more details on the evolution and functioning of the Federation Council, see Nikolai Petrov, "The Federation Council and Representation of Regional Interests," Center for Strategic and International Studies Program On New Approaches to Russian Security policy memorandum no. 96, 1999, available at www.csis.org/ruseura/PONARS/policymemos/pm_0096; and Nikolai Petrov, "Sovet federatsii i predstavitelstvo interesov regionov v tsentre," [The federation council and the representation of regional interests in the center] in *Regiony Rossii v 1998 godu* [Russia's regions in 1998] (Moscow: Gendalf, 1999), pp. 180–222.

47. For details, see Michael McFaul, *The Russian 1996 Presidential Election: The End of Polarized Politics* (Stanford, Calif.: Hoover Institution Press, 1997).

48. See Alexei Mukhin, Andrei Zapeklyi, and Nikita Tyukov, *Rossiya: presidentskaya kampaniya—1996* [Russia: the presidential campaign—1996] (Moscow: Service of Political Information and Consultation-Center, 1996).

49. David Hoffman, *The Oligarchs: Wealth and Power in the New Russia* (New York: Public Affairs, 2002).

50. Daniel Treisman and Vladimir Gimpelson, "Political Business Cycles and Russian Elections, or the Manipulation of the 'Chudar'," *British Journal of Political Science*, vol. 31, no. 2 (April 2001), pp. 225–46.

51. Boris Yeltsin, *Midnight Diaries* (New York: Public Affairs, 2000), p. 25.

52. For more details see McFaul and Petrov, eds., *Politicheskii al'manakh Rossii 1997* [A political almanac of Russia 1997], pp. 256–57.

53. For details, see Michael McFaul and Nikolai Petrov, "Russian Electoral Politics After Transition: Regional and National Assessments," *Post-Soviet Geography and Economics*, vol. 38, no. 9 (November 1997), pp. 507–49.

54. For details on Unity's creation and the contest as a whole, see Timothy J. Colton and Michael McFaul, *Popular Choice and Managed Democracy: The Russian Elections of 1999 and 2000* (Washington, D.C.: Brookings Institution Press, 2003).

55. When Seleznov ran for governor of Moscow Oblast in December 1999, Putin endorsed his candidacy in the second round, in which he faced an opponent from OVR. Seleznov lost this election.

56. For more details, see Michael McFaul, Nikolai Petrov, and Andrei Ryabov, eds., *Rossiya v izbiratelnom tsykle 1999–2000 godov* [Russia in the 1999–2000 electoral cycle] (Moscow: Carnegie Moscow Center, 2000), pp. 553–56.

57. The formula for selecting these representatives is complex. The speaker of the regional assembly selects one Federation Council representative who is confirmed by the assembly as a whole. The regional executive selects the second Federation Council representative. The regional assembly can veto the governor's nominee with a two-thirds majority. Representatives serve at the pleasure of those who select them.

58. Tuva, a small southern Siberian republic, is a good example. Initially, one of its representatives to the Federation Council was Sergei Pugachev, a banker from St. Petersburg close to Putin's team, while the other was an ethnic Tuvinian, the former local Federal Security Service chief. After elections to the local parliament in mid-2002, the latter was replaced by Lyudmila Narusova, the widow of the former St. Petersburg mayor, Anatoly Sobchak, for whom Putin had worked for five years.

59. Single-district races seem to be getting less competitive. If competitiveness is measured as the average number of candidates per seat, then it reached a relatively high level of 6.3 in the 1990 elections and was approximately the same until the 1995 Duma elections, at which point it increased even further to 11.7. The 1999 Duma elections showed a slight decrease in the number of candidates to 10.4. A look at winners' margins, however, reveals a different picture. In every successive Duma election this margin has increased by a quarter.

60. We are grateful to Jeremy Pope for providing these data.

61. Timothy J. Colton and Michael McFaul, "Are Russians Undemocratic?" *Post-Soviet Affairs*, vol. 18, no. 2 (April–June 2002), pp. 91–121.

Chapter 3

1. For comprehensive historical analysis, see Ilya Shablinsky, *Predeli vlasti: bor'ba za rossiiskuyu konstitutsionnuyu reformu, 1989–1995* [Limits of power: the struggle over Russian constitutional reform, 1989–1995], Ph.D. dissertation (Moscow: Center for Constitutional Study of the Moscow Public Science Foundation), 1997.

2. The Constitutional Commission published the full text of the first version of the draft constitution. See *Konstitutsionnyi vestnik* [Constitutional herald], no. 4 (Moscow: Constitutional Commission, 1990), pp. 55–120. It was distributed with the newspaper of the RSFSR

Supreme Soviet's Presidium, *Rossiya*, and in the weekly newspaper *Argumenty i fakty*, on November 29, 1990.

3. *Konstitutsiya (osnovnoi zakon) Rossiiskoi sovetskoi federativnoi sotsialisticheskoi respubliki* [Constitution (fundamental law) of the Russian soviet federative socialist republic] (Moscow, 1989), pp. 5, 6, 12–20.

4. *Konstitutsionnyi vestnik* [Constitutional herald], no. 4, 1990, pp. 81–87.

5. *Konstitutsionnyi vestnik* [Constitutional herald], no. 2, 1990, p. 51.

6. *Konstitutsionnyi vestnik* [Constitutional herald], no. 4, 1990, pp. 88–89.

7. *Sovetskaya Rossiya* [Soviet Russia], November 13, 16, 17, 1990, pp. 1–3; and *Konstitutsionnyi vestnik* [Constitutional herald], no. 5, 1990, p. 8.

8. See *Sravnitel'naya tablitsa: 'Proekt konstitutsii Rossiiskoi federatsii, osnovnye polozheniya kotorogo odobreny shestym S'ezdom narodnykh deputatov Rossiiskoi federatsii, i dorabotannyi proekt konstitutsii Rossiiskoi federatsii, odobrennyi v osnovnom konstitutsionnoi kommissiei'* [A comparative table: "A draft of the constitution of the Russian federation, largely approved by the sixth congress of the people's deputies of the Russian Federation, and the reworked draft of the constitution of the Russian federation, largely approved by the constitutional commission"], (Moscow, 1992), pp. 6–94.

9. *Sbornik dokumentov, prinyatykh pervym—shestym s'ezdami narodnykh deputatov Rossiiskoi federatsii* [Collection of documents ratified by the sixth congress of the people's deputies of the Russian federation], (Moscow: Republic, 1992), pp. 163–64.

10. *Chetvortiy s'ezd narodnykh deputatov RSFSR: stenograficheskii otchot* [The fourth congress of the people's deputies of the RSFSR: a stenographic report], vol. III (Moscow, Supreme Soviet Press, 1991), pp. 132–146.

11. *Pyatiy s'ezd narodnykh deputatov RSFSR: stenograficheskii otchot* [The fifth congress of the people's deputies of the RSFSR: a stenographic report], vol. III (Moscow, 1992), pp. 264–67.

12. *Shestoi s'ezd narodnykh deputatov RSFSR: stenograficheskii otchot* [The sixth congress of the people's deputies of the RSFSR: a stenographic report] (Moscow, 1992), pp. 451–90.

13. *Shestoi s'ezd narodnykh deputatov RSFSR: stenograficheskii otchot* [The sixth congress of the people's deputies of the RSFSR: a stenographic report], vol. V, p. 469.

14. G. D. G Murrel, *Russia's Transition to Democracy* (Sussex, U.K.: Academic Press, 1997), p. 101.

15. "Zakon Rossiiskoi federatsii 'ob izmeneniyakh i dopolneniyakh konstitutsii (osnovnogo zakona) Rossiiskoi federatsii—Rossii'—proekt," ["Law of the Russian federation 'on changes and amendments to the constitution (fundamental law) of the Russian federation—Russia'—a draft"] August 11, 1993. From the author's archive.

16. *Konstitutsionnoe soveshchanie: stenogramma, materialy, dokumenty* [Constitutional deliberation: stenography, materials, documents], vol. I (Moscow, 1995), pp. 11–66.

17. *Konstitutsionnoe soveshchanie: stenogramma, materialy, dokumenty* [Constitutional deliberation: stenography, materials, documents], vol. I, pp. 67–137.

18. *Konstitutsionnoe soveshchanie: stenogramma, materialy, dokumenty* [Constitutional deliberation: stenography, materials, documents], vol. I, p. 31.

19. *Proekt konstitutsii RF po sostayniyu na 12 iyulya 1993* [A draft of the constitution of the RF as of July 12, 1993], vol. 17 (Moscow, 1993), p. 361.

20. *Proekt konstitutsii RF po sostayniyu na 12 iyulya 1993* [A draft of the constitution of the RF as of July 12, 1993], pp. 389–91, and vol. 15, pp. 391–92; and *Izbiratel'nyi zakon: Materialy k obsuzhdeniyu* [Electoral law: materials for discussion], (Moscow, 1993), pp. 4–52.

21. Peter Reddaway and Dmitri Glinski, *The Tragedy of Russia's Reforms. Market Bolshevism Against Democracy* (Washington, D.C.: United States Institute of Peace, 2001), p. 633.

22. Thomas F. Remington, *Politics in Russia* (New York: Longman, 1999), p. 222.

23. Timothy J. Colton and Michael McFaul, "Are Russians Undemocratic?" working paper no. 20 (Washington, D.C.: Carnegie Endowment for International Peace), 2001, pp. 3–4.

24. George R. Urban, *End of Empire: The Demise of the Soviet Union* (Washington, D.C.: American University Press, 1993), p. 127.

25. *The CPRF in Documents (1992–1999)* (Moscow: ITRK Press, 1999), pp. 61, 102, 174.

26. Reddaway and Glinski, *The Tragedy of Russia's Reforms*, p. 633.

27. Remington, *Politics in Russia*, p. 46.

28. Article 80, paragraph 2 of the 1993 constitution.

29. Article 80, paragraph 3, and Article 83, of the 1993 constitution.

30. Robert E. Sherwood, *Roosevelt and Hopkins: An Intimate History* (New York: Harper, 1950), part II.

31. Article 93 of the 1993 constitution.

32. The Third State Duma cannot refrain from commenting on foreign political developments, however provocative or uninformed its conclusions may be. As early as 2002 it rushed to inform the president of its opinion about the activities of the Hague Court in connection with the Slobodan Milosevic trial and demanded reprisals against the Vatican after it elevated the level of its representation in Russia.

33. The amendment was introduced into article 95. See *Proekt konstitutsii Rossiiskoi federatsii: konstitutsionnoe soveshchanie: stenogrammy, materialy, dokumenty, 29 aprelya–10 noyabrya 1993* [A draft of the constitution of the RF: constitutional deliberation: stenography, materials, documents, April 29 to November 10, 1993], vol. 20 (Moscow: Judicial Literature, 1995), p. 42.

34. This idea was expressed by Yevgeny Primakov in *Izvestiya*, June 9, 2000; and by Sergei Samoilov, a high-ranking official in the presidential administration, in *Nezavisimaya gazeta*, August 2, 2000, pp. 1, 3.

35. Martin Nicholson, *Toward a Russia of Regions*, Adelphi Paper no. 330 (Oxford, U.K.: International Institute for Strategic Studies, 1999), p. 21.

36. Gordon M. Hahn, "Putin's 'Federal Revolution': Administrative Versus Judicial Methods of Federal Reform," *East European Constitutional Review*, vol. 10, no. 1 (Winter 2001), pp. 60–67.

37. *Obshchaya gazeta*, February 24–March 1, 2000.

38. *Izvestiya*, August 12, 2000; and *Obshchaya gazeta*, January 31–February 6, 2002.

39. Article 3 of the 1993 constitution.

40. Article 5 of the 1993 constitution.

41. In July the deputies gathered primarily to elect the chair of the Supreme Soviet and the October Congress session was officially regarded as a continuation of the July Congress.

42. See Article 121.6 of the 1993 constitution on the immediate cessation of the president's authority in relation to violations of constitutional norms.

43. Article 125 of the 1993 constitution.

44. Yuri Sidorenko, "Sudebnaya kontrreforma: komu vygodno ushchemlenie nezavisimosti i neprikosnovennosti sudei?" [Judicial counterreform: who gains from limiting the independence and untouchability of judges?] *Nezavisimaya gazeta*, May 16, 2002.

45. According to a national poll of 1,600 people conducted by the All-Russian Center for Public Opinion Research from January 21–24, 2001. The results were published on the Internet at www.wciom.ru.

46. For the Public Opinion Foundation survey, see www.fom.ru.

47. Author's archive.

Chapter 4

1. For more details, see Andrei Ryabov, *Filosofiya vlasti* [The philosophy of power] (Moscow: Moscow State University Press, 1993), pp. 190–193.

2. See, for example, Viktor Kuvaldin, *Prezidentstvo v kontekste rossiyskoi transformatsii: Rossiya politicheskaya* [The presidency in the context of Russian transformation: political Russia] (Moscow: Carnegie Moscow Center, 1998), p. 20.

3. Andrei Melvil, *Demokraticheskie tranziti: teoretiko-metodologicheskie i prikladnie aspekti* [Democratic transits: theoretical-methodological and applied aspects] (Moscow: Moscow Public Science Foundation, 1999), p. 63.

4. Vladimir A. Ryzhkov, *Chetvertaya respublika* [The fourth republic] (Moscow: Ad Marginem, 2000), p. 20.

5. These numbers do not include Chechnya.

6. Lilia Shevtsova, *Rezhim Borisa Yeltsina* [Boris Yeltsin's regime] (Moscow: Carnegie Moscow Center and Russian Political Encyclopedia, 1999), p. 146.

7. For details, see Michael McFaul and Andrei Ryabov, eds., *Formirovaniye partiyno-politicheskoy sistemi v Rossii* [Formation of a political party system in Russia] (Moscow: Carnegie Moscow Center, 1998), pp. 7–19.

8. For details, see Ryzhkov, *Chetvertaya respublika* [The fourth republic] pp. 35–44.

9. Theoretically, the people could have rejected the constitution in the December 1993 referendum, but Yeltsin put all his weight behind its passage. Holding the referendum at the same time as the elections for the Duma and the Federation Council also created incentives for all political groups to participate in the 1993 vote and thereby assure a voter turnout high enough to validate the vote. Though as discussed in chapter 2, whether the necessary 50 percent of eligible voters actually participated is still not clear.

10. According to Ryzhkov's calculations, in 1994 the president adopted ninety-five decrees having the force of law. Meanwhile the State Duma adopted only forty bills. At the same time, while the Duma accepted all ninety-five presidential decrees in 1994, in 1995, it accepted only fifty-one, and in 1998 only seven. See Ryzhkov, *Chetvertaya respublika* [The fourth republic], p. 48.

11. Benjamin Constant, *Principi politiki: klassicheskiy Francuzskiy liberalizm* [Principles of politics: classical French liberalism] (Moscow: Russian Political Encyclopedia, 2000), p. 38.

12. Aleksei M. Salmin, "O nekotorikh problemakh samoopredeleniya i vzaimodeystviya ispolnitelnoy i zakonodatelnoy vlastey v Rossiyskoy federatsii" [On certain problems of self-

awareness and the interaction of executive and legislative power in the Russian federation], *Polis*, no. 1 (1996), pp. 7–32.

13. Chechnya did not participate in the 1993 elections, leaving its two seats vacant.

14. Georgy Satarov, Mikhail Krasnov, Vyacheslav Kostikov, Yury Baturin, Alexander Livshits, Lyudmila Pikhoya, Alexander Ilyin, Vladimir Kadatsky, and Konstantin Nikiforov, *Epokha Yeltsina* (Moscow: Vagrius, 2000), p. 387.

15. For details, see Andrei Ryabov, "'Partiya vlasti' v politicheskoy sisteme sovremennoy Rossii" [The party of power in contemporary Russia's political system], in McFaul and Ryabov, *Formirovaniye partiyno-politicheskoy sistemi v Rossii* [Formation of a political party system in Russia], pp. 80–96.

16. Eugene Huskey, *Presidential Power in Russia* (Armonk, N.Y.: M. E. Sharp, 1999), p. 123.

17. Satarov, et. al., *Epokha Yeltsina*, pp. 558–63; and A. Kulikov, *Tiazhelie zvezdi* [Heavy stars] (Moscow: War and Peace Press, 2002), pp. 388–403, 422–23.

18. According to these transitional articles, which were valid from 1993 to 1995, the upper chamber of the parliament was formed on the basis of direct elections. As in the U.S. Senate, every subject of the federation was represented by two deputies.

19. Vladimir Gelman, Sergei Ryzhenkov, and Michael Bri, eds., *Rossiiskie regioni: transformatsiya politicheskikh rezhimov* [Russian regions: transformation of political regimes] (Moscow: The Whole World, 2000), pp. 45–60.

20. Ryzhkov, *Chetvertaya respublika* [The fourth republic], pp. 47–59.

Chapter 5

1. Seymour Martin Lipset, "The Indispensability of Parties," *Journal of Democracy*, vol. 11, no. 1 (January 2000), pp. 48–55; and John Aldrich, *Why Parties?* (Chicago: Chicago University Press, 1995).

2. For a recent review of the role of parties in democracies and democratizing regimes, see Larry Diamond and Richard Gunther, eds. *Political Parties and Democracy* (Baltimore, Md.: Johns Hopkins University Press, 2001).

3. This is a novel method of measuring party development. For other approaches for measuring party development, see Ted Brader and Joshua Tucker, "The Emergence of Mass Partisanship in Russia, 1993–1996," *American Journal of Political Science*, vol. 45, no. 1 (January 2001), pp. 69–83; Geoffrey Evans and Stephen Whitefield, "The Evolution of Left and Right in Post-Soviet Russia," *Europe-Asia Studies*, vol. 50, no. 6 (September 1998), pp. 1023–43; and Regina Smyth, *Linking Party Development and Democracy in the Russian Federation: Are the Assumptions Accurate?* unpublished manuscript, 2003.

4. The classic statement of this theory is Seymour M. Lipset and Stein Rokkan, *Party Systems and Voter Alignments: Cross-National Perspectives* (New York: Free Press, 1967).

5. Others studies that have highlighted the role of strategic actors in the formation of electoral laws include Pauline Jones Luong, "After the Break-Up: Institutional Design in Transitional States," *Comparative Political Studies*, vol. 33, no. 5 (2000), pp. 564–92; Ellen Lust-Okar and Ameney Ahmad Jamal, "Rulers and Rules: Reassessing the Influence of Regime Type on Elec-

toral Law Formation," *Comparative Political Studies*, vol. 35, no. 3 (2002), pp. 337–66; and Thomas Remington and Steve Smith, "Political Goals, Institutional Context, and the Choice of an Electoral System: The Russian Parliamentary Election Law," *American Journal of Political Science*, vol. 40, no. 4 (November 1996), pp. 1253–79. Most "actor-centric" studies highlight the correlation between the preferences of the powerful and institutional outcomes. The argument advanced in this chapter is more complex in contending that some institutional arrangements reflecting the preferences of the powerful produced the intended effect, while other institutions selected by these same powerful actors (the electoral law for the Duma, for example) produced unintentional outcomes.

6. In relation to Russia, the best comprehensive statement on this subject is Timothy Colton, *Transitional Citizens: Voters and What Influences Them in the New Russia* (Cambridge, Mass.: Harvard University Press, 2000). See also Ted Brader and Joshua Tucker, *Pathways to Partisanship in New Democracies: Evidence from Russia*, unpublished manuscript, 2001; and Mathew Wyman, Stephen White, and Sarah Oates, eds., *Elections and Voters in Post-Communist Russia* (Cheltenham, U.K.: Edward Elgar, 1998).

7. M. J. Laver and Ian Budge, eds., *Party Policy and Government Coalitions* (New York: St. Martin's Press, 1992).

8. Obviously, this causal chain can be mapped in other ways depending on the country in question.

9. V. O. Key, *Politics, Parties, and Pressure Groups* (New York: Crowell, 1964).

10. Lilia Shevtsova, *Yeltsin's Russia: Myths and Realities* (Washington, D.C.: Carnegie Endowment for International Peace, 1999).

11. Gary Cox, *Making Votes Count: Strategic Coordination in the World's Electoral Systems* (Cambridge, U.K.: Cambridge University Press, 2002).

12. Nikolai Petrov and Alexei Titkov, "Regional'noe ismerenie vyborov" [The regional dimension of elections], in Michael McFaul, Nikolai Petrov, and Andrei Ryabov, eds., *Rossiya nakanune dumskikh vyborov 1999 goda* [Russia on the eve of duma election of 1999], (Moscow: Carnegie Moscow Center, 1999), pp. 50–78.

13. The Union of Right Forces did not compete in the 1993 or 1995 elections, but the core party of this electoral bloc, Democratic Choice of Russia, did compete in the 1995 election and its predecessor, Russia's Choice, competed in 1993.

14. Not all parties share these features proportionately. For details, see Timothy J. Colton and Michael McFaul, *Popular Choice and Managed Democracy: The Russian Elections of 1999 and 2000* (Washington, D.C.: Brookings Institution Press, 2003).

15. See Mikhail Dmitriev, "Party Economic Programs and Implications," in Michael McFaul, Nikolai Petrov, and Andrei Ryabov, with Elizabeth Reisch, *Primer on Russia's 1999 Duma Elections* (Washington, D.C.: Carnegie Endowment for International Peace, 1999), pp. 31–60.

16. In answer to a question posed by the author about ideological orientation in March 2000, Vyacheslav Igrunov, deputy chairman of the party, estimated that one-third of Yabloko member are liberals and two-thirds are social democrats, but noted that most would have a difficult time answering such a question.

17. Alexei Kuzmin, "Partii v regionakh" [Parties in the regions], in Sergei Markov, Michael McFaul, and Andrei Ryabov, *Formirovanie partiino-politicheskoi sistemy v Rossii* [Formation of a political party system in Russia] (Moscow: Carnegie Moscow Center, 1998), pp. 137–51.

18. On this evolution, see Alexei Zudin, "Union of Right Forces," in McFaul et al., *Primer on Russia's 1999 Duma Elections*, pp. 103–12.

19. Of course, aggregate stability does not mean that individuals are consistently support-ing the same parties. Individual voters' preferences must be discerned from national surveys. At the individual level, partisanship looks much more unstable. For details, see Colton and McFaul, *Popular Choice and Managed Democracy*.

20. Steven Smith and Thomas Remington, *The Politics of Institutional Choice: The Formation of the Russian State Duma* (Princeton, N.J.: Princeton University Press, 2001).

21. Moshe Haspel, Thomas Remington, and Steven Smith, "Electoral Institutions and Party Cohesion in the Russian Duma," *Journal of Politics*, vol. 60, no. 2 (May 1998), pp. 417–39.

22. Alexei Sitnikov, *Power from Within: Sources of Institutional Power with the Russian Duma*, unpublished manuscript, 1999.

23. See Colton and McFaul, *Popular Choice and Managed Democracy.*

24. Timothy Colton and Michael McFaul, "Reinventing Russia's Party of Power: 'Unity' and the 1999 Duma Election," *Post-Soviet Affairs*, vol. 16, no. 3 (Summer 2000), pp. 201–24.

25. Boris Makarenko, "Fatherland-All Russia (OVR)," in McFaul et al., *Primer on Russia's 1999 Duma Elections*, pp. 61–76.

26. See Nikolai Petrov, "Fenomen 'Edinstva'" [The phenomenon of 'unity'], in *Parlamentskie vybory 1999 goda v Rossii* [Parliamentary election of 1999 in Russia], Bulletin no. 4 (Moscow: Carnegie Moscow Center, January 2000), pp. 14–17.

27. See Alexei Makarkin, "Gubernatorskie partii" [Gubernatorial parties], (pp. 178–90); Nikolai Petrov and Alexei Titkov, "Regional'noe ismerenie vyborov" [The regional dimension of elections]; and the five regional profiles of the pre-election setting in 1999 in Michael McFaul, Nikolai Petrov, and Andrei Ryabov, eds., *Rossiya nakanune dumskikh vyborov 1999 goda* [Russia on the eve of duma election of 1999], (Moscow: Carnegie Moscow Center, 1999), pp. 191–262.

28. Michael McFaul and Nikolai Petrov, "Russian Electoral Politics After Transition: Regional and National Assessments," *Post-Soviet Geography and Economics*, vol. 38, no. 9 (November 1997), pp. 507–49.

29. Vladimir Akimov, CPRF campaign adviser, interview with the author, September 1996.

30. Kathryn Stoner-Weiss, "The Limited Reach of Russia's Party System: Under-Institutionalization in Dual Transitions," *Politics and Society*, vol. 29, no. 3 (September 2001), pp. 385–414.

31. Philip Roeder, "Modernization and Participation in the Leninist Development Strategy," *American Political Science Review*, vol. 83, no. 3 (September 1989), pp. 859–84.

32. Tim McDaniel, *The Agony of the Russian Idea* (Princeton, N.J.: Princeton University Press, 1996); and Victor Sergeyev and Nikolai Biryukov, *Russia's Road to Democracy: Parliament, Communism, and Traditional Culture* (London: Edward Elgar, 1993).

33. Seymour Martin Lipset and Stein Rokkan, "Cleavage Structures, Party Systems, and Voter Alignments," in Lipset and Rokkan, eds., *Party Systems and Voter Alignments*, pp. 1–64.

34. Terry Moe, *The Organization of Interests* (Chicago: University of Chicago Press, 1980).

35. For a discussion of this literature, see Herbert Kitschelt, Zdenka Mansfeldova, Radek Markowski, and Gabor Toka, *Post-Communist Party Systems: Competition, Representation, and Inter-Party Cooperation* (New York: Cambridge University Press, 1999), pp. 391–401. More

than a decade after the collapse of communism, however, one would think that the contours of a post-communist society would have begun to form by now.

36. Stephen Whitefield and Geoffrey Evans, "The Emerging Structure of Partisan Divisions in Russian Politics," in Matthew Wyman, Stephen White, and Sarah Oates, eds., *Elections and Voters in Post-Communist Russia* (Glasgow, U.K.: Edward Elgar, 1998), pp. 68–99.

37. Michael McFaul, *Russia's 1996 Presidential Election: The End of Polarized Politics* (Stanford, Calif.: Hoover Institution Press, 1997).

38. If the past were the determining factor of all social outcomes all the time, change would never take place. The key to constructing useful, path-dependent arguments is to specify the conditions under which change could occur, the parameters within which change might occur, and the other factors that might come into play that might alter the status quo.

39. On the relationship between proportional representation and multiparty systems, see Matthew Shugart and John Carey, *Presidents and Assemblies* (Cambridge, U.K.: Cambridge University Press, 1992); and Giovanni Sartori, *Comparative Constitutional Engineering* (New York: New York University Press, 1994). On Russia, see M. Steven Fish, "The Advent of Multipartyism in Russia," *Post-Soviet Affairs*, vol. 11, no. 4 (October–December 1995), pp. 340–83; Thomas Remington and Steven Smith, "The Development of Parliamentary Parties in Russia," *Legislative Studies Quarterly*, vol. 20, no. 4 (November 1995), pp. 457–89; and Robert Moser, *Unexpected Outcomes: Electoral Systems, Political Parties, and Representation in Russia* (Pittsburgh, Pa.: University of Pittsburgh, 2001).

40. As Steven Fish presciently wrote in the summer of 1993 before the introduction of proportional representation into the electoral system: "The surest way to animate parties—and the most radical means of correcting the 'birth defects' that the elections of 1989 and 1990 created in the embryonic party system—would be a system of proportional representation (PR) that grants parties a monopoly over authority to nominate candidates in office." See M. Steven Fish, "Who Shall Speak for Whom? Democracy and Interest Representation in Post-Soviet Russia," in Alexander Dallin, ed., *Political Parties in Russia* (Berkeley, Calif.: International and Area Studies, 1993), pp. 34–48.

41. The LDPR was founded well before the 1993 elections, but assumed a national profile only after its spectacular showing in this vote. Yabloko was founded specifically to compete in the 1993 elections.

42. Guillermo O'Donnell and Philippe Schmitter, *Transitions from Authoritarian Rule: Tentative Conclusions* (Baltimore, Md.: Johns Hopkins University Press, 1986).

43. On the debatable relationship between social structure and party development in the post-communist world, see Herbert Kitschelt, "The Formation of Party Systems in East Central Europe," *Politics and Society*, vol. 20, no.1 (March 1992), pp. 7–50; Valerie Bunce and Maria Csanadi, "Uncertainty in the Transition: Post-Communism in Hungary," *East European Politics and Society*, vol. 7, no. 2 (Spring 1993), pp. 240–75; Geoffrey Evans and Stephen Whitefield, "Identifying the Bases of Party Competition in Eastern Europe," *British Journal of Political Science*, vol. 23, no. 4 (October 1993), pp. 521–48; and M. Steven Fish, "The Advent of Multipartyism."

44. In 1989, all parties except the Communist Party of the Soviet Union were illegal. In February 1990, Article 6 of the Soviet Constitution was amended to permit other parties to organize, but this amendment came too late to allow parties to participate in any substantial way in the spring 1990 elections.

45. On Yeltsin's reasons, see Michael McFaul, *Russia's Unfinished Revolution: Political Change from Gorbachev to Putin* (Ithaca, N.Y.: Cornell University Press, 2001), chapter 4.

46. M. Steven Fish, *Democracy from Scratch: Opposition and Regime in the New Russian Revolution* (Princeton, N.J.: Princeton University Press, 1995).

47. Timothy Colton and Jerry Hough, eds., *Growing Pains: Russian Democracy and the Election of 1993* (Washington, D.C.: Brookings Institution Press, 1998).

48. Mathew Shugart and John Carey, *Presidents and Assemblies* (Cambridge, U.K.: Cambridge University Press, 1992).

49. While a comparison of national and regional elections must take several important differences into account, such a comparison has the advantage of keeping structural variables relatively constant, thereby allowing the causal influence of the electoral system to be isolated.

50. Stoner-Weiss, "The Limited Reach of Russia's Party System."

51. Note that three party candidates also competed in the 1996 and 2000 U.S. presidential elections.

52. Juan Linz, "Presidential or Parliamentary Democracy: Does It Make a Difference?" in Juan Linz and Arturo Valenzuela, eds., *The Failure of Presidential Democracy: Comparative Perspectives* (Baltimore, Md.: Johns Hopkins University Press, 1994), pp. 3–90.

53. Robert Moser, "The Electoral Effects of Presidentialism in Post-Soviet Russia," *Journal of Communist Studies and Transition Politics*, vol. 14, no. 1–2 (March 1998), pp. 54–75.

54. Guillermo O'Donnell, "Delegative Democracy," *Journal of Democracy*, vol. 5, no. 1 (January 1994), pp. 55–69.

55. Thomas Remington, Steven Smith, and Moshe Haspel, "Decrees, Laws, and Inter-Branch Relations in the Russian Federation," *Post-Soviet Affairs*, vol. 14, no. 4 (October–December 1998), pp. 287–322; and Scott Parrish, "Presidential Decree Power in the Second Russian Republic, 1993–1996," in John Carey and Mathew Soberg Stugart, eds., *Executive Decree Authority* (Cambridge, U.K.: Cambridge University Press, 1998), pp. 62–103.

56. Eugene Huskey, *Presidential Power in Russia* (Armonk, NY: M.E. Sharpe, 1999).

57. Imagine how the dynamics of campaigns in U.S. presidential primaries would change if the general election took place only two weeks after the conclusion of the primary vote. Prospective candidates in both parties would have to run more centrist campaigns in the primaries and at the same time have to be more cordial to their opponents in the primary who would be crucial to remobilizing support for the party's winning candidate in the final election held just two weeks later.

58. See McFaul, *Russia's 1996 Presidential Election*, chapter 4.

59. Author's interviews with OVR consultants, September 1999.

60. According to *Vlast*, no. 31, August 10, 1999, p. 20, a July 1999 poll conducted by the All-Russian Center for Public Opinion Research (VTsIOM) showed the level of support for OVR at 28 percent, higher than for any other party. On election day, however, OVR won only 13.3 percent of the popular vote.

61. Putin's popularity eventually grew even more as people started to appreciate a leader of action. VTsIOM polls conducted during the fall of 1999 found the population to be much more optimistic about reforms and much more upbeat about the economy. For instance, in August 1999, VTsIOM asked citizens if they and their families had adapted to the changes that had occurred in their country in the last ten years. Twenty-nine percent said yes, while 42 percent said they would never adapt. In November 1999, even though the economy had not

changed appreciably since August, 40 percent had suddenly adapted and only 36 percent reported that they would never adapt. In another VTsIOM question asked in August 1999, 28 percent of respondents reported that the situation regarding payment of wages, pensions, and stipends in their region or city had improved (presumably in the last month as the question is asked every month), while 27 percent reported that the situation had become worse. In November, 51 percent reported an improvement, while only 17 percent reported the opposite.

62. Peter Ordeshook, "The Emerging Discipline of Political Economy," in James Alt and Kenneth Shepsle, eds., *Perspectives on Positive Political Economy* (Cambridge, U.K.: Cambridge University Press, 1990), pp. 9–30.

63. James March and Johan Olsen, *Rediscovering Institutions* (New York: Free Press, 1989).

64. J. Meyer, J. Boli, and G. Thomas, "Ontology and Rationalization in the Western Cultural Account," in G. Thomas, J. Meyer, F. Ramirez, and J. Boli, *Institutional Structure: Constituting State, Society, and the Individual* (Beverly Hills, Calif.: Sage Publications, 1987).

65. F. A. Hayek, "Notes on the Evolution of Systems of Rules of Conduct," in *Studies in Philosophy, Politics, and Economics* (Chicago: University of Chicago Press, 1967), pp. 66–81.

66. In the literature on institutions, this distinction is often flagged as the difference between efficient and distributional institutions. However, claiming that all institutions have varying degrees of efficiency and distributional functions and that some institutions are more efficient while others are more distributional is probably more accurate. See Jack Knight, *Institutions and Social Conflict* (Cambridge, U.K.: Cambridge University Press, 1992); S. Krasner, "Global Communications and National Power: Life on the Pareto Frontier," *World Politics*, vol. 43, no. 2 (1991), pp. 336–66; and George Tsebelis, *Nested Games* (Berkeley, Calif.: University of California Press, 1990).

67. Russell Hardin, "Why a Constitution?" in B. Grofman and D. Wittman, eds., *The Federalist Papers and the New Institutionalism* (New York: Agathon Press, 1989), pp. 100–20.

68. Paul Pierson, "Increasing Returns, Path Dependence, and the Study of Politics," *American Political Science Review*, vol. 94, no. 2 (June 2000), pp. 251–68; and Brian Arthur, *Increasing Returns and Path Dependence in the Economy* (Ann Arbor, Mich.: University of Michigan Press, 1994).

69. On Russia's cultural proclivities for autocratic rulers, see Stephen White, *Political Culture and Soviet Politics* (New York: St. Martin's Press, 1979). In searching through Russian cultural history, some evidence indicates that Russia's past is collective, if not democratic. See Nikolai Petro, *The Rebirth of Russian Democracy: An Interpretation of Political Culture* (Cambridge, Mass.: Harvard University Press, 1995); and the review of these debates in Russell Bova, "Political Culture, Authority Patterns, and the Architecture of the New Russian Democracy," in H. Eckstein, F. Fleron, E. Hoffmann, and W. Reisinger, eds., *Can Democracy Take Root in Post-Soviet Russia?* (Lanham, Md.: Rowman and Littlefield, 1998), pp. 177–200.

70. On the general argument, see Gerald Easter, "Preference for Presidentialism: Postcommunist Regime Change in Russia and the NIS," *World Politics*, vol. 49, no. 1 (January 1997), pp. 184–211.

71. Democrats is the label that this anticommunist movement adopted and that their friends and foes alike used.

72. Bruce Cain and W. T. Jones, "Madison's Theory of Representation," in Grofman and Wittman, eds., *The Federalist Papers and the New Institutionalism*, pp. 11–31.

73. On the logic of such expansions of executive power, see Terry Moe and Michael Cald-well, "The Institutional Foundations of Democratic Government: A Comparison of Presidential and Parliamentary Systems," *Journal of Institutional and Theoretical Economics*, vol. 150, no. 1 (March 1994), pp. 171–95.

74. On the other factors, see McFaul, *Russia's 1996 Presidential Election*.

75. The president's candidate for the post of governor could be vetoed by a two-thirds majority in the *oblast* soviet. In most cases, Yeltsin's *administration* agreed ahead of time with the local *oblast* soviet on a suitable candidate.

76. Grigorii Golosov, "Russian Political Parties and the 'Bosses': Evidence from the 1994 Provincial Elections in Western Siberia," *Party Politics*, vol. 3, no. 1 (January 1997), pp. 5–21.

77. Yeltsin benefited from the bipolar dynamic in the second round of the 1996 presidential election. When forced to chose between the lesser of two evils, the majority of voters supported Yeltsin against Zyuganov. In a single ballot with no runoff, however, Yeltsin would have come precariously close to losing this election, because he won only 3 percent more votes than Zyuganov in the first round. See Richard Rose and Yevgeny Tikhomirov, "Russia's Forced-Choice Presidential Election," *Post-Soviet Affairs*, vol. 12, no. 4 (October–December 1996), pp. 351–79.

78. McFaul and Petrov, "Russian Electoral Politics After Transition."

79. This winner, General Boris Gromov in Moscow Oblast, had only a weak party affiliation with OVR. Three other challengers defeated incumbents. Two of these winners were mayors and one was a former presidential representative, that is, they were nonpartisan candidates from state structures.

80. For more details, see McFaul, "Institutional Design, Uncertainty, and Path Dependency During Transitions."

81. Olga Tarasova, "Prezidenta i deputatov razdelili proportsii," *Kommersant-Daily*, February 14, 1995, p. 2.

82. Thomas Remington and Steve Smith, "Political Goals, Institutional Context, and the Choice of an Electoral System: The Russian Parliamentary Election Law," *American Journal of Political Science*, vol. 40, no. 4 (November 1996), pp. 1253–79.

83. For details, see the address by Central Election Commission Chairman Aleksandr Veshnyakov, available at www.cikrf.ru/_1_en/doc_2_1.htm.

Chapter 6

1. Accounts of the emergence of civil society during the Gorbachev period include Geoffrey Hosking, *The Awakening of the Soviet Union* (Cambridge, Mass.: Harvard University Press, 1991); Steven Fish, "The Emergence of Independent Associations and the Transformation of Russian Political Society," *Journal of Communist Studies*, vol. 7, no. 3 (September 1991), pp. 299–334; Michael McFaul and Sergei Markov, *The Troubled Birth of Russian Democracy: Political Parties, Programs, and Profiles* (Stanford, Calif.: Hoover Institution Press, 1993); M. Steven Fish, *Democracy from Scratch: Opposition and Regime in the New Russian Revolution* (Princeton, N.J.: Princeton University Press, 1995); Jane Dawson, *Eco-Nationalism: Anti-Nuclear Activism and National Identity in Russia, Lithuania, and Ukraine* (Durham, N.C.: Duke University Press,

1996); and Marcia A. Weigle, *Russia's Liberal Project: State-Society Relations in the Transition from Communism* (University Park, Pa.: Pennsylvania State University Press, 2000).

2. U.S. Agency for International Development, *The 1999 NGO Sustainability Index*, available at www.usaid.gov. Russian estimates indicate smaller numbers of NGOs. For instance, Elena Zhemkova, executive director of Memorial, put the figure at 70,000 in 2001. (Michael McFaul's interview with Zhemkova, April 27, 2001).

3. Larry Diamond, for instance, requires the realm within which organization takes place to be "open, voluntary, self-generating, at least partially self-supporting, autonomous from the state, and bound by a legal order or set of shared rules." Larry Diamond, *Developing Democracy: Toward Consolidation* (Baltimore, Md.: Johns Hopkins University Press, 1999), p. 221.

4. On why such organizations might be excluded, see Marc Morje Howard, *The Weakness of Civil Society in Post-Communist Europe* (Cambridge, U.K.: Cambridge University Press, 2003), pp. 40–41.

5. Sheri Berman, "Civil Society and the Collapse of the Weimar Republic," *World Politics*, vol. 49, no. 3 (April 1997), pp. 401–30.

6. The discussion of the proper qualities groups must exhibit does not end there. For example, some argue that "inward-looking groups" that do not engage in activities aimed at achieving some public good, such as Robert Putnam's bowling leagues, are unqualified. See Robert Putnam, "Bowling Alone: America's Declining Social Capital," *Journal of Democracy*, vol. 6, no. 1 (January 1995), pp. 65–78.

7. Howard, *The Weakness of Civil Society in Post-Communist Europe*, p. 35.

8. On the distinction between civil, political, and economic societies, see Andrew Arato and Jean Cohen, *Civil Society and Democratic Theory* (Cambridge, Mass.: MIT Press, 1992), p. ix; and Diamond "Toward Democratic Consolidation," p. 7. On the importance of opposition to the state, see Keane's definition of civil society in John Keane, *Democracy and Civil Society* (New York: Verso, 1988), p. 14. For an opposing view, that is, on the positive role that the state can play in developing civil society, see Theda Skocpol, "How Americans Became Civic," in Theda Skocpol and Morris P. Fiorina, eds., *Civic Engagement in American Democracy* (Washington, D.C.: Brookings Institution Press and the Russell Sage Foundation, 1999). On the distinction between civil society and social movements and between civil society and social capital, see Howard, *The Weakness of Civil Society in Post-Communist Europe*, chapter 3.

9. On these origins, see McFaul and Markov, *The Troubled Birth of Russian Democracy*.

10. If the essential property of political actors is that, as Cohen and Arato argue, to be "directly involved with state power…which they seek to control and manage," then many Russian parties have never attained such proximity to the state. See Cohen and Arato, *Civil Society and Political Theory*, p. x. Fish found the distinction between civil and political societies unhelpful in understanding the struggle for democracy in the late 1980s and early 1990s, and turned to the concept of "movement society" instead, which encompasses both civic and political actors. See Fish, *Democracy From Scratch*, especially chapter 3.

11. See, for example, Robert Putnam with Robert Leonardi and Raffaella Y. Nanetti, *Making Democracy Work: Civic Traditions in Modern Italy* (Princeton, N.J.: Princeton University Press, 1993); Arato and Cohen, *Civil Society and Democratic Theory*; Grzegorz Ekiert, "Democratic Processes in East Central Europe: A Theoretical Reconsideration," *British Journal of Political Science*, vol. 21, no. 3 (January 1991), pp. 285–313; Jeffery J. Mondak and Adam F. Gearing, "Civic Engagement in a Post-Communist State," *Political Psychology*, vol. 19, no. 3 (September

1998), pp. 615–37; and Daniel Nelson, "Civil Society Endangered," *Social Research*, vol. 63, no. 2 (Summer 1996), pp. 345–68. Linz and Stepan claim that the presence of a functioning civil society is one of the five major tasks a nation must engage in for democracy to become consolidated. See Juan Linz and Alfred Stepan, *Problems of Democratic Transition and Consolidation: Southern Europe, South America, and Post-Communist Europe* (Baltimore, Md.: Johns Hopkins University Press, 1996).

12. See Alexis de Tocqueville, *Democracy in America* (1984, repr. New York: Vintage, 1945). In recent scholarly parlance, this function can be described as building "social capital." See Putnam, "Bowling Alone."

13. These are not the only ways to categorize the functions that civil society supposedly performs, nor do they cover the entirety of the powers ascribed to civil society. Larry Diamond, for instance, lists thirteen distinct functions that civil society can perform to help the development of democracy that may not fit neatly into either category. These two kinds of arguments do, however, dominate prescriptive arguments for the development of civil society as a democracy-strengthening institution.

14. Putnam, "Bowling Alone."

15. Francis Fukuyama, *Trust: The Social Virtues and the Creation of Prosperity* (New York: Free Press, 1995).

16. Diamond, *Developing Democracy: Toward Consolidation*, pp. 218–260.

17. Ibid., pp. 249–250. For a more detailed account of various conceptions of civil society, see John Keane, *Civil Society: Old Images, New Visions* (Stanford, Calif.: Stanford University Press, 1998).

18. Even compared with other former communist countries, Russians' membership in all categories of organizations except labor unions is among the lowest. For details, see World Values Survey 1995–1997. Complete information is available at www.worldvaluessurvey.com.

19. In their comprehensive study of southern European, Latin American, and Eastern European democratizations, Juan Linz and Alfred Stepan argue that totalitarian and post-totalitarian regimes face a greater task in building up civil societies than other regimes, because their societies enjoyed less autonomy than other nondemocratic regime types. See Linz and Stepan, *Problems of Democratic Transition and Consolidation*, p. 56, table 4.1.

20. Fish, "The Emergence of Independent Associations and the Transformation of Russian Political Society."

21. Michael Bernard, "Civil Society After the First Transition: Dilemmas of Post-Communist Democratization in Poland and Beyond," *Communist and Post-Communist Studies*, vol. 29, no. 1 (September 1996), pp. 309–30.

22. Gail W. Lapidus, "State and Society: Toward the Emergence of Civil Society in the Soviet Union," in Seweryn Bialer, ed., *Politics, Society, and Nationality: Inside Gorbachev's Russia* (Boulder, Colo.: Westview Press, 1989), pp. 121–48.

23. This underground movement included the Communist Party of Youth, the Circle of Marxist Thought, the Leninist Union of Students, and the Moscow Logic Circle. See Michael Urban with Vyacheslav Igrunov and Sergei Mitrokhin, *The Rebirth of Politics in Russia* (Cambridge, U.K.: Cambridge University Press, 1997), pp. 30–32.

24. Leonid Polischuk, "Russian Civil Society," working paper no. 202 (College Park, Md.: Center for Institutional Reform and the Informal Sector), 1997, pp. 16–18.

25. M. Holt Ruffin, Alyssa Deutschler, Catriona Logan, and Richard Upjohn, et al., *The Post-Soviet Handbook: A Guide to Grassroots Organizations and Internet Resources* (Seattle, Wash.: Center for Civil Society International and University of Washington Press, 1999), p. xi.

26. Polish organizations represented the extreme example of this antistate approach. See Bronislaw Geremek, "Civil Society Then and Now," *Journal of Democracy*, vol. 3, no. 2 (April 1992), pp. 3–12.

27. Peter Reddaway, "The Development of Dissent in the USSR," in William E. Griffith, ed., *The Soviet Empire: Expansion and Détente* (Lexington, Mass.: Lexington Books, 1976), pp. 57–84.

28. Lapidus, "State and Society," p. 125.

29. Notable examples of mass uprising include those in Temir-Tau, Kazakhstan, in October 1959 and in Novocherkassk, Russia, in June 1962, both of which were brutally suppressed. See Vitaly Ponomarev, *Obshchestvennie Volneniya v SSSR* (Moscow: Levii Povorot, 1990).

30. Reddaway, "The Development of Dissent," p. 78.

31. Fish, *Democracy from Scratch*, p. 304.

32. Yitzhak Brudny, "The Dynamics of 'Democratic Russia,' 1990–1993," *Post-Soviet Affairs*, vol. 9, no. 2 (April–June 1993), pp. 141–70.

33. Thompson, *A Vision Unfulfilled*, p. 484.

34. Fish, *Democracy from Scratch*; and McFaul and Markov, *The Troubled Birth of Russian Democracy*.

35. Aleksandr Yakovlev, Gorbachev's adviser, helped arrange for several pro-reform progressive editors to take charge of publications such as *Novyi Mir, Argumenty i Fakty, Ogonyok*, and *Moscow News*.

36. Stephen White cites reports that only 7 percent of survey respondents regarded the defeat of the coup as a "victory of the democratic revolution," but support for the coup was sometimes estimated as high as 40 percent. See Stephen White, *Russia's New Politics: the Management of Post-communist Society* (Cambridge, U.K.: Cambridge University Press, 2000), pp. 265–66.

37. See especially Adam Przeworski, *Democracy and the Market: Political and Economic Reforms in Eastern Europe and Latin America* (Cambridge, U.K.: Cambridge University Press, 1991).

38. Section 1, chapter 2, of the 1993 constitution.

39. These are the principal, but not the only, laws governing the activities of civil society. The NGO Interlegal estimates the existence of more than 200 federal normative acts that concern the activities of public associations (which are also subject to local and regional regulations).

40. Alexander Smolar, "From Opposition to Atomization," *Journal of Democracy*, vol. 7, no. 1 (January 1996), pp. 12–23.

41. Steven Solnick, *Stealing the State: Control and Collapse in Soviet Institutions* (Cambridge, Mass.: Harvard University Press, 1998).

42. Lisa McIntosh Sundstrom, "Strength from Without? Transnational Influences on NGO Development in Russia," Ph.D. dissertation, Stanford University, 2001.

43. On this acquisition of property, as well as for a more comprehensive description of this battle over privatization, see Michael McFaul, "State Power, Institutional Change, and the Politics of Privatization in Russia," *World Politics*, vol. 47, no. 2 (January 1995), pp. 210–43.

44. Arkady Volsky was the intellectual and organizational catalyst for Civic Union. A former CPSU Central Committee member with close and longstanding ties to enterprise directors, Volsky and his organizations represented the interests of that portion of the Soviet *nomenklatura* that wanted to preserve its previous economic privileges but under new market conditions.

45. Chubais feared that too much worker control of privatized enterprises would threaten the objective of privatization—efficient, profit-seeking companies—because worker-controlled enterprises would devote all their profits to wages and salaries, leaving nothing for investment in production. Chubais, as cited in *INTERFAX News,* June 10, 1992, and in Foreign Broadcast Information Service's "Daily Report: Central Eurasia," June 11, 1992, p. 51. Chubais and his allies criticized the "political approach" of the parliament regarding privatization, warning that the achievement of "political goals of various [interest] groups" could enervate the government's privatization program. See, for example, Chubais as quoted in Russia's Informational Telegraph Agency–TASS News, February 9, 1993, and in "Daily Report: Central Eurasia," February 9, 1993, p. 22.

46. Andrei Schleifer and Daniel Treisman, *Without a Map: Political Tactics and Economic Reform in Russia* (Cambridge, Mass.: MIT Press, 2000), chapter 4.

47. Nevertheless, through their representatives in the Duma, they continued to exert influence over the budget, with devastating consequences for sound fiscal policy.

48. U.S. Agency for International Development, *The 1999 NGO Sustainability Index,* available at www.usaid.gov.

49. Colton's 1995–1996 survey produced the 8 percent number. See Timothy Colton, *Transitional Citizens: Voters and What Influences Them in the New Russia* (Cambridge, Mass.: Harvard University Press, 2000), p. 28. Using All-Russian Center for Public Opinion Research data, Rose reported in 1998 that only 9 percent of Russian citizens participated in a voluntary organization. See Richard Rose, "Getting Things Done with Social Capital: The New Russia Barometer VII," *Studies in Public Policy,* no. 3030 (Glasgow, U.K.: University of Strathclyde, 1998), p. 60.

50. Russian Public Opinion and Market Research 1999 survey results, quoted in Elena Bashkirova, "Civil Society and Changes in the Outlook of the Russian People," *Jamestown Foundation Prism,* vol. VI, no. 7, part 2 (July 2000).

51. Terry Moe, *The Organization of Interests* (Chicago: University of Chicago Press, 1980).

52. With Viktor Chernomyrdin, the former chairman of Gazprom, at the helm of government, the state rarely acted against the interests of the oil and gas sector. Two oligarchs, Vladimir Potanin and Boris Berezovsky, assumed positions in the government, while many others enjoyed special access to the president and his administration.

53. For a comprehensive overview, see Anders Åslund, "Observations on the Development of Small Private Enterprises in Russia," *Post-Soviet Geography and Economy,* vol. 38, no. 4 (April 1997), pp. 191–205.

54. See Timothy Frye and Andrei Shleifer, "The Invisible Hand and the Grabbing Hand," *American Economic Review: Papers and Proceedings,* vol. 87, no. 2 (May 1997), pp. 354–58.

55. Barry Ickes, Peter Murrell, and Randi Ryterman, "End of the Tunnel? The Effects of Financial Stabilization in Russia," *Post-Soviet Affairs,* vol. 13, no. 2 (April–June 1997), pp. 105–33.

56. Weigle, *Russia's Liberal Project,* pp. 357–59.

57. Vadim Volkov, *Violent Entrepreneurs: The Use of Force in the Making of Russian Capitalism* (Ithaca, N.Y.: Cornell University Press, 2002).

58. Arend Lijphart, "Presidentialism and Majoritarian Democracy: Theoretical Observations," in Juan Linz and Arturo Valenzuela, eds., *The Failure of Presidential Democracy: Comparative Perspectives* (Baltimore, Md.: Johns Hopkins University Press, 1994), pp. 91–105.

59. Some positive signs are, however, apparent in specific courts and sectors. See Kathryn Hendley, Peter Murrell, and Randi Ryterman, "Law, Relationships, and Private Enforcements: Transactional Strategies of Russian Enterprises," *Europe-Asia Studies*, vol. 52, no. 2 (2000), pp. 627–56; and Kathryn Hendley, "The Use of Courts by Russian Creditors," *Problems of Post-Communism*, vol. 50, no. 4 (July–August 2003), pp. 32–42. Putin has also initiated legal reforms from the top, although the actual consequences of these programs have yet to be understood. See Leon Aron, "Russia Reinvents the Rule of Law," *American Enterprise Institute for Public Policy Research Russian Outlook*, March 20, 2002; and Richard Conn, "Challenges of Implementing a New Legal System," *Russia Business Watch*, vol. 10, no. 1 (Winter 2002–2003), pp. 13–19.

60. The newspaper *Trud* cites the State Committee of the RF on Statistics estimate of bureaucratic officials at almost 1.2 million at the end of 2000, with an average addition of one more bureaucrat every eighteen minutes (*Trud*, May 16, 2001). Federal tax collections dropped from 17.8 percent of GDP during the early stages of reform in 1992 to 10.1 percent in 1997, according to World Bank data (see Shleifer and Treisman, *Without a Map*, chapter 3).

61. World Bank, *World Development Report 1997: The State in a Changing World* (New York: Oxford University Press, 1997).

62. On the stages of development of civil society in post-communist transitions, see Marcie Weigle and Jim Butterfield, "Civil Society in Reforming Communist Regimes," *Comparative Politics*, vol. 25, no. 1 (October 1992), pp. 1–23.

63. Donna Bahry and Brian Silver, "Intimidation and the Symbolic Uses of Terror in the USSR," *American Political Science Review*, vol. 81, no. 4 (December 1987), pp. 1065–98. Some would add that this trait is not only a Soviet legacy, but also an aspect of Russian culture.

64. Richard Rose, "Russia as an Hour-Glass Society: A Constitution Without Citizens," *East European Constitutional Review*, vol. 4, no. 3 (1995) pp. 34–42.

65. According to one survey, from 1993 to 1998 trust in churches ranged from 35 percent to 52 percent and in armed forces from 23 to 39 percent. During the same period, trust in political parties was at most 5 percent, in parliament was at most 9 percent, in regional governments was 17 percent, in trade unions was 13 percent, in local governments was 19 percent, in courts and the police was 17 percent, and in "government" was 18 percent. See Stephen White, *Russia's New Politics: The Management of Post-communist Society* (Cambridge, U.K.: Cambridge University Press, 2000), p. 270. Rose and Munro found similar results in 2001. The one person or institution with a trust level above 50 percent was Putin. Parties and Duma members remained in single digits. See Richard Rose and Neil Munro, *Elections Without Order: Russia's Challenge to Vladimir Putin* (Cambridge, U.K.: Cambridge University Press, 2002) p. 226.

66. William Mishler and Richard Rose, "Trust, Distrust, and Skepticism: Popular Evaluations of Civil and Political Institutions in Post-Communist Societies," *Journal of Politics*, vol. 59, no. 2 (1997), pp. 418–51. For a somewhat different conclusion, see James Gibson, "Social Networks, Civil Society, and the Prospects for Consolidating Russia's Democratic Transition," *American Journal of Political Science*, vol. 45, no. 1 (January 2001), pp. 51–68.

67. Howard, *The Weakness of Civil Society*, chapter 5.

68. Interview with Eliza Klose, director of Initiative for Social Action and Renewal in Eurasia, March 16, 2001.

69. Judyth L. Twigg, "What Has Happened to Russian Society?" in Andrew Kuchins, ed., *Russia After the Fall* (Washington, D.C.: Carnegie Endowment for International Peace, 2002), pp. 147–162. Teodor Shanin has attributed the ability of citizens to survive in rural areas to quasi-private–quasi-public "networks of mutual support." See Teodor Shanin, "Rural Russia— the Present Stage," presentation delivered at the conference on Russia: Ten Years Later, Carnegie Endowment for International Peace (June 8–9, 2001).

70. Rose, "Getting Things Done with Social Capital."

71. See especially Gibson, "Social Networks, Civil Society, and the Prospects for Consolidating Russia's Democratic Transition."

72. Meeting with the representatives on May 12, 2001. Reported on www.smi.ru.

73. "We are witnessing, for example, several continuous and persistent campaigns in the press in the last two months alone, whose organizers seek to shatter the President's Administration." Posted on May 13, 2001, on news site www.strana.ru.

74. Sergei Markov, *"Contradictions in Human Rights Movement in Russia."* Posted on January 22, 2001, on www.strana.ru.

75. Sergei Karaganov. Posted on May 7, 2001, on www.strana.ru.

76. Lev Ponomarev, interview with the authors, February 10, 2001.

77. Glasnost Public Foundation, *"Russian Authorities Force Organizations to Become Underground."* Available at www.glasnostonline.org/eng_projects/registration.htm. See also Sarah Mendelson, "The Putin Path: Civil Liberties and Human Rights in Retreat," *Problems of Post-Communism*, vol. 47, no. 5 (September–October 2000), pp. 3–12.

78. Mendelson, "The Putin Path," p. 4.

79. U.S. Department of State, Country Report on *Human Rights Practices: Russia* (Washington, D.C.: U. S. Department of State, 2000).

80. Yulia Ignatyeva, "Vremya svobody Sovesti eshchyo ne vidno" *Obshchaya Gazeta*, January 25, 2001. Reprinted in "Johnson's Russia List" newsletter in English as "The Age of Freedom of Conscience Is Nowhere to be Seen." The Slavonic Legal Center later successfully challenged this decision in court. Its experts attested that the effect previously identified as "detrimental" is characteristic of all religious services and other events such as rock concerts.

81. Ignatyeva, "Vremya Svobody Sovesti eshchyo ne vidno."

82. Elliott Abrams, "In Russia, 'Liquidating' Churches," *Washington Post*, November 14, 2000, p. A43.

83. Ignatyeva, "Vremya Svobody Sovesti eshchyo ne vidno." U.S. Department of State, Country Report on *Human Rights Practices: Russia*, states that 70 percent of organizations were able to register.

84. BBC Monitoring Service, "Russia Paper Describes Prosecution of Fringe Youth Organizations," June 7, 2001.

85. The U.S. Agency for International Development assesses the probability of favorable legislation to be uncertain at best. U.S. Agency for International Development, *1999 NGO Sustainability Report*, (Washington, D.C.: U.S. Agency for International Development, 1999), p. 85, available at www.usaid.gov/regions/europe_eurasia/dem_gov/.

86. Other provisions of the law include a fine imposed on unions that do not provide required information about workers, a possibility of a fifty-six-hour work week "with worker's consent," and a reduction in the length of maternity leave to half the current period.

87. Stephen Crowley, "Comprehending the Weakness of Russia's Unions," *Demokratizatsiya*, vol. 10, no. 2 (Spring 2002), pp. 230–257.

88. Yurii Levada, "Rech' idet o razrushenii VTsIOM" [Getting ready for VTsIOM's destruction], www.gazeta.ru, accessed August 5, 2003.

89. D. J. Peterson, "Putin Regime Pressures Russian Environmental Activists," Initiative for Social Action and Renewal in Eurasia, *Give and Take* (Fall 2000), pp. 5–6. Available on www.isar.org/isar/archive/GT/GT9djpeterson.html.

90. Joshua Handler, "Russia's Spy Trials," *Washington Post*, March 14, 2001, p. A24.

91. Complete information on the case available in American Association for the Advancement of Science's Human Rights Action Network, "Dr. Sutyagin's Moscow Trial Begins: Action Alert," http://shr.aaas.org/aaashran.htm.

92. "Russian Science Academy Orders Reports on Foreign Contacts," Agence France Presse, Moscow, May 30, 2001.

93. www.smi.ru/2001/06/12/992372090.html. [Article no longer online.]

94. Alexander Nikitin and Jane Buchanan, "The Kremlin's Civic Forum: Cooperation or Co-optation for Civil Society in Russia?" *Demokratizatsiya*, vol. 10, no. 2 (Spring 2002), pp. 147–65.

95. In interviews with the author, human rights activists Lev Ponomarev and Sergei Grigorants explained that they refused to go because they did not want to show support for the entire project. By contrast, Alexander Nikitin decided to attend. For his reflections, see Nikitin and Buchanan, "The Kremlin's Civic Forum."

96. "Political" organizations included the Institute of Civil Society Problems, the Association of Forced Settlers of Suzdal, a charity fund for infants with heart problems, the consumer rights group Zashchita, Sergei Markov's Institute for Political Studies, and the youth group "Walking Together." The latter orchestrated a mass rally for the first anniversary of Putin's rule, dressing their 15,000 to 20,000 members in Putin t-shirts. The only organization invited that was critical of the state was the Moscow Helsinki Group. Many journalists and activists viewed this event with deep skepticism about Putin's aims, claiming that he had no intention of encouraging those parts of civil society that had a record of criticizing the state. See, for example, Dmitri Polikarpov, "Civil Society Remains Merely a Dream," *Moscow Tribune*, June 15, 2001, www.tribune.ru/cgi-bin/content/content.pl?act=art&tmpl=news_a&list=news_nati&rid=992607168.

97. Mediasoyuz and the old Journalists' Union are unlikely to become allies serving the same causes, and the new union is clearly a more Kremlin-friendly group. Lyubimov claimed that even though the goals of the two groups are similar, Mediasoyuz has "more authoritative/respectable journalists." This echoes the argument, by Gazprom and the Kremlin during the NTV affair, that journalists from private networks owned by oligarchs are not "professional" or "independent." See Pyotr Belkin, "Media-Forum Our Time, First Day," June 13, 2001, www.smi.ru. "RFE/RL Security Watch," *Sovetskaya Rossiya*, November 27, 2000, had reported earlier that the Kremlin wanted to replace the current leader of the Union of Journalists, Vsevelod Bogdanov, with Lyubimov, because Bogdanov had been too vocal in defense of the freedom of the press.

98. Numerous exchanges between various environmentalists on the Center for International Civil Society e-mail list identified an organization called Ecological Forum as a Kremlin-sponsored group.

99. *Obshchaya Gazeta*, May 31, 2001.

100. Paul Goble, "The Kremlin and the Crescent," *Radio Free Europe/Radio Liberty Newsline,* March 6, 2001.

101. See www.russian-orthodox-church.org.ru/ne104113.htm. [Article no longer online]

102. Interview with Shein, July 14, 2000, www.labournet.net.

103. McFaul's interview with Irene Stevenson, director of the AFL-CIO's Moscow Solidarity Center, February 19, 2002.

104. The congress was organized by representatives of the major established human rights organizations, including the Andrei Sakharov Foundation, the Moscow Helsinki Group, Memorial, For Human Rights, the Glasnost Public Foundation, and the Glasnost Defense Foundation.

105. Cited terms are taken, in order, from Masha Lipman, "How Putin Pardons," *Washington Post*, April 17, 2001, p. A17; and Yevgenia Albats and Mikhail Berger, quoted in "Media Muzzle," *Economist*, April 21–27, 2001, p. 46.

106. See Anne Applebaum, "I Want My NTV!" April 9, 2001, www.slate.com.

107. See the VTsIOM poll results from January 25–28, 2002, available at www.polit.ru/printable/469009.html.

108. Yablokov is former environmental adviser to President Yeltsin, now executive director of the Center for Russian Environmental Policy. Quoted in Center for Russian Environmental Policy Bulletin "Towards a Sustainable Russia," no. 5 (Moscow: Center for Russian Environmental Policy, 2000), p. 8.

109. Aleksander Nikitin's Coalition for Environment and Human Rights, the Center for Russian Environmental Policy, and the World Wildlife Fund were some of the key participants.

110. According to Natalia Mironova, paper presented at the conference on "The Environmental Situation in Russia: Problems and Prospects" (Washington, D.C.: Woodrow Wilson International Center for Scholars, March 1–2, 2001).

111. Within five months, more than 200 articles on the referendum petition appeared in the national press and more than 600 in the regional press, according to Yevgeny Schwartz, paper presented at the conference on the Environmental Situation in Russia: Problems and Prospects (Washington, D.C.: Woodrow Wilson International Center for Scholars, March 1–2, 2001).

112. The minister of natural resources met with the environmentalists on numerous occasions. According to environmental activists, this was because he feared the power of this social movement (author's interview with Alexei Yablokov, March 21, 2003). The ministry also resumed the publication of a previously discontinued ecological journal, *Spasenie*.

113. Putin's concern with public opinion drove him to request that his government reconsider the proposed reorganization of ministries, which Prime Minister Kasyanov refused to do.

114. Ignatieva, "Vremya svobody Sovesti eshchyo ne vidno."

Chapter 7

1. The following are a few of the major monographs and collections of articles: A. A. Gra-belnikov, *Sredstva massovoy informacii postsovetskoy Rossii* [Mass media in post-Soviet Russia], (Moscow: Peoples' Friendship University of Russia Publishers, 1996); I. I. Zassoursky, *Mass-Media Vtoroi Respubliki* [Mass media of the second republic], (Moscow: Moscow State University Publishers, 1999); M. M. Dzyaloshinskii, D. D. Degtyarenko, M. S. Balutenko, A. P. Fedotov, I. G. Fedorov, O. U. Popova, I. V. Zadorin, A. P. Syutkina, D. O. Strebkov, E. V. Khalkina, D. N. Konovalenko, P. K. Zalesskii, S. U. Liberman, V. L. Rimskii, *SMI i politika v Rossii: sociologicheskiy analiz roli smi v izbiratelnih kampaniyah: sbornik statey* [Mass media and politics in Russia: a sociological analysis of the role of mass media in electoral campaigns: a collection of articles], (Moscow: Socio-Logos Publishers, 2000); "Rossiyskoe Obshestvo i SMI" [Russian society and the mass media] *Pro et Contra*, vol. 5, no. 4 (Fall 2000); *Sredstva massovoy informatsii i sovremennoe obshestvo: materiali seminarov Rossiysko-Skandinavskogo kursa NorFa* [Mass media and contemporary society: materials from the seminars of Russian-Scandinavian course NorFa] (St. Petersburg: 2000); A. Volkov, M. Pugacheva, S. Yarmolyuk. eds., *Pressa v obshestve* [The press in society], (Moscow: Moscow School of Political Studies, 2000); Elena Androunas, *Soviet Media in Transition: Structural and Economic Alternatives* (London: Praeger, 1993); Yassen Zassoursky and Elena Vartanova, eds., *Media: Communications, and the Open Society* (Moscow: IKAR Publishers, 1999); and J. Curran and M. J. Park, eds., *De-Westernizing Media Studies* (New York: Routlege, 2000).

2. Joseph Gibbs, *Gorbachev's Glasnost: The Soviet Media in the First Phase of Perestroika* (College Station, Tex.: A&M University Press, 1999).

3. Gibbs, *Gorbachev's Glasnost*.

4. See Ellen Mickiewicz, *Changing Channels: Television and the Struggle for Power in Russia* (Oxford, U.K.: Oxford University Press, 1997).

5. See O. N. Yanitsky, "Pressa soediniala ludey v 'grazhdanskih iniciativah'" [The press has united people in 'civil initiatives'], in *Pressa v Obshestve* [The Press in Society] (Moscow: Moscow School of Political Studies, 2000).

6. Reform Foundation, Political Department, *Sredstva massovoy informacii Rossii: socialnaya sreda i politicheskie funkcii* [Russian mass media: social environment and political function], express issue (Moscow: Reform Foundation, 1998), p. 15.

7. Zassoursky, *Mass-media vtoroi respubliki* [Mass media of the second republic], p. 54.

8. For an analysis of this law and other bills on the media in contemporary Russia, see A. G. Richter, "Pravovie osnovi svobodi pechati" [Legal foundations for freedom of the press] in Yassen Zassoursky, ed., *Sredstva massovoy informacii postsovetskoy Rossii* [Mass media in post-Soviet Russia] (Moscow: Aspect-Press, 2002).

9. Veronika Usacheva, "Vlasti i SMI v Rossii: kak izmenilis ikh vzaimootnosheniya" [The authoritites and mass media in Russia: how their relationship has changed] *Pro et Contra*, vol. 5, no. 4 (Fall 2000), pp. 112–13.

10. I. M. Dzyaloshinsky, *Informacionnoye prostranstvo Rossii: struktura, osobennosti funkcionirovanniya, perspektivi evolucii* [Russia's informational space: structure, pecularities of functioning, prospects of evolution], no. 6 (Moscow: Carnegie Moscow Center, 2001), p. 16.

11. One of the first issues of the newspaper *Segodnya* (February 23, 1993) contained a lengthy article entitled "Liberal Charter," in which the model of a social structure with minimum interference by the state was described as the social goal of democratic change. Even law enforcement was entrusted to private security as a more efficient and organized force than that sponsored by the government.

12. See Usacheva, "Vlasti i SMI v Rossii" [The authorities and mass media in Russia], p. 116–17.

13. Valery Solovei, "'Nacionalizaciya' rezhima budet prodolzhatsia" [Nationalization of the regime will continue], *Nezavisimaya gazeta*, March 7, 1995, p. 3.

14. John Dunlop, *Russia Confronts Chechnya: Roots of a Separatist Conflict* (Cambridge, U.K.: Cambridge University Press, 1998), chapter 4.

15. Reform Foundation, Political Department, *Sredstva massovoy informacii Rossii: socialnaya sreda i politicheskie funkcii* [The mass media: social environment and political function], express issue (Moscow: Reform Foundation, 1998), p. 17.

16. Zassoursky, *Mass-media vtoroi respubliki* [Mass media of the second republic] pp. 167–74, 237–41.

17. Ibid., pp. 60–80.

18. For complete information on the project, see www.freepass.ru. "Obshestvennaya ekspertiza" [Public expertise] in *Anatomiya svobodi slova* [Anatomy of the freedom of speech] (Moscow: Obshestvennaya Ekspertiza, 1999).

19. L. M. Sherova, *Rabotaem s SMI* [Working with the mass media] (Moscow: Expert Community 2002), pp. 118–21.

20. For more details on the mechanisms for manipulating public opinion with the help of the mass media, see Avtandil Tsuladze, *Bolshaya manipuliativnaya Igra* [Big manipulative game] (Moscow: Algoritm, 2000), pp. 11–104.

21. Gleb Pavlovsky, "Voyna chuzhimi rukami" [War by others' hands], *Nezavisimaya Gazeta*, December 5, 1997, p. 5.

22. Yelena Vartanova, "Media v postsovetskoi Rossii: ikh struktura i vliyanie" [The media in post-Soviet Russia: their structure and influence], *Pro et Contra*, vol. 5, no. 4 (Fall 2000), p. 64.

23. For more details, see Boris Dubin, "Ot iniciativnyh grupp k anonimnim media: massovie kommunikacii v Rossiyskom obshestve" [From initiative groups to anonymous media: mass communication in Russian society], *Pro et Contra*, vol. 5, no. 4 (Fall 2000), pp. 38–41.

24. Ibid., p. 55.

25. I. I. Zassoursky, *SMI i vlast: Rossiya devianostih* [The mass media and authority: Russia of the nineties] (Moscow: Aspect-Press, 2002), pp. 92–93.

26. Dubin, "Ot iniciativnih grupp k anonimnim media" [From initiative groups to anonymous media], p. 41.

27. Yuri Levada, *Ot mneniy k ponimaniyu: sociologicheskie ocherki, 1993–2000* [From opinion to understanding: sociological accounts] (Moscow: Moscow School of Political Studies, 2000), p. 313.

28. Ibid., p. 313.

29. N. Lazareva, *Perevorot na media-rinke: zhurnalist perestal bit chelovekom* [A coup on the media market: the journalist has ceased to be a person] www.apn.ru (December 30, 2001).

Chapter 8

1. V. Guliev, Y. Belson, V. Petrov, eds., *Marksistsko-Leninskaya obshaya teoriya gosudarstva i prava: istoricheskie tipi gosudarstva i prava* [Marxist-Leninist general theory of state and law: historical types of state and law] (Moscow: Judicial Literature, 1971), p. 418.

2. As stated in, for example, A. Sukharev, ed., *Yuridicheskiy enciklopedicheskiy slovar* [Legal encyclopedia] (Moscow: Infra-M Publishers, 1984), pp. 69, 272.

3. The Soviet Union also never recognized the idea that human rights were natural and inalienable as official doctrine. In the place of this notion was the idea that citizens' rights and freedoms were granted by the state.

4. CPSU, *Materiali XIX vsesoyuznoy konferencii kommunisticheskoy partii Sovetskogo Soyuza* [Materials from the XIX all-union conference of the communist party of the Soviet Union] (Moscow: Novasti Publishing House, 1988), p. 122. Emphasis by the author.

5. M. U. Tikhomirov, L. V. Tikhomirova, *Yuridicheskaya enciklopediya* [Legal encyclopedia] (Moscow: Yurinformcentr Publishers, 1997), p. 343.

6. Sergei Samoilov, "Ne stoit 'slizivat' u zapada" [Let's not copycat the west], *Trud*, December 20, 2000.

7. I. A. Ilyin, *O sushnosti pravosoznaniya* [On the essence of legal consciousness] (Moscow: Rarog Publishers, 1993), p. 53.

8. Ibid., p. 29.

9. Vladimir Petukhov, *Demokratiya v vospriyatii Rossiyskogo obshestva* [The perception of democracy in Russian society] (Moscow: Carnegie Moscow Center, 2001), p. 4.

10. See N. Varlamova, "Prezhdevremenniy constitucionalizm, ili Vostochno-Evropeyskiy experiment 'obratnogo hoda' istorii'" [Premature constitutionalism or the Eastern European experiment in the 'reverse flow' of history] in *Konstitucionnoe pravo: vostochnoevropeyskoe obozreniye*, no. 2 (1998), p. 65.

11. *Sochineniya Ferdinanda Lassalia* [Works of Ferdinand Lassalle], vol. 2 (St. Petersburg: N. Glagolev Publishing, 1905), p. 54.

Chapter 9

1. Vladimir Shlapentokh, Roman Levita, and Mikhail Loiberg, *From Submission to Rebellion: The Provinces Versus the Center in Russia* (Boulder, Colo.: Westview Press, 1997), p. 32.

2. See Richard Pipes, *The Formation of the Soviet Union: Communism and Nationalism, 1917–1923*, rev. ed. (Cambridge, Mass.: Harvard University Press, 1964).

3. See Pipes, *The Formation of the Soviet Union*; and Walker Connor, *The National Question in Marxist-Leninist Theory and Strategy* (Princeton, N.J.: Princeton University Press, 1984).

4. Soviet federalism, which refers to republics within the USSR, is a different case, but this disappeared in 1991 with the disintegration of USSR.

5. Richard Sakwa, *Russian Politics and Society*, 2nd ed. (London and New York: Routledge, 1996), p. 36.

6. Jeffrey Kahn, "The Parade of Sovereignties: Establishing the Vocabulary of the New Russian Federalism," *Post-Soviet Affairs*, vol. 16, no. 1 (January–March 2000), pp. 58–88.

7. *Oblasts* used to be distinguished from *krais* because *oblasts* were usually smaller and *krais* were bigger and located in border regions (the word *krai* means both the big region and the edge), but this difference no longer exists.

8. This was true, for example, in the Krasnoyarsk gubernatorial election, which saw General Aleksandr Lebed defeat incumbent Governor Valery Zubov. See Nikolai Petrov, *Aleksandr Lebed' v Krasnoyarskom Krae* [Aleksandr Lebed' in the Krasnoyar Krai], (Moscow: Carnegie Moscow Center, 1999).

9. For detailed analysis, see Jeffrey Kahn, "The Parade of Sovereignties: Establishing the Vocabulary of the New Russian Federalism," *Post-Soviet Affairs*, vol. 16, no. 1 (Winter 2000), pp. 58–88.

10. The law on autonomous republics adopted by the USSR Supreme Soviet in the fall of 1990 gave them equal status with Union republics, and in the spring of 1991 Gorbachev invited the leaders of autonomous republics to participate in the preparation of the new Union Treaty. For more details see Michael McFaul and Nikolai Petrov, eds., *Politicheskii almanakh Rossii* [Political almanac of Russia], vol. 1 (Moscow: Carnegie Moscow Center, 1997), pp. 22–43.

11. In total, three treaties were signed: one with republics, the major target of the whole undertaking; a second with Russian *krais* and *oblasts*; and a third with autonomous districts.

12. Eight of the remaining nineteen republics strongly opposed the draft. Only seventy of the eighty-seven regions where voting took place supported the draft, including thirteen where turnout was lower than the required 50 percent of voters. For more details, see McFaul and Petrov, *Politicheskii almanakh Rossii* [Political almanac of Russia], vol. 1, pp. 180–81.

13. For a detailed comparison, see Georgy Derluguian, "Ethnofederalism and Ethnonationalism in the Separatist Politics of Chechnya and Tatarstan: Sources or Resources?" *International Journal of Public Administration*, vol. 22, nos. 9–10 (1999), pp. 1402–04; and Matthew Evangelista, *The Chechen Wars: Will Russia Go the Way of the Soviet Union?* (Washington, D.C.: Brookings Institution Press, 2002).

14. Even though national movements flourished in almost every ethnic republic between 1990 and 1992, in no other case did nationalists manage to come to power by force as in Chechnya.

15. As Robert V. Daniels has pointed out: "Chechnya, of course, is an extreme instance in the relations between Moscow and its regions. However, it serves as a warning that federalism may fail in the Russian republic just as it failed in the Soviet Union as a whole, ground up between the millstones of imperial centralism and ethnic particularism." See Robert V. Daniels, "Democracy and Federalism in the Former Soviet Union and the Russian Federation," in Peter J. Stavrakis, Joel de Bardeleben and Larry Black, eds., *Beyond the Monolith: The Emergence of Regionalism in Post-Soviet Russia* (Washington, D.C.: Woodrow Wilson Center Press, 1997), p. 243. Carnegie Moscow Center researchers Dmitri Trenin and Alexei Malashenko have put the situation in a more evolutionary context: "The Chechen War is also a unique symbol of Russia's loss of imperial status. The Soviet Union was a continuation of the Russian Empire. The Russian Federation is no longer quite an empire, but neither is it a democracy in the full sense of the word. The problem of Chechnya lies between these two conditions of Russian statehood. The success of the state's positive evolution thus depends in large part on resolving the Chechen issue." Alexei Malashenko and Dmitri Trenin, *Vremya Yuga: Rossiya v Chechne, Chechnya v Rossii* [Time of the South: Russia in Chechnya, Chechnya in Russia], (Moscow: Carnegie Moscow Center, 2002), p. 257.

16. See, for example, Steven Solnick, "Russia's Asymmetric Federation: Are All Differences Alike?" unpublished manuscript (New York: Columbia University, January 31, 2000), p. 24.

17. Robert Bruce Ware and Enver Kisriyev, "Political Stability in Dagestan: Ethnic Parity and Religious Polarization," *Problems of Post-Communism*, vol. 47, no. 2 (March–April 2000), pp. 23–33.

18. The old RSFSR Supreme Soviet had a single chamber consisting of 975 deputies elected in single-member districts. See Thomas Remington, *The Russian Parliament: Institutional Evolution in a Transitional Regime, 1989–1999* (New Haven, Conn.: Yale University Press, 2001), pp. 115–16.

19. According to Stalin's design, ethnic territorial units were represented in the Council of Nationalities, the upper house of the Supreme Soviet. Similar representation was reproduced in the USSR CPD. The republics had thirty-two seats each in the CPD (eleven in the Supreme Soviet), autonomous republics had eleven seats each (four in the CPD), autonomous *oblasts* had five seats each (two in the CPD), and autonomous *okrugs* had one seat each (one in the CPD). In 1990, when the RSFSR Council of Nationalities was formed with half its seats occupied by representatives from ethnic territories, the same proportion was used: four seats were given to each autonomous republic, two seats to each autonomous *oblast*, and one seat to each autonomous *okrug*.

20. Just as at the Union level, the Supreme Soviet was defined by the constitution as a "permanently operating legislative, dispositive, and supervisory organ of state power of the RSFSR," while the RSFSR CPD, from which the Supreme Soviet was elected, was defined as the "highest organ of state power of the RSFSR." The Congress consisted of 1,068 deputies elected in single-mandate districts, of which 900 were apportioned in accordance with population (so-called territorial districts) and 168 were apportioned in accordance with the status of territorial units (so-called national-territorial districts) half the seats were given to thirty-one national autonomies and the other half to fifty-seven proper Russian regions.

21. See, for example, Alfred Stepan, "Russian Federalism in Comparative Perspective," *Post-Soviet Affairs,* vol. 16, no. 2 (April–June 2000), pp. 133–176.

22. The Kremlin used direct threats against governors. For example, the presidential representative to the State Duma told the press that law enforcement agencies were ready to jail a number of regional leaders after they lost their immunity. Nothing of the kind happened, but the threat helped the Kremlin to create an intimidating atmosphere and forced governors to defend their undeserved privileges.

23. For more details about the Federation Council's evolution and functioning, see Nikolai Petrov, "Sovet federatsii i predstavitel'stvo regional'nykh interesov v tsentre" [Federation council and the representation of regional interests in the center] in Nikolai Petrov, ed., *Regiony Rossii v 1998 godu: yezhegodnoe prilozhenie k politicheskome almanakhu Rossii* [Russia's regions in 1998: a yearly appendix to the political almanac of Russia] (Moscow: Gendalf, 1999), pp. 180–222.

24. Message to the Federal Assembly, July 8, 2000.

25. Even without Putin's appointment as prime minister, no special reasons accounted for the apocalyptic vision of relations between the center and the regions. At that time, the elites consolidated around Primakov, who combined a tough program (restoration of a vertical power hierarchy, return to the appointment of regional leaders, enlargement of the subjects of the federation) with a number of personal alliances with the strongest regional leaders, who received

favors in return. In addition to his main ally, Moscow Mayor Luzhkov, his allies included Tatarstan President Shaimiyev (in the spring of 1999, Tatarstan enjoyed an extremely advantageous prolongation of all intergovernment agreements that were to have expired five years after the signing of the bilateral treaty), Kemerovo Oblast Governor Aman Tuleyev (allocation of additional funds to miners, transfer of federally-owned shares into trust management), and Krasnoyarsk Krai Governor Aleksandr Lebed (support in his fight against regional strongman Anatoly Bykov, transfer of federally owned shares).

26. Presidential representatives were replaced in seventeen regions in January 2000 alone, while others were "suspended." During this time many FSB officials were appointed as presidential representatives.

27. Prime Minister Sergei Stepashin's inability to oppose the anti-Kremlin governors or to create an alternative pro-Kremlin bloc was one of the main reasons why Yeltsin replaced him with Putin on August 9, 1999. Later on, the center used the stick and the carrot approach more effectively and in a month and a half after Putin's appointment the inter-regional movement Unity appeared, ostensibly initiated by a number of regional leaders of the most scandal-ridden and corrupt administrations.

28. The 2000 Budget Law stipulated a gradual transition to a treasury system for regional budget implementation. The budgets of six regions (Altai Republic, Tuva, Dagestan, Kemerovo Oblast, Komi-Permyak Autonomous Okrug, and Evenki Autonomous Okrug) are already implemented through the federal treasury system. Interview with Tatyana Nesterenko, *Vremya*, February 22, 2000.

29. Eight inter-regional economic associations were formed in 1990 and early 1991 to oppose regional, and above all republican, secessionism. See Nikolai Petrov, Sergei Mikheyev, and Leonid Smirnyagin, "Russia's Regional Associations in Decline," *Post-Soviet Geography*, vol. 34, no. 1 (January 1993), pp. 59–68. As a kind of governors' private club they never played any important role except for arranging regular meetings of regional leaders with senior government officials. In the autumn of 1998 Prime Minister Primakov invited eight regional leaders, the heads of regional economic associations, to the presidium of his government and started talking about the need to enlarge regions as the next presidential campaign approached in the spring of 1999.

30. For more details on the federative reform and the military, see Nikolai Petrov, "Seven Faces of Putin's Russia: Federal Districts as the New Level of State-Territorial Composition," *Security Dialogue*, vol. 32, no. 1 (March 2002), pp. 219–37; Nikolai Petrov and Darrell Slider, "Putin and the Regions," in Dale Herspring, ed., *Putin's Russia: Past Imperfect, Future Uncertain* (Lanham, Md.: Rowman and Littlefield, 2003); and Nikolai Petrov, "The Puzzle of Federal Reform: Two and a Half Years On," *Jamestown Foundation Review*, vol. 2, no. 1, January 7, 2003.

31. Dmitri Kozak, deputy head of the President's Administration; Vladimir Kozhin, head of the Property Department of the President's Administration; Dmitri Medvedev, deputy head of the President's Administration and chairman of the board of Gazprom; Igor Sechin, deputy head of the President's Administration; and Alexei Miller, head of Gazprom.

32. Anatoly Chubais, head of Unified Energy Systems; German Gref, minister of economic development and trade; Alexei Kudrin, deputy prime minister and minister of finance; Andrei Illarionov, chief economic adviser to the president; Alfred Kokh, director of Gazprom-Media;

Mikhail Dmitriyev, first deputy minister of economic development and trade; and Dmitri Vasilyev, chairman of the Federal Securities Commission.

33. Valentina Matviyenko, deputy prime minister; Ilya Klebanov, minister of industry, science, and technology; Leonid Reiman, minister of communications; Sergei Stepashin, head of the Auditing Chamber; Yuri Shevchenko, minister of health; Ilya Yuzhanov, minister of antimonopoly policy and entrepreneurship; and Sergei Mironov, speaker of the Federation Council.

34. Each region has dozens of federal institutions. According to Novgorod Oblast Governor Mikhail Prusak's estimates, in 1999 the *oblast* had eighty-seven federal institutions with a total staff twice that of the regional bureaucracy (380,000 compared with 180,000). Many of the federal institutions, including the courts, the Ministry of Security and Internal Affairs, and the procuracy, while formally reporting to the center had long been "domesticated" by local elites and were fully dependent on, and therefore loyal to, them.

35. In terms of Yeltsin's famous 1990 formula, taking too much sovereignty is easy. Swallowing it is more difficult and digesting it is a tall order.

36. Since 1998, elections in thirty-three regions have had a turnout of less than 50 percent.

Chapter 10

1. Participants of the Institute of Humanitarian-Political Studies' project to monitor political events in the regions have produced some studies, including those published by Vladimir Gelman, the intellectual force behind this project. See Vladimir Gelman, "Regionalnyie rezhimy: zaversheniye transformatsii?" [Regional regimes: end of the transformation?] *Svobodnaya Mysl'*, no. 9 September 1996), pp. 13–22; Vladimir Gelman, Sergei Ryzhenkov, and Michael Bri, eds., *Rossiya Regionov: Transformatsiya Politicheskikh Rezhimov* [Russia of the Regions: Transformation of Political Regimes], (Moscow: All World, 2000); Sergei Ryzhenkov and Galina Luchterhandt-Mikhaleva, eds., *Politika i cul'tura v Rossiiskoi provintsii* [Politics and culture in the Russian province], (Moscow: Summer Garden, 2001); Vladimir Gelman and Grigory Golosov, "Regional Party System Formation in Russia: The Deviant Case of Sverdlovsk Oblast," *Journal of Communist Studies and Transition Politics*, vol. 14, no. 1–2 (March–June 1998), pp. 31–53; and Vladimir Gelman, "Regime Transition, Uncertainty and Prospects for Democratization: The Politics of Russia's Regions in a Comparative Perspective. Second Europe-Asia Lecture," *Europe-Asia Studies*, vol. 51, no. 6 (September 1999), pp. 939–56. See also several publications by the Carnegie Moscow Center's regional project, including Michael McFaul and Nikolai Petrov, eds., *Politicheskii al'manakh Rossii 1997* [Political Almanac of Russia], vols. 1–2 (Moscow: Carnegie Moscow Center, 1998); Nikolai Petrov, ed., *Regiony Rossii v 1998 godu: yezhegodnoe prilozhenie k 'politicheskomu al'manakhu Rossii'* [Russia's regions in 1998: a yearly appendix to the 'political almanac of Russia'] (Moscow: Carnegie Moscow Center, 1999); and Nikolai Petrov, ed., *Regiony Rossii v 1999 godu: Yezhegodnoe prilozhenie k 'Politicheskomu al'manakhu Rossii'* [Russia's Regions in 1998: a Yearly Appendix to the 'Political Almanac of Russia'], (Moscow: Carnegie Moscow Center, 1999). American and British scholars have also written a number of books and articles on the subject, including Kathryn Stoner-Weiss, *Local Heroes: The Political Economy of Russian Regional Governance* (Princeton, N.J.: Princeton University Press,

1997); Mary McAuley, *Russia's Politics of Uncertainty* (Cambridge, U.K.: Cambridge University Press, 1997); Peter Kirkow, *Russia's Provinces: Authoritarian Transformation Versus Local Autonomy?* (London: Macmillan Press, 1998); Matthew Evangelista, *The Chechen Wars: Will Russia Go the Way of the Soviet Union?* (Washington, D.C.: Brookings Institute Press, 2002); and Daniel Treisman, *After the Deluge: Regional Crises and Political Consolidation in Russia* (Ann Arbor, Mich.: University of Michigan Press, 1999). For other case studies, see Nikolai Petro, "The Novgorod Region: A Russian Success Story," *Post-Soviet Affairs*, vol. 15, no 3 (1999), pp. 235–61; Blair Ruble and Nancy Popson, "The Westernization of a Russian Province: The Case of Novgorod," *Post-Soviet Geography and Economics*, vol. 39, no. 8 (1998), pp. 433–46; Dmitri Zimin and Michael Bradshaw, "Regional Adaptation to Economic Crisis in Russia: The Case of Novgorod Oblast," *Post-Soviet Geography and Economics*, vol. 40, no. 5 (1999), pp. 335–53; and Jeffrey Hahn, *Regional Russia in Transition: Studies from Yaroslavl* (Baltimore, Md.: Johns Hopkins University Press, 2001).

2. Freedom House's annual assessments of democracy throughout the world can be found at www.freedomhouse.org. They are also published regularly in the *Journal of Democracy*.

3. See Michael McFaul and Nikolai Petrov, *Politicheskii al'manakh Rossii 1997* [Political Almanac of Russia], vol. 1, pp. 139–46; and Kelly McMann and Nikolai Petrov, "A Survey of Democracy in Russia's Regions," *Post-Soviet Geography and Economics*, vol. 41, no. 3 (April–May 2000), pp. 155–82.

4. For some of the data compiled by the Carnegie Moscow Center, see Nikolai Petrov, ed., *Regions Rossii 1998: Yezhegodnoe prilozhenie k 'Politicheskomu al'manakhu Rossii'* [Russia's regions in 1998: a yearly appendix to the 'political almanac of Russia'] (Moscow: Carnegie Moscow Center, 1999).

5. Nikolai Petrov and Alexei Titkov calculated the initial scores for all the regions in the Carnegie Moscow Center's monitoring system. In the case of notable differences between their ratings, their scores were averaged. In more complex cases of disagreement, additional experts with expertise in the region in question were consulted.

6. This is especially true for federal-level elections, but may not necessarily be the case for regional elections. Thus the value of the latter as a universal and simultaneous measurement is more limited.

7. For a detailed analysis of the different levels of democratization in the national republics and the non-national Russian regions, see Nikolai Petrov, *Po rezul'tatam issledovanii Permskaya Oblast' okazalas' demokratichnee Moskvy i Sankt Peterburga*, [Studies show Perm Oblast is more democratic than Moscow and St. Petersburg] October 16, 2002, www.regions.ru.

8. See A. Berezkin, V. Kolosov, M. Pavlovskaya, N. Petrov, and L. Smirnyagin, "The Geography of the 1989 Elections of Peoples Deputies of the USSR," *Soviet Geography*, vol. 30, no. 8 (October 1989), pp. 607–34; and V. A. Kolosov, N. V. Petrov, and L. V. Smirnyagin, eds., *Vesna 89: Geografiya i anatomiya parlamentskikh vyborov* [Spring of 89: the geography and anatomy of the parliamentary election], (Moscow: Progress, 1990).

9. Turnout for elections in the seventy-five regions that were analyzed was 53.8 percent compared with 66.1 percent for federal elections.

10. The coefficient calculated for all gubernatorial elections is 1.2, that is, turnout for gubernatorial elections was 1.2 times higher than for regional parliaments.

11. Negative voting may also be the last stage before complete voter alienation from election politics and an apathy that expresses itself in staying away from the polls. In this case, the

resulting lower turnout is not a sign of the greater health of the democracy in question but signals the deteriorating health of that democracy.

12. On the calculation of the effective number of parties, see M. Laakso and R. Taagapera, "Effective Number of Parties: A Measure with Application to Western Europe," *Comparative Political Studies*, vol. 12, no. 1 (April 1979), pp. 3–27; and R. Taagapera and M. Shugart, *Seats and Votes: The Effects and Determinants of Electoral Systems* (New Haven, Conn.: Yale University Press, 1989).

13. The effective number of candidates in gubernatorial elections is calculated similarly to the number of effective parties: the reverse of the sum of the squares of shares of votes received by each candidate. Grigory Golosov, professor at the European University in St. Petersburg, was the first to use this indicator in connection with Russian elections.

14. See Petrov, *Po rezul'tatam issedovanii Permskaya Oblast* [Studies show Perm Oblast].

15. Before a new federal law that allows only two rounds of gubernatorial elections was passed in 2002, about three-quarters of the regions had only one round of elections. Incumbent governors are much more likely to win in the first round when opposition votes are split, which is why in some cases challengers who came in second in the first round won in the second round.

16. Joseph Schumpeter is most often credited with having established the minimalist standard of holding elections for a country to qualify as a democracy. See Joseph Schumpeter, *Capitalism, Socialism, and Democracy* (New York: Harper and Row, 1976), chapters 22–23. Some have pointed to the key role of viable multiparty systems as central to such consolidation. See, for example, G. Pasquino, "Party Elites and Democratic Consolidation: Cross-National Comparison of Southern European Experience," in Geoffrey Pridham, ed., *Securing Democracy: Political Parties and Democratic Consolidation in Southern Europe* (London: Routledge, 1990), pp. 40–55. Larry Diamond has raised the bar for qualifying as a democracy beyond elections and the turnover of power to the opposition, arguing that "electoral democracies" are a lower-order form of democracy or a less advanced stage of its development than consolidated advanced or "liberal democracies," which include the full panoply of political, legal, and civic institutions buttressing a strong democratic state, the rule of law, and a vital civil society. See Larry Diamond, "Is the Third Wave Over?" *Journal of Democracy*, vol. 7, no. 3 (July 1996), pp. 20–37. Linz and Stepan include behavioral, attitudinal, social, cultural, and even market-related criteria in their definition of consolidated democracy. See Juan J. Linz and Alfred Stepan, *Problems of Democratic Transition and Consolidation: Southern Europe, South America, and Post-Communist Europe* (Baltimore, Md.: Johns Hopkins University Press, 1996), pp. 3–15.

17. Tatarstan President Mintimer Shaimiyev, Bashkortostan President Murtaza Rakhimov, and North Ossetia President Aleksandr Dzasokhov, who is a former member of the Communist Party of the Soviet Union Central Committee Politburo.

18. The Mercator group rating of electoral manageability for eighty-nine regions and 2,356 territorial electoral commissions took into account the following indicators: higher or lower turnout, invalid ballots, ballots without any marks, early voting in favor of parties that later dropped out of the race, votes against all parties, higher winners' results and winners' margins, and votes in favor of party outsiders. See Dmitri Oreshkin, "Strannosti Rossiiskoi elektoralnoi kultury" [Peculiarities of Russian electoral culture], *Golos Rossii*, vol. 1, no. 2 (February 1999), pp. 13–22; Dmitri Oreshkin, "Elektoralnaya demokratiya i tselostnost politicheskogo prostranstva Rossii" [Electoral democracy and the unity of Russia's political space], *Zhurnal o Vyb-*

orakh, vol. 1, no. 2 (February 2001), pp. 28–33; Darya Oreshkina, "A vse-taki oni upravlyayut-sya" [They're managed after all], *Golos Rossii*, vol. 2, no. 2 (February 2000), pp. 15–17; and Vladimir Tikunov and Darya Oreshkina, "'Upravlyayemaya demokratiya': rossiisky variant" [Managed democracy: the Russian version] *Ekspert*, nos. 11–12 (March 2000), pp. 61–65. Available online at www.mercator.ru.

19. See McFaul and Petrov, eds., *Politicheskii almanakh Rossii 1997* [Political Almanac of Russia 1997]; Michael McFaul, Nikolai Petrov, and Andrei Ryabov, eds., *Rossiya v izbiratelnom tsykle 1999–2000 godov* [Russia in the course of the 1999–2000 electoral cycle] (Moscow: Moscow Carnegie Center, 2000).

20. In Soviet times a phrase was coined to stress the country's enormous diversity: "It consists of parts as different as Finland and Afghanistan." Contrasts within Russia are not as great, but Karelia can be compared with Finland and Kalmykia, Tuva, and the northern Caucasian republics to Central Asian states.

21. See Mikhail Afanasyev, "Ot Volnykh Ord do Khanskoi Stavki" [From free-roaming hordes to khanates. (Power in Russian regions)] *Pro et Contra*, vol. 3, no. 3 (Autumn 1998), pp. 5–20; Dmitri Furman, "Loyalny Khan Milee Khama (Ot Avtonomii idut k nezavisimosti)" [Better a loyal Khan than an insolent (from autonomy they go to independence)] *Obshchaya gazeta*, July 2–8, 1998; and Nikolai Petrov, "Federalizm po Rossiisky" [Federalism Russian-style] *Pro et Contra*, vol. 5, no. 1 (Winter 2000), pp. 7–33.

22. Why the bottom and the top regions are invariant with regard to weighting is clear. In the first case, all partial indexes are equally small and their changes do not affect the result much, and in the second case they are equally high, and changes in a couple of them cannot influence the general picture.

23. A lack of popularity and gravitas should not be attributed to a figure such as Leningrad Oblast Governor Valery Serdyukov, who has shown himself a capable leader and won the support of the Kremlin and Putin.

24. For more on experts' approaches toward democracy in the regions see McMann and Petrov, *A Survey of Democracy.*

25. The two partial expert evaluations show that the highest correlations with a rating based on electoral democracy are free and fair elections and elites, once again underscoring the accuracy of deductive expert evaluations.

Chapter 11

1. The data presented here are the results of nationwide sociological monitoring of a representative sample of approximately 1,800 to 2,200 respondents in all economic-geographic regions of Russia conducted by the Russian Independent Institute of Social and Nationalities Problems (RIISNP) in 1995–2000. The authors have also used the results of polls conducted by other centers and institutes, such as the All-Russian Center for Public Opinion Research (VTsIOM), the Institute of Sociology of the Russian Academy of Sciences, the Public Opinion Foundation, the Center for Sociological Research at Moscow State University, and the sociological agency Monitoring.ru. All these bodies typically use representative samples of 1,600 to

1,700 respondents in eleven or twelve subjects of the Russian Federation. Their research was conducted between 1990 and 2000.

2. For elaboration, see Michael McFaul, *Russia's 1996 Presidential Election: The End of Polarized Politics* (Stanford, Calif.: Hoover Institution Press, 1997).

3. For a detailed overview, see Andrei Melvil, *Demokraticheskie tranziti: teoretiko-metodologicheskie aspekti* [Democratic transits: theoretical-methodological aspects] (Moscow: Moscow Public Science Foundation, 1999).

4. Yuri Levada, *Ot mneniy k ponimaniyu: sociologicheskie ocherki, 1993–2000* [From opinion to understanding: sociological accounts, 1993–2000] (Moscow: Moscow School of Political Studies, 2000), pp. 391–572.

5. This quotation comes from one of the interviews the Moscow State University Department for Political Science project on Russians' political priorities conducted in March 1993 before the April 1993 national referendum.

6. Not all would agree with this assessment. In particular, see Nikolai Petro, *The Rebirth of Russian Democracy: An Interpretation of Political Culture* (Cambridge, Mass.: Harvard University Press, 1995).

7. S. V. Tumanov, *Sovremennaya Rossiya: massovoe soznanie i massovoe povedenie—opit integrativnogo analiza* [Contemporary Russia: mass consciousness and mass behavior—the practice of integrated analysis] (Moscow: Moscow State University Press, 2000), p. 138.

8. Ibid., p. 139. The actual question asked in the survey was "Would you fight on to the final destruction of the political and national enemy."

9. *Obshestvennoe mnenie Rossii: otchet o rezultatah issledovaniy v 2000–2001 gg. Otchet ob issledovaniyah tsentra "monitoring.ru"* [Public opinion in Russia: a report on the results of studies in 2000–2001. Report on the studies of the "monitoring.ru" center] (Moscow: Moscow State University Publishers, 2001), p. 77.

10. Lev Gudkov and Boris Dubin, "Vse edino. Rossiyskomu obshestvu zhit stalo huzhe, zhit stalo skuchnee" [All the same. For Russian society, life has become worse and life has become boring] *Itogi*, January 23, 2001, p. 13.

11. This chapter makes wide use of data from the RIISNP's 1995–2000 sociological studies. The studies were done as a nationwide representative sampling of people from twelve social and professional groups. In the tables, the figures may total to more than 100 percent in cases where respondents could give more than one answer. In those cases where the sum of the answers is less than 100 percent, the response "difficult to say" was not counted.

12. On this point, Colton and McFaul report similar results. See Timothy Colton and Michael McFaul, "Are Russians Undemocratic?" *Post-Soviet Affairs*, vol. 18, no. 2 (April–June 2002), pp. 91–121.

13. Yuri Levada, "Mneniya i nastroeniya. Yanvar 2000 g. Analiticheskaya xapiska" [Opinions and moods. January 2000. An analytic note.] *Nezavisimaya Gazeta* (section NG-Scenarii), February 9, 2000.

14. The RNIISP conducted this study in cooperation with the Friedrich Ebert Foundation. See M. Gorshkov, ed., "Grazhdane Rossii: kem oni sebia oshushayut i v kakom obshestve hoteli bi zhit?" [Russian citizens: who do they perceive themselves to be and in what society would they like to live?] in *Rossiya na Ruzbezhe vekov* [Russia on the brink of centuries] (Moscow: Russian Independent Institute of Social and Nationalities Problems and Russian Political Encyclopedia, 2000), pp. 163–252.

15. V. Lapkin, "Demokraticheskie instituti i obshestvennoe mnenie v postsovetskoy Rossii" [Democratic institutions and public opinion in post-Soviet Russia] in T. I. Zaslavskaya, ed., *Kuda idet Rossiya? Materiali mezhdunarodnogo simpoziuma 15–16/01/1999* [Where is Russia going? Materials from the international symposium January 15–16, 1999] (Moscow: Logos, 1999), p. 162.

16. Ibid.

17. Leonid Gordon and Eduard Klopov, "Sovremennie obshestvenno-politicheskie preobrazovaniya v masshtabe socialnogo vremeni" [Contemporary public and political transformations on the scale of social time] *Sotsis,* no. 1 (1998), p. 21.

18. "Rossiya o sudbah Rossii v XX veke i svoih nadezhdah na novoe stoletie" [Russia on the fates of Russia in the 20th century and its hopes for the new century] in M. Gorshkov, ed., *Rossiya na rubezhe vekov* [Russia on the brink of centuries] (Moscow: Russian Independent Institute of Social and Nationalities Problems and Russian Political Encyclopedia, 2000) pp. 325–419. These data characterize the situation in the 1990s, when anti-American feelings were especially high because of the conflict in the former Yugoslavia.

19. V. Kalashnikov, "Chego ne khvataet Nemstam? Postyubileynie zametki o sovremennoy germanskoy zhizni" [What do the Germans lack? Post-anniversary notes on contemporary German life] *Nezavisimaya Gazeta,* November 25, 2000, p. 8.

20. *Rossiya na rubezhe vekov* [Russia on the brink of centuries], pp. 253–324.

21. M. Gorshkov, A. Chepurenko, F. Sheregi, eds., *Rossiya v zerkale reform.*

22. *Obshestvennoe mnenie Rossii: Otchet o rezultatah issledovaniy v 2000-2001 [Public opinion in Russia: a report on the results of studies in 2000–2001],* p. 81.

23. Lapkin, "Demokraticheskiye instituti i obshestvennoye mnenie" [Democratic institutions and public opinion], p. 163.

24. Colton and McFaul found a similar utopian quality to the regime most Russians preferred. See Colton and McFaul, "Are Russians Undemocratic?"

25. Igor Klyamkin and Lilia Shevtsova, *Vnesistemniy rezhim Borisa II. Nekotorie osobennosti politicheskogo razvitiya sovremennoy Rossii* [The extra-systemic regime of Boris II: some features of political development in post-Soviet Russia] (Moscow: Carnegie Moscow Center, 1999), p. 12.

26. Guillermo O'Donnell, "Delegative Democracy," *Journal of Democracy,* vol. 5, no. 1 (January 1994), pp. 56–69.

27. Andrei Melvil, "Politicheskie tsennosti i orientatsii i politicheskie institute" [Political values and orientations and political institutions] in Lilia Shevtsova, ed., *Rossiya politicheskaya* [Political Russia], (Moscow: Carnegie Moscow Center, 1998), pp. 136–194.

28. See Ronald Inglehart, "Postmodern: Menayushiyesia tsennosti i izmenayushiyesia obshestva" [Postmodern: changing values and changing societies] *Polis,* no. 4 (1997), pp. 6–32.

29. Herman Diligensky, "Politicheskoe razvitie Rossii v perehodniy period" [Political development in Russia in the transition period] in *Politicheskiy process v Rossii: sovremennie tendencii i istoricheskiy kontekst* [Political process in Russia: contemporary tendencies and historical context] Political Science Series no. 10 (Moscow: Center for Complex Social Research and Marketing, 1995), p. 21.

30. *Rossiya na rubezhe vekov* [Russia on the brink of centuries], pp. 7–46.

31. Vladimir Petukhov and Andrei Ryabov, "Sovremenniy politicheskiy process i ustanovki na politicheskoe uchastie" [Contemporary political process and instructions on political par-

ticipation] in *Rol gosudarstva v razvitii obshestva: Rossiya i mezhdunarodniy opit* [The role of the state in society's development: Russia and international experience] (Moscow: RIISNP and Friedrich Ebert Foundation Moscow Branch, 1997), p. 266.

32. E. Avraamova, "Formirovanie politicheskogo soznaniya v novom socialno-ekonomicheskom kontekste" [Formation of political consciousness in the new socioeconomic context] Moscow Carnegie Center seminar paper no. 5 (July 2001), pp. 5–6.

33. Vladimir Petukhov, "Demokratiya v vospriyatii Rossiyskogo obshestva" [The perception of democracy in Russian society] Moscow Carnegie Center seminar paper no. 2 (March 2001), p. 8.

34. For alarmist assessments, see Michael McFaul, "Russia Under Putin: One Step Forward, Two Steps Backward," *Journal of Democracy*, vol. 11, no. 3 (July 2000), pp. 19–33.

35. Dmitri Furman, "Novie sosudi zapolnili staroe vino. V Rossii zavershilos stanovlenie 'narodnoy monarhii'" [New vessels have filled old wine. The establishment of a 'people's monarchy' is concluded] *Obshaya Gazeta*, November 9–15, 2000. See also Lilia Shevtsova, *Yeltsin's Russia* (Washington, D.C.: Carnegie Endowment for International Peace, 1999).

36. Boris Kapustin, "Diktatorskiy liberalizm ili diktatura zakona" [Dictatorial liberalism or dictatorship of the law] *Izvestiya*, November 20, 2000.

37. According to VTsIOM's summer 2000 survey data.

38. Lev Gudkov and Boris Dubin, "Konetz 90h godov: zatuhanie obraztsov" [The end of the 90s: fading ideals] in *Socialnie i ekonomicheskie peremeni: monitoring obshestvennogo vremeni*, [Social and economic changes: monitoring public time] no. 1 (Moscow: Interdisciplinary Academic Center for the Social Sciences and VTsIOM, 2001).

39. Vladimir Mau and Irina Staradubrovskaya, *The Challenge of Revolution: Contemporary Russia in Historical Perspective* (Oxford, U.K.: Oxford University Press, 2001).

40. Steven Holmes, "What Russia teaches us now: how weak states threaten freedom," *The American Prospect*, no. 33 (July–August 1997), pp. 30–41.

41. *Rossiya na rubezhe vekov* [Russia on the brink of centuries], pp. 325–419.

42. V. V. Rukavishnikov, L. Halman, and P. Ester, *Politicheskie kulturi i socialnie izmeneniya: mezhdunarodnie sravneniya* [Political culture and social changes: international comparisons], (Moscow: Coincidence, 1998), p. 189.

43. V. Fedotova, "Kriminalizatsiya Rossii" [The criminalization of Russia] *Svobodnaya Misl*, vol. 21, no. 2 (2000), pp. 38–39.

Chapter 12

1. Seth Mydans, "Rare Russian Jury Acquits Scientist in Spy Case," *New York Times*, December 30, 2003, p. A7.

2. Human Rights Watch, "Russia's 'Spy Mania': A Study of the Case of Igor Sutyagin," *Human Rights Watch Briefing Paper*, October 2003.

3. "Constitutional and Due Process Violations in the Khodorkovsky/Yukpos Case," White Paper prepared by defense lawyers on behalf of Mikhail Khodorkovsky, Platon Lebedev, and Alexei Pichugin, November 2003.

4. At the same time, evidence suggests that voters have become less enamored with the actual process. Turnout in 2003 dropped by ten percentage points, the total vote for against all parties climbed to 4.7 percent, and an amazing 57 percent of respondents reported in an opinion poll before the vote that they expected falsification of the results. On the expectations about falsification, see Anna Badkhen, "Russians Believe Election Fixed; 57% in Poll Say They Mistrust Sunday's Vote for Parliament," *San Francisco Chronicle*, December 6, 2003, at www.sfgate.com/cgi-bin/article.cgi?file=/chronicle/archive/2003/12/06/MNGKJ3HPJB1.DTL.

5. For the first time ever, the Organization for Security and Cooperation in Europe (OSCE) issued a critical preliminary report on Russia's 1999 parliamentary election, stressing that "the State Duma elections failed to meet many OSCE and Council of Europe commitments for democratic elections. In addition, important safeguards in domestic legislation were not enforced by the Russian authorities. This is a worrisome development that calls into question Russia's fundamental willingness to meet European and international standard for democratic elections." OSCE/PA (Organization for Security and Cooperation in Europe/Parliamentary Assembly) International Election Observation Mission, "Statement of Preliminary Findings and Conclusions, Russian Federation State Duma Elections," December 7, 2003. The full report is available at www.osce.org/documents/odihr/2003/12/1629_en.pdf.

6. For details, see Timothy Colton and Michael McFaul, *Popular Choice and Managed Democracy: The Russian Elections of 1999 and 2000* (Washington, D.C.: Brookings Institution Press, 2003).

7. Note that exit polls and unofficial parallel vote counts showed both parties winning more than 5 percent, sparking claims of falsification. See www.fairgame.ru.

8. Citing their parallel vote count results, Yabloko and Communist Party leaders charged that government authorities falsified the result of the December 2003 vote. Yabloko has pressed for a legal investigation. See "Yabloko osporit v sude rezul'taty parlamentskikh vyborov," *Lenta.ru*, January 16, 2004, at www.lenta.ru/vybory/2004/01/16/yabloko_Printed.htm.

Index

Adygeya, democratization rating, 247*t*;
    election ratings, 259*t*, 265*t*; regional
    constitution, 72
Aga-Buryatsky, competitiveness in elections,
    254; democratization rating, 247*t*, 248;
    election ratings, 259*t*, 265*t*, 266
Agrarian Party of Russia, 108, 115*t*; 1993
    parliamentary elections, 37, 39, 131;
    1995 parliamentary elections, 309n45;
    founding elections, 121
Alekseev, Sergei, 130
Alekseeva, Lyudmila, 159
Aleksii II, Patriarch, 166, 289
All-National Congress of the Chechen
    People, 219
All-Russian Center for Public Opinion
    Research, 272–73, 318–19n61,
    338–39n1; assessments of Yeltsin, 273*t*;
    constitutional amendments, 79,
    313n45; harassment, under Putin, 163;
    NTV takeover, 168
All-Russian Emergency Conference for
    Environmental Protection, 169–70,
    328n109
Altai, 116, 215; democratization rating,

245*t*, 248; election ratings, 257, 262,
    264*t*; voter turnout, 251
Altaysky, democratization rating, 246*t*; elec-
    tion ratings, 259*t*, 265*t*
American Federation of Labor and Con-
    gress of Industrial Organizations (AFL-
    CIO), 165
Amurskaya, democratization rating, 246*t*;
    election ratings, 258*t*, 262, 263*t*, 267
The Anatomy of Free Speech, 183
Andrei Sakharov Foundation, 328n104
Anpilov, Viktor, 40, 41
Argumenty i Fakty, 175
Arkhangelskaya, 222; democratization
    rating, 244*t*; election ratings, 258*t*, 263*t*
Armenia, 31
Association of Forced Settlers of Suzdal,
    327n96
Astrakhanskaya, democratization rating,
    245*t*; election ratings, 257, 262, 264*t*
Atomic Energy Ministry, 169–71
August 1991 attempted coup, 16–17,
    32–33, 200, 323n35; dissolution of the
    KGB, 205; dissolution of the Soviet
    Union, 33, 127; public protest, 135, 148

Aushev, Ruslan, 167
autocracy in Russia, 7, 300nn15–16; *See
   also* oligarchy
Ayatskov, Dmitri, 257

Baburin, Sergei, 41
Baltic republics, 1990 elections, 31, 146;
   declaration of sovereignty, 218; democratization rating, 241
Basayev, Shamil, 293–94
Bashkortostan, democratization rating,
   247t, 248; election ratings, 257, 259t,
   262, 265t, 266; Federal Treaty, 218–19,
   221; nationalist movements, 219; political structure, 101; regional constitution,
   72; regional powers, 99
Belarus, 13
Belgorodskaya, democratization rating,
   245t; election ratings, 265t
Berezovsky, Boris, 44, 294, 297, 324n52;
   1999 parliamentary elections, 47; media
   ownership, 182, 183, 192; Sibneft ownership, 185
Berman, Sheri, 137–38
Blagoveschensk, 54
Bogdanov, Vsevelod, 327n97
borders, 214; Caucasus region, 13; elections, 217
Bova, Russell, 11
Brezhnev, Leonid, 143–44, 273–74
Bryansk, 90, 229; democratization rating,
   245t; election ratings, 263t; removal of
   governors, 54
Burlatsky, Fyodor, 196
Buryatia, democratization rating, 244t, 248;
   election ratings, 257, 264t; regional
   constitution, 72
business class. *See* oligarchy

Carey, John, 68
Carnegie Moscow Center, 178; electoral violation data, 256–57; expert evaluations
   of democratization, 242–43, 336n4
Center for Sociological Research, 271,
   338–39n1

Center on Law and the Mass Media, 183
Checheno-Ingushetia, 219
Chechen wars, 8, 20, 110, 124; 1994–1996
   war, 68, 77–78, 180–81, 294; 1999
   war, 47, 189, 293–94, 297; calls for
   peace talks, 167–68; characteristics of,
   220; Khasavyurt accord, 294; media
   criticism of, 189; Putin era, 228; terrorist acts, 193
Chechnya, 13, 72; All-National Congress of
   the Chechen People, 219; declaration of
   independence, 19, 219; democratization
   ratings, 240; election manipulation, 42,
   54, 294; Federal Treaty, 218–21; human
   rights, 5; Organization for Security and
   Cooperation in Europe, 165; participation in elections, 4, 45, 219, 307n23,
   314n13; rejection of federalism,
   219–21, 332n15; split with Ingushetia,
   219
Chelyabinsk, constitutional conflicts, 77;
   democratization rating, 244t; election
   ratings, 264t; removal of governors, 54
Cherkesov, Viktor, 231
Chernomyrdin, Viktor, 41–42, 108; 1995
   parliamentary elections, 309n45;
   Gazprom, 324n52; party affiliations,
   113; as Yeltsin's prime minister, 45,
   96–97, 324n52
Chitinskaya, democratization rating, 246t;
   election ratings, 262, 263t
Chubais, Anatoly, 44, 111, 334n32; firing
   of, by Yeltsin, 186; privatization,
   151–52, 324n44
Chukotka, 222; declaration of sovereignty,
   218; election ratings, 259t, 265t
Chukotsky, democratization rating, 247t,
   248; electoral competition, 254
Chuvashia, democratization rating, 244t,
   248, 249; election ratings, 264t
Civic Forum, 159–60, 165–66, 210,
   327nn95–96
Civic Union, 151–52, 324n44
civil society, 3, 5, 70, 135–73; alienation of
   the middle and lower classes, 283–85,

284*t*; antiwar movements, 167; Brezhnev era, 143–44; Civic Forum, 159–60,
165–66, 210, 327nn95–96; Congress in
Defense of Human Rights, 167–68; definitions, 136–42, 321n3, 321n6,
322n13; dissidents of the Soviet Union,
143–44, 322n23; economic factors,
136, 156, 158; emergence, 17–18,
102–3, 118, 136; emergence of political
parties, 139, 321n10; engrained mistrust of institutions, 157–58, 325n65;
environmental movement, 161, 163–64,
169–71, 328n98, 328nn108–12; friendship networks, 141–42, 158–59,
172–73; funding, 139, 165; Gorbachev
era, 135, 145–48, 172; grassroots, 136,
158, 170–72; historical view, 142–45;
horizontal impact, 140–41; human
rights movement, 160–61, 167,
328n104; Khordokovsky arrest, 168;
Kremlin-sponsored groups,
327–82nn95–98; legal status, 150,
323n39; legislative alliances, 155; media
independence, 139–40, 168–69;
nationalist groups, 137–38; need for
centralization, 234–35; nongovernmental organizations (NGOs), 136; nuclear
safety movement, 169–71,
328nn111–12; obstacles to development, 152–59, 161–62, 171–72; oligarchy, 324n44; participation rates,
141, 322n18; in Poland, 146, 323n26;
public opinion, 281, 281*t*; Putin era,
159–72; registration requirements,
161–62, 171–72; religious groups,
161–62, 171–72; responses to Putin,
167–72; role in elections, 25, 27; role of
intelligentsia, 147; role of the oligarchy,
153–54; role of the presidency, 136; role
of the state, 20; rule of law, 210; socioeconomic factors, 153–55; Soviet era
organizations, 14–15, 139, 142–48,
150–52, 172; state-supported, 136; taxation, 162–63; trade unions, 161; vertical impact, 140–41; weakness, 20, 95,

156–57; in Weimar Germany, 137–38;
welfare safetynet, 158, 171–72, 326n69;
Yeltsin era, 149–59; youth movement,
138, 139, 162
coalitions. *See* electoral blocs
Communist Party of the Russian Federation
(CPRF), 95, 112*t*, 115*t*, 296; 1991 presidential election, 121–22; 1993 parliamentary elections, 37, 39, 131; 1995
parliamentary elections, 41–42, 120,
309n45; 1996 presidential election,
43–45, 108, 122; 1999 parliamentary
elections, 46–48; 2003 parliamentary
elections, 342nn7–8; Duma representation, 110–14, 119–22; founding elections, 121; role in central government,
108; role in regional government, 116;
single-mandate districts, 115*t*; two-
party system, 133
Communist Party of the Soviet Union
(CPSU), 295, 317n44; 1989 elections,
24–25, 29, 306n14; constitutional role,
57–58; end of monopoly under
Gorbachev, 145; founding elections,
33–34; Nineteenth All-Union Party
Conference, 196–97; rule of law,
196–97
Communist–Working Russia–for the Soviet
Union, 41
competitive authoritarianism, 7, 300n16
Congress in Defense of Human Rights,
167–68, 328n104
Congress of People's Deputies (CPD), 17;
1989 elections, 27–31, 139, 146, 217,
306n14; 1990 elections, 216–17; during the August Republic, 87–91,
179–80; conflicts with Yeltsin, 34–37,
90–91; Constitutional Commission of
1990, 57–62; declaration of independence, 31–32; Declaration of Sovereignty of 1990, 58, 205; dissolution by
Yeltsin, 36, 62, 206–7; judicial reforms,
205–6; opposition to the CPSU, 200;
party formation, 120; power, 19–20,
305n77; regional representation,

333n19; restoration under Gorbachev,
86; role of democrats, 126, 319n71;
selection of delegates, 86; under the
Soviet Constitution, 58, 333n19;
Yeltsin's chairmanship, 32, 126, 148
Congress of Russian Communities, 41
Constant, Benjamin, 93
Constantine Palace, 231
constitution. *See* Russian Constitution
Constitutional Assembly, 63–65
Constitutional Court, 74–79, 94, 205
Constitutional Democratic Party, 146
Council of Judges of the Russian Federa-
tion, 78–79
Council of Nationalities, 224, 225*t*, 333n19
Council of the Duma, 112
Council of the Heads of Administration,
224, 225*t*
Council of the Heads of Republics, 224,
225*t*
Council of the Republics, 224, 225*t*
CPD. *See* Congress of People's Deputies
(CPD)
CPRF. *See* Communist Party of the Russian
Federation (CPRF)
CPSU. *See* Communist Party of the Soviet
Union (CPSU)

Dagestan, 1996 presidential election, 45;
1999 Chechen war, 293–94; democratization rating, 246*t*; election ratings,
257, 259*t*, 262, 265*t*; ethnicity concerns, 223; Putin's use of military force,
228; subsidies from the central government, 229; voter turnout, 251
Declaration of Sovereignty of 1990, 58
declarations of independence, 31–32
Defense Council, 68–69
Democratic Choice of Russia, 42, 112*t*,
119; 1995 parliamentary elections, 115,
120, 315n13; role in regional government, 116
Democratic Party of Russia, 146
Democratic Perestroika, 145
Democratic Russia, 1990 elections, 30–31,

146, 307n21; challenges to Soviet rule,
33, 120, 146, 157; demonstrations during 1990-1991, 148; NTV takeover,
168; Yeltsin's lack of support for, 150
Democratic Union, 147
democratization, vii–viii, 1–2, 7–9; analysis
of, 10–14, 302n39; conditions for
democracy, 2–3; correlation matrix,
261*t*; definitions of democracy, 2–7, 23;
election ratings, 258–59*t*, 263–65*t*;
electoral democracy, 2, 3, 5–7; future,
292–98; historical comparisons, 9–10,
303n2; initial push theory, 248; liberal
democracy, 2–5, 300n11; managed
democracy, 9, 160; measurements,
239–67; outsider group, 249; paternalism, 279–83; political conflicts,
264–65; public values, 269–78, 273*t*,
274*t*, 276*t*, 277*t*; ratings, 239–67;
regional elections, 249–53; regional ratings, 244–47*t*; role of elites, 264; urban
regions, 248–49
Derzhava, 41
Diamond, Larry, 2–5, 7–8, 306n6, 322n13,
337n16
Dmitriyev, Mikhail, 334n32
Dorenko, Sergei, 47
Dubin, Boris, 272
Duma, 1993 parliamentary elections,
36–39, 113, 119, 130–31, 308n32,
309n45; 1995 parliamentary elections,
40–43, 112*t*, 113, 115, 120, 309n45,
310n59; 1999 parliamentary elections,
46–48, 112*t*, 115, 250–51, 310n59,
342n5; 2003 parliamentary elections,
295–96, 342n4, 342nn7–8; antiwar
movement, 167–68; constitutional powers, 69; cooperation with Putin, 102;
Council of the Duma, 112; electoral system, 65, 109–15, 119–22, 129–31,
317n40; federalist structures, 231–35,
232*t*, 234*t*; foreign policy efforts, 69,
312n32; political block affiliations,
115*t*; political parties, 112*t*, 119–22;
political party development, 109–15;

power, 92–94, 122; proportional representation, 119–22, 129–31, 317n40;
protections of civil liberties, 150; role in
appointing prime ministers, 108–9,
226; single-mandate districts, 114–15,
115*t*, 122, 128; Yeltsin impeachment,
83, 100
Dzyaloshinsky, Iosif, 178

Eckstein, Harry, 16
Ecojuris, 169–70
Ecology and Human Rights organization,
161
economic factors, 11–12, 13, 18–19;
August 1998 financial crisis, 8, 19, 46,
108; budget deficits, 155–56; class
mobility, 284; corruption, 204; currency, 19; decline of basic services, 156,
158; depression, 18, 154–55; development of civil society, 117–18, 136; elimination of state bureaucracy, 205–6;
Gorbachev's reforms, 28, 57–58, 74,
84–85, 145–48, 195–99; income statistics, 285; media independence, 175,
178; middle classes, 18, 118, 154; presidential elections, 24; privatization,
94–95, 151–52, 181–83, 205–6,
324n44; property rights, 59; public
preferences for stability, 270–72;
regional budgets, 229, 334n28; role of
the oligarchs, 17, 97–101, 151–54;
small business problems, 154; taxation,
156, 162–63, 229, 230; Yeltsin era
reforms, 16–17, 34, 88, 92, 207–8,
270–72
Ekho Moskvy, 181–82
elections, 2–4, 23–26, 249–53, 342n5;
1989 congressional elections, 23,
27–29, 139, 146, 217, 250–51,
306n14; 1990 regional elections,
29–31, 146, 216–17, 307n21, 310n59,
317n44; 1991 presidential election,
31–32, 108, 121–22, 127, 148,
307n23; 1991 referendum, 31–32,
126–27, 307n24; 1993-1994 founding

elections, 23, 26, 33–40, 120–21,
307–8n30, 308n37, 308–9n41; 1993
parliamentary elections, 36–39, 113,
119, 130–31, 308n32, 309n45; 1993
referendum on the constitution, 35–36,
56, 219, 313n9; 1995-1997 cycle, 23,
40–46, 183; 1995 parliamentary elections, 40–43, 112*t*, 113, 115, 120,
309n45, 310n59; 1996 presidential
election, 43–45, 95, 108, 128, 153–54,
180, 204–5, 217, 269, 320n77; 1996
regional elections, 45–46; 1999-2001
cycle, 6, 23, 25, 46–52; 1999 parliamentary elections, 46–48, 112*t*, 115,
250–51, 310n59, 342n5; 2000 presidential election, 48–49, 108, 113,
250–51, 269, 306n5; 2003 parliamentary elections, 295–96, 342n4,
342nn7–8; 2004 presidential election,
6, 297; boycotts, 37; campaign funding
limits, 44; candidates/competition, 6–7,
24, 25, 28–30, 38, 54, 249–53, 261*t*,
308n41, 310n58, 337n13; certainty of
outcomes, 24; Chechen wars, 220; civil
society, 27; democratization ratings,
240–41, 258–59*t*, 263–65*t*; electoral
systems, 109–15; financial manipulation, 295–96; Gorbachev era, 23,
26–33, 85, 145, 306n14; interest
groups, 25; international standards,
342n5; local elections, 73, 85; manipulation and fraud, 25, 38, 39, 42, 45, 49,
51, 54, 209, 222–23, 249–53, 261*t*,
295, 342n5, 342nn7–8; media control,
25, 43–44, 47, 49, 54, 123, 180, 183;
minority group participation, 3–4;
mixed electoral systems, 121, 129–31,
130–31; negative voting, 249–53, 261*t*,
336n11; oligarchy, 25, 42, 47, 53–54,
153–54, 310n58; political party development, 29–30, 37, 39, 65, 91,
107–16, 119–22, 139, 218, 295–96;
political party participation, 41–42, 45,
102, 108, 115–16, 249–53, 261*t*,
308–9n41; proportional representation,

129–30, 132–33, 317n40; Putin era,
48–55; ratings, by correlation matrix,
249–53, 261*t*, 336nn9–10; regional
elections, 23, 42–43, 45–46, 49–52, 99,
115–16, 121, 216–17, 261*t*, 307–8n30,
310n57, 318n49, 335n36; removal of
incumbents, 255–56, 337n15; rule of
law, 4, 24, 42–43, 52, 65, 70, 256–57,
314–15n5; single-mandate districts,
114–15, 115*t*, 121, 122, 128; Soviet
era, 307n16; state influence in, 20, 25,
49–54, 310n55, 310n57, 310n58;
timetables, 52; voter turnout, 24, 29,
38, 73, 249–53, 261*t*, 308n37, 335n36,
336n9; Yeltsin era, 33–48, 94; *See also*
political parties
electoral blocs, 112–14, 120, 129, 132–33,
238; *See also* political parties
elites. *See* oligarchy
equality, 4, 203; *See also* human rights
ethnicity. *See* minority concerns
Eurasia movement, 138, 166
Evenkiisky, democratization rating, 247*t*,
248; election ratings, 264*t*; voter
turnout, 251
executive agencies, 205–6, 212
executive office. *See* presidency

Fatherland-All Russia (OVR) coalition,
112–14, 112*t*, 115*t*; 1999 parliamentary
elections, 46, 48, 115, 123, 217–18,
295–96; Federation Council, 109;
merger with Unity, 238; Putin's manipulation of, 229, 238
Federal Forestry Service, 169–71
federalism, 71–73, 213–38; asymmetry,
218–19, 221–23, 332n11; central institutions, 223–27, 231–35, 232*t*, 234*t*;
constitutional structure, 58, 71–73,
219, 224, 225*t*, 231–35, 232*t*, 234*t*;
elections, 216–18, 332n8, 332n12; ethnicity concerns, 214–15, 223, 332n14;
Federal Treaty of March 1992, 218–23,
332n11; Gorbachev era, 216–17,
332n10; historical aspects, 213–15,

218–19; nationalist movements, 219;
oblasts, krais, and *okrugs,* 215, 222–23,
332n7; Putin era, 221–22, 227–35;
rebellions against, 219–21; representation at the federal level, 224, 225*t*;
under the Soviet Union, 214–15; Yeltsin
era, 216–17; *See also* Federation Council; regional governments; Russian Constitution
Federal Law on the Basic Principals Underlying State Power Organization, 100
Federal Security Service. *See* FSB (Federal
Security Service)
Federation Council, 224, 225*t*; 1993 elections, 37–38, 308n32; 1995 Chechen
war, 77–78; 1999 clash with Yeltsin,
99–100; confirmation of executive
appointments, 99, 226; constitutional
role, 64, 69, 99; election of members,
99–100, 314n18; lack of electoral mandate, 34; lobbying role, 103–4; membership, 99–100, 226, 310n57; political
parties, 106, 109; powers, 93–94, 99,
224; presidential control of, 70–71, 80,
99–100, 109, 333n22; Putin era,
70–71, 103–4, 226–27, 295, 333n22
Federation of Independent Trade Unions of
Russia (FNPR), 151, 166
Fedotova, Valentina, 288
Fish, Steven, 145, 321n10
FNPR. *See* Federation of Independent Trade
Unions of Russia (FNPR)
For Human Rights, 328n104
founding elections, 23, 26, 33–40, 120–21,
307–8n32
Freedom House ratings, 7, 241–43,
300n17, 306n2
freedoms. *See* human rights
FSB (Federal Security Service), 4, 20, 92;
arrests, 294; harassment of civil society,
160–64; Putin era, 228, 231
Furman, Dmitri, 285–86
Fyodorov, Boris, 108

Gaidar, Yegor, 42, 88, 108, 111, 309n45

Gazprom, 160, 168, 205, 324n52; federal structures, 232t, 234t; media ownership, 182
Gelman, Vladimir, 100–101
Georgia, 31
Glasnost Defense Foundation, 161, 328n104
Glasnost Public Foundation, 161, 162, 328n104
Glaziev, Sergei, 296
Glinski, Dmitri, 65, 67–68
Gorbachev, Mikhail, vii; 1989 parliamentary elections, 24, 26–31, 85, 306n14; 1990-1991 regional elections, 31, 85, 146, 216–17; 1991 elections, 31–32; August 1991 attempted coup, 16–17, 32–33, 127, 135, 148, 200, 323n35; Baku, Azerbaijan action, 220; civil society, 135, 145–48, 172; constitutional modifications, 57–58; creation of the presidency, 29, 84–87; democratic ideals, 279–80; dissolution of the KGB, 205; establishment of presidency and executive branch, 87; federalism, 216–17; glasnost, 145, 175–77, 270; media independence, 146, 147, 175–77, 323n35; reforms/perestroika, 16, 28, 57–58, 74, 84–85, 145–48, 175–76, 195–99; removal from office, 74; role of soviets, 85–87; rule of law, 195–99, 205; Union Treaty, 218
Gordon, Leonid, 276, 276t
Goskomtsen, 206
Gosplan, 205–6
Gossnab, 205–6
Grachev, Pavel, 185
Greenpeace, 169–70
Grigorants, Sergei, 327n95
Gromov, Boris, 320n79
Grozny, Ivan, 21
Gudkov, Lev, 272
Gusinsky, Vladimir, 44, 168, 294, 297; media holdings, 185–86, 192, 193; media privatization, 181–82; Putin's takeover of NTV, 189–90; Svyazinvest, 185–86

Hanson, Stephen, 8
historical roots, 14–15, 303n52; civil society, 142–45; democratic tradition, 271, 273–74, 277t, 278–80; federalism, 213–15, 218–19; local self-rule, 214; paternalism, 279; political parties, 117–19, 317n38; rule of law, 201–2; Russian Constitution, 57–63
Hitler, Adolf, 138
Holmes, Stephen, 287
Hopkins, Harry, 69
Howard, Marc Morje, 138, 157–58
human rights, 4, 160–61, 167–68, 203, 269, 328n104, 331n3

Ignatenko, Vitaly, 166
Igrunov, Vyacheslav, 315n16
Illarionov, Andrei, 334n32
Ilyin, Ivan, 201–2
Ilyumzhinov, Kirsan, 266
Information Security Doctrine, 189
Inglehart, Robert, 280
Ingushetiya, 220, 229; 1991 presidential election, 307n23; democratization rating, 247t, 248; election manipulation, 54; election ratings, 259t, 262, 265t, 266; electoral competition, 254; regional constitution, 72; split with Chechnya, 219; voter turnout, 251
Institute for Political Studies, 160, 327n96
Institute of Civil Society Problems, 327n96
Institute of Sociology of the Russian Academy of Sciences, 165, 338–39n1
institutions. See specific institution, e.g. presidency
intelligentsia, 146–47, 271
interest groups. See civil society
Irkutsk, 215; democratization rating, 244t; election ratings, 263t
Isakov, Vladimir, 62
Itogi, 181–82, 189
Ivanov, Sergei, 231
Ivanov, Viktor, 231
Ivanovskaya, democratization rating, 245t; election ratings, 258t, 262, 263t, 265–66

Izhevsk, 54
Izvestiya, 63, 175, 182, 187

Jehovah's Witnesses, 171–72
Jewish Autonomous Oblast, 222; democratization rating, 247t; election ratings, 264t
journalists. See media
judicial system, 1991 reforms, 205–6; Civil Code, 209; constitutional roles, 64, 74–79; contradictory legislation, 78–79; Criminal Code, 209; development of civil society, 155; independence, 4, 78–79; jury system, 209; need for qualified judges, 212; Office of the Prosecutor General, 71–72, 211, 224–26; Pacific Fleet Military Court, 77–78; protection of rights, 209; Putin era, 189, 192, 209–12, 293, 325n59; rule of law, 195–212; Russian Constitution, 208–9; Russian Constitutional Court, 75–78; Soviet reforms, 197; suppression of the media, 78; See also law enforcement; Supreme Court

Kabardino-Balkaria, 219; democratization rating, 247t, 248; election manipulation, 54; election ratings, 257, 259t, 262, 265t, 266; electoral competition, 254; regional constitution, 72; voter turnout, 251
Kaliningrad, democratization rating, 244t; election ratings, 258t, 262, 264, 265; Kalmykiya; democratization rating, 243, 247t, 248; election manipulation, 54; election ratings, 257, 259t, 265t, 266; electoral competition, 254; political structure, 101; regional constitution, 72
Kaluzhskaya, democratization rating, 245t; election ratings, 263t
Kamchatka, 222; democratization rating, 245t; election ratings, 258t, 262, 263t, 265, 266
Kapustin, Boris, 286
Karachaevo-Cherkessia, 219, 223; democratization rating, 246t, 248; election ratings, 257, 259t, 265t
Karaganov, Sergei, 160
Karelia, declaration of sovereignty, 218; democratization rating, 243, 244t, 249; election ratings, 263t
Karl, Terry, 2–3, 10
Kasyanov, Mikhail, 97, 109
Kazakhstan, 10
Kemerovo, 215; democratization rating, 245t, 248; election ratings, 258, 259t, 265t; electoral competition, 254
KGB (Committee for State Security), 147, 205; See also FSB (Federal Security Service)
Khabarovsky, 222; democratization rating, 246t; election ratings, 263t; electoral competition, 254
Khakassia, democratization rating, 245t; election ratings, 264t
Khanty-Mansiisky Okrug, 222–23; democratization rating, 244t; election ratings, 262, 264t; electoral competition, 254
Khasbulatov, Ruslan, 34, 96
Khordokovsky, Mikhail, 151, 168, 294–97
Kiriyenko, Sergei, 108, 111, 186
Kirovskaya, 162, 245t
Kiselev, Evgeny, 169
Kissinger, Henry, 69
Klebanov, Ilya, 335n33
Klopov, Eduoard, 276, 276t
Kokh, Alfred, 334n32
Komi, declaration of sovereignty, 218; democratization rating, 245t; election ratings, 258t, 263t; regional constitution, 72
Komi-Permyatsky, democratization rating, 246t; election ratings, 264t
Kommersant-Daily, 187
Komsomolskaya Pravda, 182
Koryak, 222; democratization rating, 246t; election ratings, 264t
Korzhakov group, 180, 186
Kostromskaya, democratization rating, 244t; election ratings, 264t

Kotenkov, Aleksandr, 130
Kovalev, Sergei, 130
Kozak, Dmitri, 293
Krasnaya Zvezda, 163
Krasnodarsky, democratization rating, 246t; election ratings, 257, 264t
Krasnov, Mikhail, 130
Krasnoyarsky, democratization rating, 244t; election ratings, 262, 263t
Kudrin, Alexei, 334n32
Kurganskaya, democratization rating, 246t; election ratings, 263t
Kursk, democratization rating, 247t, 249; election manipulation, 54; election ratings, 257, 264t
Kursk (submarine), 189

labor movement, 18; Gorbachev era, 145–46; independent trade unions, 161; Labor Code, 163, 166, 327n86; media coverage, 186; media unions, 166, 329n97; Putin era, 163, 166; Soviet era, 144, 151–52, 323n29
Lapkin, Vladimir, 279
LaSalle, Ferdinand, 206
law enforcement, 79; civil society, 155, 160–61; regional level, 229; Soviet era reforms, 197; use of torture, 78; *See also* rule of law
Law on Local Self-government, 73–74
Lazareva, N., 192
Lebed, Aleksandr, 41, 43–45, 122, 185, 332n8, 333–34n25
legislature. *See* Congress of People's Deputies (CPD); parliament
Lenin, Vladimir, 85–86
Leningradskaya, democratization rating, 244t; election ratings, 258t, 262, 263t, 264
Levada, Yuri, 163, 189
Levine, Daniel, 15–16
Liberal Democratic Party of Russia, 39–40, 112t, 115t, 296, 317n41; 1991 presidential election, 121–22; 1993 parliamentary elections, 119, 130–31; 1995

parliamentary elections, 41–42, 309n45; 1996 presidential election, 122; 1999 parliamentary elections, 48, 115; Duma representation, 110–14, 119–22; founding elections, 121; role in regional government, 116
Lipetskaya, democratization rating, 245t; election ratings, 264t
lower classes, 283–85, 284t
LUKoil, 182
Luzhkov, Yuri, 46, 113, 217, 333–34n25; party affiliations, 114, 123–24; TV-Center, 182
Lyubimov, Aleksandr, 166, 327n97

Magadanskaya, democratization rating, 246t; election ratings, 264t
managed democracy, 9, 160, 298
Marii El, democratization rating, 245t; election ratings, 264t
Markov, Sergei, 160, 327n96
Mary-El Council, 219
Maskhadov, Ruslan, 167
Maslyukov, Yuri, 108
Matviyenko, Valentina, 335n33
measurements of democratization, 239–67; elections, 249–57, 336n6; electoral competition, 337n13; expert evaluations, 242–49, 336n4, 337n25; Freedom House ratings, 241–42; public opinion polling, 268–69; variables, 240–41; *See also* public opinion
media, 3–5, 20, 139–40, 174–94; advertising revenues, 178, 182; corruption, 183; coverage of labor unrest, 186; freedom of information, 3–4, 176, 183, 189; funding, 175, 178, 179–80, 182, 192; Gorbachev era, 146, 147, 175–77, 323n35; government propaganda, 191, 194; influence, 43–44, 174–81, 184–85, 191, 194, 268, 330n11; journalist unions, 166, 327n97; legal status, 178; live coverage of terrorist crises, 193; local/regional media, 187–88, 229–30; print media, 186–88;

privatization, 181–83; Putin era, 78, 162, 168–69, 189–94, 294; Putin's takeover of NTV, 160, 168–69, 189–90; readership, 187; restrictions and suppression, 78, 168–69, 189–91; rise of civil society, 176–77; role in elections, 25, 43–44, 47, 49, 54, 123; self-censorship, 193; Soviet era, 140, 175; television, 186–89; Yeltsin era, 90, 177–89

Media-Most, 181–82, 189

Mediasoyuz, 166, 327n97

Media Union, 166

Medvedev, Roy, 144

Memorial association, 145, 161, 328n104

Mercator Group ratings of freedom of elections, 256, 337n18

middle classes, alienation from civil society, 283–85, 284t; economic factors, 18, 118, 154

Mikhailov, Eugeny, 116

military involvement in the state, 3; 1991 attempted coup, 32–33; 1993 dissolution of the CPD, 36, 91; 1999 invasion of Chechnya, 47; Grigory Pasko case, 164; *See also* Chechen wars

military service alternatives, 78

Milosevic, Slobodan, 55

Ministry of Defense, 20; federalist structures, 232t, 234t; suppression of journalists, 78

Ministry of Internal Affairs, 20

Ministry of Natural Resources, 169–71, 328n112

Ministry of Security and Internal Affairs, 75, 205, 335n34

Ministry of the Interior, 232t, 234t

minority concerns, 3–4, 72, 214–15, 223, 332n14

Mironov, Sergei, 81, 335n33

Moiseev, Valentin, 164

Monitoring.ru, 271, 279, 338–39n1

Moore, Barrington, 17

Mordovia, constitutional conflicts, 77; democratization rating, 247t, 248; election ratings, 259t, 265t, 266; electoral competition, 254; removal of president, 54

Moscow, 215, 230–31; democratization rating, 239, 245t, 248, 249; election ratings, 262, 264t, 267; political structure, 100, 101

Moscow Helsinki Group, 328n104

Moscow News, 175

Moscow Theater Center terrorist attack, 193

Moskovskaya, democratization rating, 239, 244t; election ratings, 258t, 262, 263t

Movement for Nuclear Safety, 170

Murmanskaya, democratization rating, 245t; election ratings, 264t; electoral competition, 254

Murrel, G. D. G., 62

Narusova, Lyudmila, 310n58

National Association of Television and Radio Broadcasters, 166

nationalist movements, 219; disqualification of parties, 38; domination of 1993 parliamentary elections, 39; *See also* Liberal Democratic Party of Russia

National Patriotic Bloc, 45

National Patriotic Union of Russia, 116, 123

National Salvation Front, 62

natural law, 201–2

Nemtsov, Boris, 111

Nenetsky, 222; democratization rating, 247t; election ratings, 264t; electoral competition, 254

Newsweek, 181

Nezavisimaya Gazeta, 183, 187

Nicholson, Martin, 71

Nikitin, Alexander, 161, 327n95, 328n109

Nizhegorodskaya, democratization rating, 244t; election ratings, 258t, 262, 263t, 265

Nizhny Novgorod, court rulings, 78; democratization rating, 243; election ratings, 265–66; removal of mayor, 54

nongovernmental organizations, 18, 137, 152–53; *See also* civil society

North Ossetia, 1996 presidential election, 45; declaration of sovereignty, 218; democratization rating, 247t, 248; election ratings, 259t, 265t, 266

North Tyumen, 222

Novgorodskaya, democratization rating, 245t; election ratings, 257, 258, 259t, 262, 265t, 267; electoral competition, 254

Novosibirsk, democratization rating, 244t; election ratings, 258t, 262, 263t, 265; electoral competition, 254

NTV television station, 44, 181–82, 294; criticism of 1999 Chechen war, 189; takeover by Gazprom, 160, 168–69, 189–90

Obshchaya Gazeta, 162

O'Donnell, Guillermo, 11, 15, 26, 122

Office of the Prosecutor General, 71–72, 211, 224–26

Ogonyok, 175

oligarchy, 18; alienation of middle and lower classes, 283–85, 284t; civil society, 136; as closed caste, 188; elections, 25, 42, 47, 53–54, 153–54, 310n58; interest groups, 117–18; lobbying role, 102–3; media control, 44, 181–86, 191; media readership, 187; oil and gas sector, 324n52; political influence, 98–101, 153–54, 183–86, 217–18, 226, 284, 295–96, 324n47, 324n52; privatization, 94–95, 97–101, 185–86, 324n44, 324n47; Putin era, 231, 293, 294; regional power, 98–101, 128, 217; restriction of competition, 193; rule of law, 206; "wars" after 1996 election, 185–86; Yeltsin era, 92, 150–54

Omskaya, democratization rating, 245t; election ratings, 263t

ONEXIM-Bank, 182

Orel, 257, 266

Orenburgskaya, democratization rating, 246t; election ratings, 258t, 263t

Organization for Security and Cooperation in Europe, 165, 342n5

Orlovskaya, democratization rating, 247t, 249; election ratings, 259t, 265t, 266; electoral competition, 254

ORT television station, 44, 47, 49, 176, 182, 185, 294

Our Home is Russia, 41–42, 112t, 113, 115t, 309n45

OVR. *See* Fatherland-All Russia (OVR) coalition

Pacific Fleet Military Court, 77–78

pacted transitions, 15–16

parliament, 1993 constitution, 93–94; 1993 elections, 36–39; 1994 Chechen war, 77–78; 1995 elections, 40–43; 1999 elections, 46–48; alliances with civil society, 155; bicameral organization, 36–37; constitutional powers, 58, 63, 67–71; development of political parties, 109–15; elections, 25, 65, 295–96, 314n18; electoral blocs, 112–14; federal structures, 223–27, 231–35, 232t, 234t; foreign policy initiatives, 69, 312n32; power, 93–94; proportional representation, 119–22, 129–31; Putin era, 50–51, 102; *See also* Congress of People's Deputies (CPD); Duma; Federation Council

parliament, federal structures, 231–35, 232t, 234t

parties. *See* political parties

Pasko, Grigory, 78, 164

Patrushev, Nikolai, 231

Pavlovsky, Gleb, 160, 185, 186

Pentecostal religious communities, 162, 171–72

Penzenskaya, democratization rating, 246t; election ratings, 264t

People's Perceptions of Effective Ways to Influence State Authorities, 281t

perestroika, 16, 28; constitutional change, 57–58; emergence of civil society, 145–48; media pluralism, 175–76; rule of law, 74, 195–99

Permskaya, democratization rating, 243,

244t, 249; election ratings, 257, 258t, 262, 263t, 265, 266; electoral competition, 254

Pimenov, Revol't, 58

police. *See* law enforcement

political parties, 70, 105–34, 316n19; 1989 CPD elections, 29; 1990 CPD elections, 30; 1991 presidential election, 121–22; 1996 presidential election, 45; development, 39, 107–16, 139, 146; election participation, 3–4, 29, 30, 37, 45, 121–22, 253–55; future, 131–34; historical aspects, 117–19, 317n38; independence, 295–96; influence of the state, 20, 295–96; institutional roles, 124–31, 319n66; local parties of power, 116; proportional representation, 129–31, 132–33, 317n40; public opinion, 281–83; regional role, 100, 115–16; role of the Duma, 106, 109–15, 112t, 115t, 119–22, 129–31; role of the Federation Council, 109; role of the presidency, 108–9, 122–29; role of the prime ministry, 123–24; Russian Constitution, 124–31; Soviet era, 317n44; stabilization, 102; super-parties, 238; two-party system, 133–34; vs. civil society, 139, 321n10; weakness, 95, 117–24, 156–57; Yeltsin era, 149–50

Poltavchenko, Georgy, 231

Ponomarev, Lev, 160, 327n95

Pope, Edmond, 164

Poptsov, Oleg, 186

Popular Assessment of Achievements of the Yeltsin Era, 2000, 273t

Popular Expectations of Political Leaders, 1998, 283t

Popular Perceptions of the Essentials for Democracy, 274t

Potanin, Vladimir, 324n52

Power to the People, 41

Presidency, 1991 presidential election, 31–32, 108, 121–22, 127, 148, 307n23; 1991 referendum, 126–27; 1996 presidential election, 43–45, 95,

108, 128, 153–54, 180, 204–5, 217, 269, 320n77; 2000 presidential election, 48–49, 108, 113, 250–51, 269, 306n5; 2004 presidential election, 6, 297; appointments, 68–69, 92, 320n75; August Republic, 87–91, 179–80; consolidation of, by Yeltsin, 31–32, 87–101; creation of, by Gorbachev, 29, 83–104; development of civil society, 136; development of political parties, 108–9; federalist structures, 231–35, 232t, 234t; impeachment, 94; law-making role, 93, 313n10; political party system, 106, 122–29; powers, 3, 4–5, 17, 19–20, 58, 64, 67–71, 122–29, 236–38, 305n77; public opinion, 286–91; Russian Constitution, 91–94; Soviet presidency, 29, 83–104; super-presidency, 84, 122–24, 127–29, 155; weakening of civil society, 155; *See also* specific presidents, e.g. Putin

Presidential Administration, 68–69, 93

Primakov, Yevgeny, 80; 1999 parliamentary elections, 46–48; party affiliations, 113, 114, 123–24, 129; prime ministry, 97, 108–9, 333–34n25

prime ministry, conflicts with the president, 96–97; federalist structures, 231–35, 232t, 234t; political party affiliations, 123–24

Primorsky, democratization rating, 247t, 248; election ratings, 258t, 262, 263t; electoral competition, 254

private property, 59, 63

Profil', 182

Prusak, Mikhail, 258

Przeworski, Adam, 2, 6, 16

Pskov, 116; democratization rating, 245t; election ratings, 258t, 263t, 267

public opinion, 268–91; August 1991 attempted coup, 323n35; civil society, 281, 281t; constitutional amendments, 79–80, 313n45; democratic values, 269–78, 273t, 274t, 276t, 277t, 293; desire for order and stability, 102,

204–5; disappointments with democracy, 275–78; disenchantment with the West, 276–77, 340n18; dissolution of the USSR, 149; distrust in institutions, 157–58, 325n65; economic concerns, 270–72; historical factors, 271, 277t, 278–80, 281t, 282–83; human rights, 269; media manipulation of, 184–85; most significant events, 188; multiparty system, 272; NTV takeover, 168; opposition parties, 289–90; personal values, 284t; political participation, 281–83, 281t, 283t; preference for order above democracy, 285–86, 290–91, 290t; preference for paternalistic systems, 279–83, 289, 289t; presidency, 286–91, 289t; public protest, 135, 148; Putin's popularity, 289–90, 295, 318–19n61, 342n3; representative organizations, 272; research methodology, 291, 338–39n1; role of media, 268; rule of law, 198; social stratification, 283–85; support for Yeltsin, 90; tolerance of corruption, 269, 288t; trust in the media, 192; understanding of freedom, 278–79; view of equality, 203, 270–72; vulnerability to manipulation, 291
Public Opinion Foundation, 79–80, 168, 275, 338–39n1
Public Readiness to Support Authoritarian Measures, 290t
Public Views of the Importance of Democratic Institutions and Rights, 273t
publishing, 143–45
Pugachev, Sergei, 310n58
Putin, Vladimir, viii; choice as Yeltsin's successor, 46, 48, 128, 220, 228; FSB connections, 20; leadership style, 21–22; nonpartisan background, 109; as prime minister, 47–48
Putin presidency, 1–2, 6–8, 20–22, 24, 237, 292–98; 1999 Chechen war, 189, 228, 293–94, 297; 2000 presidential election, 25, 48–49, 102, 108, 113, 269; 2004 presidential election, 6, 297;

accumulation of power, 50–51, 81; antifederalism, 227–35; charges of espionage, 164–65; Civic Forum, 159–60, 165–66, 210, 327n96; civil society, 136, 139, 159–72, 327–82nn95–98; concentration on international relations, 97; concerns with public opinion, 328n113; conflicts with the Duma, 97; creation of super-regions, 229–30, 294–95; the Duma, 102; economic reforms, 191; election manipulation, 238, 310n55; environmental issues, 169–70, 171; federalist structures, 160, 231–38, 232t, 234t, 333–34n25; Federation Council reforms, 50–51, 69–71, 103–4, 109, 226–27, 295, 333n22; freedom of information, 189; FSB's role, 161–64, 228; intolerance of dissent, 159–61, 189, 297–98, 326n73; judicial reforms, 209–12, 293, 325n59; Kursk sinking, 189; managed democracy, 9, 160, 298; media control, 166, 168–69, 189–94, 294, 327n97; party affiliations, 114, 123–24, 133, 165–66, 229, 238, 295; popularity, 289–90, 318–19n61; preferences for order above democracy, 285–86; regional governments, 72, 100, 102, 218, 221, 228–35, 294–95, 334n26; rule of law, 297–98; Russian Orthodox Church, 166, 289; State Council, 227; strengthening of St. Petersburg, 230–31; traditional Russian values, 165–66; use of military force, 228; youth movement, 139
Putnam, Robert, 140–41

Rabochaya Tribuna, 182
Rakhimov, Murtaza, 266
Reddaway, Peter, 65, 67–68, 144
regional governments, 1990 elections, 148; 1991 referendum, 307n24, 307n27; 1993 constitutional referendum, 332n12; 1993 elections, 307–8n30; 1999-2001 elections, 49–51; 2002 electoral law, 134; appointments of gover-

nors, 89, 320n75, 333n22; asymmetric relationships with the center, 218–19; August Republic, 89–90; authoritarian tendencies, 103–4; budgets, 229, 334n28; constitutional powers, 19–20, 64–65, 71–74; constitutions, 72; contradictions with federal law, 71–73, 155, 211–12, 229; creation of super-regions, 229–30, 294–95; democratization ratings, 239–67, 244–47t, 261t; election manipulation, 222–23, 255–56, 295; elections, 100, 121, 218, 238, 249–67, 251–52, 261t, 318n49, 336n6, 337n13; executive powers, 128–29; federalist structures, 231–35, 232t, 233, 234t, 335n34; Federal Treaty of March 1992, 218–23, 332n11; Federation Council, 69–71, 310nn57–58; immunity of governors, 73; law enforcement, 229; media, 176, 229–30; mixed election systems, 100; negative voting, 252–53, 336n11; negotiations with the center, 221–23; *oblasts, krais,* and *okrugs,* 215, 222–23, 332n7; oligarchy, 98–101, 128, 218; political parties, 100, 106, 113–16, 129, 229, 238, 253–55, 320n79; political structures, 99–101; Putin era, 218, 221–22, 228–35, 294–95, 333n22; representation in the center, 69–71, 224, 225t, 310n57, 310n58, 333n19; rule of law, 211–12, 256–57; separatist tendencies, 235–36; Soviet era, 266, 333n19; super-parties, 238; taxation, 229, 230; voter turnout, 335n36
Reiman, Leonid, 335n33
religious groups, 161–62, 171–72
Remington, Thomas, 66–67, 68
research. *See* measurements of democratization
revolution model, 12, 199–208, 302n42
Rhyzhkov, Vladimir, 8–9
Rodina party, 296
Roeder, Philip, 15
Rogozin, Dmitry, 296
Roosevelt, Franklin D., 69

Rossel, Eduard, 129
Rostov-on-Don, democratization rating, 246t; election manipulation, 54; election ratings, 259t, 265t
RSFSR Constitution of 1978, 206–7
RTR television station, 44, 47, 49, 176, 182, 186, 294
rule of law, 4, 24, 195–212; bureaucracy, 212; civil society, 210; Communist Party of the Soviet Union (CPSU), 196–97; conflicts of interest, 211–12; failure of reforms, 199–208; Gorbachev era, 195–99, 205; historical aspects, 201–2; limitations of reforms, 203–4; natural law, 201–2; oligarchy, 206; paternalism of the state, 201–2, 210, 211; public opinion, 198; Putin era, 297–98; regional governments, 211–12; relationship of the state to the individual, 203–4; Soviet era, 195–99, 331n3; Yeltsin era, 155–56, 198–208; *See also* human rights
Rumyantsev, Oleg, 57
Russian Attitudes Toward Democratic Procedures, Selected Years, 276t
Russian Constitution, 8–9, 17, 56–82, 207–8; 1993 referendum, 35–36, 56, 219, 313n9; amendments, 79–82, 313n45; central government organization, 58–59; civil rights, 81, 150; civil society, 210; consolidation of the presidency, 91–94; contradictions with regional constitutions, 71–73, 155; division of power, 20; federal structure, 58, 71–73, 219, 224, 225t; historical aspects, 57–63; illiberal features, 66–67; impact on political parties, 124–31; judicial system, 74–79, 208–9; liberal features, 66; local self-government, 73–74, 211–12; parliamentary powers, 93–94, 305n77; political parties, 124–31, 210, 319n66; presidential power, 17, 64–65, 67–71, 125–29; provisions for impeachment, 94; Putin's reforms, 50–51, 102; regional divisions,

215; separation of powers, 67–71;
Soviet era interests groups, 152; voter
participation, 4; Yeltsin's early reforms,
90–91; Yeltsin's "presidential" draft,
63–65, 84
Russian Constitutional Court, 75–78
Russian Independent Institute for Social
and Nationalities Problems (RIISNP),
272, 273t, 275–76, 276t, 278–79, 288t,
289t, 338–39n1, 339n11
Russian Journalists' Union, 166, 327n97
Russian Movement for Democratic Reforms,
309n45
Russian Orthodox Church, 81, 162, 166,
289
Russian Press Institute, 166
Russian Soviet Federative Socialist Republic
(RSFSR), 214–15, 333n20; 1990 system
of soviets, 86–87, 224; dissolution of
soviets, 216–17; Supreme Soviet, 86,
89–90, 179–86, 333n18, 333n20
Russian Television and Radio Company,
186
Russian Union of Industrialists and Entre-
preneurs, 152
Russia's Choice, 108, 130, 309n45; 1993
parliamentary elections, 38–39, 113,
119, 130–31; 1995 parliamentary elec-
tions, 309n45, 315n13
Russia's Pacific Fleet, 164
Rutskoi, Aleksandr, 36, 41, 90, 96
Ryazan, democratization rating, 246t; election ratings, 258t, 263t, 267; removal of
mayor, 54
Rybkin, Ivan, 41
Ryzhkov, Nikolai, 41, 307n23
Ryzhkov, Vladimir, 89

Sagalayev, Eduard, 166
Sakhalinskaya, democratization rating,
244t; election ratings, 258t, 262, 263t,
265
Sakharov, Andrei, 86, 144, 147, 306n14
Salmin, Alexei, 93
Salvation Army, 162

Samarsakaya, democratization rating, 244t;
election ratings, 264t, 267
samizdat, 143–44
Saratov, democratization rating, 246t, 248;
election manipulation, 54; election rat-
ings, 257, 259t, 265t
Satarov, Georgy, 130
Schmitter, Philippe, 10, 11, 15, 26
Schumpeter, Joseph, 2, 23, 337n16
Sechin, Ivor, 231
Security Council, 68–69, 230, 233
Segodnya, 181–82, 189, 330n11
Seleznov, Gennady, 48, 310n55
separation of powers, 83–104, 198; August
Republic, 87–91; presidential law-mak-
ing, 93, 313n10; presidential republic,
91–94
Sergei Alekseev, 74
Shaimiev, Mintimer, 72, 113, 217, 266,
333–34n25
Shakhnazarov, Georgy, 196
Shein, Oleg, 166
Sheinis, Viktor, 58, 63, 130
Shevchenko, Yuri, 335n33
Shevtsova, Lilia, 91
Shugart, Matthew, 68
Sidorenko, Yuri, 78–79
Skokov, Yuri, 41
Slavonic Legal Center, 171, 326n80
Smolenskaya, democratization rating, 246t;
election ratings, 263t, 267
Sobchak, Anatoly, 63, 231, 310n58
Sobyanin, Aleksandr, 38
Social Democratic Party of Russia, 146
social stratification, 283–85, 285t
Socio-Ecological Union, 169–70
Solidarity (Poland), 146
Solzhenitsyn, Alexander, 144, 289
Soros, George, 163
Sovetskaya Rossiya, 58
Soviet Union, 18–20; 1936 Constitution,
142–43; 1978 "Brezhnev" Constitution,
57–58; 1989 elections, 23, 26–33,
306n14; 1991 military coup, 32–33;
1993 dissolution of the soviets, 216–17;

anti-Stalinist movement, 143; civil society, 14–15, 142–48, 150–52, 172; Congress of People's Deputies, 27–31, 86; Constitutional Oversight Committee (KKN), 74–75; creation of presidency, 29; declarations of independence from, 31–32; dissidents, 143–44, 322n23; dissolution in 1991, vii, 33–34, 120, 127, 149, 177; elections, 33–34, 307n16; federalist structures, 214–15, 218, 236–37; media, 175; perestroika, 28, 57–58, 74; political parties, 317n44; public opinion, 273–74; role of soviets, 85–87, 89–90, 216–17; rule of law, 195–99, 331n3

SPS. *See* Union of Right Forces (SPS)

St. Petersburg, 215, 230–31; democratization rating, 243, 244*t*; election ratings, 257, 258*t*, 262, 263*t*, 267; voter turnout, 251

Stalin, Joseph, 21, 142–43

State Committee for Environmental Protection, 169–71

State Council, 227

State Duma. *See* Duma

Stavropolksy, democratization rating, 246*t*; election ratings, 263*t*

Stepashin, Sergei, 109, 115, 334n27, 335n33

Stevenson, Irene, 165

Stoner-Weiss, Kathryn, 116, 121

Stroyev, Yegor, 257, 266

super-presidency, 84, 122–24, 127–29, 155

super-regions, 229–30, 294–95

Supreme Court, 78–79, 206; environmental protection suits, 170; presidential impeachment, 94

Supreme Soviet, 86, 333nn18–20; 1993 conflict with Yeltsin, 89–90, 179–86, 269; creation of the Russian Constitution, 59–63; under the Soviet "Brezhnev" Constitution, 58; transitional body of 1990, 224, 332n10

Sutyagin, Igor, 164–65

Sverdlovsk, democratization rating, 243, 244*t*; election ratings, 258*t*, 263*t*, 266–67; political structure, 101; regional powers, 99

Svyazinvest, 185–86

Tambovskaya, democratization rating, 246*t*; election ratings, 258*t*, 262, 263*t*, 265, 267

Tatarstan, 1991 presidential election, 307n23; 1993 constitutional referendum, 219; 1996 presidential election, 45; declaration of independence, 19, 218; democratization rating, 247*t*, 249; election manipulation, 54; election participation, 219; election ratings, 257, 259*t*, 265*t*, 266; Federal Treaty, 218–21; nationalist movements, 219; political structure, 101; regional constitution, 72; regional powers, 99

Tatar World Congress, 219

taxation, 129, 192; impact on civil society, 162–63; regional governments, 229, 230

Taymyrsky, 222; democratization rating, 246*t*; election ratings, 263*t*

television, 186–89; elections, 25, 44, 49; National Association of Television and Radio Broadcasters, 166; NTV, 44, 160, 168–69, 181–82, 189–90, 294; ORT, 44, 47, 49, 176, 182, 185, 294; RTR television station, 44, 47, 49, 176, 182, 186, 294; Russian Television and Radio Company, 186; support of Yeltsin, 179–81; TVS television station, 169, 190

The Marxist-Leninist General Theory of the State and Law, 195

Tomskaya, 215; democratization rating, 245*t*; election ratings, 263*t*

transitions, 10–17; decolonization model, 13; elections, 26–27; imposed, 16–17; pacted, 15–16; revolution model, 12, 302n42

Transitions from Authoritarian Rule (O'Donnell, Schmitter, & Whitehead), 11, 15

Tretyakov, Vitaly, 183
Trud, 182, 198
Tuleyev, Aman, 258, 333–34n25
Tulskaya, democratization rating, 246t;
    election ratings, 263t, 267
Tumenskaya, 258t
Tuva, 310n58; 1991 presidential election,
    307n23; democratization rating, 247t,
    248; election ratings, 259t, 265t, 266,
    267; electoral competition, 254;
    regional constitution, 72
TV-6, 168–69, 182, 190
TV-Center, 182
Tverskaya, democratization rating, 245t;
    election ratings, 263t
TVS television station, 169, 190
Tyulkin, Viktor, 40, 41
Tyumen, 215; democratization rating, 245t;
    election ratings, 257, 262, 263t

Udmurtia, declaration of sovereignty, 218;
    democratization rating, 244t, 249; elec-
    tion ratings, 264t
Ukraine, 1989 miners' strikes, 145–46;
    declaration of sovereignty, 218
Ulyanovskaya, democratization rating,
    247t, 249; election ratings, 263t, 267
Unified Russia, 133
Union of Distributors of Press Productions
    and Titles, 183
Union of Right Forces (SPS), 112t, 115t,
    129, 296, 315n13; 1995 parliamentary
    elections, 120; 1999 parliamentary elec-
    tions, 48, 115; Duma representation,
    110–14, 119–22; NTV takeover, 168;
    Putin's endorsement, 123
Union of Russian Journalists, 183
United Ministry of Railroads, 232t, 234t
United Russia, 295
United States, 300n11; AID support of civil
    society, 152–53, 326n85; Edmond Pope
    case, 164; Peace Corps, 165
Unity party, 25; 1999 parliamentary elec-
    tions, 112–14, 132–33, 295–96; 1999
    presidential elections, 47–48; Duma

representation, 112t, 115t, 132–33,
    238; Federation Council, 109; national
    super-parties, 238; Putin's endorsement,
    47, 123; regional role, 334n27; regional
    support, 218, 229; support of Putin, 70;
    youth movement, 165–66
Urban, George, 67
USA Canada Institute, 164–65
USSR. See Soviet Union
Ust-Orda okrug, 215; democratization rat-
    ing, 247t, 248; election ratings, 257,
    259t, 265t
Uzbekistan, 10

Vasilyev, Dmitri, 334n32
Video International, 182
Vladimirskaya, democratization rating,
    245t; election ratings, 263t
Vladivostok, 54
Volgogradskaya, democratization rating,
    244t; election ratings, 263t
Volkov, Leonid, 58
Vologodskaya, democratization rating,
    244t; election ratings, 264t
Volsky, Arkady, 324n44
Voronezhskaya, democratization rating,
    246t; election ratings, 263t
voters' clubs, 139
voter turnout, 24, 29, 38, 73, 249–53,
    261t, 308n37, 335n36
VTsIOM. See All-Russian Center for Public
    Opinion Research

Walking Together, 138, 139, 166, 327n96
Weimar Germany, 137–38
Whitehead, Laurence, 11
World Bank, 156, 170
World Chuvashy Council, 219
World Development Report, 1997(World
    Bank), 156
World Wildlife Fund, 171

Yabloko, 42, 95, 296, 309n45, 315n16,
    317n41; 1993 parliamentary elections,
    119; 1995 parliamentary elections,

309n45; 1996 presidential election, 122; 1999 parliamentary elections, 48; 2003 parliamentary elections, 342nn7–8; civil society, 168, 170; constitutional amendments, 80–81; Duma representation, 110–14, 112t, 115t, 119–22; NTV takeover, 168; regional government, 116; single-mandate districts, 115t

Yablokov, Alexei, 169–70, 328n108

Yakovlev, Aleksandr, 196, 217, 323n35

Yakutia, declaration of sovereignty, 218; democratization rating, 247t; election ratings, 257, 264t; Federal Treaty, 218–19, 221; regional constitution, 72–73

Yamalo-Nenetsky, democratization rating, 245t; election ratings, 262, 264t; electoral competition, 254

Yaroslavl, 89–90; democratization rating, 244t; election ratings, 264t, 267

Yavlinsky, Grigory, 42, 49, 110, 122, 309n45

Yeltsin, Boris, vii, 11; August 1991 attempted coup, 16–17, 127, 135; chairmanship of Russian CPD, 32, 87, 126, 146, 148; chairmanship of Supreme Soviet, 176; creation of RTR television station, 176; creation of Russian presidency, 31–32, 126–27; health, 46, 208; leadership style, 21; negotiation of the end of the Soviet Union, 33; party affiliations, 117, 122, 123–24; retirement, 8, 48, 228, 306n5

Yeltsin presidency, 17, 24, 34, 91–94, 292; 1991 presidential election, 31–32, 108, 121–22, 127, 148, 307n23; 1991 referendum, 31–32, 126–27, 307n24; 1993 founding elections, 33–40; 1993 referendum on the constitution, 35–36, 56, 219, 313n9; 1996 presidential election, 43–45, 128, 153–54, 180, 184, 204–5, 217, 269, 320n77; August Republic, 17, 62, 75–76, 87–91, 149, 179–80, 304n66; basic social services, 156, 158;

bicameral parliament, 36–37, 308n32; campaign funding violations, 44; Chechen wars, 68, 77–78, 180–81, 220, 224, 228; choice of a successor, 46, 48, 220, 228; civil society, 95, 149–59; conflicts with the Constitutional Court, 75–78; conflicts with the CPD, 36, 90–91, 206–7; conflicts with the Duma, 96–97, 127; conflicts with the Supreme Soviet, 88–91, 179–80, 186, 269; consolidation of the presidency, 87–101, 126–29; Constitutional Commission, 57; constitutional reforms, 206–8; consultative bodies, 224, 225t; control over elections, 308n37, 308n40; decentralization process, 228; Decree Number 1400, 90–91, 200, 206–7; desire for order and stability, 204–5; dismissal of Chubais, 186; dismissal of Primakov, 108–9; dissolution of soviets in 1993, 216–17; dissolution of the Russian CPD, 36; dissolution of the Soviet Union, 34, 127, 149; economic reforms, 16–17, 34, 88, 127, 149, 151–52, 207–8; election manipulation, 39; federal structures, 206–8, 216–17; Federal Treaty of March 1992, 218–21; Federation Council, 80, 99–100, 109, 333n22; growth of bureaucracy, 156, 205–6, 325n60; impeachment proceedings, 83, 100; law-making activities, 93, 313n10; media, 90, 177–89; Ministry of Security and Internal Affairs, 75, 205; oligarchy, 94–95, 98–101, 150–54, 183–86, 324n47; political parties, 120–22, 150; preservation of power, 95–97, 184–86; "presidential" draft of the Russian Constitution, 63–65; prime minister appointments, 48, 109, 226, 334n27; privatization, 151–52, 181–83, 324n44; proportional representation, 129–31; prosecutors general replacements, 224–26; public opinion, 272–73, 273t, 275–78; regional power, 89, 98–101, 217, 320n75; relationship with

Tatarstan president Shaimiyev, 72; religious practice, 162; resignation in 1999, 228, 306n5; rule of law, 198–208; Russian Constitution, 58–63, 84, 127–28, 129–30; voter turnout, 308n37

youth movement, 138, 139; FSB harassment of, 162; Komsomol, 151; Walking Together, 138, 139, 166, 327n96

Youth Unity, 165–66

Yukos, 103

Yuzhanov, Ilya, 335n33

Zadornov, Mikhail, 115

Zashchita, 327n96

Zhirinovsky, Vladimir, 39–42, 108, 296; 1991 presidential election, 307n23; 1995 parliamentary elections, 309n45; 1999 parliamentary elections, 48; *See also* Liberal Democratic Party of Russia

Zorkin, Valery, 58, 75

Zubakin, Semen, 116

Zubkov, Viktor, 231

Zyuganov, Gennady, 110; 1996 presidential election, 43–45, 108, 320n77; 1999 parliamentary elections, 48; 2000 presidential election, 49; National Patriotic Union of Russia, 45; party affiliations, 123–24

About the Authors

Michael McFaul is the Peter and Helen Bing Senior Fellow at the Hoover Institution. He is also an Associate Professor of Political Science at Stanford University and a nonresident Senior Associate at the Carnegie Endowment for International Peace. Before joining the Stanford faculty in 1995, he worked for two years as a Senior Associate for the Carnegie Endowment for International Peace in residence at the Carnegie Moscow Center. McFaul is also a Research Associate at the Center for International Security and Cooperation, and the Center for Democracy, Development, and the Rule of Law, both at Stanford. He is a widely published author, with articles appearing in magazines, newspapers, and journals worldwide. He received his B.A. in International Relations and Slavic Languages and his M.A. in Slavic and East European Studies, both from Stanford University, and his Ph.D. in International Relations from Oxford University in 1991.

Nikolai Petrov is head of the Center for Political Geographic Research and is a leading research associate with the Institute of Geography at the Russian Academy of Sciences. From 1990–1995, he served as an adviser to the Russian parliament, government, and presidential apparatus. Petrov was the chief organizer of the Analysis and Forecast Division in the Supreme Soviet and head of a governmental working group on regional problems. He also served as an analyst in the Analytical Center of the President. From

1996 to 2000, he led the regional project at the Carnegie Moscow Center, where he published the *Political Almanac of Russia 1997*, and the annual supplements *Russian Regions* in 1999 and 2000, as well as numerous essays on elections, federalism, and regionalism. From 2000 to 2002, he taught at Macalester College, St. Paul, Minnesota. He earned his Ph.D. in Geography from Moscow State University in 1982.

Andrei Ryabov is a leading political scientist in Russia. Since October 2002, he has been editor-in-chief of the Russian academic journal *The World Economy and International Relations*. Prior to joining the Carnegie Moscow Center, he worked as a senior researcher at the Center of International Programs of the Russian Independent Institute of Social and National Problems and as senior researcher at the department of modern Russian political process of Moscow State University. He was previously deputy chief editor of *Vestnik*, the Moscow University Political Science series. Ryabov coauthored several books, including *Philosophy of Power* and *Party-Political Elites and Electoral Processes in Russia*. In addition to his work with the Carnegie Endowment, Ryabov is deputy director of the Center of Political Science Programs at the Gorbachev Foundation. He received his Ph.D. from the Moscow State Historical Archive Institute.

Carnegie Endowment for International Peace

The Carnegie Endowment is a private, nonprofit organization dedicated to advancing cooperation between nations and promoting active international engagement by the United States. Founded in 1910, its work is nonpartisan and dedicated to achieving practical results.

Through research, publishing, convening, and, on occasion, creating new institutions and international networks, Endowment associates shape fresh policy approaches. Their interests span geographic regions and the relations between governments, business, international organizations, and civil society, focusing on the economic, political, and technological forces driving global change. Through its Carnegie Moscow Center, the Endowment helps to develop a tradition of public policy analysis in the states of the former Soviet Union and to improve relations between Russia and the United States. The Endowment publishes *Foreign Policy*, one of the world's leading magazines of international politics and economics.